INTEGRATION AND DISINTEGRATION IN EUROPEAN ECONOMIES

INTEGRATION AND DISINTEGRATION IN EUROPEAN ECONOMIES

Edited by

BRUNO DALLAGO
University of Trento

GIOVANNI PEGORETTI
University of Trento

Dartmouth

Aldershot • Brookfield USA • Singapore • Sydney

11 2 11946

Published by
Dartmouth Publishing Company Limited
Gower House
Croft Road
Aldershot
Hants GU11 3HR
England

Dartmouth Publishing Company
Old Post Road
Brookfield
Vermont 05036
USA

Learning Resources
Centre

British Library Cataloguing in Publication Data
Integration and Disintegration in
European Economies
  I. Dallago, Bruno II. Pegoretti, Giovanni
  330.940559

Library of Congress Cataloging-in-Publication Data
Integration and disintegration in European economies / edited by Bruno
  Dallago, Giovanni Pegoretti.
      p.   cm.
    Includes index.
    ISBN 1-85521-552 7
    1. Europe–History–Economic integration–Congresses. 2. Europe,
  Central–Economic conditions–Congresses. 3. Europe, Eastern–Economic
  conditions–1989- –Congresses. 4. Post-communism–Congresses.
  I. Dallago, Bruno, 1950-   . II. Pegoretti, Giovanni.
  HC241.I566   1995
  357.1'47–dc20

                                                                    95-5683
                                                                         CIP

ISBN 1 85521 552 7
Printed in Great Britain by Ipswich Book Co. Ltd., Ipswich, Suffolk.

CONTENTS

FOREWORD

The complexity of the processes triggered after 1989 by the onset of transition to democratic society and a market economy in the central and Eastern part of the continent and the time required for them to settle and stabilize means that the economic - as well as political and strategic - situation of the continent remains uncertain. However, the decisions already taken and implemented, and the manifest will of the protagonists already allow the observer and the scholar to analyse the new situation. The importance of the topic, the novelty and complexity of the processes involved, and their intellectual, scientific and professional interest have prompted the present book, which collects analyses by twelve scholars from various European countries on diverse aspects of the processes of integration and disintegration under way in the European countries. With the exception of those by Szamuely and Dallago, the essays are the revised versions of papers presented to the Third Trento Workshop organised jointly by the European Association for Comparative Economic Studies (EACES) and the Department of Economics of the University of Trento. The theme of the Workshop was 'Integration and Disintegration in European Countries', and it was held at the University of Trento on 4-5 March 1993, with other European and extra-European scholars also participating.

The Workshop was made possible by the cooperation of various members of the EACES and the Trento Department of Economics, by the sponsorship provided by the Department of Economics of the University of Trento, by the Autonomous Province of Trento and by the *Cassa Rurale di Villazzano e Trento*.

The conference, as well as the preparation of the present book, would not have been possible without the work of Edith J. Kismarjay. Adrian Belton provided valuable help in revising and translating the texts into English, while Marco Margoni and his colleagues at CRASI had the patience to page-set the text, scrupulously following the instructions of the editors. Only the latter, therefore, are to be blamed for any remaining errors or omissions in the book.

ABOUT THE AUTHORS

MADELEINE ANDREFF, lecturer of Statistics at the University Pierre Mendés-France, Grenoble, has published Statistique: *traitement des données d'échantillon,* Presses Universitaires de Grenoble, 2 volumes, 1993. She has participated in a research on CMEA-EC trade for the French Planning Commission in 1991.

WLADIMIR ANDREFF, Professor of Economics at the University of Paris 1 Panthéon-Sorbonne, has published several books among which *La crise des économies socialistes: la rupture d'un systéme,* Presses Universitaires de Grenoble, 1993, and has edited *Réforme et échanges extérieurs dans les pays de l'Est,* Editions L'Harmattan, Paris, 1990, *Privatisations et secteur public dans les pays de l'Est,* Centre Franéais du Commerce Extérieur, Paris, 1992, *Convergence and System Change: The Convergence Hypothesis in the Light of Transition in Eastern Europe* (with H. Brezinski, B. Dallago), Dartmouth, Aldershot, 1992. He is Deputy-President of the Social Sciences Committee in the French Commission at the UNESCO and member of the Executive Committee of the European Association for Comparative Economic Studies.

IVO BICANIC, was born in Zagreb, Yugoslavia. He completed a B. Phil. in

Economics at Oxford University and later received a doctorate from the University of Zagreb, where he has been teaching since 1977. He has published articles on such topics as economic theory, economic history and the Yugoslav economy. His main research interest is the study of income inequality with special reference to Yugoslavia.

LUIGI BOSCO graduated in Economics (1984) at the University of Siena. He received a Master of Arts in Economics (1986) at the Department of Economics of the University of Warwick. Between 1987-1990 he served as a research student (1987-90) at the Department of Economics, European University Institute, in Florence. He is presently Assistant Professor at the Department of Economics, University of Trento.

HORST BREZINSKI is Professor of Economics and Dean at the Faculty of Economics and Business Administration, University of Freiberg. He is also Secretary of the European Association for Comparative Economic Studies. He has published articles on COMECON and the second economy in the Soviet Union and Eastern Europe. His book *The Shadow Economy in East, West and South: a Comparative View* is forthcoming. His main research interests are comparative economic systems and international economic relations.

MAREK DABROWSKI graduated in 1974 (Warsaw University). He received his PhD in 1979 from the Institute of Planning in Warsaw and 'habilitation' degree from toD2 University in 1987. In September 1991 he became the founder of the CASE - Center for Social and Economic Research.

Since September 1989 until September 1990 he took a position of the First Deputy Minister of Finance in Tadeusz Mazowiecki's government. Since November 1990 until April 1992 he was a member of the Supervisory Board of the Polish Development Bank. Since April 1991 he is the Chairman of the Council of Ownership Transformation, the advisory body to the Prime Minister. From October 1991 to May 1993 - Member of the Polish Parliament. From November 1991 he was invited as the economic consultant to the Russian Government. From Spring 1993 he co-operates also with Ukrainian and Lithuanian governments.

BRUNO DALLAGO graduated at the University of Trento (1993) and received his PhD at the Hungarian Academy of Sciences (1980). He was a visiting scholar at the University of California at Berkeley (1982-83) and at the University of Illinois at Urbana Champaign (1984). He is presently Associate Professor of Economic Policy and Comparative Economic Systems at the University of Trento, Italy. His publications include *The Irregular Economy* (Dartmouth, 1990), *Privatisation and Entrepreneurship in Post Socialist Countries: Economy, Law and Society* with G. Ajani and B. Grancelli (Macmillan, 1992), and *Comparative Economic Systems* (in Italian, la Nuova Italia, 1993).

PETER KALMBACH is Professor of Economics at the University of Bremen, Germany. He has published books and articles on theory of income distribution, technological change, employment and the labour market.

SEIJA LAINELA, MA, is economist in the Unit of Eastern European Economies, Bank of Finland

GIOVANNI PEGORETTI received his degree at the University of Bologna. He followed his studies at the London School of Economics and Political Science. He is presently professor of economics at the University of Trento and chairman of the Foundation of the Trento and Rovereto Savings Bank. His research interests are for structural dynamics of the economic system, with particular reference to the role of resources, environment and technical progress, finance and industrial capital. His publications include the following books: *Financial Capital, Profit, Interest* (in Italian, Angeli, Milano, 1983), *Resources, Production, Distribution* (in Italian, Angeli, Milano, 1986), *Finanz, Industrie und Währung in Italien und im deutschsprachigen Raum*, Dunker & Humblot, Berlin, 1990 (in cooperation with O. Clauser and P. Mooslechner), *Technological Innovation, Competitiveness and Economic Growth*, Dunker & Humblot, Berlin, 1992 (in cooperation with O. Clauser, P. Kalmbach and M.L. Segnana).

ROSSITSA RANGELOVA is Senior Research Associate at the Institute of Economics, Bulgarian Academy of Sciences and Head of the Information and Statistical De-partment. She also teaches international macroeconomic comparisons at the University for National and World Economy in Sofia. Her main research area is East/West economic performance comparisons. She has specialised on macroeconomic modelling in Moscow and Novosibirsk and on international economic comparisons in the United States. She has published several books in co-authorship and many articles and papers mainly on macroeconomic analyses and prognoses of Bulgaria's development compared with other European countries and some regions; has taken part in several international research projects.

MARCO ŠKREB is Executive Director of Research and Statistics Department at the National Bank of Kroatia. Formerly he was working full time at the Economics Faculty, University of Zagreb as Assistant Professor where he still lectures. After studying at the University of Pittsburgh, Department of Economics for a year he received his PhD at the Zagreb University. On top of monetary analysis his main topic of interests include anti-inflationary (stabilisation) policies and economic transformation.

PEKKA SUTELA, PhD, is special advisor in the Unit of Eastern European Economies, Bank of Finland.

LÁSZLÓ SZAMUELY (b. 1936) graduated at the Moscow State University in 1959, got his PhD in Economics in 1971 and DSc in 1992 (both in Budapest, Hungary). Since 1959 he has had different jobs: taught economics in the Budapest Polytechnical University, edited the economic monthly Közgazdasági Szemle, made research work in some economic institutions attached to the Hungarian Academy of Sciences. Now he is a scientific adviser to the Kopint-Datoring Institute for Economic, Market Research and Informatics, Inc. (Budapest). Dr. Szamuely published a number of books of socialist and capitalist economy and on the history of economic thought. Among them: *First Models of the Socialist Economic Systems* (published in Hungarian, English, Italian and Chinese). *Industrial Democracy in Western Europe?* (in Hungarian). *The Welfare State Today* (in Hungarian). *The Development of Economic Thought in Hungary. 1954-1978.* Selected Readings (in Hungarian), (editor). *Changing Structure, Changing Industrial Society* (in Hungarian).

FERDINANDO TARGETTI graduated from Bocconi University in 1970 and pursued his studies at the London School of Economics, University of Cambridge and Pembroke College, New York University. He is now full Professor of Economic Policy at the University of Trento. He published various books and articles in Italy and abroad on the Italian development, the theory of prices, income distribution, technical progress, the theory of growth, the history of economic thought, the international economy, stagflation and inflation, monetary policy, comparative economic systems, privatisation. He has given lectures at various universities and research institutes in Italy and various other countries. In 1989 he was awarded the Prix Saint Vincent for the year's best book on economics.

GIJSBERTUS VAN SELM is a PhD student at the University of Groningen, Holland. The present study is part of his forthcoming dissertation *The Economics of Soviet Breakup*. Previous studies related to this project were published in *Osteuropa Wirtschaft* and *MOST, Economic Journal on Eastern Europe and the Soviet Union*.

INTRODUCTION

Bruno Dallago and Giovanni Pegoretti

Since the Second World War, Europe has been both protagonist and spectator of major processes of political, economic and military disintegration and integration. Post-war Europe, in fact, was born from the disaggregation of the traditional order based on the dominant role of the colonial powers, Great Britain's above all. This order was brought to an end by the entry onto the European scene of the two new super-powers, the United States and the Soviet Union, and by the weakening of the old European powers. For the first time in its history, Europe was split sharply between two blocs which, for many years, were militarily and politically opposed. Consequently, also economic relationships between the countries belonging to the two blocs were drastically reduced and obstructed, and this broke up Germany's old area of influence in Central-Eastern Europe.

Both in parallel with and subsequently to the breakdown of the old order, however, new processes of political, economic and military integration rapidly arose within each of the two blocs. Western European integration, in which the United States played a leading but partly - in the economic field - external role, was based on substantially favourable economic, cultural and political circumstances. By contrast, integration among the countries of the East was brought about by only two cohesive factors: the dominant role of the Soviet Union and the political factor of the shared ideology of the parties in power. All other factors either hampered or wholly obstructed the process. The economic system, moreover, was not only inefficient but hindered integration among the economies of these countries, relationships among which in fact went no further than the centralised management of exchanges and payments on a bilateral basis, and a limited amount of productive specialisation, which was also centrally administered.

This order evolved over the years, but its basic coordinates remained unchanged until the end of the 1980s. The collapse of the Eastern bloc between 1989 and 1991 apparently enabled the restoration of the traditional European order based on the nucleus of the leading countries of Western Europe. Today the most striking differences with respect to the past are the central role assumed by the European Union, the great influence of united Germany and the decline of Great Britain, the role of the United States, and the situation that has arisen in the ex-Soviet area. These factors induce one to suppose that the present situation, more than a return to the past, is entirely new.

Matters are made more complex by the various attempts under way in the countries of Central Eastern Europe to join the European Union or to establish close relations with it, to re-establish national or regional integrations in the place of those that existed previously, or to create new ones. The role assumed by the regional powers of the Islamic world, most notably Turkey and Iran has further important consequences. In the background to all these developments is the disintegration of the Eastern bloc and - although in different ways - of certain of its major countries (the Soviet Union, Czechoslovakia and East Germany) and peripheral ones (Yugoslavia). Some of these processes have been accompanied by tragic conflict and war.

And in fact an intriguing aspect of these events is their magnitude, not solely in geographical terms but also as regards their capacity to generate forces which influence the dynamics of different systems. The disintegration of the Soviet bloc, already important in itself, has had immediate knock-on effects both in its immediate periphery and in distant areas of the Third World. But a striking feature, one not widely predicted, is that the shock-waves have spread to richer European neighbours. Of course, it would be incorrect to blame developments in the East for the change of atmosphere, the slowdown, and the recent difficulties encountered by the process of integration in Western Europe. There are, however, certain features that have undoubtedly influenced this state of affairs, albeit to different extents and in different areas:

(a) the disappearance of the threat of war consequent on the collapse of the 'historic' enemy and the slackening of the most compelling political-strategic reasons for the compactness of the Western European countries;
(b) the prediction (perhaps rather hasty) of massive shifts in the centre of gravities of production and trade as the free market 'conquers' East Europe;
(c) the unification of Germany, with the fading of the German inferiority complex and of the principal reason for seeking Western support (that has been uncertain on this specific matter) on the one hand, and the economic difficulties involved in integrating the Eastern *Länder* on the other.

Because of these and other factors, Europe, which until a few years ago was moving along two distinct and predictable trajectories - the Western one of growing integration, and the Eastern one of stagnation after forced integration - has been affected *as a whole* by forces which have rendered the former trajectory unstable and led to the latter's collapse. The reason why the essays collected in this book speak of 'integration' and 'disintegration', but also of Eastern Europe and Western Europe, lies precisely in this twofold intersection of tendencies: the East which, now that the old supranational system has *disintegrated*, interrogates itself concerning possible new (or old) *integrations*; the West which, practically at the culmination of a process of complete economic integration and on the verge of political integration, has begun to falter and to allow what was the most conspicuous (although not necessarily the most important) outcome of the process of union, i.e. the European monetary system, to break up.

It is therefore important to discuss jointly and to juxtapose assessments of both European trajectories. Without claiming to identify a single linking theme in all the complex events of recent years, nor, even less, to establish unilateral cause/effect relations between developments on each side of the 'curtain' that divides the European continent, it seems inadvisable to separate areas of discussion which can benefit from comparison between the two. The common denominator - the integration/disintegration process - emerges in all the essays collected in this book. It is precisely this shared problematic (if not methodological) framework which makes any sharp division of the book into three parts difficult.

By adopting a somewhat 'fuzzy' approach, therefore, *Part One* of the book contains three papers, the first of which seeks to give a theoretical framework for processes of national integration/disintegration, while the other two deal mainly with the disintegration of the former economic system of Eastern Europe and with its consequences.

In his paper Dallago considers integration and disintegration as if these processes were public goods. The outcome of the processes depends on the existence of a majority in favour of their 'supply', where this majority can be either numerical (number of individuals) or (more likely) constituted by strength of the individuals and organisations in favour of the event.

These agents see their effort as an investment in the public good that will give them a substantial return in economic, political and social terms. As a consequence, a relevant problem of collective actions exists and is implemented through an asymmetrical game (considering the preferences of the players and information) which favours small but determined privileged groups endowed with effective selective incentives over large but loosely motivated latent groups. This creates numerous opportunities for free riders.

The existence of some agents (individuals or organisations) in favour of integration or disintegration does not imply that the events necessarily take place. In fact, change may be impeded by path dependency, uncertainty over the results of the future situation, transition costs, lack of the cooperation necessary to implement the change and free riding.

When integration or disintegration take place and some agents as disadvantaged, they can choose between two different options, which following Hirschman, are defined as 'exit' and 'voice'. These two options are constrained by the action of the government (repression, co-option of the leaders of the integration or disintegration movements if they are contrary to the government's will) and the loyalty of the individuals and organisations to existing institutions and to economic, political and social structures. In order for the opposition not to take over, some conditions of collective action must be fulfilled. In particular, a privileged group endowed with relevant selective incentives and retaliation power must exist, and it must be interested in pursuing the objective of integration or disintegration.

Collective action is strengthened by individual processes that take place within it. The promoters of collective action can be compared to people who invest in the present in order to obtain a profit in the future. When collective action starts to achieve success (the processes of integration and disintegration begin to display their effects), other people imitate the promoters in order to participate in return on the investment (in the economic, political, social or ethical sense). For this development to be effective, free riders must be effectively controlled by promoters of collective action.

Integration and disintegration usually involve redistributive processes, especially when disintegration takes places. The latter implies that if expropriation of non-nationals takes place at market prices, and considering that the building of a new structure (e.g. a national state, or even regional autonomy) usually involves the creation of new, well paid jobs and other privileges for some individuals of the former national minority (now majority), redistribution (of income, wealth, power) takes place *within* the national group. This 'zero-sum' redistribution may not happen in the case of integration, provided that only the net returns of integration are distributed among the promoters of collective action and their supporters.

To understand whether the 'investment' in nationality (leading to disintegration) and supranationality (leading to integration) is economically, politically and socially positive, one must determine the extent of the return on the investment compared to alternative uses of the same resources, how equally the return is distributed among participants in collective action and the strength of the forces (e.g. national sentiments) which can ensure the permanence of the result of collective action.

In his paper, Szamuely begins by examining the features of economic inter-relations among the countries belonging to the CMEA, as a system which tended towards overall autarky and internally to which trade radiated outwards from the Soviet Union. This system had markedly negative consequences on the capacity of individual member states to develop a system of production and trade able to compete on international markets; by contrast, the member states developed an obsolete economic structure, strongly oriented by the centre towards strategic productions, unable to satisfy internal demand for consumption goods, and with a highly unequal distribution of costs and benefits among the various countries (even if these costs and benefits are difficult to calculate, given the complex and unrealistic criteria used to attribute values).

In early years, the dissolution of the system provoked a steep fall in the national products of these countries. Szamuely identifies three processes which - beyond the crisis of political and social systems - helped to aggravate the situation:

(a) the restructuring required to compete on international markets,
(b) the abandonment of the autarky policy, which internalized this competition,
(c) the decline in trade with the other ex-CMEA countries caused by the sudden, rather than gradual, abandonment of the system.

The dramatic fall in these countries' trade (with the collapse of their exports) has been accompanied by its geographical reorientation. By this means, some countries - Poland, Hungary and the Czech Republic - have managed to revive their exports, which are now directed not towards the interior of the area but towards Western markets. This has also altered the order of importance of their trading partners. For these countries, Germany has taken the place of the Soviet Union, whose role is nonetheless still important.

The reorientation of commercial flows, however, has chiefly concerned the countries of Central Europe with economies more compatible with that of the West; and, moreover, it has been the outcome of necessity imposed by economic depression rather than being a matter of choice. Finally, it has not given rise to well-defined and sustainable specialization in the long period. In fact, Szamuely points out, transition to a market economy requires institutional changes which have not yet been accomplished, and the resolving of the unprecedented depression into which these economies have lapsed; problems, these, whose solution requires active assistance from the international community.

While Szamuely's essay dwells on the countries formerly belonging to the CMEA - and in particular on the potentialities and problems of the central-European economies - Bicanic and Skreb address the problem of the break-up, with the tragic consequences so universally evident, of ex-Yugoslavia. Apart from the difficulty of the disintegration of the economic system, there are other pressing problems in the Yugoslavian case, such as definition of the new national states, of peace and reconstruction.

After reviewing the reasons for the break-up of the Yugoslavian state, Bicanic and Skreb raise the problem of quantification of the costs and benefits deriving from the creation of new states in the Balkans; a problem which resists easy solution, given the incomplete definition of the geopolitical situation and the lack of reliable data. The differences among the countries to have emerged from the disaggregation are extremely wide, as are the differences among the paths followed by these countries in transition. These are institutional differences (property regime, worker participation, role of the state in the economy, etc.), differences in economic structure (degree of development and of competitiveness, macroeconomic structure, inflation, etc.), and differences of attitude towards international partnerships. The disintegration process imposes extremely high costs, which are not only the costs of war but also those arising from institutional change, from restructuring the economy, and from competing on markets. It is more difficult to define the benefits of transition, which for the moment can only be clearly distinguished in the countries least affected by war, i.e. Slovenia and Macedonia.

Part Two of the book contains a number of essays which analyse the prospects and problems of possible new processes of integration.

Van Selm's paper surveys some of the principal conclusions concerning the possible advantages of a customs union or of a monetary union. As regards the former, van Selm indicates the principal criteria for assessment of the economic convenience of the initiative: with the benefits, which principally derive from a 'volume of trade effect' (which requires an increase in specialization that is only possible if the partners have activities in common and comparable levels of development) on the one hand; and the possible negative effects deriving from 'terms of trade effects'.

As regards monetary unions, their possible benefits (in terms of a reduction in risks and transaction costs, of an increase in capital mobility, and - according to some - of credibility) are correlated with the economy's degree of openness towards potential partners. Their costs derive mainly from the divergent levels of development of the partners (who can no longer resolve differing preferences for inflation and real interest rates), as well as those deriving from the adjustments required to absorb asymmetric demand or supply shocks. Also in the case of monetary union, the similarity of the partners' levels of development and the reciprocal openness of their economies are positive features; factor mobility and the budget redistributive capacities of the union are also of major importance.

Having identified what may be called the 'success indicators' of economic integration initiatives, van Selm applies this 'grid' in assessment of the economic rationality of the processes ongoing in Europe. As regards the European Union, van Selm's analysis causes him to be doubtful about possible benefits, mainly because of the reduced labour mobility and scant redistributive capacity of the community budget. As regards the Soviet Union, his conclusion is that there is insufficient space for the advantageous reconstitution of a monetary area, whereas the creation of a customs union might have positive effects on the development of the area.

The topic of a possible new integration among the economies of Eastern Europe is addressed by the two essays by Andreff and Andreff and by Brezinski. The former examine the diverse alternative aggregations available to the countries already belonging to the CMEA; a hypothesis which necessarily entails breaking the links that have tied them together. The authors analyse the effects of the dissolution of the CMEA (together with the disintegration of the USSR), and they apply to disintegration the conclusions drawn, *in the reverse direction*, by the theory on international economic integration.

The figures for the period 1988-92 confirm the predictions, based on this theory of a collapse of trade in the ex-CMEA area, of trade diversion among the ex-partners and of trade creation with the Western economies by certain countries more committed than others to transition - Hungary and Poland especially. Given the close links of interdependence among the countries of the ex-USSR, the distintegration of the latter has had even more devastating effects on the trade of the new states than those which have affected the other ex-CMEA countries. Given this situation, it is natural that the countries of Central-Eastern Europe (CCEEs) should seek closer integration with Western markets, in particular in Europe; a process which may be encouraged by the creation of new integrated areas among the CCEEs which will cooperate with the European Union with a view to eventually joining it. Madeleine and Wladimir Andreff examine five of these possible areas of aggregation, analysing the possible advantages of their integration with the EU on the basis of prerequisites drawn from the theory. Using a set of statistical indices on trade relations among the countries concerned and a further qualitative criterion (the dynamics of the transition process in each CCEE), they reach the conclusion - subject to political, ethnic, military, etc. uncertainties - that the potentially best solution would pass through the so-called 'Visegrád Channel', or through a free trade area in Central-Eastern Europe comprising six countries which already have agreements with the EU. Much more uncertain would be the advantages of solutions involving the countries formerly belonging to the USSR or Yugoslavia.

While the Andreffs' analysis concerns all the countries of the ex-CMEA, but focuses principally on those in Central-Eastern Europe, Brezinski concentrates on the economies of the countries which formerly belonged to the USSR. He highlights the distortions in the use of resources, in commercial flows, in the mentality and in the social behaviour that the Soviet system produced. The structure of trade relations which ties the various republics together, which was exposed by the break-up of the USSR, is such to render full economic independence difficult to achieve under current conditions. In fact, for many republics, a fall in inter-republic trade has immediate counter-effects on the national income. In addition to the problems of openness towards the world economy, which Russia has sought to resolve in the 1990s, is the problem of monetary relations among the ex-USSR countries brought about by the dissolution of the ruble zone. Given the interdependence among the economies of the republics, a system of payments should be maintained and improved; however, various republics must now also cope with problems of monetary and fiscal sovereignty, which they must conciliate with the needs of coordination.

Brezinski considers three possible alternatives for economic relations among the republics. The first is that of complete independence; given the close real interdependence among the respective economies this option seems unrealistic. The second alternative is concentric circles of association, with a core group of republics forming a currency union and a common market; but this scenario also encounters the obstacle of interdependence, which would impede most of the republics from adopting differentiated forms of association. The third alternative - the one that Brezinski regards as most realistic - consists of the creation of an economic union on the basis of equal membership, with a uniform monetary and fiscal policy; this, however, would come about *after* a system of independent convertible currencies had been created. This option, Brezinski stresses, requires determined steps to be taken in integrating the individual republican economies with the world economy - the which entails substantial help (as does the modernization process) from Western countries and from the international institutions.

Leaving the context of the Soviet Union behind, the paper by Rangelova examines the situation of the Balkan area (Albania, Bulgaria, Greece, Romania, ex-Yugoslavia and Turkey) *vis-à-vis* processes of disintegration and reintegration; an area characterized by socio-cultural similarities and, in the past, by political and economic ones as well. Rangelova examines the two principal groups of countries in the area (those formerly with planned economies, and those with market economies) and briefly surveys the economic situation and prospects of each of them. As regards prospects for cooperation among the countries in the area, an important role could be played by Turkey, which has ambitions as a regional power and has already promoted the Black Sea cooperation agreement. On the other side, the principal task falls to Western Europe and in particular to the European Union, whose current tendencies towards integration are examined. Western Europe could do a great deal to encourage the development of the Balkan countries and the transition of those now orienting themselves to the market, for which the rigorous stabilization policies required by the international institutions have had heavy recessionary effects. At the moment, however, the tendency is towards exploiting outlets in the East for Western products instead of encouraging flows in the opposite direction, in the spirit of a joint effort for integration.

The final essay in Part Two, by Kalmbach, is of particular interest because it presents the case of *already achieved* integration - at least at the political level - with the effects that it has had on the various subjects involved compared with their initial expectations.

After surveying the political and economic premises for German unification, Kalmbach focuses on the evolution of the labour market in the new *Länder*. The period following unification saw in the ex-GDR - as in the other countries caught up by the collapse of the Soviet empire - a fall in industrial production and an equally dramatic and unprecedented increase in unemployment. This, however, was accompanied by a growth of wages (both nominal and real) which, according to agreements between workers and employers, should have brought wages and salaries in the Eastern *Länder* into line with those in the Western ones. The principal aim of this policy (apart from raising living standards in the East, as promised prior to unification) was to discourage emigration to the West. In fact, according to Kalmbach, this policy could only lead to the reverse result: high wages helped to push firms in the East out of the market (since it was impossible for productivity to adjust with sufficient rapidity) and this exacerbated the unemployment problem; with the additional outcome that a decreasing proportion of workers in the East enjoyed the new living standards. Furthermore, high unemployment has had markedly negative effects on the federal budget, since the social security system has been extended to the new *Länder*, while the economic burden for it predictably falls on the Western Germans despite promises that unification would not be financed by tax increases. After analysing, on the basis of original calculations, the consequences of these policies on the labour market and on productivity in the East, Kalmbach addresses the problem of the distribution of the costs and benefits of unification which, according to the initial promises, should have had progressive Paretian effects. His striking conclusion is the following: that the citizens of the erstwhile FGR expected a cost-free unification process, with a strong impact on the development of economic activity in the West as well (which in fact happened in the early stages). The Easterners expected to enjoy living standards equal to those of their 'rich cousins' after a process of painless and brief transition. Instead, employment in the East has fallen steeply, and the group of workers who have obtained high wage increases are counter-weighted by the mass of people who live on unemployment benefit.

Social groups in the West, for their part, have been affected differently by unification. The financial burden has fallen in fact on low-income groups, which have benefited least from the positive effects. This is also due to a mechanism which Kalmbach highlights with extreme clarity: the exchange between flows (financial assistance to the East for transition) and stocks (property rights in the East). In fact, on the one hand, property collectivized after the Second World War and assigned to the *Treuhandanstalt* has been sold at very low prices, mainly to firms in the Western *Länder* which could guarantee investments to revive employment. On the other, property collectivized after 1949 has been restored to its legitimate owners, most of whom are also citizens of the West. Independently of good intentions, therefore, the strategy adopted has not only caused discontent among broad sections of the population in both East and West as regards living standards (flows), it has also had major consequences which will be prolonged in the future (stocks).

Finally, *Part Three* of the book collects together essays which deal with the monetary aspects of ongoing processes and whose principal focus is the role of the monetary institutions, although the importance of the topic is such that it is also treated in Parts One and Two. Of the four essays in this final part, two examine the transition from the Soviet ruble to the national currencies of Eastern Europe, while the other two discuss the role of the European monetary system in the light of its recent crisis and the prospects for the economic and monetary union of Western Europe.

With the disintegration of the Soviet Union, the various republics faced the problem of a monetary system previously based on the ruble as the common currency and (within the Union) controlled by the Moscow central bank. Hyperinflation, the need to render national economic policies independent and to undertake reforms towards a market system, and not least the effect on national sentiments within each republic exerted by the symbolic power of its own national currency, applied powerful centrifugal forces on the currency issued by Moscow. On the other hand, the commercial and financial links that tied the various republics together, as well as problems of internal stabilization and credibility, made immediate passage to full monetary sovereignty a formidable undertaking. At the centre of the ex-Union, the Russian government tackled the difficulties of managing a currency in common with economies which were beginning to manifest somewhat diverse problems and tendencies. The transition from the Soviet ruble to a system of national currencies, which with its intricacies and the various solutions proposed and tried, is the subject of Dabrowski's essay.

After describing the endemic hyperinflation of the last years of the USSR, Dabrowski describes the effects of the cessation of coordination among the macroeconomic policies, in a situation characterized by a single currency and with fifteen *independent* central banks. In this situation, the strategies of the various republics inevitably diverge: some may be tempted to reap the benefits (in terms of spending capacity and the inflow of reserves) of credit expansion, at the expense of those which pursue more restrictive policies: with the outcome, as Dabrowski points out, of producing generalized hyperinflation in the medium-to-long run. Faced with the inflationary effects of uncontrolled liquidity, the Russian government employed various devices to limit the external circulation of the ruble (cash) thereby provoking, at the beginning, an increase in monetary chaos. Subsequently it restricted foreign payments in rubles, establishing a bilateral clearing system with the other republics and halting access by the firms and financial institutions of the latter to the Russian foreign exchange market and investments in Russia through ruble accounts in Russian banks. These and other measures spelt the end of the ruble as a common currency. A number of republics (among them the Baltic ones, which will be discussed below) began to take steps to leave the ruble area definitively.

However, inflationary monetary expansion did not cease as a result of these measures: on the one hand because of the granting of a large amount of credit for exports to the other republics (for political reasons and on account of pressure by exporting Russian enterprises) accompanied by the under-pricing of the raw materials exported; on the other, because of the expansion of internal credit and financing of the huge budget deficit.

A new exchange market between the ruble and the currencies (the official currencies and the parallel ones) of the republics began to grow. The trend of quotations on this market was clearly influenced both by commercial and financial relations among the republics, and by the ability to each of them to stabilize its currency against Western ones. In its turn, the disintegration of the Soviet system of payments inevitably affected trade among the republics; added to which were the effects of the raising of trade barriers and the imposing of export controls, the consequences of regional political conflicts, and the differing evolution of reform and liberalization processes in the various republics.

This system is not yet satisfactory, but it is amenable to further development. A first step in this direction are the agreements of Bishkek and Minsk signed by eight republics (Russia included) which discipline the payments systems and the issue of rubles, regulate debts among the central banks and attempt to coordinate macroeconomic policies. Dabrowski considers a variety of possible future developments in the monetary system, ranging from the maintenance of a system of only partially convertible currencies to fully-fledged monetary union. Achievement of the latter, although possible, will be extremely difficult because of the problems of stabilization (above all in Russia) and the need to coordinate the macroeconomic policies of countries which have not synchronized their reform paths towards the market and which, apart from their sovereignty, they are now loath to renounce. This links with the theme of the *prerequisites* for an economic and monetary union already explored in this book (see, for example, the essay by Brezinski).

Within the picture outlined above, a number of the countries of the ex-Soviet Union have already begun to move in different directions. Lainela and Sutela examine the evolution of the monetary systems in the Baltic countries in their paper. After setting out the arguments in favour of the introduction of national currencies, they consider the situation in the Baltic countries, each of which has adopted different strategies. Lainela and Sutela concentrate in particular on Estonia and Latvia, which were the first to undertake monetary reform.

In Estonia, the new currency, the kroon, was introduced even before all the conditions deemed necessary by the IMF were in place. Moreover, the introduction of national currencies in the ruble area also required bargaining over trade and payments with the other countries in an area involving numerous and conflicting interests. One of the principal problems to be addressed was undoubtedly the attitude of Russia; apart from political frictions (also the decline in trade with Russia was seen by the Estonians as an act of retaliation), there were such concrete problems as the sharing of the debt of the ex-USSR and the destination of the rubles circulating in the country. Russia's attitude to Estonian monetary sovereignty only became favourable when it beacme clear that a shrinking ruble area was in its interests. By accepting to return the rubles collected with the conversion to the new currency, Estonia has in fact replaced the Soviet bank's liabilities with its own liabilities issued against foreign currency reserves.

The regulations governing notes and coin in circulation and the pegging of the kroon to the DM at a rate which overvalues the latter has had the important consequences of reducing trade with Russia (although there are other reasons for this) and stimulating exports to the countries with strong currencies. This, however, has been accompanied by a rise in the price of imports. A major problem which arises (here too) is that of stabilization policies, with the consequent fall in internal production and in employment. The instrument chosen for the first stage of monetary reform, the 'currency board', gives rigidity to the system because it ties the money supply to currency earned by exports. If, as has happened, the latter grows more rapidly than domestic production, inflation is generated; if it falls, then a monetary squeeze comes about. According to Lainela and Sutela, the passage to a fully-fledged central bank system, with monetary policy powers, is therefore necessary.

As has already been mentioned, the Baltic countries have followed different paths of monetary reform. Whereas Lithuania has encountered major difficulties in monetary stabilization (which is not discussed in detail by Lainela and Sutela), Latvia, like Estonia, has been able rapidly to stabilize its inflation rate and exchange rate. The latter, however, is allowed to fluctuate, partly out of deliberate choice. The timing of monetary reform in Latvia has differed with respect to Estonia, with the introduction of an interim currency and then the definitive conversion, in 1993, to the lats. This policy initially increased the inflow of rubles (the restitution of which to Russia was obstructed by the difficulty of reaching agreement on the Soviet debt), a phenomenon which probably induced the central bank to suspend the absorption of currencies from the CIS countries. Despite freedom of exchange, the Latvian currency has been highly unstable against the dollar. A large money market has been created in Riga, which is regulated towards the CIS currencies with the fixing of maximum exchange rates. Since this system can be circumvented by three-way currency dealings, it has penalized enterprises exporting to the ruble area.

Lainela and Sutela stress that while withdrawal from the ruble area has allowed the Baltic countries to distance themselves from the monetary chaos of Russia, the stability of their new currencies depends in the short term on stabilization policies and, in the long term, on the ability of these countries to undertake structural reforms of their economies (which, at least initially, will probably have negative effects on standards of living), to build the institutions adequate for the purpose, to manage them efficiently, and, not least, to obtain resources from abroad.

The problem of economic and monetary union, as we have seen, is frequently examined in this book. Whereas in the essays discussed previously, argument focused on countries already belonging to the ruble area, the papers by Targetti and Bosco discuss the complex problems that the countries of the European Union, already well advanced towards integration, encounter on the road to monetary union (EMU).

Targetti analyses the (intermediate and final) goals of the EMU constitution. He dwells in particular on the European Monetary System (EMS) mechanisms, on the rules - optional and compulsory - governing intervention by the central banks, and on the norms regulating their short-term financing and medium and long-term financial assistance. These rules have apparently created a more secure system than that devised at Bretton Woods. However, like the latter system, the EMS is asymmetric, in the sense that one of the countries (Germany) occupies a dominant role, with monetary and fiscal policies to which the others must adjust if they wish to maintain exchange rate parities. It was believed (until the crisis of 1992) that the autonomy of monetary policy in this country, the independence of its central bank, and the possibility for the other countries to 'import credibility' from it, were sufficient to ensure stability. Targetti argues that in fact the system contains structural and persistent inflationary differentials. This is a key element in interpretation of the crisis of the system, together with the quasi-fixity of nominal exchange rates and with German economic policy, which leads to a raising of the interest rate. According to Targetti, therefore, the fragility of the system is due on the one hand to the rigidity produced by quasi-fixed exchange rates and to the above-mentioned asymmetry, in the presence of free capital movement, and, on the other, to the persistent divergences among the economies of the member states at both the real and the monetary and financial levels. In Targetti's view, the Treaty of Maastricht gives excessive importance to monetary union compared with other important objectives, such as the strengthening of the community political institutions, of budget capacities, and so on. However, he argues, monetary union is a goal worth pursuing in its own right; the problem is that it conflicts with the intermediate goals set by the Treaty itself. Targetti criticises the 'Euro-orthodox' positions which advocate a Europe on the German model. Europe is characterized by a dual economy, with institutional and structural differences, also in fiscal behaviour; these are the factors responsible for divergences in rates of inflation. To the 'Euro-orthodox' opinion that the real factors at the basis of divergence should first be adjusted and then proceed with monetary union, Targetti advances the contrary view that monetary union should be achieved rapidly, without intermediate stages, and then real divergences should be addressed using the instruments of the community budget (did not Germany do so with the ex-DDR?). The process of convergence and cohesion, which is closely connected with the growth of employment and income, should be accelerated by designing the new European institutions for this purpose. Targetti concludes by describing two scenarios of transition: one in which the need to fulfil the pre-established prerequisites entails a two-speed system; and another in which the system is cooperative and the intermediate goals of individual countries are assumed by the community institutions.

Also the essay by Bosco analyses the nature and the mechanisms of the EMS. Taking his cue from the crisis of 1992, which saw two countries - Italy and Great Britain - forced temporarily to leave the system, Bosco asks whether its cause was contingent in nature or whether the system no longer meets the needs of the European economy; and, moreover, whether it will continue to be advantageous for a country like Italy to stay in the system if it does not change. Clearly these questions require assessment of the benefits and costs of EMS membership. Bosco explores this theme by examining various arguments for and against Italy's rejoining the EMS. As regards one of the most obvious (theoretical) advantages of the EMS - the reduction of uncertainty in intra-community exchanges - Bosco notes that Italy has in fact been penalized by the constant revaluation of the lira in real terms. Another possible advantage of the system is the monetary discipline that it imposes on member countries. The above-mentioned asymmetry of the system also increases its credibility, which is particularly to the advantage of the countries with weaker currencies. Bosco notes, however, that in the first half of the 1980s the system was unable to act as an instrument of inflationary discipline; subsequently, when the EMS acquired credibility, the liberalization of the capital markets and the establishment of practically fixed exchange rates exposed the persistent causes of inflation in various countries; causes other than a lack of credibility in monetary policy. Bosco then analyses the role of the EMS within the framework of the Treaty of Maastricht and shows that such a rigid system is not best able to bring about monetary union without risks and at acceptable costs. Costs which consist in the loss of full monetary sovereignty and of the ability to alter exchange rates. In a system without mechanisms of fiscal compensation (at the community level), the loss of the exchange rate instrument renders the absorption of asymmetric shocks more costly, especially for the weak countries. Commitment to a pre-established disinflation path, moreover, may lead an economy to diverge in the short period from the desired trade-off between unemployment and inflation. This loss of autonomy, however, could be more than compensated, for a high-inflation country, by the advantages of long-term credibility.

Overall, according to Bosco, in the specific case of Italy, the costs of the loss of monetary autonomy and of competitiveness do not seem to be offset by the advantages of belonging to the system.

We pointed out at the outset that the vicissitudes of the EMS are particularly interesting because they concern countries which - unlike those of Eastern Europe - have already achieved considerable integration among market economies. The evidence provided by the last two essays in the book clearly shows that the path towards economic and monetary union is neither simple nor straightforward. Significant here is the fact that the EMS broke down at precisely the moment when it had acquired its long-sought-after credibility and when the inflation rates of its member countries at last seemed to be moving towards convergence. This once again seems to confirm the dominance of the real economy over the monetary economy: divergence in the efficiency of production and of the bureaucracy, in real competitiveness and in the capacity for growth can only be remedied by intervention in the real economy. This evidence does not contradict the observation of the damage that the currency's loss of value, especially in situations of hyperinflation, causes: for instance, in terms of the distortion in the use of resources and in the distribution of income. Inflation must certainly be curbed, in the shortest time possible, compatibly with the necessity to safeguard and reinforce productive capacity: and it is precisely as regards this requirement that the role of international cooperation both in the East and West is crucial. Whereas in the West cooperation signifies principally the mobilization of budget resources, in the East it also means constructing a system of regional relationships which does not pursue solely the objectives of individual countries but takes account - in a dynamic process which should profoundly change the overall system - of interdependencies which have grown and consolidated over time.

PART ONE

Integration and Disintegration: an Economic Interpretation[1]

Bruno Dallago

1. Introduction

Economic theory has traditionally paid scant attention to the processes of integration among different economies and the disintegration of national economic systems.[2] Applied analysis of these processes, moreover, have been concerned less with understanding their causes than with description, analysis and evaluation of their consequences. This applies principally to processes of disintegration, and for essentially two reasons.

On the one hand, dominant economic theory generally presupposes rational behaviour (or at least a constant level of rationality) in individuals and consequently in groups of individuals at any level and in organizations. It has therefore occupied itself with the consequences of this behaviour and with the conditions necessary for there to be no obstacles against its free expression. This approach restricts its analysis to cases of 'rational' integration and disintegration processes; cases, that is, in which the initial situation was sub-optimal due to the predominance of economic institutions less efficient than the free market, or to the excessively limited nature of the national market, or again to the existence of the forced and therefore inefficient integration of national economies.

The first of these cases evidences the need to change the economic system and is either irrelevant to our purposes or belongs among the ones that follow. The second and third cases open the way to, respectively, supranational integration and disintegration. This latter case has been the least studied and is the most difficult to analyse and comprehend, because it entails renunciation of the benefits of a larger market: division of labour, economies of scale, comparative advantages. This is even truer when one bears in mind that the disintegration of a previously unitary, if inefficient, system is often followed by a rapid breakdown in the economic relationships among its previous, now independent components which is not offset by integration with other economies.

An illuminating example is forthcoming from analysis of the commercial flows and economic relationships in general among the member countries, until 1991, of Comecon and among the republics of the ex-Soviet Union. In all these cases, the relationships among these countries have rapidly declined in both relative and absolute terms, and they have been replaced only in part by relationships with Western countries. These may yield their benefits only in the long period, while in the meantime they impose the major costs stemming from the necessary change to the institutions and from the restructuring of the economy and of international economic relations. In this sense, the disintegration of a complex (supranational) economic system presents analogies with the break-up of a multinational company due to its inability efficiently to coordinate its activity (the activity of its various components based on mutual advantage) in order to respond to market stimuli and to a deterioration in quality when unitary costs are constant or increasing; an inability which therefore induces its exit from the market.

Alternative lines of theoretical enquiry have recently highlighted how individuals, groups of individuals and organizations may exhibit behaviours which correspond to different kinds of rationality, and that they may not necessarily seek to maximize the typical goals of economic activity (some sort of income, a certain quantity of output, a share of the market). Attempts have also been made to adjust the concept of utility so that it encompasses anything that individuals wish effectively to accomplish. However, this development blurs the concept of utility and reduces its applicability, and it also ignores the fact that the integration and disintegration of an economic system are sometimes the unwanted and unexpected outcomes of action by individuals, groups and organizations (or at least a large part of them) explicitly geared to a more restricted goal, such as changing certain aspects of the economic system. At the same time, the freedom of choice available to the promoters of change is not limitless, because the final result is always in some way conditioned by the initial situation (path dependency).

The second reason for orthodox economic theory's lack of interest in these processes, and for the lack of relevance of the orthodox approach to their analysis, lies in its predominantly static approach or, better, in that of comparative statics, which prevents evaluation of the richness and the implications of integration and disintegration processes and their often 'unpredictable' or 'irrational' consequences.

The effects of this approach are particularly evident in the case of the disintegration of an economy characterized by the strong and long-lasting economic and institutional integration of its individual components; an integration induced by endogenous reasons (the economic advantages obtained by at least one of the parties) or exogenous reasons (political, for example). These cases are usually ignored and attributed to the prevalence of extraeconomic constraints. They are thus 'left' to other disciplines, and their major economic implications are therefore neglected. The static inspiration of the orthodox approach therefore does not provide the flexibility required to handle processes of change which involve the institutions. Moreover, according to the orthodox approach, an 'irrational' and therefore sub-optimal integration cannot last for long because it would incur losses for all participants. This eventuality would soon force the government to reverse direction towards disintegration or to introduce a form of reintegration which would re-establish optimal conditions. And yet these developments often do not occur, or else they have only come about after considerable delay and for diverse reasons. It should also be pointed out that this approach overlooks the implications of these processes for economic development, as well as for institutional factors, most notably incentives .

This approach to the question fails to assess whether, in what circum-stances, and how, an apparently irrational process may yield positive results for at least one of the parties concerned. After all, this is one of the strongest economic motivations (as well as others of a non-economic nature) for secessionist tendencies in the (usually) most economically advanced area of a country. It is this, among other things, that has driven the behaviour of the ex-Soviet republics of the Baltic (Estonia, Latvia and Lithuania), of the Czech Republic, and of Slovenia and Croatia. It also partly explains the separatist or federalist demands of the *Lega Nord* in Italy, of the Catalan and Basque autonomist/independentist movement in Spain and of the Tyroleans in Italy. And it accounts in part for the behaviour of Hungary and Poland in Comecon during the 1980s and which led to its disintegration.

History shows that apparently strange and unforeseeable processes often appear: the separation of a smaller geographical unit from a much larger body has, in several cases, led to great economic progress in the smaller area, when economic theory has predicted exactly the opposite. It thus appears that disintegration may trigger energies which were previously concealed or else dissipated in constant attrition against the larger body, and that it enables more efficient use to be made of the favourable conditions concentrated in a small territorial area. This has been the case of, for example, Finland (which split off from Russia), the Czech regions (from the Hapsburg Empire), Greece (from the Ottoman Empire), Panama (from Colombia). Static analysis fails to explain these events, in which disaggregation serves only as the catalyst for a set of changes in the country's most important institutions.

The case of integration is apparently less problematic, for it enables countries to benefit from the expansion of their market. However, already at the level of theory, one discerns other effectively or potentially less advantageous aspects. Although on the one hand integration creates trade by removing internal barriers (trade creation), on the other it usually leads to the raising of stronger barriers against trade with third countries, and therefore to its reduction in at least relative but often also absolute terms (trade diversion). The effects of integration are positive whenever the former effect prevails over the latter, and this occurs when the integration is between economies which are complementary to each other and which already engage in a considerable amount of reciprocal trade.

However, these economies - precisely because they are complementary - trade among themselves even before integration takes place. Trade creation may then be less significant than in the case of integrating competitive economies. In the latter event, economies which formerly competed on world markets because they were specialised in the same industries must now restructure their specialisation. This creates a good amount of new trade flows which did not exist before and which could not have come into being without integration.[3]

This approach, however, is less useful in explanation of various recent phenomena, most of them interconnected, in Europe. There are four cases of particular salience here: the reasons for the failure and consequent dissaggregation of Comecon, of the Soviet Union, of Yugoslavia, and the recent difficulties in Western European monetary integration. To these can be added the unexpected difficulties - due to major economic and non-economic factors - hampering the integration of the two Germanies and also the scant success of the attempt at the partial reintegration of Eastern Europe (Visegrad Agreement), of the Black Sea area, and of a large part of the ex-Soviet Union (Commonwealth of Independent States or CIS).

For all these reasons, the traditional approach, though useful and decisive in several cases, appears unable to give a satisfactory explanation of the violent turmoil and apparently inexplicable and irrational changes that have occurred in the countries and economies of Europe in the last five years. Fortunately, as we shall see, less orthodox approaches exist (those, for example, of Hirschman and Olson) which, originally applied to problems similar or assimilable with those examined in this book, are particularly useful for those who seek a more satisfactory solution. Moreover, an opportune modification of the orthodox approach (as expounded by Breton) and the use of certain suitably adapted concepts and tools (such as the demand and supply curve and the concept of public good) may be of help in explaining certain essential aspects of the problems examined here.

2. THE ECONOMIC NATURE OF INTEGRATION AND DISINTEGRATION

The integration and disintegration of economic systems, as well as political and social ones, are institutional changes of such magnitude that they decisively influence all the variables of the socio-economic system. They often stem from contingent changes in the environment that provides the framework for the operation of the socio-economic systems and comprises all phenomena not strictly and wholly economic in nature. Of great importance among these are nationalism and supranationalism - phenomena which may be engendered by motives and events of various kinds, and which are discussed below. Other important aspects are, for example, geopolitical changes (such as the Cold War with the Soviet Union) which induce expansion of the economic basis of defence;[4] or the realization by various economies previously dominant on the world stage, like those of Western Europe, that unless they integrate they will inevitably lose out in competition against the new economic powers, most notably the United States and Japan.

Apart from the environment, deliberate policies (economic or otherwise) introduced following a specific political decision taken by the government may activate processes of integration and disintegration. However, they may also be the unintended and unforeseen consequence of economic (and non-economic) policy decisions taken either erroneously or as the unavoidable choice of the lesser evil. The history of the European Union provides several examples. Centrifugal forces may be unleashed, for example, by the scrapping of an obsolete industry incurring grave losses for the country but which is concentrated in a region or a republic belonging to a federation or confederation. In this case, if the consequences are undesirable they can be remedied with appropriate compensatory policies, but the lack of these or their failure may activate processes of disintegration.

Finally, integration and disintegration processes may derive from substantial changes in the performance of one or more economies. Usually, the deterioration or destabilization of an economy leads, because of its loss of competitiveness, to the exacerbation of internal economic, social and political tensions which may give rise to the disaggregation, first, and then to the disintegration of the economic system. Conversely, a prolonged period of economic growth, and the prospect of sustaining it by expanding the market, are usually factors favourable to the integration of various economic systems - as has been the case of Western Europe and of Germany.

Evidently, there is feedback and reciprocal influence among all these elements. However, given that our interest here is analysis of the integration and disintegration of economies, we shall concentrate on the factors that lead to these outcomes, on how they come about, and on the changes produced in socio-economic systems.

The results of integration and disintegration can be usefully compared to public goods (or 'bads'). This possibility stems from two of their key features. First, their 'supply' is indivisible: the integration and disintegration of a economic system affect all the individuals, groups and organizations living and operating in that particular economic system. Secondly, the 'consumption' of both these goods by an individual, group or organization in no way reduces the consumption of others. Indeed the opposite is the case: the ability of everyone to consume these goods presupposes that at least the decisive part of those living and operating in the economic system (the majority, a group of individuals or organizations with the power to impose their will on others) wish to consume that good. It is therefore the majority - or better the choice made by the median individual, group or organization - or the group in power which determines whether or not consumption by everyone takes place.

Two further key features of integration and disintegration now emerge with especial clarity. Because supply depends on the existence of a majority in favour of it, integration and disintegration pose a major problem for collective action. However, the diversified nature of the individuals, groups and organizations involved ensures that the relationship between 'demand' and 'supply' - that is, the process itself of collective action - is not symmetrical. Since certain groups have a stronger interest (preference) than others in obtaining supply of the good (more intense 'demand'), individual demands cannot simply be summed. This means that production may take place even though the demand is advanced by a qualified minority (a privileged group) in a particularly intense and organized manner compared with the disorganized majority of actors (a latent group) which does not pursue the goal of collective action - namely, integration or disintegration - or which attributes minor importance to it. It is indeed possible to demonstrate that the larger the group, the more difficulties it encounters in organizing itself to pursue an interest. The opposite applies to small groups distinguished by a distinct and important interest which is shared by all its members.[5] This becomes more evident the less efficiently the institutions promote collective action by large latent groups.

The second fundamental feature derives from the first and from the similarity with public goods. Because the consumption of the good (or the 'bad') is enjoyed (or suffered) by all the individuals, groups and organizations that constitute the socio-economic system, this holds also for those who abstain from the collective action necessary to reveal the preference for the good (or the dispreference for the bad) and therefore to activate its supply. In this manner, in fact, they avoid paying the private cost entailed by the collective action and thus operate as free riders.

In normal circumstances, the workings of a socio-economic system are regulated by the routines adopted by economic agents.[6] Routines tend to preserve the basic characteristics of the system over time; but they may nevertheless change, because systems are obliged to deal with new problems caused by changes in the environment. If these changes are sufficiently important and enduring, they lead to either the spontaneous development of new routines or to reforms designed to introduce a new set of routines better adapted to the new situation. However, as in biological organisms and in microeconomic organizations, system control processes seek to resist changes in routines.[7]

Change may first of all be obstructed by uncertainty over the results and advantages of the future system. This concerns uncertainty both over the future situation and over possible undesirable outcomes, which reinforces the former kind of uncertainty. A second obstacle is the costs entailed by transition from one system to the other; costs which may be, or appear to be, so high as to block the change.[8] Consider, for example, the conflicts among social groups defending opposing interests that accompany every change, or the inevitable economic and social upheaval which ensues until the new institutions and the new rules have been established and internalized. This applies both to change which is expected to be slow - in which lower costs must be borne for a longer period of time - and to change with a more stronger but more immediate impact. This is not to imply that change is impossible in all cases because of uncertainty and the costs of transition; it means, rather, that only certain strategies of change are likely to succeed. These strategies should reduce the number of people and organizations damaged by the change to the minimum, and they should raise the number benefiting from it to the maximum.

Thirdly, the collective action required to achieve a better system may be blocked by a lack of cooperation. This situation can be described in terms of the prisoner's dilemma. All those concerned want collective action to take place, but individually they prefer to abstain from it. Change usually involves conflict, and this entails costs of a private nature. On the other hand, the benefits accruing from the collective action are public goods. In this situation, therefore, individuals who do not cooperate (free riders) may enjoy a free benefit which is greater, the larger the group affected by the change. Consequently the collective action may not take place.[9]

There exist a number of organizations - such as political parties, trade unions, pressure groups, associations, and so on - which help to overcome this problem; but they do not always suffice. Especially in periods of rapid and profound change, these organizations may themselves enter crisis and lose their authority. However, the constant interaction of individuals in a society favours cooperation, so that the society itself is able to promote evolution and change even in a prisoner's dilemma situation.

Finally, problems of path dependency[10] and of irreversibility may render the final outcome dependent on the initial state, and therefore on the history of the system and of the country in question.

If despite all these factors, and despite the unpredictable consequences of purely exogenous factors, collective action does indeed take place and achieves its goal, then this will be for two concomitant reasons. First the promoters of the collective action (the privileged group) view their effort as an investment in a collective good which will pay off in the future, usually in terms of political, economic and social power (for example, by enabling the members of the group to take control of the government and firms), of earnings in terms of stock (for example, through privatization at prices lower than market ones, or the assignation of property expropriated from a minority to the members of the group), and of increased income flow (usually in the form of well-paid jobs). These features of collective action often appear in clusters and mutually reinforce each other.

The second reason for collective action to take place, even though it has been promoted by a minority, is that it may be able to offer efficient selective incentives;

that is, incentives able to discriminate among the individuals in a group or among individual organizations according to their contribution to the group's or society's achievement of its goal or interest. Incentives may be positive when they reward those acting in the interest of the group or society, or they may be negative when they punish those who refuse to assume their share of the costs or to accept the disadvantages of collective action. Selective incentives therefore induce passive individuals, groups and organizations to accept the leadership of the privileged group, thereby reinforcing - or at least not obstructing - its action. Examples of selective incentives are the co-option of other organizations' leaders, the threat of excluding other individuals from the returns on the investment in integration or in disintegration, ideological or moral campaigns designed to convince other individuals, groups and organizations of the political and moral importance and value of the chosen goal (for example, by exploiting nationalist sentiments), terrorist attacks against the individuals, groups and organizations actively opposing the collective action in order to induce them (or their constituency) to side with the privileged group.[11]

The dynamics of collective action are therefore of decisive importance for the outcomes of integration and disintegration. Before investigating them, however, we must first establish what it is that triggers the processes of integration and disintegration, as well as the ways - alternative or complementary - in which the problems that arise in the economic system and then lead to integration or disintegration can be dealt with.

The point of departure is a series of events which precipitate an economic situation which some deem unacceptable or damaging and as preventing rapid and substantial improvements if acceptable effort is made, or else induce them to believe that not all the options have been taken up and that the economy is excessively inside the production frontier potentially achievable by integrating various complementary economies. The first of these possibilities - which recalls events in the Soviet Union - threatens to activate processes which may lead to the disintegration of the economic system, while the second - which calls to mind the situation of post-war Western Europe - indicates that it is advisable to integrate two or more economies in order to reap the benefits. I shall examine the case of disintegration, treating that of integration only marginally because it is better known.

3. THE ONSET OF DISINTEGRATION PROCESSES

An economic system may disintegrate for various reasons.[12] Firstly, fortuitous and often non-economic factors may be involved. In any economic (or social or political) system, agents - be they individuals, groups or organizations - often deviate from behaviour which is efficient, rational, law-abiding or in any case functional to fulfilling their institutional goal. However, it may happen that the normal workings of the market will cause - in the presence of an initial disequilibrium in the quantitative and qualitative endowment of production factors - further disequilibria in the location of the benefits of growth, as well as conventional problems of distribution and social stratification. We know, for example, that investments tend to cluster in regions where conditions are more favourable to them, especially if demand is concentrated in the area, if transport costs and other transaction costs are high, and if prices are not perfectly flexible. If left to itself, therefore, the market rapidly widens the gap between the most developed and the least developed areas of a country. This may provoke a reaction by the more disadvantaged area (a region, a state in a federation, a colony). It is superfluous to add that this widening gap may also be the deliberate or unexpected result of economic policy or of politics *tout court*.

At this point, individuals and organizations with resources located in the more disadvantaged area of the country have various options available to them. They may not react at all to the unfavourable processes in progress and adapt to the widening gap. In a world in which information is of massive importance in politics too, this situation is highly improbable if extended to all participants; this case is therefore not examined here. It is in fact very likely that some agent will react in some way. Since these marginal reactions may trigger collective action, it is on them that we concentrate our analysis.

A certain number of individuals may decide to transfer themselves physically from the disadvantaged to the advantaged area of the country (Hirschman's 'exit'[13]). Organizations may behave in the same way: for example, a certain number of firms may transfer their offices and operations. Or it may only be capital that transfers itself in search of more profitable investments in the more developed area. This behaviour has two consequences. First, it impoverishes the most disadvantaged part of the country by depriving it of essential human, financial and material resources, and it correspondingly enriches the more advantaged part. The gap between them therefore widens rapidly, and this may provoke severe social tensions which a democratic country cannot withstand for very long. At the same time, this exit signals to the government that all is not well in one area of the country. The cases of Italy and Germany are extremely interesting in this regard.

There is a further kind of exit which takes the form of discrimination against the products or resources of one area of the country. For example, individuals and organizations in the most disadvantaged area may refuse to purchase products or to accept personnel (workers, technicians, managers, tourists) from the more advantaged one. This may happen for political reasons: consider the boycott on the tea imported by the British to the port of Boston which sparked the American War of Independence, and the many cases of the boycotting of products from colonial powers organized by independence movements. It may also involve mafia or criminal methods, such as mafia restrictions on bids for tender made by companies from other regions. Similar results can be achieved by applying discriminatory taxation. A specular case, but with the same consequences, occurred after German unification when the citizens of the Eastern *Länder* refused to purchase products from firms located in ex-East Germany. In these cases the internal market becomes highly segmented for social and political reasons.

Exit signals to the goverment that it must intervene with policies designed to re-establish equilibrium between the two regions of the country. This may result, for example, from an income transfer policy implemented directly or through either differential income taxes or credit policies in the two regions. The government may also resort to a policy of public works or investment incentives in the more disadvantaged part of the country. Whichever option it chooses, a transfer of income resources moves in the reverse direction, and this may provoke discontent in the more advantaged part of the country. The same consequences may also arise if one region develops much more rapidly than the rest of the country for reasons other than income or resources transfer as happened for instance in South-Eastern China since the 1980s.

Exit is a typically individual response which may be organized into mass proportions. Discontented individuals and organizations may, however, resort to a different kind of behaviour: they may protest in words or deeds (Hirschman's 'voice'). Protest is often individual at the beginning. For example, single individuals or representatives of organizations apply to local politicians in order to obtain advantages: guaranteed transfers, jobs, the favouring of one of the competing bidders for public works. As long as this situation persists, the economic, political and social stability of the disadvantaged region may be enhanced. Individual protest, however, may spill over into destructiveness: disadvantaged individuals, those for example who have lost their jobs, may resort to vandalism or crime. Protest may assume a collective and organized character, however, if it is motivated by reasons that are widespread and significantly affect a large number of people.

As long as exit and voice remain individual actions, they may be viewed as attempts to avoid the private costs imposed by the disadvantaged situation in the absence of the collective benefits available in normal circumstances. In a certain sense, therefore, those who effectively exit and protest in a disadvantaged situation may be compared to an individual or organization seeking, by different means, to achieve the same results that comparable individuals and organizations would obtain simply by supplying their resources in a country with the characteristics of the more advantaged part. Since the situation is disadvantaged, individual action entails that at least some of the private costs should be off-loaded onto other individuals or organizations, or that the results of the collective advantages may somehow be privatized by the promoters of the collective action in order to off-set the greater costs sustained.

The government, of course, possesses effective instruments with which to discourage or to impede both exit and voice, and to reinforce loyalty. Some of these instruments can only be activated indirectly: for example, moral sentiments such as patriotism and nationalism, or an external threat, which mobilize the cohesive forces of society and stimulate loyalty to the country among individuals and organizations. Other instruments are employed directly: for example, the government may stifle protest and may impede the internal and external exit (migration) of people, organizations and resources. For many years the Soviet Union adopted a system of internal passports which considerably restricted internal mobility in the country, while exit abroad was virtually impossible. The German Democratic Republic built the Berlin Wall for the same purpose. The centralized allocation of capital and, to a much more limited extent, of education and work also prevented the exit of resources.

Governments that react in this manner behave like a monopolist which, unable to control costs, raises the price of its product or, unable to maintain its quality, does not reduce its price. This also implies that the monopolist will seek to acquire patents, or firms planning to enter a market made attractive by the inefficiency of the monopolist, in order to control them or neutralize them.

Action of this kind may, at least in the short term, achieve the results desired, so that the situation temporarily stabilizes. This outcome may also be encouraged by the interaction between the various possible kinds of response (exit, voice, loyalty) and the government's action. The government may selectively allow exit or voice by certain individuals and organizations and instead seek to strengthen the loyalty of the majority of the population and organizations. For example, it may permit protest by a limited number of people, such as intellectuals in rigidly controlled private clubs or black marketeers. The government may even enable them or force them to defect: for example, it may grant them permission to travel abroad on the condition that they do not return, or send a deposed politician into exile. At the same time, these individuals and organizations are subjected to an intense political and ideological campaign designed to portray them as enemies and as damaging to the interests of the great majority of the loyal population and organizations.

The Soviet Union made great use of these strategies, isolating dissident intellectuals and allowing them to leave the country as long as they did not return, and supporting patriotic and social organizations designed to strengthen loyalty to the Soviet Union among its citizens. It also allowed more economically enterprising individuals (including numerous managers of state economic organizations) to operate freely in the black market, albeit to a limited extent, but circumscribed their action with periodic repression in order to prevent the phenomenon from spreading and to ensure the continuing loyalty of economic organizations.

One factor helping the government, in fact, is that the two destructive responses of exit and voice are often mutually exclusive, while loyalty delays recourse to them. Individuals and organizations who choose to exit do not usually resort to protest unless their choice is impeded in some way: consider, for example, the Soviet dissidents and Jews who wanted to emigrate but who were refused permission. Those who protest usually do so because they have no intention of exiting - unless their protest proves wholly ineffectual - because they have a high sense of loyalty and have already invested a great deal of resources and energy in their protest.

If the government reacts to signals of distress and inefficiency by prohibiting their expression, or if for some other reason (inability to mount collective action) individuals and groups fail to organize themselves, problems gradually worsen and the decay of the socio-economic system continues. Expressions of dissent (exit and voice), in fact, perform the crucial role of making it plain to the government that the situation is becoming untenable, and loyalty - together with the time required for exit and voice to reach mass proportions - thereby gives it time to make the necessary changes. However, for these expressions effectively to lead to the removal of their causes, collective action must take place and be crowned with success.

4. COLLECTIVE ACTION

For collective action to occur a set of favourable circumstances are required which depend only in part on the volition of those involved. Only thus can individuals, groups and organizations coordinate their collective action sufficiently to achieve their common goal. The first necessary condition, therefore, is the existence of a nucleus of individuals or organizations (privileged groups) vigorously pursuing a given objective because this will bring considerable economic, political, social or moral advantages, achievement of which will justify the collective action. This common goal may be, for example, national political and economic independence, or the integration of two or more systems into a single unit, such as a free trade area, a customs union, a common market, an economic community, or economic, political and monetary union.

A second and usually necessary circumstance is that each of the individuals and organizations pursuing a common goal must be willing to negotiate a clearly defined agreement with all other potential participants in the collective action. This often requires compromises to be reached which inevitably leave certain issues undefined and therefore increase the costs of collective action. Well known examples are provided by all processes of international bargaining and agreement.

The pursuit of national independence, moreover, usually entails a slackening or halting of trade with the other areas of the country into which the national group was previously integrated, which is not necessarily offset by an immediate increase in trade with other countries. Similarly, the accomplishment of integration between two or more countries strengthens customs barriers against third countries and therefore reduces trade with them. The transaction costs created when this accord is reached and implemented must naturally be lower than the benefits expected when the goal of collective action has been achieved. It often happens in these circumstances that certain participants seek to avoid these costs but nevertheless benefit from the collective outcome. In order that this eventuality does not obstruct collective action and causes it to fail, their range of action must be restricted and controlled by means of selective incentives. As a corollary to this, these processes usually take a considerable amount of time. They are always incremental processes, therefore, which achieve success when they reach a critical mass.[14] At this point they may also accelerate rapidly.[15]

Achieving control over free riders and the promotion of collective action requires the joint action of two crucial factors: the existence of appropriate institutions, and the use by organizations of a certain number of selective incentives. The key institutions in the promotion of collective action - in the case discussed here - are the nationalist parties and movements, including the regional governments, in the case of disintegration; and authoritative central governments and federalist movements in the case of integration. Particularly efficacious selective incentives in this case are the organized boycotting and ostracism of those who do not join in the collective action - strategies which may degenerate into physical threats - and promises that those who actively participate will be rewarded with economic, political and administrative advantages once the objective has been achieved. In the case of integration it is much easier than in that of disintegration to stagger the advantages accruing to those who participate in the process over time, from the earliest stage onwards. The building of the European Union provides numerous examples. In the case of disintegration, those engaging in collective action may initially find themselves in a situation in which they only sustain costs, while the enjoyment of any advantage is postponed until the moment of success.

There are, however, external restraints on collective action. The path followed by the action and its final outcome cannot be wholly determined from the outset. They therefore cannot be freely chosen. The selection of goals and the path of action - that is to say, the desired future state of the economy and the manner in which this is to be achieved - are governed by the initial conditions, by the diversity of agents and the interaction among them, by the role and transformation of the institutions, by the extent to which the goals are effectively achievable and desirable to economic agents (and this may vary over time according to the extent to which these goals have been realized and according to agents' contingent circumstances), and by exogenous and unforeseen factors.

When the collective action is successful, under the pressure exerted by a group of individuals or one or several organizations which launch a nationalist or autonomist movement (for disintegration), or a federalist or unionist movement (for integration), exit, voice and loyalty change their nature and significance. In the case of disintegration, exit loses its individual character, especially when it takes the form of emigration, and - as already mentioned in the previous section - transforms itself into collective and organized defection. This form of exit resembles what happens in the market when a certain number of consumers decide not to purchase the output of a certain monopolist enterprise, because of an increase in its price or a decline in its quality. These consumers decide to purchase the same product supplied by a competing enterprise (for example, the services supplied by a national state instead of the previous multinational one) which may enter the market or strengthen its position thanks to this new demand detrimental to the former monopolist.

This type of collective defection obviously proceeds *pari passu* with the new forms assumed by protest. This is most obviously manifest in the formation of nationalist and autonomist, or alternatively federalist or unionist, movements which organize demonstrations, protests, boycotts, and apply pressure on governments. When collective action is successful, therefore, exit and protest are no longer alternative to each other, as they often are at the individual level; they become complementary and thus acquire greater impact.

Loyalty, too, changes in object and form, and it assumes great significance as a selective incentive. From often passive endorsement of the previous situation, it assumes the more active features of national or ethnic group cohesion (in the case of disintegration) or of commitment to the ideals and practices of federalism and unionism (in the case of integration). This new loyalty thus becomes the basis for exit and protest in the former case, and for entry and commitment in the latter, heightening their impact and effects.

These changes are favoured by individual processes operating within the collective action. Because the promoters of the action have entered first and are most actively engaged in it, they rapidly assume leadership of the movement and take over its economic, political and administrative structures. This prompts imitative behaviour by those who arrive later and seek to join the movement (also) in order not to miss the advantages available should it prove successful. In contrast to Schumpeter's vision of a competitive system, where imitation spreads innovation and wipes out (extra) profit, the case of collective action is rather similar to that of monopoly. The imitation of consumption of a good expands the market. Because of their position in the hierarchy and their control over (asymmetric) information, those who govern supply (the leaders and promoters of the collective action) also control the distribution of pay-offs (the difference between the individual advantages and costs of the collective action) and are able to draw personal advantage from the situation.

Participation in the 'monopoly's' activity can be viewed as a sort of investment, the returns on which are a function of its duration but which are only enjoyed at some time in the future and are the greater in per capita terms the higher the overall investment. The investment, that is, yields increasing returns as it grows in size and duration since, other conditions remaining equal, it ensures greater control over the structure and inner life of the 'monopoly' itself. Imitation of the first 'investors' by the new arrivals leads to the formation of political and economic coalitions aiming to increase the collective return on the investment. The collective outcome and individual returns are curtailed by the resistance raised by agents of the old system under threat. This resistance can be viewed as the investment production cost, which usually takes the form of the high transaction costs caused by protracted and difficult bargaining prior to reaching agreement or by the imposition of a solution through political pressure or violence. If free riders are effectively controlled, this cost is uniformly distributed among the 'investors' according to the amount and duration of their investment.

These features have been highlighted by the recent GATT agreements, although the analysis given below seems over-simplified and somewhat contentious. The goal was an important economic gain for all concerned which can be approximately quantified:

> "For decades, GATT has been the world's most successful forum for global cooperation. Its premise is that *like-minded nations, with a shared interest in liberal trade and market economics, can better achieve those goals by acting together*. ... With the socialist model in ruins, pro-market politicians made ground everywhere, especially in the third world. And this was an important reason why the Uruguay round worked out as it did: the developing countries are keen as never before to liberalise trade and embrace market economics ... Protectionist sentiment in Europe and America dragged this round out for seven years, and it imperilled it until the very end. There are reasons to believe that this sentiment will continue to gain strength in the industrial countries, so the further spread of liberal trade certainly cannot be taken for granted ... the main lesson for the West ... is that *liberalism, which benefits all people in general but each only lightly, will continue to be assailed by special interests*."[16]

More detailed analysis of the economic effects of collective action is required in the case of nationalism and of supranationalism as engines of collective action.

5. NATIONALISM AND SUPRANATIONALISM AS INTEGRATING AND DISINTEGRATING FORCES: A QUASI-ECONOMIC ACCOUNT

Nationality and supranationality may be treated in analogous fashion to a public capital good which can be augmented by investment and reduced by depreciation.[17] They correspond to the two key features proposed by Samuelson: indivisibility and the non-excludibility of consumption.[18] On account of these factors, individuals who seek to evade costs - wholly or in part - by concealing their preferences cannot be excluded from consumption based on pure market processes. It thus proves impossible to fix a demand price for the good and an equilibrium price is therefore lacking. This fact prevents the formation in the market of a distribution corresponding to the marginal contribution of each participant in production of the good.[19]

The market is therefore unable to identify an equilibrium point, and a solution can only be found via collective action - of which the state is an example but not the only one. Nationalist (supranationalist) policies may be introduced by the state, or else they may be the outcome of collective action from below. Only in this way, in fact, is it possible to address and solve the problem of the collective choice mechanisms whereby public activities are made to correspond to the preferences of individuals and organizations.

Nationalism[20] and its opposite, supranationalism, may in turn be defined as movements for economic as well as political and social ends which induce individuals and organizations to favour and justify investment in nationality (supranationality). This encourages the use (investment) at the present moment of scarce resources in order to alter the inter-ethnic or inter-national distribution of property and incomes[21] or in order to increase the international division of labour within a group of two or more countries - according to comparative advantages - and to exploit economies of scale at an international level.

The more complex case arises when national (supranational) goals are pursued contrary to the wishes of the existing state, because in this case the action must begin and be organized from below against the resistance of the state. The private costs of pursuit of the collective goal are thus increased, since every individual and organization that wishes to participate is threatened with persecution, repression and punishment. They must therefore camouflage their preferences and activity, thereby increasing transaction costs and uncertainty; and this reduces the net collective benefit accruing from achievement of the objective. In these cases, however, opposition and repression by the state may add value to pursuit of the collective goal: the more the state opposes and represses, the more intense the preference of individuals and organizations to pursue the goal may become, because the state's action makes it more costly for them to remain in their current situation. Consequently, the private cost of the collective action increases and the investment required becomes greater; but the rate of return on it also substantially increases. The economic convenience of the collective action may be enhanced as a result. Moreover, the promoters of the collective action may considerably raise the cost of non-participation, in the manner described above. In this sense, the investor in nationality and supranationality is enabled to set close constraints on the action of free riders.

The pursuit of national (supranational) goals - that is to say, investment in nationality (supranationality) - is therefore a form of cooperation fostered by nationalist (supranationalist) movements imposed by virtue of their political power in order to condition individuals and organizations. As in the case analysed by Axelrod, these are endowed with great power to exercise positive or negative sanctions which enable them to impose a cooperative game - protracted in time and therefore repetitive[22] - in which they are also helped by the existence of an external threat, for example by the state.

Investment in nationality differs crucially from investment in supranationality in terms of the return obtained from it. Although in both cases the investment is made in order to yield a profit for those promoting and financing the investment, from a social point of view the consequences are the reverse. In fact, while investment in nationality (which leads to disintegration) primarily yields individual profit through the redistribution of property rights, of wealth, of income and of extant power, investment in supranationality - provided that it is made on a voluntary basis among equal partners - leads to an overall increase in property rights, wealth and income, while it is the incremental part that is distributed to the investors.

The different outcomes derive from the economic (and geographical) setting in which the investment takes place. In the case of nationality, this is an investment made by a part of society in activities geared directly to the appropriation of already existing property rights, wealth, income and power which previously belonged to another national group. The investment therefore yields a return - this indeed is why it was made - but this return only accrues to the national group which promoted it. The losing social-national group consequently makes a negative investment in that it has failed to protect its interests by correctly investing its resources. Alternatively, this group has preferred to consume its scarce resources in the present period, thereby reducing the capital available to it.

One notes with interest, however, that the redistribution is often less to the detriment of the losing social-ethnic group than within the winning one.[23] This effect is only averted when the 'outsiders' are expropriated without compensation or else are compensated at a price lower than the market one. In this case, which is usually motivated by the poverty of the country,[24] or by crimes committed by those whose assets are confiscated, or by nationalist or racist ideology (consider the confiscation of Jewish property in Nazi Germany, or that of Nazis and German citizens in general after the war), a net transfer of wealth and income takes place to the advantage of the national group as a whole. In the extreme case, the individuals and organizations that have promoted and implemented the nationalist policies are able entirely to appropriate what has been confiscated, while leaving unaltered the situation of the individuals and organizations of their own national group which abstained from the action or only participated in it passively.

If one excludes confiscation under the above conditions - if, that is, the confiscation takes place at market prices - the distribution can only occur within the winning national group. In this case, in fact, the nationalist group which acts does nothing but pay the 'extraneous' group the current value of the future flow of incomes as compensation. The overall value of the assets of the two national groups therefore remains invariant, even though the ratio between wealth and income (between stock and flows) changes. The national group that confiscates exchanges a stock (the price of the compensation or of the purchase) for a flow (the annual returns on the activity expropriated). In this case, the entire return on the investment in nationality accrues to those individuals and to those organizations which directly control the investment or which profit from it: those who occupy managerial positions in firms and in all the 'nationalized' economic and political activities, including the new national government, and those who obtain jobs or better paid ones by replacing workers of the confiscated national group. If the number of these posts increases as a result of 'nationalization', and if their unitary remuneration increases as well

- which is inevitable if a new national state is created - there must be a transfer of wealth and income from the nation as a whole to the emerging individuals and groups. If, moreover, the overall volume of the economy is reduced (for example, because of the lower volume of exports which is likely to result from disintegration), the redistribution of income within society must be all the greater. Consequently, the middle and - above all - upper classes will inevitably benefit, to the detriment of the working class. This aspect has been amply documented by events in the countries of Central-Eastern Europe and especially in the newly-independent countries.

In reality, nationalist policies often involve the use of various instruments. For example, if the confiscation takes place at market prices, the nationalist government may employ tariffs, taxes, duties, subsidies, as well as different combinations of these and other instruments, and is thus able to attenuate or further to increase the scope of direct redistributive processes internal to society.

These zero-sum processes do not occur in the case of investment in supranationality (integration), because in this case (apart from situations of forced integration or integration for imperial ends which are not considered here) the aim of the investment is to increase the social product in favour of all the entities involved in the integration process, chiefly by lowering trade barriers. In this manner, although distribution does indeed take place, it only concerns the net social product created by the investment. Even though the greatest return on the investment will probably accrue to its promoters,[25] the individuals and organizations in the new supranational entity will not lose out - at least not as a whole and apart from those who fail because of increased internal competition and because of the removal of customs barriers. It is indeed probable that they will enjoy some return on the investment, for example in the form of increased employment. This return is equal to the overall return yielded by integration net of the additional remuneration to the promoters of the investment. Thus, the interest of the small privileged integration-promoting group is probably not in conflict with the large latent group supporting it. The building of the European Union provides numerous and interesting examples in this regard.[26]

In the case of investments in nationality, however, redistibutive processes may have serious social consequences, and they may undermine the stability of the new state formation. The privileged group of investment-promoters pursues a goal which may be in conflict - as regards its direct economic consequences - with that of the latent group constituting the majority of the population. However, as we have already pointed out, national processes arouse strong emotions and large-scale political participation. By dismantling a structure which was previously seen as oppressive and which deployed a vast bureaucratic, police or military apparatus to maintain its authority, the investment in nationality may radically diminish transaction costs, strengthen the impact of incentives, and improve the allocation of resources. In this way, the gains accruing to the privileged group are at least partly off-set by the destruction of the privileges and structures utilized by the former privileged group to preserve its economic and political power, and by the effect of the new incentives. Should this happen, national policies increase the net social product and endow society with a net quantity of resources and goods greater, other conditions remaining equal, than before. We shall return to this point in the next section.

6. THE ADVANTAGES AND DISADVANTAGES OF INTEGRATION AND DISINTEGRATION: EFFICIENCY AND STABILITY

We have seen that when a certain number of individuals and organizations manage to act collectively, exit and voice as individual phenomena become of secondary importance. If the collective action is successful, the national (supranational) group acts as if it were undertaking an investment in a public capital good in order to obtain a positive return. In this way, exit and voice disappear and a new form of loyalty takes over.

In order to decide whether investment in nationality or supranationality is economically and socially positive, one must determine the extent to which it is efficient (in both the static and dynamic senses) and stable. That is to say, one must establish the amount of return on the investment compared with alternative uses of the same resources, the extent to which it is equitably distributed among the participants in the collective action, and the extent to which the new situation is stable over time. In short, one must decide the extent to which the new formation arising out of integration or disintegration is economically and socially superior to its predecessor. Here too, the cases of integration and disintegration differ and must be treated separately. However, given that generally speaking the advantages and disadvantages deriving from investment in nationality become respectively disadvantages and advantages when the investment is made in supranationality, we shall not dwell on discussion of this case either.

It has been usually argued that investment in nationality, in the static sense,[27] moves the economy further away from the frontier of production possibilities, while investment in supranationality moves it towards the frontier and often shifts the frontier itself towards the outside.[28] The negative effect of investment derives from the fact that the criterion employed in selecting the investment is not that of maximizing the current aggregate value of future returns on the investment of a certain quantity of resources. On the contrary, the criterion usually adopted is that of maximizing the return on the investment for the privileged group which has decided to undertake it. It is therefore the analogy itself between nationality and public capital goods than engenders a lower return than that available from alternative investments.

The new situation is stable over time only if the overall return on the investment net of all costs is positive and distributed in such a manner that it does not excessively increase distributive disparities. In other words, it must respect the condition of the Paretan optimum, moving the economy towards the frontier. Although the situation of some may have improved, the quantity of property rights, wealth, income and power previously possessed by each must not have diminished (at least not to a significant extent) and, if possible, the return must accrue in minimal measure to all participants. That is, it must not consist solely of a transfer from one social class to another within the same national group. Should this happen, the privileged group, which has decided and now manages the investment, must take action either to increase the stock and flows of non-monetary remuneration (such as national pride and cohesion) for the components of the latent group who have supported the privileged group in its action, or to increase the cost (in the form of repression) that these latter would incur by making an investment in the redistribution of property rights, wealth, income and power in their favour through exit and voice and perhaps new collective action. These actions by the privileged group, however, require the commitment of further resources in an economically non-remunerative manner; by which is meant that they entail a further redistribution to the detriment of the latent group. This is a clearly unequitable situation and it persists as long as the non-monetary remuneration is deemed higher than the advantages (return) that would accrue from an investment in the redistribution of property rights, wealth, income and power, minus the costs involved in acquiring them.

If the collective gain is nil, or if indeed the investment is at diminishing returns for the collectivity and is only to the advantage of the privileged group, there will be an inevitable resumption of exit and voice by the losing individuals and organizations, even though they belong to the winning privileged group, and loyalty to the new leading national group will diminish. Since this outcome creates powerful interests determined to change the situation once again, a new (potentially) privileged group will probably form to promote new collective action against the winning national group. This process can be observed in various countries of Central-Eastern Europe, where transformation has led to the radical polarization of the distribution of incomes. And it explains why in recent elections there have been increasing numbers of votes for the socialist parties (comparable to privileged groups), heirs to the reformist wing of the communist parties in power prior to transition, or for populist parties.

Other costs increased by investment in nationality are the so-called 'dead weight costs'[29] due, for example, to the need to introduce customs barriers where none existed before, to set up a new government, a new diplomatic corps and a new civil service (or to expand, upgrade already existing structures and therefore finance them better), to organize bodies for the defence and maintenance of public order, to raise obstacles against the mobility of persons, goods and resources, to reorganize transport and telecommunications.

Probably the most serious negative effects stem from the loss of advantages ensured by the economies of scale and positive externalities consequent on the reduction of the market. Moreover, internal competition diminishes and, if the new country resorts to protectionism in order to protect its economy during reorganization and restructuring, its place is not taken by external competition. All this gives rise to a less efficient allocation of resources and to less efficient production.

With the rise of national governments, decision-lines become shorter in the sense that decisions are taken closer to production sites. Apart from the advantages discussed below, this has the disadvantage of making the decision process more sensitive to particular circumstances and pressures, so that it becomes more difficult to gain a global view of the situation and easier to make less efficient decisions. Control certainly improves (as we explain below) but it may also become more difficult, because the number of organizations and individuals that exercise it diminishes and their skill level may be lower.

However, as we saw in the previous section, investment in nationality changes both the costs structure and institutions. If the previous situation failed to match the preferences of the repressed ethnic or national group, investment in nationality may bring an improvement in both the passive sense by eliminating previous costs, and in the active one through the action of new incentives. In the former case, the previous situation could only survive by means of repression, which required the economically unproductive use of considerable resources (for example, to maintain a strong police apparatus and to co-opt or corrupt the most influential representatives of the repressed ethnic-national group), while the efficient allocation of others (work and the capital of the repressed ethnic-national group) were obstructed by political and administrative controls. The success of the collective action eliminated these costs. One should also bear in mind that if an ethnic-national group was previously part of a much larger country and with a strong military presence, exit from that country may lead to a substantial reduction in military investments. This may be the case, for example, of certain ex-Soviet republics, although recent events seem to indicate the reverse.

A supranational unit by definition comprises disparities among its various (geographical, economic and ethnic) components. The pursuit of political and social stability requires the transfer of income and resources - especially capital - to the most disadvantaged parts of the country. Because this policy serves to prevent investment in nationality by seeking to anticipate its effects, it displays features similar to those of public goods. The policy therefore is influenced by pressure groups which increases its implementation costs and restricts its efficiency. The disaggregation of the country along ethnic-national lines also eliminates these costs (which are ultimately transaction costs) and exposes - mainly through trade - the real differences between one area and another of the country. This may induce attempts, where possible, to resolve the country's underlying problems. A further advantage may be that, as we have seen, the disaggregation abbreviates decision-making processes. This enables decisions to be based on more precise knowledge of the specific features of the economy and of society, and it will probably reduce conflict and uncertainty. Moreover, control is facilitated by the greater closeness of managers to the individuals and organizations affected by decisions.

Finally, by reducing or eliminating redistributive processes and by disaggregating the labour market on a national basis, disintegration brings wages more closely in line with marginal productivity at the local level. This probably fosters technical progress, given that higher wages with respect to marginal productivity tends to stimulate it, and it also has major consequences on price formation and reduces the need for state intervention in the economy.[30] Suppose, for instance, that an economy consists of two (ethnic-geographical) sectors with differing levels of productivity, but that it has a single labour market and therefore a single wage rate. If, in this situation, the state wishes to preserve unchanged the gap between the two sectors (for example, by maintaining each sector's share of national income unchanged), it must increasingly intervene with redistributive instruments.[31] These may take the form, for example, of the financing of a proportion of the labour cost in the more disadvantaged sector, in order to decrease it for employers to the level coinciding with marginal productivity, or they may take the form of the direct transfer of income to workers forced into unemployment by excessively high labour costs in the disadvantaged sector.

A second positive consequence of disintegration arises when the new situation corresponds to the preferences and expectations of both the privileged and the latent group: for example, because there is a closer correspondence between taxes paid and services delivered. It is probable in these circumstances that - also because of the stock and flows of non-monetary remuneration in favour of all components of the ethnic-national group - there will be a radical alteration in the nature and amount of incentives. This development may lead to a substantial increase in work effort, to a more rapid flow of capital towards more efficient investments, and in general to a sizeable reduction in transaction costs.

Should at least one of these possibilities come to pass, the return on the investment in nationality may, other conditions remaining equal, be greater than that deriving from any alternative use of the same resources in a static situation. Consequently, all participants may benefit from the distribution of this return, and the situation may be stable over the long period.

However, one should remember that processes of national disintegration and supranational integration may stimulate free riding behaviour. This occurs, for example, when an ethnic-national group has enjoyed net transfers from other groups or parts of the country in the past. Now, faced with the possible cancellation of these net transfers (for political reasons, or because a previously disadvantaged group or area has managed to catch up so that the net transfer is no longer justified), and indeed apprehensive that it may have to finance transfers to other disadvantaged groups or regions, and aware that protest has no effect, the group or region may decide to exit. In other cases, the disintegration of a country may be to the exclusive advantage of only one part of it, while the other part or parts find that they must meet the additional costs. In the ex-Soviet Union, for example, one part (Russia) has been able to appropriate the Central Bank and currency of the former integrated country, while the other parts (the other ex-Soviet republics, that is) have had to meet the costs of creating their own National Banks and introducing their own currencies (unless the former does not compensate the others in proportion to the economic advantage obtained). Or again, an ethnic-national group or region which splits off from a larger country may refuse to accept the proportion of national indebtedness or public debt which corresponds to its economic weight; or it may refuse to pay for supplies received. Finally, the part of the country that controls the central economic organizations may refuse to hand over to the exiting part the share of external or internal credit due to it.

7. CONCLUSIONS

The foregoing analysis points to the conclusion that the final outcome of the processes of integration and disintegration is not univocally determined by the initial situation and by the quantity of resources invested in nationality or supranationality. The consequences, in fact, depend on the numerous other factors that we have sought to illustrate: the distributive effects of investment, the balance between increased costs and reduced costs, the effect of new institutions and changed incentives, the characteristics of collective action, the role of loyalty, the possibilities of exit and voice and their significance. Only joint consideration of all these factors can determine when and under what circumstances the result of the investment will be positive at the aggregate level and the new situation therefore stable over the long period.

A final issue of great importance concerns the self-sufficiency of bottom-up and decentralized processes in provoking disintegration and integration. We have already pointed out that nationalistic policies are usually adopted as a last-ditch attempt to maintain control over the situation when other strategies have proved unsuccessful. It is equally evident that the less determined case is that of disintegration, since the technical complexity alone of integration processes is sufficient to make intervention by the central authorities inevitable. In the case of disintegration, instead, one could maintain that decentralized processes are sufficient, without intervention by the central authorities, if one excepts the braking role performed by the central authorities of the entity in disintegration.

In reality, the decisive presence of some state authority (that is, of the new national entity) is made necessary, in the case of disintegration as well, by the nature itself of the good 'nationality' and in order to avert the onset of anarchy. As we have seen, nationality is similar to a public capital good. It is well known that in this case the impossibility that a market price will form, and consequently the impossibility of an efficient allocation of resources, renders central intervention inevitable. There is only one case when this may not occur: if transaction costs are zero, agents possess complete information and property rights are freely negotiable.[32] It is superfluous to add that the nature itself of the good in question rules out this eventuality. In all other cases, although decentralized collective action is necessary, it is not enough to bring the investment in nationality to maturity.

The situation is even more evident if the disintegration of the old system comes about as the result of an anarchic explosion in which the dominant figure is that of the free rider. In this case, the refusal to pay the (private) costs necessary to set collective action in train so that the investment in nationality can be effected and brought to fruition is so high and universal that the option chosen is exit. Consider, for example, a routed army in which all forms of command and organization have broken down. Two possibilities arise. The first is that the void is filled by an external authority (an invading army, a foreign country, an international organization) which assumes the role of a new central authority.

The second possibility - which is much more important in our case - is that a process is somehow set in motion which leads to successful collective action. For example, despite the situation of anarchy a group may for some reason form which manages to gain the upper hand over the others and to impose itself as the dominant group. Consider for example an initial situation characterized by atomistic and perfect competition. If just one industry operates at increasing returns, this is sufficient for a more efficient enterprise to expand until it has imposed its monopolistic power on the market and then extended it to others. Alternatively, a group of firms may decide to coordinate themselves so that they can jointly manage certain phases of the productive process - for example, the marketing or storage of the raw materials they need - in order to reduce costs and to guarantee supplies. A similar result can also be achieved with illicit or illegal methods - intimidation or mafia methods, for example.

At this point, the stabilization of the new situation - that is, the possibility of reaping the fruits of the investment - renders the emergence of a new central authority inevitable, for two distinct reasons. First, it is the similarity itself of nationality to a public capital good that necessitates the presence of a state authority to coordinate collective action and to curb free riders. This is even truer in a situation where it is necessary to supply further public goods and therefore to exact the corresponding payments in the form of taxes and duties. Intervention by the central authority is in fact necessary whenever transaction costs are positive, or information is asymmetric, or property rights are not perfectly negotiable.

The second reason for the presence of a central authority applies when, apart from the above conditions, the game is repetitive in nature. In this case, as Axelrod[33] has shown, cooperation is better than competition. Axelrod considers games which are repeated an infinite (or very large) number of times. Strategies that are cooperative from the outset in this case invariably yield better long-term results than opportunistic and non-cooperative ones. The crucial question, however, is why and how a cooperative solution comes about. Although in principle cooperation may arise spontaneously among rational or socially educated individuals or organizations, in reality this spontaneous development is obstructed by the threat of free riders, who immediately benefit from opportunistic and non-cooperative behaviour. Consequently a cooperative solution in a repetitive game can only derive from an explicit accord among the individuals and organizations concerned which is guaranteed by an external or internal authority endowed with retaliatory power and selective incentives to control free riders. Or, more straightforwardly, it may be the result of intervention by the state.[34]

Therefore, it is not during the construction and assertion of collective action that a central authority is necessary. On the contrary, the distinguishing feature of this process is the attempt to overthrow the former supranational authority or to change its characteristics and functions. However, once this goal has been achieved, the constitution of a new central authority is necessary if the fruits of the investment in nationality are to be enjoyed. This central authority is also necessary in order to confer stability on the new situation, since only central authority can ensure that distributive processes do not predominate in the victorious ethnic-national group, curb transaction costs, control and enforce the implementation of contracts, and reduce uncertainty over the final outcome of collective action.

NOTES

1 I wish to thank Giovanni Pegoretti (University of Trento), Wladimir Andreff (University of Paris I) and the participants to the third general Conference of the European Association of Comparative Economic Studies on *Transformation of Economic Systems,* Budapest, 8-10 September 1994, for helpful comments on an earlier draft of this paper. All the remaining errors are my own.

2 By the term 'integration' is meant any form of greater coordination - from custom union to economic, monetary or political union - among previously independent economies. Disintegration is this process in reverse.

3 See Andreff and Andreff, this volume.

4 On the role of these factors in the creation of NATO see the interesting minutes of off-the-record talks between Truman, top members of the American politico-military establishment and the foreign ministers of the countries forming the Atlantic Alliance held at the White House on 3 April 1949. See *LiMes,* 1993.

5 For detailed treatment of these concepts and proof of these points, see Olson, 1965. See also Becker, 1983.

6 Routines "... play the role that genes play in biological evolutionary

theory. They are a persistent feature of the organism and determine its possible behavior [...]; they are heritable in the sense that tomorrow's organisms generated from today's [...] have many of the same characteristics, and they are selectable in the sense that organisms with certain routines may do better than others, and, if so, their relative importance in the population [...] is augmented over time". Nelson and Winter, 1982, p. 14.

7 "... (I)n functioning complex systems with many highly differentiated and tightly interdependent parts, it is highly unlikely that undirected change in a single part will have beneficial effects on the system; this, of course, is the basis for the biological proposition that mutations tend to be deleterious on the average ... It is not surprising, therefore, that the control processes of (surviving) organizations tend to resist mutations, even ones that present themselves as desirable innovations". Nelson and Winter, 1982, p. 116. See also Roland, 1990.

8 If the old sys..m is defended by a minority (for example, by agents of the state), a compensations policy may be devised to persuade them to accept the change. This may raise the Paretan optimum. But it is obvious that this solution would be optimal only before the change takes place. Once the minority has lost its power, in fact, the optimal solution is to stop the compensation. Since the minority anticipates behaviour of this kind, it is probable that the minority will rationally prefer the existing situation. See Eggertsson, 1990; Roland, 1990; Winiecki, 1986.

9 See, for example, Axelrod, 1984; Bacharach, 1977; Elster, 1985; Olson, 1965; Stigler, 1974.

10 This may be taken in both the deterministic and the stochastic senses. In the former, passage from one economic system to another may be blocked in certain directions and encouraged in others. In the stochastic version, specific and unknown events occurring in the change process may have an enduring influence upon it.

11 For example, the killing of collaborators by radical Palestinian groups or by the anti-apartheid movement in South Africa, the attacks on centralist parties and social organizations in the periphery of the ex-Soviet Union.

12 For well-documented analysis of the economic reasons for secession - and therefore possibly disintegration - see Zarkowic Bookman, 1993.

13 Hirschman, 1970.

14 Marwell and Oliver, 1993.

15 Glance and Huberman, 1994.

16 *The Economist*, 18 December 1993, pp. 11-13, emphasis added.

17 See Breton, 1964, p. 377. Breton examines the case of a society in which nationalist demands have considerable economic weight but which nevertheless remains cohesive (Canada). However, the processes at work are the same as those in cases of disintegration. See also Johnson, 1967b.

18 Samuelson, 1955.

19 Pejovich, 1994 proposes the market for institutions as an alternative solution.

20 For a fine and well-documented analysis of the role of nationalism in former socialst countries, see Ferrero, 1992, who stresses that "... the current resurgence of nationalism in post-communist societies is meaningfully understood not as the surfacing of primordial cleavages from pre-communist times ... but as the direct, rational, albeit unintended, consequence of the very success of the socialist solution to the national question." (p. 5). See also Pejovich, 1993, who examines the effects of nationalism on the direction and rate of institutional change in Central-Eastern Europe.

21 Note that this solution is usually adopted when the promoters of change have failed to take up other less costly and sometimes more remunerative options for the ethnic-national group as a whole: "The appearance of nationalism is dependent on the existence or on the burgeoning of a new middle class, because nationalism is a tool used by the new middle class to accede to wealth and power ... It is only if the new middle class is incapable of dealing with changes in institutional structures, with technology, and with other important social forces that it will elect nationalism as its tool": Breton, 1964, pp. 381-2.

22 Although the game is played only once - thus providing considerable opportunities for opportunist behaviour - it is made up of innumerable actions among individuals and organizations which will most probably continue their relations once the game is over.

23 This point has been shown very clearly by Breton, 1964, both in theory (pp. 386 and 378-80) and in the case of Canada (p. 385).

24 "Investment in nationality implies a transfer of resources from the working class to the middle class. Where the working class is poor, a nationalist government will generally abandon the policy of partial or complete compensation of assets taken over and confiscated, because it cannot, without creating social and political chaos, alter the distribution of income against the working class ... One implication of the foregoing argument, as well as of the hypothesis, is that we should expect the working class to be less nationalist than the middle class." Breton, 1964, p. 381.

25 For example, they will occupy the posts (usually very well paid) created in the common structures and financed by the greater net product generated by the investment, and it will be they who appropriate the additional profit deriving from the expansion of the market.

26 Note that free-riding and rent-seeking behaviour can also be discerned in the attempt by certain countries (e.g. Central European countries like the Czech Republic) to join existing integrations (e.g. the European Union). See also the behaviour of Britain and Italy in the European Union.

27 On this see Breton, 1964, p. 379.
28 As we shall see, these conclusions must be moderated or even changed in sign if there is a dualism in the economy which prevents it from functioning normally. In this case, investment in nationality may lead to better results than those achieved previously.
29 See Breton, 1989, pp. 738-41.
30 At least in the manner envisaged by the market failure school.
31 This point can be illustrated using Baumol's (1967) model of unbalanced growth.
32 This is the case considered in Coase's theorem. See Coase, 1960.
33 See Axelrod, 1984.
34 See also Zamagni, 1991.

BIBLIOGRAPHY

Andreff, M. and Andreff, W. (1994), 'Economic Disintegration in Eastern Europe: Towards a New Integration?', this volume.
Axelrod, R. (1984), *The Evolution of Cooperation*, Basic Books, New York.
Bacharach, M. (1977), *Economics and the Theory of Games*, Westview Press, Boulder, Col .
Baumol, W.J. (1967), 'Macroeconomics of Unbalanced Growth: The Anatomy of Urban Crisis', *American Economic Review*, June: pp. 415-426.
Becker, G.S. (1983), 'A Theory of Competition among Pressure Groups for Political Influence', *The Quarterly Journal of Economics*, Vol. XCVIII, August, no. 3, pp. 371-400.
Breton, A. (1964), 'The Economics of Nationalism', *The Journal of Political Economy*, vol. 72, August, no. 4, pp. 376-386.
Breton, A. (1989), 'The Growth of Competitive Governments', *Canadian Journal of Economics*, November, no. 4, pp. 717-750.
Coase, R. (1960), 'The Problem of Social Cost', *Journal of Law and Economics*, October, pp. 1-44.
Dallago, B. and Mittore L. (1995), eds., *Economic Institutions, Markets and Competition,* Edward Elgar, Cheltenham (forthcoming).
Eggertsson, T. (1990), *Economic Behavior and Institutions*, Cambridge University Press, Cambridge.
Elster, J. (1985), *Making Sense of Marx,* Cambridge University Press, Cambridge.
Ferrero, M. (1992), *The Economics of Socialist Nationalism: Evidence and*

Theory, in *Nationalism and Its Re-emergence*, proceedings of the Fifth Villa Colombella Seminar, 3-4 September 1992 (forthcoming).

Glance, N.S. and Huberman, B.A. (1994), 'La dinamica delle scelte nelle interazioni sociali', *Le Scienze*, n. 309, May, pp. 68-73.

Hirschman, A.O. (1970), *Exit, Voice, and Loyalty*, Harvard University Press, Cambridge, Mass.

Johnson, H.G. (1967a), ed. *Economic Nationalism in Old and New States*, University of Chicago Press, Chicago.

Johnson, H.G. (1967b), 'A Theoretical Model of Economic Nationalism in New and Developing States', in H.G. Johnson (1967a), pp. 1-16.

LiMes (1993), 'La strategia segreta della Nato', *LiMes*, no. 4, pp. 111-122.

Marwell, G. and Oliver, P. (1993), *The Critical Mass in Collective Action. A Micro-Social Theory*, Cambridge University Press, Cambridge.

Nelson, R.R. and Winter, S.G. (1982), *An Evolutionary Theory of Economic Change*, The Belknap Press, Cambridge, Mass.

Olson, M. (1965), *The Logic of Collective Action*, Harvard University Press, Cambridge, Mass.

Pejovich, S. (1993), 'Institutions, Nationalism, and the Transition Process in Eastern Europe', *Social Philosophy & Policy*, vol. 10, no. 2, Summer, pp. 65-78.

Pejovich, S. (1994), *The Market for Institutions v. the-Strong-Hand-of-the-State: The Case of Eastern Europe*, in B. Dallago and L. Mittone (1994).

Roland, G. (1990), 'Gorbachev and the Common European Home: The Convergence Debate Revived?', *Kyklos*, vol. 43, no. 3, pp. 385-409.

Samuelson, P.A. (1955), 'The Pure Theory of Public Expenditure', *Review of Economics and Statistics*, November, pp. 350-356.

Stigler, G.J. (1974), 'Free Riders and Collective Action', *Bell Journal of Economics*, vol. 5, no. 2, pp. 359-365.

Winiecki, J. (1986), *Why Economic Reforms fail in the Soviet System: A Property Rights-Based Approach*, Seminar Paper no. 374, The Institute for International Economic Studies, Stockholm.

Zamagni, S. (1991), *Il rapporto tra stato e mercato e la teoria dell'intervento pubblico: un riesame critico*, Bologna, Dipartimento di Scienze Economiche, Università degli Studi di Bologna, Working Paper no. 109.

Zarkovic Bookman, M. (1993), *The Economics of Secession*, Macmillan, Houndmills, Basingstoke.

THE OPENING PROCESS IN EAST EUROPEAN ECONOMIES

László Szamuely

The notion of *'opening'* is used in economic parlance synonymously with the *liberalization* of external economic relations. The accepted textbook sense of the term is the freeing of such relations from all restrictions in order to secure free international trade and the free movement of capital. However, just as every synonym conveys a subtle distinction in meaning, so the notion of opening is applied nowadays to the particular case of the liberalization of the former centrally planned economies (CPEs); that is, to their reintegration into the world economy. Hence the process of opening is part and parcel of the transformation of these economies into market ones.

This paper examines the process since the end of the 1980s in the European member countries of the now defunct Council of Mutual Economic Assistance (CMEA), or COMECON in Western terminology. These countries include six Central and East European countries: Poland, the Czech Republic and Slovakia (the former Czechoslovakia or CSFR), Hungary, Romania, Bulgaria and the successor states of the former Soviet Union. (The former Yugoslavia and Albania are not involved as they did not belong to the CMEA).

Section 1 presents the peculiarities of the external economic relations of the CPEs - the reasons for their inward-looking, autarkic developments and the consequences which have made their restructuring and reorientation so difficult. *Section 2* gives an overview of the reasons for the collapse of the CMEA/COMECON and the outcomes of this process, while *Section 3* describes the impact of ongoing systemic change on the geographical reorientation of trade flows in Eastern Europe.

1. WHY THE CLOSED CMEA 'MARKET' EMERGED AND HOW IT WORKED

The socialist centrally planned economy *in statu nascendi* was an autarkic one. In the hostile environment in which Soviet Russia found itself after the Bolshevik revolution of 1917, this was to a certain extent understandable. Seclusion was in any case a feasible policy for a huge country with enormous human and natural resources. Soviet industrialization policy both before and after the Second World War had a distinctly import-substituting character.

Enormous volumes of technologically advanced machinery and other equipment were imported from the West in order to render such imports unnecessary in the future. The paramount aim of this kind of industrialization, with the great sacrifices that it entailed, was to build a firstclass defence industry.

However, it was not only the opportunism and pragmatism of the great power policy, aimed at military expansion, which envisaged the socialist economy as a closed one. The idea of closed economy can in a sense also be traced back to a possible interpretation of Marxian economics.

The well-known Marxian thesis of the withering away of commodity production (i.e. of the market economy) under socialism logically entailed the Marxian and Engelsian vision of a socialist economy with a central body assessing needs in physical terms and distributing goods and allocating the production factors accordingly. This vision would appear to rest on the implicit assumption that an economy of this kind is both closed and self-supporting.

The relatively small countries of Central and Eastern Europe which fell under Soviet influence after the Second World War followed the same well-trodden path of Stalinist industrialization. They even accepted the idea of autarky - which was absurd for small countries, and the serious consequences of which were already being felt in the mid-1950s.

The idea of national autarky was replaced in the early 1960s by the more feasible notion of CMEA-scale autarky. It should be remembered, however, that even in the more relaxed atmosphere of the 1960s, the CMEA countries still pursued the Stalinist strategy of economic development that had characterized the 1930s. Industries that enjoyed priority in development policy (mostly defence-oriented ones) obtained the lion's share of imports from the West, while they manufactured products primarily not for Western export but for domestic use or for export to the CMEA region.

A heavy price was paid for this curious bifurcation of the CMEA economies under the altered world economic conditions of the next decade. Heavy industry, which enjoyed preferences and had often been established with the help of Western imports (and partly financed out of loans), was unable to produce the export outputs with which to balance the Western import inputs necessary for its maintenance. At the same time, the production of the food and consumer goods that created export earnings was hampered, and proved to be the most vulnerable to world market competition and most severely hit by open protectionism and disguised discrimination. It was this rather bleak situation that led to the first major increase in the international debt of the smaller CMEA member countries.

Simultaneously, it reinforced the conscious striving for a defensive isolation from world market effects and for reliance on a 'secure' CMEA market that operated according to quite different rules.

There is no need to describe in detail how the CMEA system worked, since the literature on the topic abounds.[1] Suffice it to mention the working principles of the system, which were in full accordance with the rules of the game in the domestic economies of CPEs:

(i) Intra-CMEA trade was a system of *state trading*. Governments undertook mutual commitments to supply and to purchase commodity quotas specified in agreements and expressed in kind. These quotas were based on long-term (five-year) intergovernmental agreements on plan coordination and bilateral (five-year and one-year) trade agreements. Trading itself was conducted by two or three dozen specialized, large, state foreign-trade companies (as in the case of Hungary).

(ii) Although there was much talk about the multilateral settlement of payments, the CMEA was until its demise nothing more than a *system of bilateral clearing relations*. Although the accounting unit within the CMEA was called the 'transferable ruble' (TR), it was neither convertible nor transferable among the CMEA member countries, and its nominal rate of exchange *vis-à-vis* convertible currencies was artificially fixed and overvalued. The settlement of mutual claims was carried out within a strictly bilateral relationship by mutual deliveries of goods predetermined by an intergovernmental agreement.

(iii) Since the mutual deliveries of goods had been decided upon and specified in physical terms (in kind) by intergovernmental agreement, *price formation played a secondary role*. Prices were determined - at least in principle - on the basis of the average world market prices of the five years preceding the year in question (the principle of the so-called 'moving average'). In practice, however, this principle could only be followed more or less consistently in the case of raw materials and energy. Determining the 'world market' price of manufactured goods - a great many of which had never been marketable outside the CMEA - was simply impossible. Price-setting was subject to bargaining within an intricate web of price and commodity tie-ins which wove bilateral trade together. This led to the practice whereby actual prices for the same article were different not only on the Western and Eastern markets but in individual bilateral relations within the CMEA as well.

This closed, inward-looking system of regional autarky seeking to achieve full independence from the 'hostile' world market managed to survive for some forty years. The reason why CMEA-scale autarky was relatively stable was the overwhelming share of intra-CMEA trade, which on average surpassed 50% of total trade in each member country. A perhaps even more important reason was *the radial character* of this trade; that is, the fact that approximately 60-70% of the intra-CMEA trade of each member country was conducted with the Soviet Union. This meant that about *one third of each CMEA country's trade was with the Soviet Union.*

Because of its radial character, CMEA integration was mostly based on, and held together by, the exchange of Soviet energy and raw materials for East-European manufactured goods and food.

Despite a great deal of research, it is impossible to establish definitively who were the winners and losers in this exchange precisely because of the intricate web of price and commodity tie-ins within a bilateral inter-governmental relationship that I mentioned above.

For instance, Marrese and Vanous[2] computed the value of Soviet exports to, and imports from, the six former CMEA member countries (East Germany included) in 1971-1982 at world market prices (used in East-West trade). Since the fixed contractual prices of energy and raw materials within the CMEA were lower than the prices to be obtained on the world market, while the prices of manufactured goods (mainly machinery) were higher, Marrese and Vanous calculated that the Soviet Union suffered substantial losses, whereas her partners in the CMEA apparently gained a great deal from this situation.

However, the dynamic advantages or disadvantages resulting from this exchange cannot be judged on the basis of foreign trade prices alone. One must also know how efficient the economies based on the mutual trade of this kind are, and how marketable their output is in international trade. A good illustration of this has been provided by Köves in arguing the conclusions of Marrese and Vanous:

> No doubt, it was very advantageous to buy oil from the USSR at half of world market prices - and against rouble payment - but if this oil is used, for example, as the fuel of trucks[3] whose specific consumption is about double of the average international consumption level, then this advantage will disappear. Of course, it is also true that in the short run the trucks available in a country should be filled with the possible cheapest fuel. But, in the longer run trucks with high fuel consumption ... are a consequence of the same system of economic relations that enabled buying oil cheaper than on the world market.[4]

One thing is certain, however: this was not a zero-sum game because *all* partners suffered long-lasting losses due to the creation and maintenance of an obsolete economic structure based on smoke-stack industry with the world's highest specific energy- and material-intensity. It was rather ironic that the very dynamic growth of intra-CMEA trade in previous decades was due mostly to precisely this obsolete, energy- and material-intensive structure.

I have already mentioned that the Soviet Union's extremely costly pattern of industrial development inevitably led to the spectacular rise and accumulation of its *huge foreign indebtedness* to Western banks and governments. Less well-known is the other negative aspect of the autarkic development of intra-CMEA trade; namely, that its dynamic growth certainly included an immense share of so-called *overtrading*, i.e. the mutual deliveries of non-marketable goods impossible to sell elsewhere. The reason for this phenomenon was primarily political, but the aims of defence policy were also involved. The major effects of protection on the closed CMEA market, the preservation of obsolete economic structures, and so on, were also contributory factors.

It is impossible, of course, to make exact determination of the share of overtrading in mutual trade. However, some conclusions can be drawn from, for instance, comparative analysis of the intensity of trade flows between countries or regions. In the 1980s, the Hungarian economist András Nagy conducted comparative research on the intensity of the main flows in international trade.[5] Applying his method to the analysis of intra-CMEA trade flows, he reached the conclusion that trade intensity with the Soviet Union in the case of the smaller member countries (including Hungary) was two or three times higher than it would be in a 'normal' case. Concerning Hungary, he wrote that the 'normal' share of the Soviet Union in total Hungarian trade - according to international experiences - amounted to around 10-12%, i.e. about one third of the share actually existing in the mid-1980s.[6]

It was perhaps no coincidence that after the collapse of the CMEA system - discussed later - the share of Hungarian trade with the post-Soviet successor states fell precisely to this level.

2. THE COLLAPSE OF THE CMEA/COMECON

The year of the great change, the *annus mirabilis* of 1989, promised to usher in the regeneration of the Central and Eastern European societies situated on the eastern side of the former Iron Curtain. Although the promise still exists, a great many hopes have been dashed. The area of the now defunct CMEA/COMECON has become a crisis zone of the world economy.

The GDP of these countries in 1992 was at least one-third below the level of 1989. (Even in relatively better-performing Hungary the fall was at least 20%). According to a comparison made by the experts of the UN Economic Commission for Europe, the present decline in the GDP of six Central and East European countries (without the former Soviet Union and Albania, but including Yugoslavia) is steeper than it was during the Great Depression of 1929-34.[7] This region has never suffered such a major loss of national income in peacetime (this statement does not apply, of course, to the warring successor states of former Yugoslavia). This is still not the end of the story, however: at the time of writing (1993) we can only hope that the bottom of the trough will at last be reached this or next year.

This real economic disaster was caused by the simultaneous unfolding of different but interconnected processes of political, economic and social change, by the dissolution of established state formations, by the explosion of old national and ethnic enmities.

If we confine ourselves to the economy sphere alone, it is evident that the emergence of a mixed market economy in the place of the centrally-managed, non-market one - through privatization and the introduction of profit-orientation, the appearance of market competition, etc. - itself provokes considerable social shocks and tensions. In the former CMEA member countries, the crisis situation is aggravated by three additional processes.

First is the *process of economic opening* itself. The adjustment of the East-European economies to the relative price and cost levels of the world market means that they must now undergo the same process of economic restructuring that the other countries of the world experienced at least from the mid-1970s, after the two oil price shocks.

At that time the market economies were afflicted by the deepest economic recession since the Great Depression of the 1930s. Today, the former socialist countries are being tormented by this process, in addition to their other troubles. They should wind up or 'streamline' those economic branches which do not fit the structure of the modern world economy.

The other factor is *the abandonment of the policy of economic autarky*. This is a part and also a consequence of economic opening. Because of the collapse of central planning, domestic producers have suddenly found themselves exposed to competition by imported goods even on their home market.

These goods pour in from every part of the globe and are very often superior both in quality and in price. Although the wide assortment of goods entering as a result of liberalized imports and/or foreign aid are a blessing for domestic consumers, they can be a curse for domestic producers, because these imports push them out of the market. This may provoke a variety of xenophobic, anti-liberal and protectionist tendencies. However, the *single most important factor* accounting for the unprecedented slump in the ex-CMEA countries - besides depressed domestic demand and the fall in output - *was the rapid and sharp contraction of trade with the former CPEs*. We should bear in mind the fact that, in every former CMEA member country's foreign trade, the share of the other member countries was around 50% during the last decades, because of 'overtrading' and other reasons.

Now (see charts 1 and 2) this share is (excepting Bulgaria) around 20% in exports and - in the case of the five smaller countries - a few percentage points higher in imports.

*Chart 1   European transition countries: geographical structure of exports
1989-1992* (Percentages)

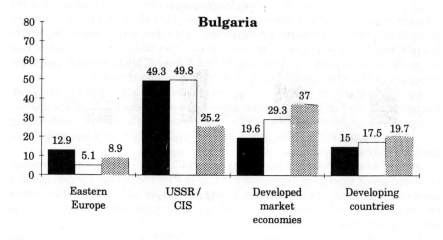

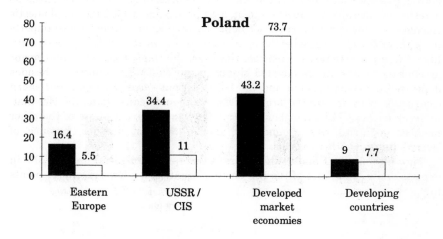

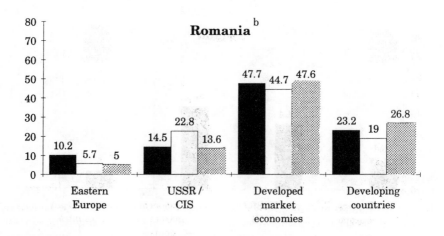

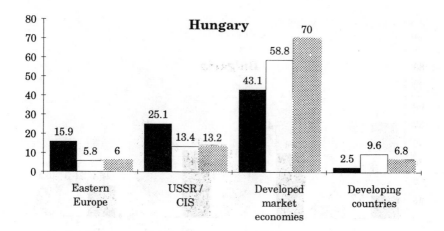

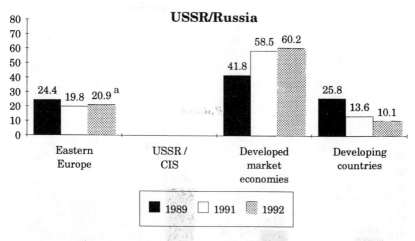

a 1992 January-November.
b 1992 (QI-III).

Note: 1989 figures are calculated at standardized rouble dollar cross-rates (see
United Nations Economic Commission for Europe, *Economic Bulletin for
Europe,* vol. 43, 1991, New York, 1991). The former GDR is included in the
Eastern Europe aggregates. Figures do not add up to 100 because trade with
some smaller 'socialist' partners (China, Cuba etc.) is not shown.

Source: ECE, 1993, p.116.

Chart 2   European transition countries: geographical structure of imports,
1989-1992 (Percentages)

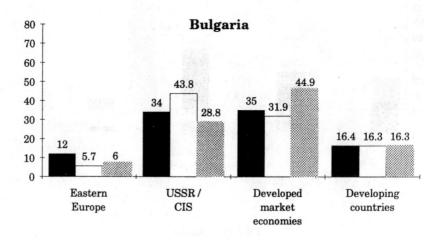

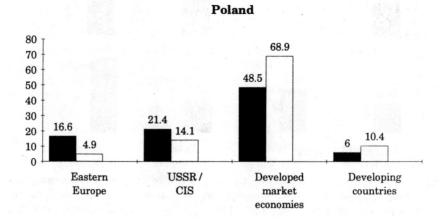

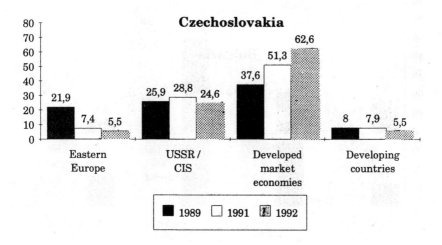

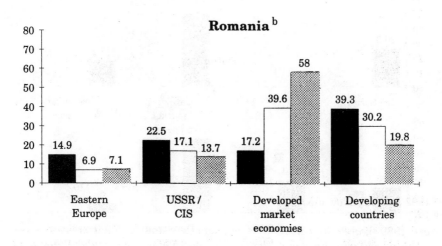

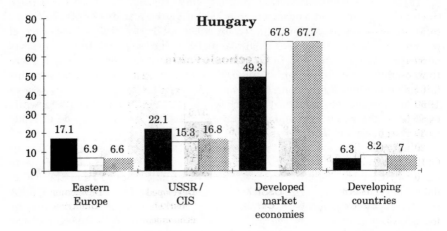

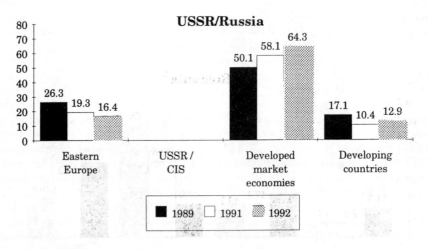

a 1992 January-November.

b 1992 (QI-III).

Note: 1989 figures are calculated at standardized rouble dollar crossrates (see United Nations Economic Commission for Europe, *Economic Bulletin for Europe,* vol. 43, 1991, New York, 1991). The former GDR is included in the Eastern Europe aggregates. Figures do not add up to 100 because trade with some smaller 'socialist' partners (China, Cuba etc.) is not shown.

Source: ECE, 1993, p.118.

Table 1[8] demonstrates this process very clearly. In Eastern Europe (including Albania and Yugoslavia, but excluding the former USSR) the fall in total exports seems to have halted in 1992 after the three-year-period of permanent decline. (Between 1988 and 1991 the region's annual exports decreased steadily from 66 to 59 billion USD). The rate of contraction more than doubled, from less than 3% in 1990 to almost 7% in 1991. However, this fall reflects primarily the contraction of trade with the former CPEs (by 16% in 1990 and around 24% both in 1991 and in the first nine months of 1992), while exports to the market economies expanded rapidly. The import side of trade turnover shows a more or less similar picture.

What was the reason for this almost free fall in trade among the former CMEA partners? Some experts both in the East and the West continue to maintain that the collapse was caused by the rapid change from the TR to dollar payments and world market prices in trade among the former CMEA countries. (This changeover came into effect on 1 January 1991). It would be foolish, of course, to deny the harmful, even disastrous consequences of the rapid abandonment of the previous trade system. And perhaps it is not only by benefit of hindsight if we stress that opportunities for the gradual phasing out the state trading certainly existed and were even elaborated in an embryonic state by a group of Hungarian government experts in 1988.[9] Nevertheless, the abrupt change to dollar payments was not the cause but an effect of the deep-seated crisis of the system of intra-CMEA trade. And since the hub of CMEA integration was the economy of the Soviet Union, it was its crisis and its inability to pay either in goods or money that caused the collapse of intra-CMEA trade. It is enough to cast a cursory glance at Table 1 to realize that the exports of the Soviet Union to Eastern Europe fell by nearly 27% already in 1990 - that is, *before* the change from the TR to dollar payments - while its imports from this region diminished only by some 12%. In fact, the decline in Soviet exports to the CMEA partners started even earlier. After 1986 their value (in current prices) diminished by 3-4% annually. In 1989, however, the fall in Soviet exports to Eastern Europe already amounted to 11.1%.[10] In short: contraction of the Soviet exports has been a continuous and accelerating process for half a decade and has undetermined the foundations of CMEA cooperation. Intra-CMEA trade would have broken down even if the change from TR to dollar payments and world market prices had not taken place on 1 January 1991.

There is neither need nor space for an analysis of the well-known *internal reasons* for the under-performance of Soviet-type economies in general and of the USSR economy in particular. The official dissolution of the CMEA/CO-MECON in the summer of 1991 was the logical outcome of the entire process. It was no accident that the dissolution of the CMEA preceded the disintegration of the USSR itself. It would have happened anyway.

Could the CMEA have been saved by more intelligent and skilful inter-governmental management of its reorganization? As a system of state trading of the CPEs certainly not, because its Central European member countries (Poland, Czechoslovakia, Hungary) were no longer centrally planned economies.

Table 1 - European transition countries: Foreign trade, by direction, 1990-1992 (values in billion USD; growth rates in percentages)[a]

Country or country group[b]	Exports				Imports			
	Value	Growth rates			Value	Growth rates		
	1991	1990	1991	1992	1991	1992	1991	1992
Eastern Europe, to or from:								
World	58.6	-2.8	-6.9	0.1	62.1	4.6	-4.1	1.4
Transition economies	17.3	-15.6	-24.6	-23.5[c]	17.2	-11.2	-19.8	-8.0[c]
Soviet Union successor states	10.6	-16.1	-25.1	-35.9[c]	11.4	-10.8	-9.3	-3.4[c]
Eastern Europe[d]	4.8	-25.6	-20.1	-7.6[c]	4.5	-17.3	-25.8	-11.0[c]
Developed market economies	34.9	9.9	6.6	24.3[c]	37.0	19.1	7.8	22.3[c]
Developing countries	6.4	-12.6	-11.8	15.4[c]	7.9	6.7	-9.2	-38.1[c]
Soviet Union / Russia,[e] to or from:								
World	46.7	-5.2	-24.6	-25.2	45.4	-	-35.9	-21.3
Transition economies	14.0	-24.3	-35.0	-25.8	14.3	-10.6	-43.4	-42.8
Eastern Europe[d]	9.2	-26.9	-40.8	-32.7[f]	8.8	-12.1	-51.6	-49.7[f]
Developed market economies	26.4	12.3	-16.2	-20.3	26.4	5.6	-31.0	-13.0
Developing countries	6.3	-9.5	-29.0	-44.0	4.7	3.8	-35.8	-2.6

a Growth rates are calculated on values expressed in US dollars. Trade with 'transition' and East European countries throughout 1990 was valued on the basis of an adjusted dollar measure reflecting consistent ruble/dollar cross-rates. All trade values for 1991 and 1992 were either originally reported in dollars or were converted to dollars at the appropriate national conversion coefficient (usually the 'commercial' rate quoted by national banks).

b 'Eastern Europe' refers to Albania, Bulgaria, Czechoslovakia, Hungary, Poland, Romania and Yugoslavia. The partner country grouping follows the practice until recently prevalent in the national statistical sources, which differs from the breakdown usually employed in United Nations publications. Thus, 'transition economies', which covers the ex-socialist trade partners, in addition to the East European countries, the Soviet Union, and the Asian centrally planned economies, includes Yugoslavia and Cuba.

c Four countries only (Bulgaria, Czechoslovakia, Hungary and Romania), from January-September 1991 to January-September 1992.

d Without Yugoslavia.

e 1992 data refer to the Russian Federation.

f Trade with all former CMEA members (i.e. including Cuba, Mongolia, Vietnam). It can be assumed that trade with the non-European CMEA members fell more steeply than that with Eastern Europe.

Source: ECE, 1993, p. 112.

Their reintegration into the world economy demanded *inter alia* market-conforming systems of pricing and payment - that is, the abandonment of TR payments and CMEA-specific pricing. Exactly as was done in 1991.

3. CHANGES IN FOREIGN TRADE FLOWS

How did the former member countries of the CMEA/COMECON react to the collapse of their economic bloc?

3.1. CHANGES IN LEVELS AND DIRECTIONS OF TRADE

The immediate - negative - outcome was the *sharp contraction* of their trade. However, a simultaneous positive process of the *geographical reorientation* of their trade towards markets in developed Western countries also began. The general overview given by Table 1 already shows that only the figures relating to trade with the developed market economies in 1990-1992 were a positive sign. However, this general trend has to date only been valid for the countries of Central and Eastern Europe. The situation in the USSR/Russia, before and after the disintegration of the empire, showed a steep decline in its trade in all directions.

A much more concrete (and somewhat different) picture emerges from Table 2, which is compiled on a country-by-country basis. Although the data collected by the experts of the Secretariat of the UN ECE should be taken *cum grano salis*, like any statistics concerning the former CPEs,[11] to the best of my knowledge they accurately reflect general trends.

Compared with the level of 1988 total exports by the *USSR/Russia* fell by almost half. Even worse, however, was the contraction of exports in *Bulgaria* and *Romania*. In 1992, the former country's total exports were 46% of the 1988 level, while the latter's were just below 49%. Perhaps the slightly favourable difference *vis-à-vis* the Russian situation can be seen in the slowdown of total export decline and in the positive growth rates of exports to developed market economies and developing countries in 1992. However, according to current statistics, a turning-point came in the first half of 1993: whereas in Russia the decline in exports seems to have come to a halt, it continued both in Bulgaria and Romania.

A different picture emerges as regards the countries of the Central European *troika* (Poland, Czechoslovakia, Hungary) - which after the break-up of Czechoslovakia might be called a *quadriga*. Because of the dynamic growth in these countries' exports to the developed market economies, the fall in their total exports was much less marked than in the countries of the former group. According to the data given in Table 2, both *Poland* and *Hungary* were, within two years, able to reach and surpass the earlier level of their total exports.

Table 2 - *European transition countries: Change in foreign trade values and trade balances by partner region, 1989-1992 (growth rates in percentages)*

Country and trade partner groups[a]	Growth rates							
	Exports				Imports			
	1989	1990	1991	1992	1989	1990	1991	1992
Bulgaria								
World	-12.0	-21.3	-34.2	1.6	-9.9	-23.7	-51.5	27.5
Transition economies	-10.6	-32.0	-27.8	-25.7	-16.7	-23.8	-43.1	-4.3
Developed market economies	17.2	-11.1	-36.3	61.6	0.6	-25.9	-59.8	79.3
Developing countries	-35.8	9.7	-47.6	14.2	-8.7	-19.0	-54.4	26.7
Czechoslovakia								
World	-3.2	-10.5	5.6	3.2	-2.4	0.3	-7.2	14.6
Transition economies	-11.7	-27.4	6.8	-33.0	-6.9	-17.1	0.3	-10.2
Developed market economies	10.9	13.4	6.9	26.4	-1.6	24.6	-13.7	39.6
Developing countries	0.1	-10.9	-6.0	27.4	17	-12.0	4.4	-20.4
Hungary								
World	-3.3	-0.6	5.1	4.1	-5.4	-0.7	30.2	-3.2
Transition economies	-9.5	-21.5	-26.8	3.2	-14.4	-18.8	2.8	1.8
Developed market economies	5.6	27.9	21.4	9.1	7.7	8.6	44.3	-3.4
Developing countries	-6.8	-12.8	21.8	-27.4	-22.2	52.9	29.0	-16.6
Poland								
World	0.6	24.7	-18.5	9.7[b]	-1.1	-2.5	24.3	6.1[b]
Transition economies	-2.5	14.9	-62.0	-	-5.7	1.8	-42.8	-
Developed market economies	5.3	40.0	13.7	-	7.1	-4.7	71.7	-
Developing countries	-3.6	3.2	-15.5	-	-8.8	-17.1	151.0	-
Romania								
World	-10.0	-43.4	-7.1	0.9	8.8	18.1	-17.6	-1.4
Transition economies	-14.7	-45.5	29.2	-17.6[c]	-2.3	-13.7	-8.9	-33.7[c]
Developed market economies	-3.9	-38.4	-22.8	2.5[c]	1.7	116.7	-9.4	42.6[c]
Developing countries	-15.2	-51.0	-11.9	43.8[c]	29.0	10.1	-32.7	-46.2[c]
Soviet Union, Russia[d]								
World	0.4	-5.2	-24.6	-25.2	12.0	-	-35.9	-21.3
Transition economies	-8.7	-24.3	-35.1	-25.8	-4.5	-10.6	-35.9	-42.8
of which Eastern Europe[e]	-11.1	-26.9	-40.8	-32.7[f]	-5.7	-12.1	-51.6	-49.7[f]
Developed market economies	7.8	12.3	-16.2	-20.3	21.1	5.6	-31.0	-13.0
Developing countries	2.0	-9.5	-29.0	-44.0	26.0	3.9	-35.8	-2.6

a The partner country grouping follows the practice of the national statistical sources, which differed from the breakdown usually employed in United

Nations publications. Thus, 'transition economies' - the former 'socialist countries' - include Yugoslavia and Cuba, in addition to the East European countries, the Soviet Union, and the Asian centrally planned economies.

b On the basis of balance-of-payments data.

c January-September 1992 relative to the same period in 1991.

d 1992 data refer to the Russian Federation only.

e Excluding Yugoslavia. The former German Democratic Republic is included in the data for 1990, but not in those for 1991.

f Russian Federation trade with all former CMEA members (i.e. including Cuba, Mongolia and Vietnam).

Source: For 1989: ECE, 1992, p. 80 and 111; for the following years: ECE, 1993, p. 114.

This means that the steep fall in their 'Eastern' exports gave way to growth in their exports to the West. Hence the 'Operation Reorientation' of these countries seems to have been successful.

The position of the *former Czechoslovakia* was somewhat different. The calculation based on the figures in Table 2 shows that the level of total exports in 1992 was slightly below the level of 1988. However, because of the different situations of the *Czech Republic* and Slovakia, we can confidently assume that the foreign trade performance of the more developed Czech Republic - which is in much better economic shape than the Slovak Republic - was at least as good as that of Poland and Hungary. This fact, however, leaves serious doubts concerning the future international economic position of the already independent *Slovakia*.

3.2. THE NEW GEOGRAPHICAL PATTERN OF TRADE

The changes of the past three years in most countries have resulted in striking shifts of market shares *from* the former CMEA trade partners *towards* the rest of the world (and first and foremost towards the OECD countries). The changes are shown in graphic form in Charts 1 and 2.

Shifts in trade patterns, especially in the countries of East-Central Europe, have been very large indeed: the 'East-West' shift in *exports* over a three-year span amounted to some 20 to 30 percentage points; in *imports* the changes were smaller and the range wider - generally 10 to 20 percentage points. According to the data on the former Soviet Union, the 'East-West' shift was much smaller.

The dominant feature of the new geographical pattern of trade is the *overwhelming share of the OECD countries* in both the exports and imports of *all* the former CMEA/COMECON member countries. Particularly impressive in the four-year period covered by Table 2 was the growth in the export share of the developed market economies due to the burgeoning exports of the three Central European countries. (Compared with the 1988 level, Polish, Hungarian,

Czechoslovak exports to the OECD as a whole rose by 70 to 80%).

At the individual country level, *Germany has become the largest trading partner* of the Central and Eastern European countries. In the case of Hungary, Czechoslovakia and Poland, Germany had already replaced the Soviet Union as their principal partner in 1991. According to Inotai,[12] most advantage of the positive impact of Germany's unification on its import demand has been taken not by the neighbouring EC countries but by four non-EC-members, namely China, Czechoslovakia, Poland and Hungary. Again according to Inotai, Czechoslovakian and Polish exports to Germany were 130% higher, and Hungarian exports 80% higher, in 1991 than in 1989.

The other important feature of the new geographical pattern of trade is that despite large 'East-West' shifts, *the CIS* (that is, Russia and the other successor states of the USSR) *is still a major partner* of all the Central and Eastern European countries in both their export and especially import activity (see Charts 1 and 2). For example, even in the case of Hungary, a country that was rather successful in shifting its trade towards the West, Hungarian trade with the CIS grew rapidly in 1992 and moved into second place after Germany. In spite of the growing political and financial uncertainties of their economic relationships with the CIS-area, mutual trade will remain important for the Central and Eastern European countries, which are heavily (in some cases unilaterally) dependent on the previously established intra-CMEA network of energy and raw material supplies.

Perhaps the most striking phenomenon was *the sharp fall in mutual trade among East-European countries*. This, however, was not as steep as appears from Charts 1 and 2, where the figures for 1989 include both the former GDR and Yugoslavia. Neither of these countries exist now, and disintegrated Yugoslavia, torn by a protracted and bloody civil war, did not belong to the CMEA in any case. If we only consider mutual trade among the five former CMEA member countries - Bulgaria, Czechoslovakia, Hungary, Poland and Romania (which we may call Group 5) - and if we inspect the figures for the years prior to 1989, there emerges the rather different picture given by Charts 3 and 4, which are based on data collected by Richter and Tóth from national trade statistics.[13]

A few interesting conclusions can be drawn from these two charts. As can be seen, the decline in the share of mutual trade started neither with political change (in 1989) nor with the changeover to payments in hard currency (in 1991), but earlier, in the mid-1980s. In the case of Poland, Hungary and Czechoslovakia, this can be straightforwardly explained by the process of the geographical reorientation of their trade that started before the systemic change. Richter and Tóth's analysis shows that the trade of the three countries at constant prices with non-CMEA economies grew in the period 1985-1990 at a substantially faster rate than that with CMEA member countries.

Chart 3 Group 5: shares of intragroup exports in total trade, 1985-1991
(percentages)

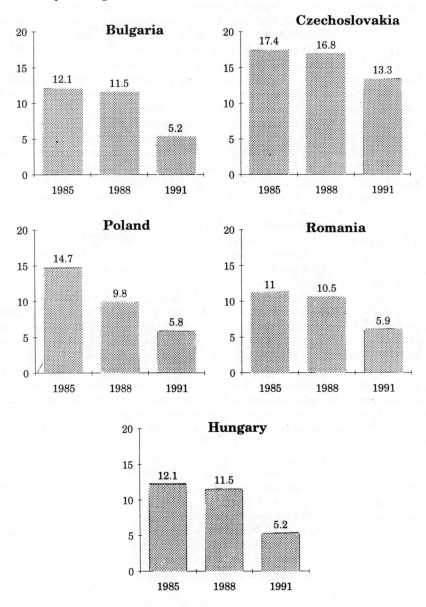

Source: Richter and Tòth, 1993, Table 7-11

Chart 4   *Group 5: shares of intra-group imports in total trade, 1985-1991*
         (percentages)

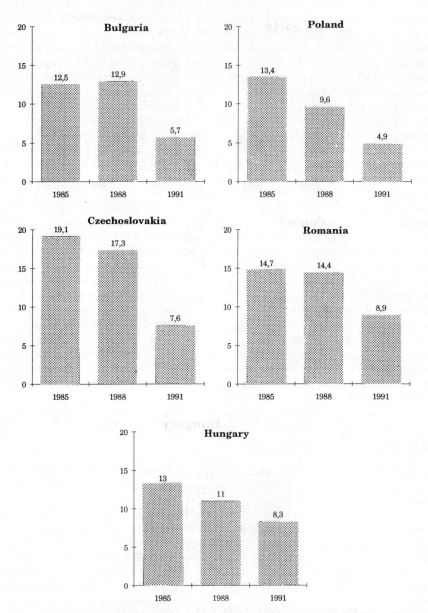

Source: Richter and Tòth, 1993, Table 7-11

Hence it follows that the fall in the trade among the three countries in question, comprising the so-called Visegrád Group, was neither accidental nor the outcome of either the insolvency of the economies or of a lack of hard currency, as was the case of the former USSR and her successor states. On the contrary, not only did all three countries of the Visegrád Group boost their exports to the West, as has been mentioned, and significantly improve their external payment positions, they also very quickly liberalized their imports. Consequently, the fall in their mutual trade was brought about by other factors, such as the structural incompatibility of their economies (as a result of radial integration within the CMEA), low competitiveness and the attractiveness of their goods for each other (caused by the technological gap between East and West), as well as other factors.

Will the new *Central European Free Trade Agreement (CEFTA)* established by Poland, the Czech Republic, Slovakia and Hungary (the agreement came into effect on an interim basis on 1 March 1993) revive the earlier intensity of mutual trade? There is no doubt that the CEFTA will be very helpful *in preventing the further shrinkage* of mutual trade. The member countries of the Visegrád Group - which established the CEFTA[14] - are now associate members of the European Community. In fact, the tariff and other consessions granted to, and obtained from the EC under the association agreements concluded at the end of 1991 discriminated against trade with third parties, including the members of the Visegrád Group. The CEFTA should prevent these potential disadvantages. Of course, the prospect of the step-by-step elimination of the major restrictions on free trade will lead to a more efficient allocation of the factors of production and may attract more foreign direct investment into the free trade area, now that it has a chance of joining the EC. This will certainly induce both the growth of output and mutual trade within the area. However, whether it will substantially increase the *relative share* of mutual trade under the strong attraction of, and competition from, the Common Market remains an open question.

3.3. THE LIMITS OF REORIENTATION

Although the geographical reorientation of the foreign trade of the former CPEs was achieved in an unexpectedly short time, this success is questionable in at least three respects.

First, as the statistical data show, the process of reorientation has so far been implemented only by the westernmost countries of the former CMEA (and Slovakia's place among them is uncertain in this respect). The other countries born out of the ruins of the Soviet Union, and the two former Balkan members of the CMEA (Romania and Bulgaria), have not yet been able either to create the framework for a market economy or to replace their lost CMEA market by expanding on Western markets. The prospects for this sub-region are therefore gloomy.

Second, the dynamic growth in exports to developed market economies achieved by the former group of the ex-CPEs should be placed against the background of the protracted depression and steep decline in domestic demand. Manufacturers and agricultural producers export to the West because they simply have no other option. They are frequently forced to export at a loss, thereby 'eating up' their assets in order to survive. These developments have their well-known limits, and after a while economic decline no longer boosts exports but impedes them.

Third, the export offensive of the Central European countries did not rely on well-defined sectors or products which would have determined their export performance. These countries seem to have increased their market shares across-the-board in all major product groups, ranging from labour-intensive ones (textiles, clothing) to material-intensive goods (steel, paper, metals) to technology-intensive sectors (machinery, instruments, pharmaceuticals). This pattern of export growth has already proved to be unsustainable. According to statistical data for the first five to six months it was only the Czech Republic among the six Central and East European countries that was able to raise its exports. The exports of the others (Bulgaria, Hungary, Poland, Romania, Slovakia) contracted,[15] proving to be vulnerable to both international and domestic recession.

CONCLUSIONS

The process of opening, for all its importance, is only one part of the general process of the transformation of centrally planned economies into market ones. The success of the latter, however, depends not only on the introduction of institutional changes (like privatization or creation of modern banking, a fiscal system, and so on) but at the moment first and foremost on bottoming out from unprecedented economic decline and achieving sustainable economic growth. It seems that the former CPEs will be unable to solve this complex problem without effective assistance from the international community. But what must be done in this regard is the subject of another study.

NOTES

1 See the comprehensive analyses of the topic in Ausch, 1972; Marer and Montias, 1980; Köves, 1985.
2 Marrese and Vanous, 1983.
3 As a rule also made in the USSR.
4 Köves, 1983, p. 127.
5 The methodology and partial results of Nagy's research have been

published in English in Nagy, 1985.

6 Nagy, 1989.

7 ECE, 1992, p. 44.

8 Compiled by the Secretariat of the UN Economic Commission for Europe.

9 The proposals of the working group were published a year later in Hungarian: see Szamuely, 1989. See also in English Csaba, 1991/1992, and Köves, 1992, pp. 59-77.

10 ECE, 1992, Table 4.1.5, p. 111.

11 See, for example, in Table 1 the discrepancy between the growth rates of exports from the transition economies to the Soviet successor states and the matching figures on imports by the latter states from the transition economies.

12 See Inotai, 1992.

13 See Richter and Tóth, 1993.

14 Visegrád is the ancient town in Hungary where the leaders of Czechoslovakia, Hungary and Poland held their first summit in February 1991 and agreed to begin negotiations on the establishment of a free trade area. The CEFTA was signed in Cracow on 21 December 1992.

15 See Kopint-Datorg, 1993.

BIBLIOGRAPHY

Ausch, S. (1972), *Theory and Practice of CMEA Cooperation*, Budapest: Akadémiai Kiadó.

Csaba, L. (1991/1992), 'What comes after COMECON', *Soviet and Eastern European Foreign Trade*. vol. 26, no. 4, Winter.

ECE (1992), *Economic Survey of Europe in 1991-1992*, New York: UN Economic Commission for Europe.

ECE (1993), *Economic Survey of Europe in 1992-1993*, New York: UN Economic Commission for Europe.

Inotai, A. (1992), 'External Economic Policies and Challenges During the Transformation Process', keynote address at the conference on 'The Future of Eastern and Central Europe in the World Economy'. mimeo, Institute for World Economics of the Hungarian Academy of Sciences, Budapest, November 17-18.

Kopint-Datorg (1993), *Economic Trends in Eastern Europe*, vol. 3, no. 3, Kopint-Datorg Institute for Economic and Market Research and Informatics, Vienna-New York: Budapest and Springer Verlag.

Köves, A. (1983), 'Implicit Subsidies' and some Issues of Economic Relations within the CMEA. (Remarks on the analyses made by Michael Marrese and Jan Vanous)', *Acta Oeconomica* (Budapest), vol. 31, no. 1-2. pp. 125-36.

Köves, A. (1985), *The CMEA Countries in the World Economy: Turning Inwards* or *Turning Outwards*, Budapest: Akadémiai Kiadó.

Köves, A. (1992), *Central and East European Economies in Transition: The International Dimension*, Boulder-San Francisco-Oxford: Westview Press.

Marer, P., Montias, I. (1980), *East European Integration and East-West Trade*, Bloomington: Indiana University Press.

Marrese, M., Vanous, I. (1983), *Soviet Subsidization of Trade with Eastern Europe: A Soviet Perspective*, Berkeley: University of California Institute of International Studies.

Nagy, A. (1985), 'Changes in the Structure and Intensity of East-West Trade', *Acta Oeconomica*, vol. 35, nos. 3-4, pp. 359-75.

Nagy, A. (1989), 'Külkereskedelmi orientációváltást!' ('A change is needed in foreign trade orientation!'), *Közgazdasági Szemle*, vol. 36, no. 9, September, pp. 1033-46.

Richter, S., Tòth, L.G. (1993), *After the Agreement on Free Trade Among the Visegrád Group Countries: Perspectives for Intra-Regional Trade in East-Central Europe*. WIIW-Forschungsberichte, no. 195 (Vienna), April.

Szamuely, L. (ed.) (1989), *A világgazdasági nyitás: gazdaságpolitikai fordulat és intézményi reform* (The opening towards world economy: A turn in the economic policy and an institutional reform), Budapest: Közgazdasági és Jogi Könyvkiadó.

Differing Approaches to the Transition to Post-Socialist Development in the Newly-Formed Balkan States

Ivo Bicanic and Marko Škreb

1. Introduction[1]

In the early 1990s Yugoslavia irreversibly split up into five independent states: namely, from north to south, the Republic of Slovenia, the Republic of Croatia, the Republic of Bosnia and Herzegovina, the Republic of Macedonia[2] and the Federal Republic of Yugoslavia (composed of the former Yugoslav republics of Serbia and Montenegro, by September 1993 Yugoslavia had not yet gained international recognition because of its role in the still ongoing Wars of Yugoslav Succession). This decomposition, together with the brutal way in which it is being conducted, has vastly increased the problems faced by all these newly-formed states. Since the beginning, each has sought to solve its problems differently, and as time passes they will go their increasingly divergent ways.

As a result, the economic problems of these countries - and their economic problems are the only ones addressed by this paper - are more numerous than those faced by other small European post-socialist economies (but not some of the newly-formed economies emerging from the break-up of the Soviet Union). In addition to the two problems placed on the agenda by post-socialist development, they face two further ones. Like all other economies on the path to post-socialist development, they have the double task of economic transition and of catching-up. The first of their two additional problems, namely the task of establishing a national economy, they share with other newly-formed states; the second one, the issues raised by war and reconstruction, they share with a small number of other newly formed states.

The break-up of Yugoslavia raises many tasks for the analyst, two of which seem central. The first is understanding how the process of disintegration evolved over time and induced the newly formed Balkan states to prefer 'go-it-alone' transition policies in spite of the increased complexity of economic problems that they necessarily entail. The second and perhaps even more interesting (and arguably important) question is quantitative analysis of the economic benefits and costs of establishing new Balkan states.

The first section of the paper will attempt to deal briefly with the most important issues relating to the process which led to the break-up of Yugoslavia. The second and third sections are concerned with the issue of the costs and benefits of 'go-it-alone' transition, even though this question at present cannot be answered with precision (firstly, because of the still unresolved Wars of Yugoslav Succession which constantly change the balance sheets of all the newly-established states, and secondly because of the obvious lack of data required for rigorous quantitative analysis). As a result, this paper will offer tentative analysis by dealing with those areas in which research is possible. Thus the second section will deal with the different transition paths now emerging in the newly-formed states, while the third section addresses aspects of the economic impact of the disintegration. The fourth and final section of the paper offers some tentative conclusions.

2. THE DISINTEGRATION OF YUGOSLAVIA

The crises of the 1980s began in Yugoslavia, as elsewhere, with the debt crises of the world economy. External insolvency, given the then existing economic system and policies (both those formally declared and those on the double agenda of the party in power at the time) soon spilled over into internal disequilibrium. Regardless of their intention, when economic policies were implemented they became 'soft' policies, and instead of dealing with the crises they deepened and prolonged them, making the 1980s a decade of increasingly poor economic performance. The crises of the 1980s have been well documented[3] and need no further elaboration here, except perhaps to draw attention to one of their less-frequently mentioned features. In the case of the Yugoslav economy, the 1980s were a period of deeper, longer and more severe depression than the world slump of the 1930s.[4]

This prolonged economic depression understandably highlighted all the weaknesses of the economic system in its institutional and historical setting. In the case of Yugoslavia, these were: (a) the role of self-management and socialism as a generator of crises and depression; (b) the consistent failure of attempts to generate 'modern economic growth'; (c) the inability satisfactorily to deal with regional issues and establish an unbiased central brokerage of regional interests, thus failing to create a uniform economic space; and (d) the inability to design and implement efficient crisis management policies. Of course, many issues overlap and the above compartmentalization is not 'watertight'.

(a) Self-management

Concerning the role of self-management in generating crises, "... the difficulty lies, not in the new ideas, but in escaping from old ones which ramify ... into every corner of our minds".[5] Throughout the 1980s, a maturing process took place among economists and politicians which slowly generated demands for increasingly more radical reforms. In the early 1980s, it was not self-management as such that was held to be the main culprit, but the form in which it had been applied since the mid-1970s (i.e. the 'associated labour paradigm'[6]). This was the main thesis of published official blueprints for reform, crises management and growth promotion (issued in 1983[7] and 1986[8]) and one ambitious last-ditch effort to build new socialism (in 1989[9]). Under their influence, by the end of the 1980s the legal and institutional structure started to show changes, each of which was increasingly radical and one step behind events. As the crises continued, the 'real world' demanded additional changes, while society in general, as well as many politicians, came to recognize the need for radical transformation. This maturing process is perhaps best evidenced by the changes concerning ownership. The 1980s began with the inherited system of social ownership and limited areas of private ownership. By 1990 (i.e. before the post-socialist phase began), institutional changes had significantly limited self-management, equalizing all forms of ownership (i.e. private and socialized), legislation for 'spontaneous privatization' had been passed, capital and labor markets accepted, and a multi-party system planned. The importance of this decade-long process is that the taboos on socialism and self-management (and with it the role of the party) were significantly weakened by the time post-socialism and disintegration came onto the scene.

(b) Modern economic growth

During Yugoslavia's 73-year-long history,[10] which started with the country's amalgamation in 1918 and lasted until its decomposition in 1991, it never achieved 'modern economic growth', i.e. it never achieved "a long term rise in the capacity to supply increasingly diverse economic goods to its population, this growing capacity based on advancing technology and its institutional and ideological adjustments that it demands".[11] This failure was not due to lack of effort and sacrifice by the population nor of ambitious proposals advanced by politicians. During the period, numerous growth-promoting policies were attempted both in 'clear' and 'mixed' (i.e. transitional) institutional frameworks.

Four 'clear' frameworks can be distinguished while: The four 'mixed' frameworks represent interregnums (i.e. transitions) between clear systems and thus tend to include features of two 'clear' systems. These four frameworks are: restructuring for state capitalism, 1925-36; state investment policies with limited self-management and limited markets, 1950-65; associated labour paradigm 1971-88, reformed associated labour paradigm, 1988-90. Even though these policies coincided with spurts in growth of varying lengths (notable among them being the 'agricultural boom' that followed World War I, the 'state-led' pre-World War II spurt, the high growth rates of the so-called 'golden era of self-management' in the late 1950s and 'import led growth' of the mid-1970s), they never lasted more than five years and they never led to sustained economic growth. Furthermore, high growth rates can frequently be more convincingly attributed to other causes than the implementation of growth-promoting policies.[12] The inefficiency of growth since the Second World War has been measured in four ways. The first addresses the century-long slowdown of growth and its determinants; the second analyses Yugoslavia's unchanged relative position on Europe's development gradient; the third matches its economic performance against that of comparable economies; and the fourth deals with the inefficiency of achieved growth rates. In all four respects Yugoslavia's performance has been increasingly poor, placing the country firmly among Europe's semi-peripheral economies.[13] As a cumulative effect of this failure, the myth of post-war growth leading to abundance and wealth was proved false and, furthermore, it became acceptable to evaluate socialist performance.

(c) Regional development, brokerage of regional interests and creation of uniform economic space

When analysing Yugoslavia's disintegration, regional development and the representation (brokerage) of regional interests must be given special consideration. This is because of the intricate relationship among geographical regions (most of which do not cover more than one republic) and ethnic regions, which has often meant that regional issues have coincided with national ones. This identification of national and geographical areas became increasingly important during the post-war period, when the boundaries among the federal republics of Yugoslavia were drawn largely in order to respect ethnic and historical criteria. Three comparative aspects were singled out regarding regional development, while two principal issues relating to the Yugoslav economy were discussed.

The first set of issues concerning regional development arose when the growth of Yugoslavia's regions was compared with that of regions outside Yugoslavia. This aspect was emphasised in particular by the most developed Yugoslav republic, Slovenia. It was claimed that in 1918 (before the amalgamation of Yugoslavia) Slovenia was almost equally as developed as southern Austria, thereafter it increasingly lagged behind ('falling behind') the comparable regions of Austria. The second important aspect concerned the position of regions on the Yugoslav development gradient in absolute and relative terms. These discussions turned into heated debates. For example, papers were published for every region which pointed out that 'it' was losing out in Yugoslavia's development while 'others' were gaining (not unexpectedly, there was a high correlation between the author's domicile and the loser region). It was claimed that Serbia was dropping below the average Yugoslav growth indicators, falling behind the developed regions and growing increasingly similar to the less developed regions.[14] These latter drew attention to the widening inequalities among regions and that they were falling behind. Finally in Croatia it was argued that its growth was below the capacity of its economy.[15] The last aspect of regional development relevant to the break-up of the country centred on inter-regional redistribution.

There were two kinds of redistribution that were important. The first was aid to the less developed regions, the second was redistribution through administrative prices and government decisions. The aid issue covered the usual arguments between donor (the more developed 'north', i.e. Slovenia, Croatia and Vojvodina) and recipient (the 'south', i.e. the rest of former Yugoslavia). Regarding redistribution through prices, once again every region contended that it was losing due to this redistribution. The main exporters, Slovenia and Croatia, were losing because of an over-valued exchange rate and foreign currency regulations, the less developed regions and Serbia because of administratively low energy prices and low prices for semi-processed goods (with the developed regions gaining through high market prices for industrial goods). From the mid-1980s onwards, these discussions broke down the taboos which restricted inter-regional comparisons in the name of 'brotherhood and unity'. In spite of major differences both in the data used, analyses and conclusions regarding the level of integration and its changes over time (and especially regarding 1974 as a year of discontinuity), all participants in the discussion agreed that regional differences had increased during post World War II development. The data in Table 1 illustrate these differences.

Two types of issues relating to the Yugoslav economy were discussed: the first came under the heading of the 'unity' of the economy; the second concerned inter-regional redistributions. The unity arguments were a recurrent topic[16] of discussion and controversy among mutually irreconcilable opinions, which never led to a professional consensus or found academic resolution.[17] During the 1980s this discussion centred on three topics: the first was whether the Yugoslav economy was disintegrating; the second was whether a single institutional framework was possible in such a diverse economic environment; the third concerned the levels of centralization required for efficient economic policy.

The opinions expressed were regularly backed by economic analysis supplied by impressively titled authors and institutions. However, as already mentioned, there was a surprisingly close correlation between the author's region of residence and the arguments advanced.

Table 1 - Comparison of republics (Yugoslavia = 100)

Republic	A		B		C		D		E
	1955	1988	1955	1988	1955	1988	1955	1988	1955-88
B & H	80	65	107	94	100	67	14.4	12.7	4.6%
Croatia	120	129	100	110	100	133	26.7	25.5	4.6%
Montenegro	80	71	49	137	200	67	1.8	2.0	5.0%
Macedonia	60	65	68	75	100	67	5.2	5.7	5.2%
Serbia	80	88	93	87	100	100	37.6	37.5	5.1%
Slovenia	160	200	124	137	200	233	14.3	16.6	5.2%

A - social product per capital.
B - capital/labour ratio.
C - gross investment in fixed assets per capita.
D - the share of social product of Republics in total Yugoslav social product (in %)
E - average yearly rate of growth of social product from 1955 to 1988.

Source: Computed by the authors from *Statistical Yearbook of Yugoslavia* (SYY), various years.

The intra-regional homogeneity of opinions and their inter-regional diversity increased the importance of non-economic arguments.[18] A similar fate befell the second set of issues concerning regional income and wealth redistribution. Depending on the author, every region was losing and every region was gaining. Thus it was claimed that major redistributions were taking place from the less developed regions (the 'south') and Serbia to the developed regions (the 'north'). The redistribution came about through government-regulated artificially low prices for energy and semi-processed goods (supplied by the south) and market-determined relatively high prices for finished products and consumer goods (produced by the north), which created unfavourable terms of trade for the undeveloped regions.

Table 2 - Sold goods and services in %

Republic	A		B		C		D	
	1968	1987	1968	1987	1968	1987	1968	1987
B & H	61.7	69.5	29.1	19.7	7.4	9.5	1.8	1.3
Croatia	65.1	68.6	21.6	19.1	10.1	10.8	3.2	1.5
Montenegro	56.8	59.8	32.0	26.3	8.8	10.0	2.4	3.5
Macedonia	65.6	66.5	22.7	23.5	8.9	9.2	2.8	0.8
Serbia	66.5	76.2	17.4	14.8	14.0	8.7	2.1	0.3
Slovenia	60.0	62.9	27.5	22.2	10.7	13.4	1.8	1.5

A - sold goods and services within republic (in %).
B - sold goods and services to other republics (in %).

C - exported goods and services outside Yugoslavia.
D - statistical discrepancy.

Source: Compiled by authors from Grubisic, 1990.

The developed regions, Croatia and Slovenia, pointed out that they were the main providers of aid to the 'south', and that the over-valued dinar and their above-average earnings of foreign currency brought about a redistribution in the other direction. The unity discussions also focused on the appropriate level of centralization for efficient economic policy, which was discussed in the context of federalist and confederalist options. The inability to build an equitable, coherent and robust policy was attributed to the consensus requirement and to confederalist elements. The counter-arguments pointed to the legacy of the biased centralized brokerage of regional interests and 'soft' policy implementation. The level of intra and inter-regional sales and their changes (see Table 2) were especially important in the unity arguments. Some interpreted the data as showing high levels of integration with a falling trend since the institutional changes of 1974. Others stressed the low level of integration and questioned the identification of any point of discontinuity, explaining changes as resulting from other causes and not from the 1974 institutional change.

(d) Inability to design and implement efficient crisis management policies

As can be seen from this brief survey, by the late 1980s and early 1990s the Yugoslav economy was plunging ever deeper into crisis and all its underpinnings were under discussion and review. Various stabilization programmes were proposed, comprising a wide range of approaches (from bans and regulations to market-oriented ones). None of them succeeded and the economic crises deepened. In the face of this persistent inability, the attractiveness of as yet untried 'go-it-alone' policies increased. This argument will be thoroughly explored in the next section.

3. DIVERGENT PATHS OF TRANSITION

All periodizations are subject to criticism, and the following one will be no exception. Yugoslavia will be considered a uniform economy until the emergence of inter-republic institutional differences and the raising of formal barriers to internal trade.[19] On this criterion, institutional segmentation began in 1990, in which year multi-party elections were held in all of the republics. These elections led to a major shift of political power since in all but two republics, Serbia and Montenegro,[20] the communist parties (which participated in the elections under new names) were voted out of power and post-socialist development began. The constitutions passed by the individual republics introduced different socio-economic systems (Croatia abolished self-manage-ment, Slovenia extended the power of managers at the expense of workers).

Even formal inter-regional barriers to trade were erected by republican legislation. In October 1990 Serbia introduced special taxes on Slovenian and Croatian goods and blocked all payments to those republics. In September 1990, Serbia stopped transferring part of its fiscal revenues to the then federal authorities. By the end of that year, Slovenia and Croatia did the same, and the federal fiscal system collapsed. Hostile takeovers 'Balkan style' started in the summer of 1990. For example, branches of Croatian enterprises in Serbia declared themselves independent from their parent companies and sometimes merged with similar Serbian companies. Other republics followed suit, and in anticipation of these moves enterprises from different republics exchanged plants and offices. No legal action was possible. Thus, a common legal system ceased to exist as well.

Institutional segmentation was paralleled by political negotiations intended to redesign the country by 'recontracting' it. Three options were mooted: the first envisaging a confederation of republics (implying looser relations than existing ones), the second a 'asymmetrical' federation ('two-track' Yugoslavia), and the third a tightening federation (reducing the autonomy of the republics). Interestingly, with the exception of the third option, economics did not figure prominently (the third option entailed centralization with its claim that only a centralized economic policy is effective for crises management) since all the other options accepted one economic space (i.e. a common currency, a tariff system, and free internal free trade).

After a brief period of segmentation, the final disintegration of the Yugoslav economy (and of Yugoslavia) into its successor states came with the international recognition of Croatia and Slovenia in January 1992. Already by the end of 1991, the economies of the successor states of Yugoslavia were institutionally, structurally and environmentally so different as to render disintegration irreversible, and different paths of transition were defined which the ongoing wars of the Yugoslav Succession have only made more visible.[21]

Institutionally the differences were enormous. As regards workers' self management and their participation in enterprise decision-making (the basis of the 'Yugoslav road' to communism), some states eliminated the system entirely (Croatia), some redefined it (Slovenia), some left it almost intact ('rump' Yugoslavia and Macedonia) while others had no opportunity to deal with it (Bosnia and Herzegovina). Different privatization legislation led to quite different methods for changing property rights. One plan (Slovenia's, passed in November 1992) envisaged a complicated partial voucher system and extended the time horizon for privatization, assigning a prominent role to managers and a minor one to the state. Croatia's plan, passed in May 1991, favoured speed but relied on state-dominated and revenue-oriented privatization. Serbia's plan, passed in August 1991, retained socialized ownership coupled with increasing state control. Macedonia's, passed in June 1993, gave a prominent place to leveraged buy-outs, permitted numerous methods of privatization and resisted any voucher scheme, while that of Bosnia and Herzegovina pushed it far down the agenda.

These different privatization paths, together with their implementation, have changed property rights to differing extents and are likely to result in different distributions of economic power. The newly-formed states have also chosen different methods for introducing new currencies and monetary systems, and they are at different places along the path towards complete monetary reform. Slovenia introduced its new temporary currency in October 1991 and completed its transition by replacing a temporary currency with a permanent one in early 1993. Croatia introduced its own temporary currency (the Croatian dinar) in December 1991, and hopes to complete its transition to a stable currency quite soon. 'Rump Yugoslavia' introduced a new permanent currency immediately (the 'new' dinar). Macedonia introduced a temporary currency (the Macedonian denar) in April 1992. A new Bosnian dinar was introduced by the Bosnian government in August 1992 (although in the territory of Bosnia and Herzegovina multiple currencies are in use: the Yugoslav dinar, Croatian dinar, Bosnian dinar, and the currency of the self-proclaimed Republic of Serbian Krajina).[22] The picture becomes even more confused if one remembers that in all the former republics with high inflation (that is, all of them with the notable exception of Slovenia) German marks are widely used in daily transactions not only as a measure of value (i.e. all monetary variables in legal contracts are pegged to German marks) but as a medium of exchange as well (on the 'green market', the real estate market, etc.) - in short, the opposite of Gresham's law. Interestingly, all the countries have adopted a floating exchange-rate regime.

Similar differences can be seen in the foreign trade and tariff systems, the fiscal and tax systems, and the payments and accounting systems as all the successor states replace their federal legislation with one better suited to their own circumstances.

These economies have diverged structurally as well. Their inherited levels of development have made some of them similar to newly-industrialized economies and others to low-income economies. The patterns of foreign trade vary, with some economies (Slovenia) exporting mainly industrial goods, others mixed agricultural and industrial goods together with services (Croatia), one which has remained an agricultural exporter (Macedonia) and two which have 'imploded' ('rump' Yugoslavia and Bosnia and Herzegovina).

The newly-formed states have grown further apart regarding macro-economic disequilibrium and inflation: only one has achieved stabilization and low levels of inflation (Slovenia) while the others are suffering from varying degrees of hyperinflation (Croatia, 'rump' Yugoslavia and, until recently, Macedonia) or have seen their economies disintegrate (Bosnia and Herzegovina). Although comparable data are difficult to obtain, it is possible to provide some general macroeconomic indicators.[23]

For example, at the beginning of 1993 inflation in Slovenia was about 1%, in Croatia about 25% and in Serbia ('rump' Yugoslavia) about 225%, all these expressed as monthly rates. According to the *Financial Times*,[24] Serbia's annual inflation rate of about 20,000% is the highest in the world. In Bosnia and Herzegovina no attempt at all is made to measure inflation. Following a period of high inflation, the introduction of the Macedonian dinar led to a fall in monthly inflation rates: the June 1992-June 1993 average monthly rate was 12.9%.[25] Unemployment figures show a very similar pattern. Croatia's very high rate of 17.9%, compared to Serbia's 40%, seems manageable.[26] By the beginning of 1993, Slovenia's rate was close to 14%. Data on industrial production depict a quite similar pattern and ranking. All the former Yugoslav republics have suffered from a dramatic fall in production, the greatest being in Serbia and Montenegro (27% in 1992), followed closely by Croatia (23.6%), and the smallest in Slovenia (6.5%). The dramatic economic conditions of 'rump' Yugoslavia can be attributed (in addition to other reasons) to the economic sanctions imposed by the international community.

Finally, the economic environments of these states vary enormously. Two of them (Croatia and Slovenia) have become fully-fledged members of international financial institutions (e.g. the IMF, IBRD and its affiliates, EBRD, etc.), one has been only partially recognized (Macedonia), and one is subject to international embargo and isolation ('rump' Yugoslavia).

4. ECONOMIC ASPECTS OF THE DISINTEGRATION

The previous two sections argued, first, that Yugoslavia found transition and the crises of the 1980s 'unsolvable', which led to the lengthy maturation of alternative transition policies, crises management and development policies, and second that disintegration became irreversible as 'go-it-yourself' transition policies prevailed and produced increasing divergence. This course of events raises the question of the costs and benefits of 'go-it-yourself' transition policies. These are questions that the economist must answer even though political considerations played a dominant role in the actual decision making.

The issue becomes especially interesting when related to economic theory. The corpus of economic theory explains the process of integration as rational (customs union theories, free trade, etc.) and most study (and research finance) has been devoted to the benefits of introducing larger units in terms of scale economies (e.g. the European Community). The transition has, however, led to the break-up of all the federations established after World War I (the Yugoslavia and Czechoslovakia created by the Treaty of Versailles, and the Soviet Union created by the October Revolution). Those seeking to explain this manifold process of disintegration in terms of economic theory, and thus as a process based on rational economic behaviour, find that ready-made theoretical explanations and models do not exist.

The question of the costs and benefits of disintegration for Yugoslavia's successor states cannot yet be answered unambiguously. It is a counter-factual question since alternative paths are not known, the data are sparse or non-existent, and with the war still unresolved some of the main determinants of costs are still changing (by mid-1993, the war had finished for only one of the newly-formed states, Slovenia, so that a final balance-sheet cannot be drawn up). Another major element missing from the calculation is the result of the 'divorce proceedings' now in progress, which at the time of writing, mid-1993, are stalemated in Geneva. These proceedings concern such important issues as the distribution of federal property in the country and abroad, the distribution of the resources of the military forces, appropriation of the National Bank of Yugoslavia's reserves, and the foreign debt.

Although this is obviously an issue for economic history to decide, tentative analysis is nevertheless possible (bearing the above considerations in mind).

In the case of Yugoslavia's successor states, the short-run costs of establishing the new national economies have been great. Two types of costs prevail: substantial ones stemming from the Wars of Yugoslav Succession, and more minor ones resulting from the creation of the institutional framework for a national economy.

The immediate effect of The Wars of Yugoslav Succession have been direct war damage. Although negligible in Slovenia, this in Croatia currently amounts to somewhere around 22 billion US $ - twice Croatia's annual GNP - and is obviously even greater (but not yet calculated) in Bosnia and Herzegovina. The war is not being waged on the soil of 'rump' Yugoslavia, but about 20% of GNP goes to supporting ethnic Serbs in Bosnia and Croatia.[27]

Other factors are the international embargo (which hits 'rump' Yugoslavia and Macedonia hardest, at times Croatia, and least of all Slovenia), military expenditure measured in billions of dollars (since all but 'rump' Yugoslavia have had to establish and finance new armies), the loss of former Yugoslavia's internal markets because of the conflict, and the breakdown of transport links[28] (the main east-west road and rail links have been cut). Finally, and in terms of human suffering, the largest cost is taking care of people driven from their homes by ethnic cleansing (so far more than 2.5 million people have at some time left their homes, with only a small number finding sanctuary outside former Yugoslavia.[29]

The indirect costs, in addition to demographic ones, represent the income lost because of the war. Most notable among these are the decline in Croatia's tourist trade (which has fallen to one-half of its pre-war and pre-transition level), the costs of the embargoes, and the income lost from mutual trade. Besides the already-mentioned macroeconomic indicators, the fact that the average wage in Serbia by the end of April 1992 was 27 DM, in Croatia around 150 DM, and in Macedonia 219 DM is highly significant. As regards the whole territory of the former Yugoslavia, the fact that its GNP was about 77 billion US $ in 1989, and now when combined for all former republics should not exceed 40 billions US $,[30] or only slightly more than half its 1989 level, is indicative.

The costs of establishing national economies are closely intertwined with the costs of transition. The extent to which it is impossible to isolate the influence of the two is best illustrated by the disastrous macroeconomic indicators. In each of the new states, production has fallen and unemployment has risen. Most of them have to cope with hyperinflation and dramatically falling real wage rates and living standards. However, in international comparitive terms these statistics are not so exceptionally bad: many economies in transition are experiencing the same economic disaster without being caught up in a war. Table 3 clearly illustrates this point.[31]

Table 3 - Real GDP growth rates in %

Country	1990	1991	1992	Cumulat. 90-92[*]
Albania	-10.0	-27.7	-7.8	-40.0
Bulgaria	-11.8	-23.3	-8.7	-38.2
Hungary	-4.3	-10.2	-5.0	-18.4
Poland	-11.6	-7.2	1.0	-16.2
Romania	-7.7	-13.7	-10.0	-28.3
Former Yugoslavia	-7.5	-17.0	-24.0	-41.6
Former USSR	-2.2	-9.0	-18.5	-27.5
Former Czechoslovakia	-0.4	-15.9	-8.5	-23.4

* Cumulative decline in the period 1990-1992.

Source: Computed from *World Economic Outlook, 1993*, p. 138.

What is the price of disintegration? Although former Yugoslavia registers the largest decline in GDP compared with 1989, Bulgaria and Albania, which have not broken up (and have not been involved in the war), have experienced similar declines. Since former Czechoslovakia divided on January 1 1993, this split is not shown in the data. All the countries undergoing transition register a decline in GDP. But whether separation by itself has 'added' to this decline, is difficult to decide from the data.

The second category of costs are those produced by the creation of a new economic space. Two kinds of cost are involved here: those relating to the setting-up of the new institutions of national economies (e.g. a monetary system, international trade and tariff system, etc.) and the costs of adjusting existing institutions and legislative adaptation. These costs were relatively minor for the successor states of Yugoslavia because they emerged from a loose federation (each republic had a national bank with limited authority in monetary policy, and fiscal semi-independence). They have been further reduced because they largely coincide with some of the costs of transition (liberalizing foreign trade, new payments system, etc.). The loss of the Yugoslav market provides a important example of how these costs cannot be distinguished. The Yugoslav republics mutually traded an important proportion of their social product.[32] The change cannot be attributed only to the breakdown of trade links and the extension of trade among adversaries caused by the war. With the establishment of the successor states, internal trade (i.e.

inter-republic) becomes international trade. As a result, the competitive position of the agents involved changes. With the loss of previous protection, competition increases as they compete in 'old' markets with the rest of the world. This applies equally to agricultural products (for example, Macedonian paprika lost its virtual monopoly on the Yugoslav market and now competes with Bulgarian paprika) and industrial products (Slovenian home appliances, which once dominated the former Yugoslav market, have now, like all European products, become imports in its major regional markets).

The major exporters (e.g. Croatian shipbuilders) have a much narrower domestic capital market to finance their production. The negative impact depends on their ability to increase competitiveness or to change their product mix. Both strategies are medium-term at best and require significant economic restructuring, namely capital influx.

Inflation can be regarded as a cost (tax) on consumers. Table 4 gives a comparative view of the growth of consumer prices. Obviously, for former Yugoslavia the war has its price (beyond the loss of human life and the destruction of national wealth) in inflation. Of course, this figure is grossly misleading because of the wide variations among different states that we have already discussed.

Table 4 - Growth rates of consumer prices in %

Country	1990	1991	1992
Albania	-	35.5	226.0
Bulgaria	26.3	339.0	79.6
Hungary	28.9	37.0	24.7
Poland	585.8	70.3	43.0
Romania	4.7	161.1	202.3
FormerYugoslavia	584.0	270.0	15,021.0[*]
FormerUSSR	5.4	94.7	1,201.8
FormerCzechosl.	10.8	57.7	10.8

* This figure is nonsensical due to the huge differences among the newly-formed states.

Source: Computed from *World Economic Outlook, 1993*, p. 146.

5. TENTATIVE CONCLUSIONS

Yugoslavia disintegrated into five independent Balkan states in the early 1990s. This disintegration, combined with the brutal war presently being conducted in some of the states, has exacerbated their economic problems. For these reasons, the transitional problems (and costs) that other small European post-socialist economies are having to cope with seem much greater for the states that have formed on the territory of the former Yugoslavia.

It should be stressed that Yugoslavia was not the only country to disintegrate with the collapse of the communist system. The former Soviet Union split into fifteen sovereign countries in 1991 and former Czechoslovakia divided into two republics. To date only former Czechoslovakia has managed to avoid open military conflict between its previously constituent parts.

This paper has attempted to show how the process of disintegration has evolved over time, and to assess the economic costs and benefits of establishing new states. Because of the still ongoing war and vast war damages, a sophisticated cost-benefit approach to the go-it-alone transition path chosen by these newly-formed independent states is almost impossible at this point in time. The two facts that the combined GNP for the new states in 1992 is estimated at slightly more than half its value in 1989, and that war damage is calculated in tens of billions of US \$, indicate by themselves that these states are facing very large short-term costs. Yet high unemployment, rising inflation and falling production is a fact of life for all the transitional economies.

The costs of establishing independent states (i.e. a monetary and fiscal system, payments system, tariffs, etc.) have not been prohibitively high because of the loose federal arrangement that the newly-formed states were able to build upon.

If costs are high in the short and medium term, the question of benefits arises. These are perhaps best illustrated by the case of Slovenia, which has been least influenced by the Wars of Yugoslav Succession. Slovenia has achieved macroeconomic stability (low inflation, balanced trade balance) within two years of economic independence. Furthermore, it has defined a transition path (privatization, the introduction of capital and labour markets, a new economic system, etc.) best suited to local circumstances. The advantages enjoyed by Slovenia could become accessible to the other newly-formed economies once the costs of war have diminished.

Bearing in mind that Yugoslavia never managed to attain sustained economic growth and (arguably) never functioned as an efficient and well-organized economic unit - the republics constantly complained about their status in the Federation - its disintegration need not necessarily be discouraging, in spite of the worldwide trend towards integration. On the contrary, the formation of new states (war apart) might lay solid foundations on which to base the better economic development of this area. Of course, a political settlement is a necessary condition for the macroeconomic stability and structural change that will secure a sustainable increase in the living standards of these countries. We should not forget that divorce is sometimes much better than a failed marriage - even for the children.

NOTES

1 The opinions expressed here are those of the authors and do not necessarily represent the views of the National Bank of Croatia. We would like to thank Mrs. Lidija Pleadin for her assistance.

2 Macedonia has been admitted to UN under the curious name of 'The Former Yugoslav Republic of Macedonia'.

3 See, for example, Rusinow, 1988; Bicanic and Škreb, 1992; Škreb and Bicanic, 1993; ECE, 1991.

4 Bicanic, 1986.

5 Keynes, 1936, p. xxiii.

6 This paradigm was criticised by both Yugoslav and foreign economists from the moment when it was first implemented in the early 1970s. Prominent among the Yugoslav critics were adherents of the 'costs of production' theory, who claimed that the theoretical underpinnings of this theory in 'income theory' were an misinterpretation of the Marxian 'law of value'.

7 The first of these blueprints was the report of the so-called 'Kraigher Commission' which appeared in three volumes, of which an abridged English version was prepared by Lazovic, 1983. On publication, it was duly approved by a Party Congress, parliament, and all other 'socio-political' organizations, thereby becoming 'official'. It inspired (with the help of IMF recommendations) a initially successful stabilization policy (achieving external equilibrium and internally stabilizing the inflation rate), which was then abandoned because the ruling elite feared its destabilizing effects (caused by a fall in real wages and rising unemployment). A restrictive economic policy aimed at establishing external liquidity and internal 'real' prices was introduced, but once it started to show results and its further implementation required additional restrictive policies, it was replaced by soft policies.

8 The second blueprint was the report of the so-called 'Vrhovec Commission' (or 'Pasic' after the editor: see Pasic, 1986), which on publication was duly approved by the party apparatus. Although this report was in partial backlash to the previous one, it initiated major changes in the legislature.

9 Introduced in the inaugural speech by the then President of the Federal Executive Council. See Markovic, 1989.

10 For a more detailed analysis see Bicanic and Škreb, 1992.

11 Kuznets, 1973, pp. 165-6.

12 On the interwar period see Durovic, 1986, and on the post-war period, Bicanic, 1990.

13 Based on data and arguments from: Bajt, 1989; Bicanic and Škreb, 1992; Burkett and Škegro, 1988; World Development Report, 1991; ECE, 1991; *IMF Yearbook*, 1991.

14 This interpretation gained ground following publication of Mihajlovic,

1981, and a special issue of *Ekonomska misao*, no. 3, vol. XIV, 1981, which discussed the book. It later generated a voluminous literature, the most notable contributions to which were the 'unity' papers: for a review see Bicanic, 1988. The climax of its influence came with the infamous Memorandum: see Isakovic, 1986. This unpublished but widely circulated and discussed manuscript provided the intellectual base for Serbia's demands, first during the attempts of 1991 to re-contract Yugoslavia, subsequently during the Wars of the Yugoslavian Succession.

15 See for example Dodan, 1992. For a survey of the 'Croatian case', see Škreb and Bicanic, 1993.

16 During the period of 'socialist development', unity issues entered the public limelight three times. The first time was in the late 1960s and early 1970s and debate centred on re-defining the scope of federal economic policy by relating multi-nationalist environment, decentralization, markets and unified control together. The most notable contributions were by Novak *et al.*, 1971, and Horvat *et al.*, 1971. The second time came with the crises of the 1980s when the 're-publicanization' of the economy and efficiency of crises management were discussed. The literature on this was voluminous: for a survey see Bicanic, 1988. The third time was prior to the country's disintegration.

17 The first period of discussion was resolved by the 1971 political purge in the party and a politically imposed institutional reorganization; the second by rising nationalism, which simplified arguments into a nationalist 'black-versus-white' context; the third was left unresolved because the country broke up.

18 The first period of discussion was brought to an end by the 1971 political purges in Slovenia, Croatia, Serbia and Macedonia, and by a party-imposed institutional reorganization. The second was curtailed by the rising nationalism which, as said, reduced debate into a nationalistic 'black/white' stand-off. The third was left unresolved since the country disintegrated and communication between discussants broke down.

19 Thus the opportunity for more vocal expression of regional interests used by those regarding the 1974 Constitution as marking the beginning of Yugoslavia's break-up will not be used here as a sign of segmentation.

20 The presidents of Slovenia and Macedonia were also members of the re-named party but in neither case did the president's party obtain a parliamentary majority or a prime ministerial post.

21 The wars started in Slovenia with a ten-day conflict in summer 1991. In Croatia they started in the summer of 1990 and still continue, while the most ruthless and brutal war to date, in Bosnia and Herzegovina, began in spring 1992. One should not forget the 'events' in Kosovo, which started back in spring 1981.

22 See *World Economic Outlook*, 1993; Vidovic, 1992a and 1992b; *'Slovenien/Kroatien'*, *Frankfurter Allgemeine Zeitung*, *Informations*

Dienste, January, 1993; Vreme, 1993; Martic and Škreb, 1993; Uvalic, 1993.

23 Data compiled from: *Financial Times*, April 22, 1993; Vreme, 1993; Vidovic, 1992a and 1992b; *The Economist*, December 12, 1992; WIIW, 1993/7.

24 *Financial Times*, 22 April, 1993.

25 See Wyzan, 1993.

26 The unreliability of data is evidenced by the fact that WIIW 1993/7 estimates the unemployment rate in Serbia/Montenegro at around 24.5%.

27 See *Financial Times*, 22 April, 1993.

28 The importance of the transport sector in transforming economies is described in Škreb, 1993.

29 For a more detailed survey see Dominis *et al.*, 1993. In addition to this, the death toll is extremely high and unfortunately still rising. In Bosnia alone more than 200,000 people have lost their lives.

30 This figure is our own estimate: in 1992 GNP was about 9 billion US $ in Croatia, about 12 billion in Serbia, no more than 9 billion in Slovenia. No data are available for Montenegro, Macedonia (isolated) and Bosnia/Herzegovina (torn apart by war) taken together, but most probably did not amount to more than 10 billion US $. An implicit IMF estimate (see Table 2) is about 10% higher than ours.

31 See also Mencinger, 1993.

32 See Škreb and Bicanic, 1993; Uvalic, 1993.

BIBLIOGRAPHY

Aerst, E., Milward, A. (eds) (1990), *Economic Planning in the Post-1945 Period*, Leuven: University of Leuven Press.

Bajt, A. (1989), *Alternativna ekonomska politika*, Zagreb: Globus.

Berend, I., Borchardt, K. (eds) (1986), *The Impact of the Depression of the 1930's and its Relevance for the Contemporary World*, Budapest: Academy Research Center for Eastern Europe.

Bicanic, I. (1986), 'Some General Comparisons of the Impact of the Two World Crises of the Twentieth Century on the Yugoslav Economy' in I. Berend and K. Borchardt (1986).

Bicanic, I. (1988), 'Fractured Economy', in Rusinow (1988).

Bicanic, I. (1990), 'The Failures of Post-War Yugoslav Planning', in Milward (1990).

Bicanic, I., Škreb, M. (1992), 'The Political Economy of Crises Management and Long Term Growth Promotion in Yugoslavia 1918-1991', paper presented at the conference *The Economic Future of Central Europe: Lessons and Legacies from the Past*, Minneapolis, 1992.

Burkett, W., Škegro, B. (1988), 'Are Economic Fractures Widening?', in Rusinow

(1988).

Dodan, S. (1991), *Hrvatsko pitanje 1918-1990*, Zagreb: Alfa.

ECE (1991), *Economic Survey of Europe in 1990-1991*, Economic Commission for Europe, UN, New York.

Durovic, S. (1986), *Drzavna intervencija u industriji Jugoslavije 1918-1941*, Belgrade: ISI.

Horvat, B. *et al.* (1971), *Ekonomske funkcije federacije*, Belgrade: Institut ekonomskih nauka.

IMF Yearbook 1991, International Financial Statistics.

Isakovic, A. (ed.) (1986), *Memorandum Srpske akademije znanosti i umetnosti o aktuelnim drustvenim pitanjima u nasoj zemlji*, unpublished manuscript, Belgrade: SANU.

Keynes, J.M. (1936), *General Theory of Employment, Interest and Money*, London: Macmillan.

Kuznets, S. (1973), *Population, Capital and Growth*, New York: W.W. Norton, New York.

Lazovic, B. (ed.) (1983), 'Long-Term Programme of Economic Stabilization', *Yugoslav Survey*, vol. 24, no. 4, pp. 3-26.

Markovic, A. (1989), 'Statement by Ante Markovic in the Assembly of the SFRY on the Occasion of His Election to the Office of President of the Federal Executive Council', *Yugoslav Survey*, vol. 30, no. 1, pp. 39-60.

Martic, R., Škreb, M. (1993), 'The Recent State and Future Developments of the Financial System in Croatia', *Razvoj/Development*, nos. 2-3, vol. VII, pp. 293-86.

Mencinger, J. (1993), 'Transformacijska kriza 1989 - 199?', *Gospodarska gibanja*, no. 238, April.

Mihajlovic, K. (1981), *Ekonomska stvarnost Jugoslavija*, Belgrade: Ekonomika.

Mirkovic, M. (1956), *Ekonomska historija Jugoslavije*, Zagreb: Informator.

Novak, M. *et al.* (1971), *Trziste u visenacionalnoj samoupravnoj zajednici*, Zagreb: Institut za ekonomska istrazivanja.

Pasic, N. (ed.) (1986), *Kriticka analiza funkcioniranja politickog sistema sociialistickog samoupravljanja* (The critical analysis of the functioning of the socialist self-management system), Belgrade: Centar za radnicko samoupravljanje, Belgrade.

Rusinow, D. (ed.) (1988), *Yugoslavia: A Fractured Federalism*, Washington: Wilson Center Perspectives.

Škreb, M. (1992), 'Transport Sector in Transforming Economies: A Comparative Approach'. *Economic Analysis*, no. 4, vol. XXVI, pp. 384-99.

Škreb, M., Bicanic, I. (1993), 'The Independence of Croatia. Economic Causes and Consequences', mimeo, paper presented at the Conference *Assets and Liabilities of Independence*, Trento 10-11 December 1992 (to be published in the conference proceedings).

Uvalic, M. (1993), 'The Disintegration of Yugoslavia - Its Costs and Benefits', mimeo, paper presented at the Conference *Assets and Liabilities of Independence*, Trento 10-11 December 1992 (to be published in the conference proceedings).

Vidovic, H. (1992a), 'Croatia: A Storm is Brewing', *WIIW Mitgliederinformation*, no. 10.

Vidovic, H. (1992b), 'Slovenia: Suffering from Secession', *WIIW Mitglieder-information*, no. 10.

Vreme (1993), *A Belgrade Weekly*, no. 131, April 1993.

WIIW (1993), *Mitgliederinformation*, no. 7.

World Development Report (1991), published by Oxford University Press for the World Bank.

World Economic Outlook (1993), International Monetary Fund, Washington.

Wyzan, M. (1993), 'Macedonia: An Economically Viable Nation?', paper presented at the Conference *First Steps Towards Economic Independence: New States of the Postcommunist World*, Stockholm, 23-24 August 1993.

PART TWO

INTEGRATION AND DISINTEGRATION IN EUROPE: THE EC VERSUS THE FORMER USSR

Gijsbertus van Selm[1]

1. INTRODUCTION

Discussion of the mixed blessings of economic integration has a long history in the economic literature. Mr Methuen's Treaty of 1703, which admitted Portuguese wines into Great Britain on preferential terms in return for the removal of a prohibition on British woollen exports to Portugal, was hailed for 'gaining Great Britain above a Million a Year'. Adam Smith, however, called the treaty 'evidently disadvantageous to Great Britain', on account of what would be called 'trade diversion' today.[2]

Recent events in both Eastern Europe (the disintegration of the Soviet Union, Yugoslavia, Czechoslovakia and the collapse of the Council for Mutual Economic Assistance) and Western Europe (the creation of the European Economic Area and the Maastricht decisions on a common European currency), as well as in America (the NAFTA agreement), have provided new impetus for the development of economic integration theory. This paper presents an overview of both old and new ideas, identifies the relevant success indicators of economic integration and applies them to the cases of the EC and the former USSR.

The literature of economic integration theory concentrates on two main forms: customs unions and monetary unions.[3] These can be defined as a group of geographical entities which, in the former case, have agreed both to abolish internal barriers to trade and to adopt common external tariffs, and in the latter to adopt a common currency.[4] The handbooks on economic integration often present monetary union as a higher form of economic integration than customs union, sometimes implying that it can be achieved only at a later stage in the process of convergence among the participating members. As a consequence, a monetary union is defined as containing a customs union. However, in principle the two concepts can very well be separated, and I shall do so in this paper. Customs union and monetary union theory are dealt with in Sections 2 and 3 respectively. Section 4 combines the results obtained, and Section 5 sets out my conclusions.

2. CUSTOMS UNIONS

Why do countries join customs unions? In order to answer this question it should be split into two sub-components: (i) why do countries liberalize their trade with *some* other countries? (ii) why do they not liberalize their trade with *all* other countries?

The textbook answer to the first question is that by joining a customs union and hence by freeing mutual trade, economic gain may possibly arise from a more efficient allocation of resources. Specialisation according to the comparative advantage and increased output deriving from better exploitation of scale economies are possible. Also, the partners may profit from the forced changes in X-efficiency arising from increased competition within the group. However, these are arguments in favour of world-wide free trade, not in favour of bilateral free trade. Yet customs unions are an important fact of life. By what forces can their existence be explained?

Arguments of political economy have been adduced to answer this question. For example, Hirschman suggested that customs unions are formed because of political support by the small group of people who stand to gain from them; that is, the people who benefit from 'trade diversion'. If country A joins country B in a customs union, exporters in B obtain a competitive advantage in A's market over exporters in C who also try to sell their goods in A. Similarly, a group of exporters from A obtains a competitive advantage on B's market. If A and B buy each other's products, even though C offers the same products at a lower price, then total welfare in both A and B is reduced, and the price is paid by the consumers in the two countries. Unfortunately, their losses are dispersed over a multitude of subjects who are difficult to organize politically. In this interpretation, therefore, customs unions are formed for the wrong reason.

An alternative, 'right reason' explanation for the existence of customs unions is yielded by application of dynamic instead of static arguments. Free trade is beneficial to all the parties concerned in static terms.[5] In a dynamic setting, however, free trade reinforces existing divisions of labour. It is common knowledge that, in world history, the leading economy has often promoted free trade (Holland in the seventeenth century,[6] the United Kingdom in the nineteenth, and the United States in the twentieth). Customs unions can be used as a protective device with which to promote infant industries, as

Friedrich List noted.[7] More recently, arguments against free trade employing dynamic analysis have been formulated by Krugman,[8] whose notion of a strategic trade policy is directly relevant to customs union analysis. If international trade is not governed by comparative advantage and factor endowments, but rather by increasing returns to scale, then 'whichever firm manages to establish itself in the industry will earn super-normal profits that will not be competed away'.[9] If A and B form a customs union, this might help A and B firms to establish such a position.

Once worldwide free trade has been ruled out, the question arises as to whom, if anyone, should be picked as an integration partner. This requires a comparison between the welfare effects of no economic integration and those of biased integration. This is the field of customs union analysis, which usually takes Viner's classic work as its starting point. According to Viner,[10] the welfare effects of a customs union can be divided between 'trade creation' and 'trade diversion'. Viewed from the perspective of country A, the benefits of economic integration - 'trade creation' - arise because production that formerly took place in A now takes place in partner country B. The welfare reducing 'trade diversion' effect stems from imports that used to come from a third country C and now come from B. The relative magnitude of these effects depends on a number of variables, such as the elasticities of the demand and supply schedules and the magnitude of the difference between domestic and foreign prices. The total welfare effect can be obtained by subtracting trade diversion from trade creation. Of course, the result thus obtained hinges on a long list of assumptions, and not surprisingly, changing the assumptions also changes the results. In this way, many other effects have been 'discovered' (trade suppression, trade modification, and trade destruction to mention just a few[11]).

More crucially, the results become ambiguous if Viner's one-good partial equilibrium analysis is extended to two-good general equilibrium analysis. Lipsey[12] showed that a customs union may increase welfare without any 'trade creation' as defined above. For this reason, customs union theory has been dubbed 'one of the more disappointing branches of postwar economics'[13] and the terms 'trade creation' and 'trade diversion' have been called inadequate and even blamed for retarding progress in customs union analysis for forty years.[14] Kowalczyk has proposed using the concepts of 'terms of trade effect' and 'volume of trade effect' instead. Indeed, using this terminology, he provides rigorous proof of Lipsey's proposition that 'A Customs union is more likely to raise welfare, *given the total volume of imports of the country*, the larger the proportion of these imports obtained from the country's union partners and the smaller the proportion devoted to imports from the outside world'.[15]

Lipsey's proposition is intuitively appealing. It is clear that the negative effects stemming from a switch in trade from buying something from a third party to buying something from the partner country should be avoided as far as possible, irrespectively of whether this effect is called 'trade diversion' or 'terms of trade effect'. From this proposition it is possible to derive an operational variable that can be used to decide who is a suitable partner; that is, a partner or group of partners constituting an important part of foreign trade should be selected.[16]

Also, it seems obvious that whether we talk about 'volume of trade effect' or 'trade creation effect', benefits should somehow accrue from a different division of labour between the two partners concerned. Trade creation - that is, a shift from domestic production to foreign production - cannot exist if no products are produced in either country. If one country is a producer of raw materials and the other is a producer of advanced industrial products, then the division of labour will probably be little affected by the customs union. The link that empirical studies have often been found between international economic integration and intra-industry trade is no coincidence.[17] The two partners involved should have activities in common which allow for an increase in specialization.[18] From this derives a second operational variable: the countries that join in a customs union should have comparable levels of development.

To recapitulate, numerous as its shortcomings may be, customs union analysis provides us with two determinants that can be operationalized empirically. The countries chosen as partners in a customs union should (i) already be important trading partners (so that the risk of trade diversion is minimized) and (ii) have a comparable level of development (so that the possibilities for trade creation are maximized). These findings are confirmed by real-world experience. The EC has been a success because intra-EC trade has been part of total trade for the participating member states and because levels of development are comparable, especially among the original six members (see Tables 2 and 3 below). Conversely, attempts to create trade blocs in Latin America and Africa have failed because of too limited potential for internal trade[19] and too widely diverging levels of development.[20]

3. MONETARY UNIONS

The Maastricht decisions on a single European currency, envisaged for 1999, have placed the economics of monetary unions in the spotlight. As in the case of a customs union, the decision whether or not to join a currency area depends on an assessment of the costs and benefits involved. The benefits of a monetary union are the reduction of risks and transaction costs. In the European community, at present, a round trip by an amount of money among the twelve member states would produce a 50% loss on the original sum.[21] Probably more important is the reduction of risk and uncertainties. In a world of risk-averse agents, adopting a single currency amounts to providing free and perfect foreign exchange hedging for everyone. Because the losses stemming from a devaluation are ruled out once a monetary union has been created, capital mobility (both portfolio investment and foreign direct investment) is increased, giving rise to potential welfare improvements. Moreover, the negative incentives stemming from exchange rate over- or undervaluation can be avoided. Finally, 'credibility' arguments in favour of a monetary union have recently been advanced. It has been contended, for example, that by adopting the ECU a country like Italy can import 'Bundesbank' reliability and hence price stability. However, it is doubtful whether this can effectively be counted an advantage: Italy could also create its own Bundesbank.[22]

The benefits of a monetary union can be linked to the intensity of mutual trade. This is so because decreasing uncertainty and transaction costs are not particularly helpful if there is no trade with the country concerned. The benefits of a monetary union increase *pari passu* with openness towards the potential partner.

On the cost side of monetary unions, a distinction should be drawn between arguments that relate to economic 'fundamentals' and arguments related to 'shock adjustment'. To begin with the former, countries with widely divergent levels of development may incur high costs when entering a monetary union because they have different inflation preferences. This argument was originally used in the context of a Phillips curve.[23] Different countries may opt for a different choice in the trade-off between unemployment and inflation. This would create the need for nominal exchange rate adjustment at regular time intervals. However, this argument breaks down if the faith in a stable Phillips curve disappears. Alternatively, countries may have different inflation preferences because the optimal levels of monetary financing of the government budget may diverge. For developing countries especially, this level may be high because of the difficulties encountered in levying taxes on the population. A developed economy would normally prefer to have income and value added taxes in combination with price stability. Hence, the costs of a common currency are related to the level of development of the countries considering a monetary union.

'Real' arguments have also been advanced.[24] In the long run, real interest rates are determined by time preference and capital productivity. In turn, time preference is determined by such factors as a country's age structure and 'national character'. Countries with different attitudes to time should have different real interest rates. The argument is that the option of having different real interest rates is lost if a common currency is adopted. However, this possibility is lost not because of a single currency, but rather because of a single market. It is capital mobility that leads to a common real interest rate, not a common currency. Only to the extent that a common currency increases capital mobility can this effect be blamed on the common currency.

In the 'shock adjustment' line of reasoning, the exchange rate is lost as an instrument of economic policy if a common currency is formed. The basic idea is that if two countries united in a common currency area suffer from an asymmetric demand or a supply shock giving rise to a balance of payments disequilibrium and diverging patterns of economic performance, an adjustment mechanism is needed to redress the balance. Three questions are relevant here:

(i)   Do the parties involved suffer from asymmetric shocks?

(ii) Is the exchange rate an appropriate instrument with which to bring about adjustment?

(iii) Is an alternative instrument available?

On the first question, the more 'similar' the two countries involved, the less need there is for exchange rate adjustment. In his classic article on optimum currency areas, Mundell[25] criticized the Canadian experiment with a flexible exchange rate because of the similarity between the economies of the USA and Canada. In section 4 below, I use levels of development as a rough approximation of the similarity among countries or regions. Yet even if economies have 'similar' levels of development, asymmetric shocks will remain because countries or regions specialise in different economic sectors. In an attempt to quantify the correlation of shocks among regions in the United States and also among member states of the European Community, Bayoumi and Eichengreen[26] found that both demand and supply shocks are far from perfectly correlated.

On the second question, McKinnon stressed in an equally classic article[27] the importance of openness. In his view, a monetary union is beneficial if there is a high degree of openness within the region and a low degree of openness between the area and the rest of the world. If a country is open, a change in the exchange rate does not improve the balance of trade, since a change in the exchange rate increases the price of tradables relative to non-tradables. This stimulates the production of tradables and consumption shifts from tradables to non-tradables. Hence, on the cost side of monetary union analysis, openness is an important variable.

If the two partners suffer from asymmetric shocks, but decide to join in a monetary union anyway, the need for an alternative mechanism of adjustment arises. In Mundell's classical theory of the optimum currency area, this mechanism is provided by labour mobility. The idea is that in the case of an asymmetric shock, such as a shift in tastes from the output of region A to that of region B, unemployment might result if prices and wages are slow to adjust and the exchange rate cannot be adjusted, unless labour is mobile and can move from region A to region B.

The importance of labour mobility as an adjustment mechanism is reinforced by recent empirical findings on shock adjustment in the American economy. Here we have a monetary union that suffers from asymmetric shocks because the regional concentration of economic sectors in the USA is high. Blanchard and Katz[28] found that in the case of a negative demand shock, labour moves out of a US state. Even though wages decline, few jobs move in. This result surprised those who expected capital mobility to be higher than labour mobility.[29] An explanation can be found in modern international trade theory, as De la Dehesa and Krugman suggest.[30] In a traditional neoclassical framework, one would expect capital to move to a region where labour is abundant and where wages are low. In a modern increasing returns to scale setting, however, capital moves to places where a certain amount of capital has already settled. This implies that if a region is hit by an asymmetric demand shock, capital mobility increases the problem.

A second important adjustment mechanism found in the case of the United States is fiscal redistribution. Sala-i-Martin and Sachs[31] explained the success of the USA as a monetary union by pointing out that 40% of an initial demand shock consists of automatic fiscal transfers.[32] Eichengreen[33] confirms this result by showing that, apart from labour mobility, fiscal redistribution played an important role in dealing with an asymmetric shock to Michigan caused by the second oil crisis. This mechanism of adjustment could be especially important in circumstances where labour mobility is a less desirable mechanism for adjustment. In the monetary unification of Germany, for example, wages in the Eastern part were set relatively close to wage levels in the Western *Länder*, the aim being precisely that of restraining migration flows. Instead, the adjustment mechanism used in Germany was a large-scale fiscal transfer.[34]

The case for a substantial union budget with redistribution capacities in a monetary union is strengthened by the fact that room for an independent fiscal policy at the sub-federal level decreases as one enters a monetary union.[35] The Maastricht Treaty even sets out explicit rules for the members' budget deficits, although the economic rationality of these rules has been vehemently contested.[36] However, even if no rules are formulated explicitly, the degrees of freedom diminish. For example, member states cannot afford to raise significantly higher taxes than other member states, because of possible tax evasion on productive factors.

4. THEORY APPLIED TO THE EC AND THE FORMER USSR

We can summarize the argument so far as follows. Openness increases the benefits and reduces the costs of monetary union. Moreover, the costs of a monetary union are lower, the more similar the levels of development of the two partners. We have here the same two determinants that we found in the case of customs union. If the mutual exchange of goods is high and if the levels of development are similar, both a customs union and a monetary union will probably be a success from an economic point of view. In the case of a monetary union, however, more variables (factor mobility and budget redistributive capacities) are relevant. This could serve as an economic explanation for the fact that monetary unions are often customs unions as well, although the reverse does not hold.

The ideas discussed in this paper are set out in comprehensive form in Table 1. The institutional setting is expressed horizontally in the table, and the success indicators vertically. The relevant paradigms have been given a (+) sign if they relate to the benefit side of union and a (-) sign if they are connected to the cost side.

Table 1 - Economic integration theory

	Customs Unions	Monetary Unions
openness	trade diversion (-)	transaction costs and/or uncertainty reduction (+) shock absorption (-)
level of development	trade creation (+)	'inflation tax' (-)
factor mobility and/or budget redistributive capacities		shock absorption (-)

It is important to differentiate between *ex-ante* and *ex-post* success requirements. Openness should be high *before* the two partners form a customs union. Once a customs union has been formed, the level of goods exchange may be quite high, but this may be trade of the 'trade-diverting' type. Hence, high relative openness is an *ex-ante* requirement.

As regards the level of development, the question of *ex ante* versus *ex post* can be converted into the convergence/divergence debate. If economic integration leads to economic convergence, then the disadvantages that derive from an integration partner with a different level of development will disappear over time. It is by no means certain that economic integration does lead to economic convergence integration, however. On the contrary, modern economic models predict higher interregional inequalities over time on account of scale economies.[37] A similar level of development is an *ex-ante* requirement only if we assume that there is no or slow convergence.

High factor mobility in the case of a monetary union is in principle an *ex-post* requirement. That is, even if factor mobility is not very high, if *by the creation of a monetary union* it is made very high, then there is no problem. Indeed, the creation of a common currency can be expected to raise the level of capital mobility significantly. However, as we have seen, capital mobility is an unreliable mechanism of adjustment. It seems unlikely that the creation of a common currency would have an important bearing on labour mobility. Hence, even though strictly speaking the requirement that labour mobility should be high is an *ex-post* requirement, in practice the level of *ex-ante* labour mobility can be taken as a good proxy.

4.1. EC MONETARY INTEGRATION

The debate whether the EC is an optimum currency area or not is hardly new. In the 1950s, Meade[38] considered labour mobility to be too low in Europe although, according to Scitovsky,[39] something should and could be done about it. Evidently, they applied Mundellian arguments *avant la lettre*. On the benefit side of monetary union, the EC Commission[40] recently estimated the benefits from reduction in transaction costs at some 0.5% of Community GNP and the benefits from the reduction of risk and uncertainty at 5 to 10% of European GNP. An idea of the distribution of the gains from monetary union among the member state can be obtained from EC openness ratios, which are presented in Table 2. These ratios suggest that the benefits deriving from the creation of a single currency have not been equally distributed. The reduction in transaction costs and uncertainty has been most significant for Ireland, Belgium, Portugal and the Netherlands. These countries have high internal EC openness, both expressed as a percentage of GNP and relative to extra-EC openness.

Table 2 - EC openness

Country	Share in union GNP (1)	Intra-union trade/GNP (2)	Extra-union trade/GNP (3)	Ratio of intra- to extra-union (4)
Belgium/Lux.	3.31	42.91	16.45	2.61
Denmark	2.26	12.97	12.11	1.07
Germany	25.23	12.81	11.02	1.10
Greece	1.10	10.73	6.30	1.70
Spain	7.14	8.56	6.16	1.40
France	19.94	11.88	6.86	1.73
Ireland	0.68	38.25	14.30	2.67
Italy	17.40	9.21	6.87	1.34
Netherlands	4.79	31.58	14.73	2.14
Portugal	0.88	22.48	10.40	2.16
United Kindom	17.27	10.25	10.47	0.97
EC	100.00	13.8	9.37	1.43

Source: Author's calculations from Eurostat, 1991, p. 37, p. 259. Data for 1988. The figures in columns (1), (2) and (3) are percentages.

Openness also reduces the costs of monetary union. However, on the cost side more factors are relevant. Differences in levels of development (see Table 3 below) indicate that countries may have different preferences regarding the use of the inflation tax and that they may be susceptible to asymmetric shocks. The former argument is irrelevant in Western Europe because even the lowest developed countries make little use of inflation tax, so that there is no real problem in this area.[41] The latter argument is more important in discussion of the costs of a common currency for the EC member states. Portugal, Greece, Spain and Ireland exhibit all the characteristics of countries at an earlier stage of economic development: lower GNP per capita, a larger share of output in agriculture, and a lower share in services. If, for example, a worldwide slump in agriculture occurred, these countries would be hit harder than the more developed group. Devaluation might be the appropriate response, but this will be impossible once there is a single currency.[42]

Table 3 - EC levels of development

Country	GDP/cap	Economic structure (% in economy):		
	current US$	Agriculture	Industry	Services
	(1)	(2)	(3)	(4)
Belgium	15,180	2.0	31.1	66.9
Denmark	20,926	4.2	28.1	67.7
Germany	19,581	1.5	39.9	58.6
Greece	5,244	15.8	28.3	55.9
Spain	8,722	5.1	37.4	57.5
France	17,002	3.5	30.6	65.9
Ireland	9,182	9.7	36.8	53.5
Italy	14,430	3.7	34.3	62.0
Luxembourg	17,592	2.1	32.6	65.3
Netherlands	15,461	4.3	32.5	63.2
Portugal	4,264	6.3	38.0	55.7
United Kingdom	14,413	1.0	35.5	63.5
EC		3.0	35.4	61.6

Sources: Eurostat, 1991, p. 43, for economic structure; OECD, Economic Survey (any issue) for GDP per capita at current prices. Data for 1988.

Asymmetric shocks would not pose a problem if an alternative to the exchange rate as a mechanism for adjustment existed. This alternative, however, is lacking in the EC. Budget redistribution among member states is low. The present EC budget (some 1% of EC GNP) is not capable of fulfilling a significant redistribution function. A simple calculation by Eichengreen[43] makes it clear that if a USA level of shock absorption via the budget is to be achieved, the EC budget needs to be significantly enlarged. This conclusion is reinforced by empirical evidence on intra-EC transfers in 1980.[44] For all the member states except Ireland, net grants to or donations from other member states amounted to less than 1% of GNP. Moreover, if the EC budget is to play a redistributive role, its principles should be changed fundamentally. At present, on the receipts side the EC budget system is regressive instead of progressive. Value added tax (VAT) hits the poor more than proportionally, because a higher fraction of a low income is consumed, and VAT is a tax on consumption.[45] The main entry on the expenditure side, the common agricultural policy, does not lead to rich-to-poor redistribution either.

Hence, factor mobility should carry the main burden of adjustment if a common currency is introduced. It is doubtful if it can, though, because Western European labour mobility is low.[46] Conversely, capital mobility is both high and equality-promoting.[47] It remains to be seen, however, whether capital flows will continue to play this beneficial role. The American experience is not encouraging in this regard.

In conclusion, the economic success of a common currency in Western

Europe is questionable. The central problem is that there is no well-developed mechanism that can assume the role of the exchange rate in the case of asymmetric shocks. Interestingly, support for monetary union in the various EC member states is to some extent reflected in the costs and benefits involved. The openness ratios indicate that the two countries which have shown least enthusiasm for monetary union - Denmark and the United Kingdom - are those who have little to gain from it. On the other hand, countries like Belgium and the Netherlands which have the most to gain because of their high openness, have been most supportive.

Beneficial or otherwise, the Maastricht Treaty, with its commitment to a common currency, has now been ratified by all the member states. The introduction of a common currency, however, is far from certain because the Treaty has made it contingent on a number of stringent criteria. One of these is that the countries must keep to stable exchange rates - that is, ones within their normal EMS fluctuation bands - for two years prior to entry. With the demise and redefinition of the EMS, it is unclear how this requirement is to be interpreted. And the same goes for the fiscal criteria set by the Maastricht Treaty. Since these are met by very few members, they must be either neglected or renegotiated.[48] The monetary future of Western Europe is still undecided.

4.2. The Disintegration of the Former USSR

Recent events in Europe make it clear that the creation of new currencies is easier than the abandonment of old ones. Western Europe is moving slowly towards the ECU, while *crowns* (Estonia), *lats* (Latvia), *litas* (Lithuania), *kupons* (Ukraine) and *soms* (Kyrgyzstan) have been introduced in the Newly Independent States. Political factors have played an important role in the decision to leave the ruble area. Together with the flag and the national anthem, the currency is one of the principal symbols of statehood; symbols which are particularly important for new states trying to put themselves on the world map. The question I address here is whether the decision to introduce a national currency can be justified from an economic point of view as well.

On the cost side of using the ruble as a common currency for the former Soviet republics, there exists a problem corresponding to that for the EC: there is no alternative adjustment mechanism that can replace the exchange rate. The federal Soviet budget has disappeared, and inter-republican distribution is rapidly declining.[49] Furthermore, free mobility of labour is very unlikely, to say the least, since present ethnic tensions preclude it. Capital mobility cannot be expected to come to the rescue either because capital markets are virtually non-existent in the former Soviet Union. If the exchange rate is given up as a mechanism for adjustment, neither the budget nor factor mobility can be used as a substitute.

Table 4 - USSR levels of development

	GNP/cap.	Economic structure (% of economy)				
	USSR=100	Agriculture	Industry	Construction	Transport	Other
	(1)	(2)	(3)	(4)	(5)	(6)
Russia	118.9	19.9	42.2	12.7	6.9	18.3
Ukraine	90.1	30.3	41.3	9.7	6.0	19.4
Belarus	116.8	29.3	44.0	11.8	5.1	9.8
Uzbekistan	47.3	44.0	23.8	14.9	5.7	11.4
Kazakhstan	74.0	39.9	27.6	15.3	9.3	7.9
Georgia	85.2	37.2	35.0	11.0	4.9	11.9
Azerbaijan	70.4	37.6	34.8	11.7	5.2	10.8
Lithuania	109.7	33.4	34.1	13.4	5.9	13.3
Moldova	80.7	41.7	34.4	9.0	4.8	10.1
Latvia	118.8	21.8	51.2	8.1	7.5	11.3
Kyrgyzstan	53.0	43.1	31.8	11.9	3.8	9.2
Tajikistan	43.8	38.3	28.6	14.7	4.2	14.3
Armenia	80.2	17.3	45.4	25.4	4.1	7.8
Turkmenistan	60.5	47.9	15.7	17.9	8.5	10.1
Estonia	118.5	20.3	50.5	10.5	7.2	11.5

Sources: Van Selm and Wagener, 1993, p. 33, for GNP per capita (data for 1988); World Bank, 1992, pp. 6-7, for the economic structure (data for 1990).

The data set out in Table 4 show that asymmetric shocks are highly unlikely in the ex-Soviet Union. The levels of development differ greatly and, moreover, the inflation tax argument is relevant in this case. At the moment, all the former Soviet republics are trying to develop a new tax system. Under communism, the state's receipts relied heavily on profit taxes and turnover taxes; in a market setting, personal income tax and value added tax are more important. The introduction of these new tax systems is likely to be much easier in the more developed republics. Hence, especially during the period of transition to a new tax system, the less developed republics will probably have to rely much more on inflation tax than the more developed ones.

With respect to the benefits of a common ruble, the data on openness in Table 5 show that the intra-union ratio and the ratio between intra- and extra-union trade are considerably higher than in the case of the EC. However, we have here what is clearly an *ex-ante* problem. For the peripheral republics, extra-USSR trade was seriously hampered by the central foreign trade monopoly. Today, the level of goods exchange among the republics is decreasing at a rapid pace. Gravity models can be used to find more 'natural' levels of intra-former USSR and extra-former USSR trade. For example, Gros and Dautrebande[50] found that trade with the West should increase relative to inter-republican trade by a factor of 16 to 20 for most of the former republics. The benefits of a common currency might be less than suggested by Table 5.

Table 5 - USSR openness

	Share in (1)	Intra-union (2)	Extra-union (3)	Ratio of intra-to (4)
Russia	61.08	12.92	9.37	1.38
Ukraine	16.24	26.89	7.14	3.77
Belarus	4.15	44.54	7.38	6.03
Uzbekistan	3.28	34.08	5.62	6.06
Kazakhstan	4.26	29.47	4.69	6.28
Georgia	1.62	37.87	5.90	6.42
Azerbaijan	1.73	35.37	5.95	5.94
Lithuania	1.41	47.24	7.21	6.55
Moldova	1.22	45.86	6.36	7.21
Latvia	1.11	46.84	7.21	6.50
Kyrgyzstan	0.79	39.63	5.98	6.63
Tajikistan	0.79	36.17	5.76	6.28
Armenia	0.92	47.83	5.84	8.19
Turkmenistan	0.74	37.56	4.60	8.16
Estonia	0.65	50.09	8.79	5.70
USSR	100.0	21.10	8.27	2.55

Sources: Van Selm and Wagener, 1993, p. 28. Data for 1988. The data in columns (1), (2) and (3) are percentages.

In the short run, however, goods exchange among the former Soviet republics is still substantial, and this might be an argument for keeping the ruble for a certain transition period. Up until April 1992 this was the reason why the IMF advised the former Soviet republics to continue with the ruble. However, the disadvantage of keeping the ruble as a common currency in the short run was that it might create a free rider problem. With numerous fiscal authorities sharing a common currency, there are strong incentives to create money because the benefits of increased spending only accrue to the spending republic, whereas the costs (increased inflation) are spread over the entire area. This arrangement provoked considerable inflation in 1991, with the Russian Government as the biggest spender: Russia's fiscal deficit in 1991 was 20% of its GNP! The Ukraine came a good second with 14.4%. Many of the other republics apparently failed to understand the game and ran fiscal surpluses.[51] When the Soviet Union ceased to exist, the Russian government made stabilization its primary economic goal and saw its attempts at stabilization frustrated by inflationary policies in the other republics. Attempts are now being made to stem the flow of peripheral rubles to Russia. Republican account rubles were made non-convertible to Russian account rubles in July 1992. One year later, central bank president Gerashenko defended his monetary reform as an attempt to do the same for cash rubles. Indeed, for Georgia, Turkmenistan, Azerbaijan and Moldova the events of July 1993 were reasons for leaving, or for accelerating the process of leaving, the ruble zone (Ukraine, Estonia, Latvia,

Lithuania and Kyrgyzstan had already left it). However, a new agreement among Russia, Kazakhstan, Uzbekistan, Armenia, Tajikistan and Belarus to form a ruble zone was signed on 7 September 1993. Many such agreements have been made in the past few years, and it remains to be seen what will become of them. However, it is clear that the idea of a ruble zone has not yet been abandoned. And it is also clear that the remaining group of six contains two of the most advanced former Soviet republics (Russia and Belarus: see Table 4) and two of the most backward ones (Uzbekistan and Tajikistan). The wisdom of this new ruble zone is therefore questionable.

What, then, are the prospects for a customs union covering the area of the former USSR? We have seen that a customs union is likely to be successful if the members are 'natural' trading partners and if their economies have similar levels of development. Again, high as the openness ratios may have been under Soviet rule (Table 5), it remains to be seen whether there will be much room for trade among the former Soviet republics in the future. If extra-former USSR trade becomes far more important than intra-former USSR trade, in line with the predictions of Gros and Dautrebande's gravity model, the danger of trade diversion is imminent. Moreover, differences in levels of development are quite substantial (Table 4), and hence the possibilities for trade creation may be limited. The economic success of a former Soviet customs area is far from evident.

The case for a customs union among the states of the former Soviet Union can be made stronger if it is interpreted in a dynamic sense. This 'Listian' argument has recently been repeated by Dornbusch,[52] who states that "freeing regional trade and discriminating somewhat in favour of the region is a good development policy."[53]

5. CONCLUSIONS

In this paper, I have derived four success indicators from customs union and monetary union theory. A surprising finding has been that, although the two bodies of theory are quite different, the relevant variables overlap. Greater openness among potential integration partners increases the benefits of a monetary union and reduces the costs of a customs union. Conversely more similarity of levels of development increase the benefits of a monetary union and reduces the costs of a customs union. Two additional variables - factor mobility and federal budget redistribution - are relevant to monetary union analysis: the higher factor mobility and budget redistribution are, the lower the costs of a monetary union.

I have used this result to assess the economic rationality of current processes of integration and disintegration in Europe. On account of the limited labour mobility and redistribution capacities of the budget in the EC, monetary unification of the EC may prove costly, since private capital flows will have to accommodate asymmetric shocks. Openness ratios indicate that the benefits of monetary unification are unequally distributed, and that small countries like Belgium and the Netherlands have most to gain from it.

In the former USSR, the future prospects for budget redistribution and factor mobility are even gloomier. This implies that the decision of the majority of the republics to introduce their own currencies might be not only beneficial in the short term (because it avoids sharing a common currency with a number of independent fiscal authorities), but also rational from a long-term economic point of view. A high degree of openness among the Newly Independent States indicates that important benefits from a common currency do exist, although inter-republican trade is at the moment in steep decline and it remains to be seen at what level it will stabilize. The preconditions for a successful customs union are less demanding, and a customs union might therefore be a useful tool of development policy in the former Soviet area.

NOTES

1 My thanks are due to Hans-Jürgen Wagener, Beppo van Leeuwen, Ger Lanjouw, Leendert Colijn, Harry Garretsen, Elmer Sterken and Emiel Dölle for their comments on an earlier draft of this paper. This research was sponsored by the Economic Research Foundation of the Dutch Organization for Scientific Research (NWO).

2 Smith, 1976, pp. 546-47.

3 Two other forms of integration, free trade areas and common markets, are obliquely referred to in this paper. The economics of free trade areas (i.e. customs unions without a common external tariff) and customs unions are basically similar (but see El-Agraa, 1982, p. 22, on some of the differences). A common market adds the free mobility of production factors to the free mobility of goods. This form of integration is encountered in the case study of integration in Western Europe (section 4.1).

4 The term 'monetary union' should be reserved for a common currency alone, and not used in the case of fixed exchange rates. Withdrawal from a fixed exchange rate area may occur at any time, whereas the introduction of a new currency takes time and effort.

5 If the parties concerned are too small for their terms of trade to be affected. See the literature on optimum tariffs: for example, Krugman and Obstfeld, 1991, p. 217.

6 For an overview of Dutch economic thought in its heyday, see Wagener, 1993.

7 List, 1922, p. 538 ff. used 'infant industry'-like arguments in defence of the German *Zollverein*. Conversely, the example of the aforementioned Methuen Treaty led List to this generalization: '*Schädliche illegitime Handelsverträge sind solche, wodurch eine bereits in der Entwicklung begriffene Manufakturkraft einer andern Nation zum Opfer gebracht wird*'; (p. 73).

8 Krugman, 1987.

9 Krugman, 1987, p. 135.

10 Viner, 1950, p. 44 ff.

11 See Robson, 1980, p. 36; Ethier, 1985, p. 478; and Holzman, 1987, p. 171, respectively.

12 Lipsey, 1970, ch. 4.

13 Pomfret, 1986.

14 Kowalczyk, 1990.

15 Lipsey, 1970, p. 56, italics in the original.

16 The words 'more likely' in Lipsey's proposition should be emphasised. Even if A trades a great deal with B and little with C, union with B may be harmful to A and a union with C beneficial. This depends on the magnitude of the price differences and the tariffs.

17 Greeneway, 1989.

18 Pelkmans, 1984, p. 14; Robson, 1980, p. 17.

19 Foroutan, 1993, p. 253; Nogués and Quintanilla, 1993, p. 298.

20 Foroutan, 1993, p. 257; Nogués and Quintanilla, 1993, p. 296.

21 European Commission, 1990, p. 66.

22 Bean, 1992, p. 41.

23 Fleming, reproduced in El-Agraa, 1990, p. 102

24 Melitz, 1991.

25 Mundell, 1961, p. 659.

26 Bayoumi and Eichengreen, 1992.

27 McKinnon, 1963.

28 Blanchard and Katz, 1992, p. 52.

29 Shiller (in reaction to Blanchard and Katz, 1992, p. 71) has argued that *a priori* one would expect capital mobility to be higher than labour mobility, because the value of residential housing stock depreciates more slowly than the value of venture capital. Hence, moving capital would normally be cheaper.

30 De la Dehesa and Krugman, 1992, p. 6.

31 Sala-i-Martin and Sachs, 1991, pp. 18-19.

32 The 40% is made up of an increase in federal grants of 6% and a decrease in taxes paid of 34%. Note, however, that von Hagen (1992, p. 344-5) has recently counter-argued that this 40% cannot be interpreted as a response to a transitory regional shock, but rather reflects the long-run redistributive properties of the system. 'The US fiscal system is designed to alleviate persisting inequalities, but does little to buffer transitory regional shocks'. Masson and Taylor (1993, p. 40) find results for Canada that bear out the conclusion reached by Sala-i-Martin and Sachs - namely that fiscal redistribution is important as an adjustment mechanism in monetary unions.

33 Eichengreen, 1991, p. 24.

34 De Grauwe, 1992.

35 However, the *effectiveness* of fiscal policy might be increased by joining a

monetary union, as suggested by the well known Mundell-Fleming model. In this framework, with flexible exchange rates, monetary policy is effective, whereas fiscal policy is not; under fixed exchange rates, these results are reversed. Of course, entering a monetary union entails the fixing of the exchange rate with a part of the outside world.

36 See, for example, Buiter, Corsetti and Roubini, 1993.

37 See, for example, Krugman, 1991.

38 Meade, 1957, pp. 385-6.

39 Scitovsky, 1958, ch. 2.

40 European Commission, 1990, p. 21, p. 63.

41 European Commission, 1990, p.121.

42 A more sophisticated indicator for the likelihood of asymmetric shocks can be found in Gros and Thygesen, 1992, pp. 257-8. Their conclusion is the same: the least developed member states have the most to lose from monetary unification because their economic structures differ from the EC average.

43 Eichengreen, 1990, p. 141.

44 Swann, 1988, p. 77.

45 Dehesa and Krugman, 1992, p. 21.

46 European Commission, 1990, p. 46.

47 De la Dehesa and Krugman, 1992, p. 21.

48 In 1991, Germany, France, the UK and Luxembourg fulfilled both fiscal criteria, i.e. a debt ratio of less than 60% and a deficit/GDP ratio of less than 3%. In 1992, only France and Luxembourg passed the test. See Buiter, Corsetti and Roubini, 1993, pp. 64-5.

49 Van Selm and Dölle, 1993.

50 Gros and Dautrebande, 1992, p.16.

51 IMF, 1992, p. 39.

52 Dornbusch, 1992, p. 419.

53 The literature on Soviet disintegration abounds with misinterpretations of customs union analysis. For example, in a recent World Bank publication, Michalopoulos and Tarr argue that 'preferential trade areas are intended to provide an incentive to the importer to buy the produce within the region of preference', i.e. customs unions are intended to lead to trade diversion! Economists can only hope that politicians have better intentions when they create customs unions.

BIBLIOGRAPHY

Bayoumi, T. Eichengreen, B (1992), 'Shocking Aspects of European Monetary Integration', *NBER Working Paper*, no. 3949, January.

Bean, C.R. (1992), 'Economic and Monetary Union in Europe', *Journal of Economic Perspectives*, vol. 6, no. 4, pp. 31-53.

Blanchard, O.J., Katz, L.F. (1992), 'Regional Evolutions', *Brookings Papers on*

Economic Activity, no. 1, pp. 1-75.

Buiter, W., Corsettti, G., Roubini, N. (1993), 'Excessive Deficits: Sense and Nonsense in the Treaty of Maastricht', *Economic Policy*, April, pp. 58-100.

Dehesa, G. de la, Krugman, P. (1992), *EMU and the Regions*, Washington.

Dornbusch, R. (1992), 'Monetary Problems of Post-Communism: Lessons from the End of the Austro-Hungarian Empire, *Weltwirtschaftliches Archiv*, pp. 391-423.

Eichengreen, B. (1990), 'One Money for Europe? Lessons from the US Currency and Customs Union', *Economic Policy*, no. 10, pp. 117-87.

Eichengreen, B. (1991), 'Is Europe an Optimum Currency Area?', *NBER Working Paper*, no. 3579.

El-Agraa, A. (1982), 'The Theory of Economic Integration' in El-Agraa, A. (1990), 'European Monetary Integration' in El-Agraa, A. (ed.), *Economics of the European Community*, Cambridge.

Ethier, W. (1985), *Modern International Economics*, New York.

European Commission (1990), 'One Market, One Money - an Evaluation of the Potential Benefits and Costs of Forming an Economic and Monetary Union', *European Economy*, no. 44.

Eurostat (1991), *Basic Statistics of the Community*, Brussels.

Foroutan, F., 'Regional Integration in Sub-Saharan Africa' in De Melo, J. and Panagariya eds, *New Dimensions in Regional Integration*, Cambridge, 1933, pp. 234-277.

Grauwe, P. de (1992), 'German Monetary Unification', *European Economic Review 36*, pp. 435-45.

Greeneway, D. (1989), 'Regional Trading Arrangements and Intra-industry Trade', in Greeneway, D., Hyclak, T., Thornton, R. (eds), *Economic Aspects of Regional Trading Arrangements*, Exeter, 1989, pp. 31-42.

Gros, D., Dautrebande, B. (1992), 'International Trade of Former Republics in the Long Run: An Analysis based on the "Gravity" Approach', *CEPS Working Document*, no. 71, Brussels.

Gros, D., Thygesen, N. (1992), *European Monetary Integration. From the European Monetary System to European Monetary Union*, London.

Hagen, J. von (1992), 'Fiscal Arrangements in a Monetary Union: Evidence from the US', in *Fiscal Policy, Taxation and the Financial System in an Increasingly Integrated Europe*, Dordrecht, 1992, pp. 337-59.

Holzman, (1987), *The Economics of Soviet Bloc Trade and Finance*, Colorado.

IMF (1992), *Common Issues and Interrepublic Relations in the Former USSR*, April.

Kowalczyk, C. (1990), 'Welfare and Customs Union', *NBER Working Papers*, no. 3476, October.

Krugman, P. (1987), 'Is Free Trade Passé?', *The Journal of Economic Perspectives*, 1, no. 2, pp. 131-44.

Krugman, P. (1991), 'Increasing Returns and Economic Geography', *Journal of Political Economy*, pp. 483-99.

Krugman, P., Obstfeld, M. (1991), *International Economics. Theory and Policy*,

2nd edition, New York.

Lipsey, R.G. (1970), *The Theory of Customs Unions: A General Equilibrium Analysis*, London.

Lipton, D., Sachs J.D. (1992), 'Prospects for Russia's Economic Reforms', *Brookings Papers on Economic Activity*, 2, pp. 213-83.

List, F. (1922), *Das Nationale System der Politischen Oekonomie. Der Internationale Handel, die Handelspolitik und der Deutsche Zollverein*, Jena (original 1841).

Masson, P.R., Taylor M.P. (1993), 'Fiscal Policy within Common Currency Areas', *Journal of Common Market Studies*, no. 1, pp. 29-44.

McKinnon, R.I. (1963), 'Optimum Currency Areas', *American Economic Review*, pp. 717-25.

Meade, J.E. (1957), 'The Balance of Payments Problems of a Free Trade Area', *Economic Journal*, pp. 379-96.

Melitz, J. (1991), 'A Suggested Reformulation of the Theory of Optimal Currency Areas', *CEPR Discussion Paper Series*, no. 590, October.

Michalopoulos C., Tarr, D. (1992), *Trade and Payments Arrangements for States of the Former USSR*, Washington.

Mundell, R. (1961), 'A Theory of Optimal Currency Areas', *American Economic Review*, no. 51, pp. 509-17.

Nogués, J.J., Quintanilla, R. (1993), 'Latin America's Integration and the Multilateral Trading System', in De Melo, J., Panagariya, A. (eds), *New Dimensions in Regional Integration*, Cambridge, pp. 278-318.

Pelkmans, J. (1984), *Market Integration in the European Community,* The Hague.

Pomfret, R. (1986), 'The Theory of Preferential Trading Arrangements', *Weltwirtschaftliches Archiv*, 122, pp. 439-99.

Robson, P. (1980), *The Economics of International Integration*, London.

Sala-i-Martin, X., Sachs, J. (1991), 'Fiscal Federalism and Optimum Currency Areas: Evidence for Europe from the United States', *NBER Working Paper,* no. 3855, Cambridge (Ma.).

Scitovsky, T. (1958), *Economic Theory and West European Integration*, Stanford.

Selm, G. van, Wagener H.-J. (1993), 'Soviet Republics' Economic Interdependence', *Osteuropa Wirtschaft*, no. 1, pp. 23-40.

Selm, G. van, Dölle, E. (1993), 'Soviet Interrepublican Capital Transfers and the Republics' Level of Development 1966-91', *Most. Economic Journal on Eastern Europe and the Former Soviet Union*, no. 1, pp. 133-49.

Smith, A. (1976), *An Enquiry into the Nature and Causes of the Wealth of Nations*, Oxford.

Swann, D. (1988), *The Economics of the Common Market*, London.

Viner, J. (1950), *The Customs Union Issue*, London.

Wagener, H.-J. (1992), *Free Seas, Free Trade, Free People. Early Dutch Institutionalism*, Groningen, mimeo.

World Bank (1992), *Statistical Handbook. States of the Former USSR*, Washington.

ECONOMIC DISINTEGRATION IN EASTERN EUROPE: TOWARDS A NEW INTEGRATION?

Madeleine Andreff and Wladimir Andreff

1. INTRODUCTION

The fall of the Soviet empire was brought about by several causes: a deepening economic crisis in all the countries belonging to the Council of Mutual Economic Assistance (CMEA); the increasingly inefficient operation of CMEA integrative mechanisms; the impact of falling oil prices on the USSR; and, last but not least, political will, which included both new Gorbachevian policies and the increasing reluctance of the Central Eastern European countries (CEECs) to gear most of their trade to the Soviet market. Decision-makers in these countries were increasingly willing to develop trade with Western markets, and it might well have also been in the Soviet interest to support this trade reorientation.[1] This new orientation was even backed by Gorbachev when he promoted a 'new thinking' on the relations between Socialist countries and the world economy according to which former CMEA members must seek closer integration with the world network of commodity and capital flows.

In the former CMEA area, the channel to this new integration into the world economy is quite the opposite of the Western European integration process: countries should first destroy their mutual economic links which isolated them from the rest of the world economy. Thereafter application for membership of another regional union - namely the EC (European Community) - might well be envisaged. In waiting to join another European economic union, the former CMEA countries should seek to deal with the drawbacks inherent in any process involving the dismantling of previously-established international any process involving the dismantling of previously-established international economic relations - whatever one may think about the real benefits of a CMEA-type economic union. Economic performances in the CEECs and in the Commonwealth of Independent States (CIS) dramatically deteriorated in 1990-1992. One of the main reasons for this deterioration was the international economic disintegration of the CMEA and the break-up of the USSR. A painful process of transition from one economic union to another might well last for a decade at least, given that none of the CEECs has a chance of joining the EC before the year 2000. It has already proved rather difficult to conclude association agreements between the EC and Hungary, Poland and the CSFR (the Czech and Slovak Federative Republic).[2]

Several other options are available to the former CMEA members willing to join a new economic union instead of waiting for straight EC membership. The Viségrad triangle, comprising Hungary, Poland and the CSFR, is already in operation as a free trade area. Among the much-discussed projects are an Eastern European Union of Payments, the already achieved European Economic Area consisting of the EC and the EFTA (European Free Trade Area) but not yet the former CMEA members, and even some kind of economic union between Turkey, Iran, Central Asia and Caucasus, not to mention the Baltic and the Black Sea free trade areas. The Bridge project, for instance, is based on the principle of creating a fifth common market as a bridge between East and West. Some kind of comprehensive European integration - even stretching from the Atlantic to the Pacific - has been envisaged by various economists. Although political factors will be decisive in any process of new European integration, economic analysis can provide some insights into the most advantageous way of reshaping a new economic union in Europe. This chapter must hence be regarded as an 'economic exercise' to the extent that the real outcome of the process geared towards a new integration of CEECs in the European economy will depend primarily on politics and diplomacy.

We start this chapter with theoretical examination of the foreseeable consequences for trade of the twofold break-up of the USSR and of the CMEA. We then outline some empirical evidence which confirms the expected trade consequences. Building new economic links in Europe is an urgent necessity, and one of the crucial issues is which a 'sample' of countries should be incorporated into a new framework of European economic integration. The third part of the chapter suggests five Eastern European areas whose union with the EC might have some economic relevance. A new economic union involving the CEECs, however, entails several economic pre-conditions. The fourth section briefly draws a set of criteria from the previous theoretical analysis of what should be the prerequisites for a new integrated economic area in Europe, while the final section considers, on the basis of these criteria, how far it is economically worthwhile to envisage various common economic areas which integrate the former CMEA and CIS members with the EC countries in new projects of an European economic union.

2. THE THEORETICAL ANALYSIS OF ECONOMIC DISINTEGRATION IN EASTERN EUROPE

In January 1990, at the 45th CMEA session in Sofia, an agreement was reached to settle trade among members at world prices and in hard currency from 1 January 1991 onwards. Throughout 1990, bilateral trade agreements were signed between the USSR and each CEEC (except the former GDR) in order to implement the decision taken in Sofia. Thereafter CMEA trade mechanisms ceased to operate and settlements at CMEA international prices and in transferable rubles were doomed to disappear; and they did indeed start to unravel. After January 1991, trade among the former CMEA members was no longer privileged and it was definitively superseded by national economic protection among the former partners. Within the USSR, in 1990, new protectionism even started to develop among republics, most of whom erected tariff and non-tariff barriers against trade with other republics. They restricted 'exports' (deliveries) of goods in short supply to other republics.[3] Restrictions and prohibitions were imposed on the intended exports of several products to now 'alien' republics, affecting especially food, basic consumables and materials. Inter-republic customs barriers were erected. Goods in shortage were rationed on the basis of republican 'citizenship': rationing cards were delivered only to residents. Trade bargaining over so-called 'hard goods' (i.e. those in shortage) among the newly-independent CIS states became extremely tough.

In the face of this process of disintegration, our initial premise is that the theory of international economic integration may provide the relevant framework for analysis of international disintegration as well, once this latter is accepted as the exact opposite of an integrating process. It would then suffice to reverse the main theoretical conclusions concerning integration to sketch out the expected trade consequences of economic disintegration.

1. In 1945, J. Tinbergen[4] defined integration as an economic policy aimed at an optimal centralization which entails the regulation of economic relations among integrated nations. Beggar-my-neighbour policies, particularly competitive devaluations, are thus considered as the exact opposite of integration. From the point of view of Tinbergen's analysis, the former CMEA countries are of course involved today in a process of economic disintegration because they have abandoned mutual regulation of their international economic relations, and they have not coordinated anti-inflationary stabilization and exchange rate policies since 1990. Uncoordinated devaluations of Central Eastern European currencies have borne out this statement. Devaluations or downward floating exchange rates were decided and implemented, between 1990 and 1993, for the Polish zloty, the Hungarian forint, the Czechoslovak crown (and the Slovak crown in 1993), the Romanian leu and the Bulgarian lev. All these downward fluctuations of the exchange rate must obviously be viewed as competitive devaluations insofar as their overt aim is to reduce trade imbalances in hard currency by restricting imports[5] and stimulating exports. They are not greatly

different from classic beggar-my-neighbour policies. Before the CMEA disbanded, any possible fluctuation in the exchange rate between a member's currency and hard currency affected, at worst, trade with Western markets (proportionately to import and export elasticities). Since the dissolution of the CMEA, the devaluation of a member's currency has hindered imports from the former CMEA partners as well, while all these countries have problems with their settlements in hard currency and are in search of outlets for their exports.

When the USSR was disbanded, the level of economic centralization suddenly decreased. Mandatory planning was abandoned and this thwarted all attempts at unified regulation or economic policy for all republics. The agreement which created the CIS has apparently not reversed this trend. Since none of the CIS states has so far been able to implement an autonomous economic policy, each newly-independent state has attempted to create its own currency, with varying degrees of success: the Estonian crown, the Latvian lat, the Lithuanian litas, the Ukrainian grivna, the Armenian tram, the Moldavian leu, the Kazakh tumen, the Tadzhik somon, or the Azeri manat, for instance. A new currency, distinct from the ruble, is only one of the elements which reflect the willingness of the new states to escape any kind of centralization within a Russian ruling economic order. Before they actually issue a new currency, all the CIS members behave as free riders in utilizing and creating rubles (through credit) beyond the supervisory capacity of the Russian central bank. The downward floating rate of the ruble since 1992 is to be viewed much more as the consequence of an uncontrolled excess supply of money than as a discretionary competitive devaluation; it appears to be an outcome of economic disintegration.

2. The theory of customs unions[6] envisages two effects in particular as arising from a free trade union (area) and from a common tariff throughout the union: the first effect is trade creation, the second of trade diversion. Every integration process may simultaneously involve both effects; and, of course, disintegration may do so as well. Thus the simplest index of disintegration lies in trade re-orientation after the USSR and CMEA break-up. Viner maintained that, in principle, a union will create trade more than deviate it, and most empirical studies have shown predominant trade creation as a result of EC unification.[7] Taking the union's net trade creation for granted in the case of integration, we may roughly infer that a symmetrical effect of disintegration is the triggering of a trade diversion which gains over trade creation in the former CMEA countries and the former Soviet republics. The trade to be diverted is greater, the tighter the former and now disbanded economic union.

3. Since Viner's analysis, it has been generally admitted that integration yields more benefits than inconveniences if it unifies similar (competing) economies. J.E. Meade[8] followed up Viner's assertion by pointing out that an integration process would breed greater net trade creation if it gathered together similar and competing, rather than different and complementary,

economies. A complementary partner is usually already a supplier prior to union; a competing economy is not. Thus the best prerequisite for a successful union is the assembly of economies of close similarity now (before union) but of potential complementarity in the future (after union). Consequently, disintegration would probably be more trade deviating than trade creating if it were to split up complementary economies, especially if these were to compete on third markets after disunion. Specialization within the CMEA, even though limited and inefficient, had increased complementarity among its members to some extent without obliterating the similar development pattern which had given priority, in all CMEA countries, to heavy industry producing intermediary products and now outdated machinery. This scheme of specialization is precisely this: it diverts trade among former complementary partners and makes them compete on hard currency markets in the future because of a roughly similar industrial structure. The CEECs are together in potential or real competition on Western markets;[9] and as regards some products, like steel for example, they even withstand Soviet export competition.

4. Union, and here the reference is again to Meade, is all the more beneficial to each participant country if each is the main supplier and the main customer of the other. In this situation, disintegration is obviously more disadvantageous. This unfavourable effect of disintegration is likely to occur due to the high concentration of trade on the USSR within the CMEA[10] and on Russia within the USSR. Meade also stressed that union is profitable if it occurs in a world of tough quantitative restrictions on trade. Disintegration can thus be expected to bring the worst effects in an economic environment of restrictions and quotas. These were predominant CMEA trade on the one hand, and on the other the European Community's raising of non-tariff barriers against imports from Eastern Europe for foodstuffs, textiles and steel. These barriers still impede the implementation of association agreements between the EC and CEECs. The worst effects of disintegration will not be dispelled as long as the EC's smallest quantitative restrictions remain in force.

5. A further question must now be addressed: how does a newly created union distribute gains from trade among its participants? The distribution is likely to be determined by countries' relative economic sizes.[11] For instance, if a large country like the USA unionizes with a small country like Canada, the former is so much larger that its domestic relative prices will remain unchanged after the removal of trade barriers, while the latter's prices will stick to US ones. Triggered by prices, shifts in resource allocation should be wider in the Canadian rather than in the US economy. In Eastern Europe too, economic disintegration should imply an asymmetric impact on resource allocation. The loss of the Soviet market for their exports today imposes a more dramatic resource reallocation on CEECs than that implied by the loss of Central European markets for Soviet exports (or even for Russian exports).

6. Economies of scale are being created by integration.[12] The disintegration of Eastern Europe entails diseconomies of scale that already hit those enterprises which previously supplied the Soviet market and whose outlets have started shrinking in recent years. Diseconomies of scale linked to disintegration would have disappeared, of course, had Western markets been instantly substituted for CMEA and Soviet outlets. This substitution is a long-term change insofar as Soviet and CMEA exports do not meet the technical standards and quality requirements of Western markets, and so will be scarcely competitive for a while.

7. An international economic union builds up a less divided market, so that it attracts foreign direct investment. We may thus infer that disintegration would put a brake on foreign capital inflow, or that it would at least weaken foreigners' incentives to invest in a fragmented economic area. On the other hand, by erecting protection (new tariffs or non-tariff barriers) at the border of each newly disintegrated nation, disintegration is likely to fuel capital inflows. Indeed, it seems that the splitting up of the Soviet Union into autonomous republics, and then independent states, has been felt by foreign investors as a disincentive to invest, and the growth of foreign investment in the CIS dropped in 1991-92. The shrinking market effect has thus surpassed the barrier to trade effect in Soviet disunion. The same tendency is not to be found in CEECs. Foreign capital is also attracted by a better investment climate, as evidenced by countries closely backed by foreign (Western) economic aid and most deeply involved in a stabilization policy (the Czech Republic, Hungary, Poland and Slovakia).

3. TRADE CONSEQUENCES OF DISINTEGRATION

Foreign trade among the five CEECs (Bulgaria, the CSFR, Hungary, Poland and Romania) shows, between 1989 and 1992, a dramatic shift of the kind expected from the analysis of international disintegration. In value terms, trade among CEECs began to decrease in 1989, and then collapsed in 1990 and even more sharply in 1991 and 1992 (Table 1).

Trade diversion among former CMEA participants is crystal clear, including the USSR's trade: Soviet exports and imports with the CEECs collapsed as well. By contrast, Central Eastern European trade in hard currency with Western market economies has continued to increase since 1988. We may assume that trade creation is at work here, although we cannot take it for granted because, since 1991, EC trade has included the data for the former GDR as well. EC-CEEC trade has nevertheless increased, although to a lesser extent than shown by the available figures. As regards the USSR, trade with the West continued to grow in 1989 and 1990, but it collapsed in 1991 despite the improvement in Soviet terms of trade on Western markets. For the Soviet Union, trade diversion obviously prevails over trade creation.

Table 1 - Eastern European and Soviet Foreign Trade, by main areas, 1988-
1992 (annual rate of change calculated from values in current dollars)

Areas	Eastern Europe									
	Exports					Imports				
	1988	1989	1990	1991	1992*	1988	1989	1990	1991	1992*
with:										
Eastern Europe	5.8	-8.6	-15.6	-24.6	-25.4	0.3	-9.4	-11.2	-19.8	-13.6
DMEs	10.7	6.5	9.9	6.6	17.0	10.9	4.8	19.1	7.8	4.2
DCs	1.8	-12.5	-12.6	-11.8	9.5	0.5	5.5	6.7	-9.2	-33.7

Areas	Soviet Union									
	Exports					Imports				
	1988	1989	1990	1991	1992*	1988	1989	1990	1991	1992*
with:										
Eastern Europe	-4.6	-11.1	-24.3	-35.0	-35.7	2.6	-5.7	-10.6	-43.4	-46.4
DMEs	7.8	7.8	12.3	-16.2	-34.3	22.6	21.1	5.6	-31.0	-4.5
DCs	2.2	2.1	-9.5	-29.0	-32.7	17.4	25.9	3.8	-35.8	10.6

Eastern Europe: European countries in the CMEA, including the GDR up to
1990.
DMEs: developed market economies.
DCs: developing countries.
* First semester only, compared with the first semester 1991.

Source: Economic Commission for Europe, United Nations.

Trade diversion appears to be a general phenomenon among the former
CMEA countries, whereas trade creation has been mainly due to Hungary and
Poland, and to a lesser extent to the CSFR[13] and Romania. In Hungary, trade
with Eastern Europe has decreased every year since 1988, except in the first six
months of 1992; and it has increased every year with the West (Table 2).

Hungary, and to some extent Poland, provide a successful test for the
theoretical analysis of economic disintegration: for these two countries, one
finds both trade diversion from the former CMEA high-cost suppliers and trade
creation with the Western lower-cost or higher-quality market economies. It is
worth pointing out that Poland and Hungary were the two major host countries
of foreign direct investment in Eastern Europe up to 1992. At the margin of
these main results, it should be stressed that trade decline for the CSFR,
Hungary and Poland has been less pronounced than trade collapse in the rest of
the former CMEA area. This better performance might be attributed to the
Viségrad agreement, but it is more probably due to the fact that the countries
involved are more committed to achieving transition to a fully-fledged market
economy, and to their willingness to bring the possibility of rather significant
mutual trade into negotiation of their possible membership of the EC.

Table 2 - *Eastern European Foreign Trade: annual rate of change by main areas, 1988-1992 (calculated from values in current dollars)*

Eastern European Countries	Exports				Imports			
	1989	1990	1991	1992*	1989	1990	1991	1992*
Bulgaria								
Socialist countries	-10.6	-32.0	-27.8	-34.5	-16.7	-23.8	-43.1	9.3
DMEs	17.2	-11.1	-36.3	35.0	0.6	-25.9	-59.8	84.3
DCs	-35.8	9.7	-47.6	32.6	-8.7	-19.0	-54.4	82.5
Hungary								
Socialist countries	-9.5	-21.4	-27.0	10.5	-14.4	-19.1	3.2	11.9
DMEs	5.6	20.6	28.0	13.4	7.7	3.8	53.8	-9.5
DCs	-6.8	-0.2	7.7	-10.7	-22.1	60.9	3.3	-61.4
Poland								
Socialist countries	-2.5	14.9	-62.0	n.a	-5.7	1.8	-42.8	n.a.
DMEs	5.3	40.0	13.7	n.a	7.1	-4.7	71.7	n.a.
DCs	-3.6	3.2	-15.5	n.a	-8.8	-17.1	151.0	n.a.
GDR								
Socialist countries	-7.4	-5.5	-	-	-10.4	-30.1	-	-
DMEs	9.5	11.3	-	-	6.7	54.4	-	-
DCs	-0.2	-5.1	-	-	5.3	-10.9	-	-
Romania								
Socialist countries	-14.7	-45.5	29.2	-19.8	-2.3	-13.7	-8.9	-29.8
DMEs	-3.9	-38.4	-22.8	2.5	1.7	116.7	-9.4	38.3
DCs	-15.2	-50.9	-11.9	6.2	28.9	10.1	-32.7	-32.9
Czechoslovakia								
Socialist countries	-11.7	-27.4	6.8	-43.5	-6.9	-17.1	0.3	-27.6
DMEs	10.9	13.4	6.9	28.6	-1.6	24.6	-13.7	-4.0
DCs	0.1	-10.9	-6.0	15.9	17.1	-12.0	4.4	-42.7

Socialist countries: CMEA countries, Yugoslavia and Asian Socialist countries. DMEs and DCs: as in Table 3.

Source: Economic Commission for Europe, United Nations.

Replacing settlements in transferable rubles with settlements in hard currency has also reduced trade among the former CMEA countries. Scarce currency usually hinders trade, and former intra-CMEA trade especially, insofar as this latter can be substituted now, for the same hard currency, by higher-quality, lower-cost, higher-tech products purchased on Western markets. Tradable goods available within the former CMEA countries have lost their chief comparative advantage, which was that they could be settled in transferable rubles. Increasingly scarce currency now compels the CEECs and the CIS states to promote lower-cost and higher-quality goods in trade (trade creation with the West) and to reduce high-cost trade with the East (trade diversion). The shortage of hard currency will be a lasting hindrance to foreign trade in the former CMEA area because of heavy foreign debt and of interests to service. The increased scarcity of currency for trade is one of the major signs of international economic disintegration.

Table 3 - Inter-republican trade and trade of Soviet republics with the rest of the world in 1988 (%), and change in this trade in 1991

Republics	Imports in 1988			Exports in 1988			Change in 1991*
	Inter-republican	Rest of the world	Relative weight (+)	Inter-republican	Rest of the world	Relative weight (+)	In % of 1990
Armenia	81.6	18.4	1.7	97.4	2.6	1.7	78.4
Azerbaijan	75.4	24.6	2.1	94.1	5.9	2.9	57.9
Belarus	79.8	20.2	6.3	91.5	8.5	8.6	55.3
Estonia	81.1	18.9	1.3	90.1	9.9	1.3	-
Georgia	80.1	19.9	2.3	93.2	6.8	2.6	-
Kazakhstan	83.5	16.5	5.8	91.2	8.8	3.9	60.9
Kyrgyzstan	78.9	21.1	1.3	96.2	3.8	1.1	57.6
Latvia	82.1	17.9	1.9	91.8	8.2	2.1	-
Lithuania	82.7	17.3	2.7	89.9	10.1	2.6	-
Moldavia	81.9	18.1	2.2	94.1	5.9	2.2	51.1
Uzbekistan	61.8	38.2	4.3	85.7	14.3	4.6	60.2
RSFS Russia	50.8	49.2	48.1	67.5	32.5	44.2	62.9
Tajikistan	85.7	14.3	1.2	86.9	13.1	0.9	56.4
Turkmenistan	86.2	13.8	1.1	92.3	7.7	1.1	62.9
Ukraine	72.9	27.1	17.7	85.5	14.5	20.2	57.8
Total (x)	184.8	97.6	282.4	184.7	47.2	231.9	61.5

*   Index of the foreign trade value (exports + imports) with all partners outside the republic concerned in 1991, 1990 = 100.
(+) Share of each republic in the value of total imports and total exports, in billion rubles, at domestic prices.
(x) Value in billion dollars, at domestic prices.

Sources: Calculated from the *Statistical Yearbook of the Soviet Union and East European Statistics Service*, no. 189, 20 February, 1992.

In 1991 and 1992, Soviet trade with all areas of the world economy collapsed. This was partly due to the total disruption of the Soviet economy from within: indeed, the Soviet Union disintegrated into fifteen national independent states, all of which are willing to monitor their own foreign trade with the rest of the world, this latter including now the rest of the former USSR. On the other hand, the political will of the new independent state leaders clashed with the reality of the strong integration of the former republics by means of their mutual trade and of their inter- and intra-industry links. For instance, in 1988 each republic of the Soviet Union registered a substantially larger share of its trade with other republics than with foreign countries (Table 3).

This integration through trade has been commented on as follows: 'considering trade intensity and monopoly, Soviet republics are more interdependent than national States within the EC, so that the cost of a splitting up could be very high insofar as efficiency is concerned'.[14] It is therefore quite logical that trade consequences of the disintegrating Soviet economy should be much more devastating for the former republics of the Soviet Union than the effects of the CMEA disintegration on the former participants' trade. Table 3 shows the extent to which the foreign trade of former Soviet republics collapsed in 1991 compared with 1990 - that is, only one year after the Soviet integrated economy was disbanded and less than one month after the official independence of eleven new states. Trade diversion was all the more devastating for the republics that had been highly specialized in the past: 'exports' (delivery) of steel and machinery were only provided by Russia, Ukraine and Belarus, energy and chemicals only by Russia, Azerbaijan, Kazakhstan and Turkmenistan, light industry products mainly by Moldova, the Caucasian republics and the Baltic states. The amount of foreign debt in hard currency[15] prevents large-scale trade creation with the rest of the world in most of the former Soviet republics. The agreement between the independent states and Russia whereby the latter is to pay the overall debt of the former USSR is hardly encouraging for foreign creditors.

4. FIVE SAMPLES OF COUNTRIES FOR A NEW ECONOMIC INTEGRATION IN EUROPE

The most obvious target today for each Eastern European economy is to develop trade with Western market economies in the short run, to integrate into the world market and mainly into Western European markets in the medium term, and, for this purpose, to apply for membership of existing European economic unions. So far as membership of the EC is concerned, it is obvious that the CEECs firmly intend to apply; but the CEEC export structure towards the EC is biased in favour of the so-called 'sensitive products'[16] against which EC non-tariff barriers have been largely maintained.[17] EC membership for these countries cannot be taken for granted before the year 2000. An application to the EFTA might have been a necessary or intermediary stage, but it is now of decreasing interest,[18] to the extent that the EFTA itself has signed an agreement with the EC creating the European Economic Area. Moreover several EFTA countries have already applied for EC membership and are thus competing successfully with the CEECs in this respect. A few hypotheses may nevertheless be advanced as far as a new integration of the CEECs and the CIS countries is concerned, although everything will be hampered until the former Soviet and East European puzzle has been somehow recomposed and stabilized.

Almost all lines of thought converge on the idea of creating a new integrated economic area conceived as either a channel (or a bridge) to the EC, or as a new grouping of countries willing to cooperate while they wait to apply for EC membership.

A first line of thought suggests new bilateral or multilateral trade and clearing arrangements among the former CMEA countries, including the new CIS States, in order to boost their mutual trade: mutually balanced lists or indicative lists of products for trade have even been defined in intergovernmental agreements since 1990. These latter are thus reminiscent of former CMEA arrangements. Heated debate has broken out among economists over the idea of forming an Eastern European union of payments covering almost the same set of countries as the former CMEA. Although it soon proved politically unrealistic, we must still consider a scheme of this kind which integrates the entire former CMEA area with the EC. Let us use the term 'Old-Style European Agreement' (OSEA) for the Eastern component - and thus for the corresponding sample of all former CMEA countries - of this common EC-CMEA hypothetical area.[19]

A second hypothesis deserves some comment. The Bridge Project[20] suggests assembling those countries now left 'in the middle of nowhere' or, to quote Horvat, "in a sandwich between the EC and the Soviet Union". These countries (now) number eighteen, ranked here according to their populations: Turkey, Poland, (now) five Yugoslav States, Romania, the two states of the former CSFR, Hungary, Bulgaria, Lithuania, Albania, Latvia, Estonia, Cyprus and Malta. Horvat advocates the idea of a fifth common market which gathers all these countries together. Such a so-called 'European Union' would be complemented by a monetary union based on an EM (*Evropska Moneta* or European Money); the EM should be convertible, pegged to the ECU and stabilized at the parity of one EM for one ECU. In the long run, some sort of association might be envisaged between this Bridge area and the EC. Although obviously appealing to countries 'in the middle of nowhere', this proposal probably raises more political problems than it solves. Not even the number of countries concerned can be fixed before the war in the former Yugoslav states is brought to an end. We should nevertheless assess whether integrating the Bridge countries, called jointly the 'European Bridge', into an economic union with the EC meets our criteria. From a statistical point of view, the data on the three Baltic states' trade are not coherent with the data, published by the OECD, that we utilize for other countries. The foreign trade of these three states will be omitted from the following calculations, and so too will the relatively tiny trade flows of Malta and Cyprus.

A. Steinherr[21] has called for a 'New Europe from the Atlantic to the Urals' (or even to the Pacific). Again appealing and ambitious, this call strikes one as being over-optimistic until the CEECs, the CIS states, and the states painfully emerging from former Yugoslavia, have definitively stabilized their economies and their political regimes. Of course, a new Europe as wide as this in scope might fulfil our prerequisites listed below, including economic leadership by some Western European country or, as Steinherr puts it, with the EC as the centre of gravity and, within the EC, Germany as the epicentre. Although this wishful thinking has very few chances of materializing even in the early twenty-first century, we shall neverthless examine it. The name 'Continental Europe'[22] is given to the sample of countries supposed to join the EC in this scheme: all the European countries except EFTA members, that is, all CIS participants and all European Bridge countries.

Two other schemes, which are probably more realistic as springboards to an economic union with the EC, must also be examined. One envisages the combination of the Viségrad free trade area, in operation since December 1992, with the EC. Let us call this scheme the 'Viségrad Channel' to full EC membership, a channel consisting of four countries since the break-up of the CSFR. The other scheme covers the five (now six, including independent Slovakia) CEECs already linked to the EC by the above-mentioned agreements. A 'Central Eastern European Free Trade Area' (CEEFTA), for instance, might be the appropriate term for the sample of these six CEECs. The CEEFTA hypothesis was strengthened somewhat in early 1993 when Romania and Bulgaria reached, in their turn, an association agreement with the EC.

5. CRITERIA FOR INTEGRATING EASTERN EUROPEAN COUNTRIES IN A NEW ECONOMIC UNION

For all these integrating schemes or hypotheses, the previous analysis of economic disintegration, and thus the underlying theory of integration, provides a set of basic criteria which can tell us whether an economic union or area (of integration) is viable and beneficial, or whether it is not. We translate these integration criteria into the indices and ratios usually utilized in quantitative analysis of international trade and specialization, and which can be calculated from the existing data on the foreign trade of the CEECs, the CIS countries and the members of the EC. The assumption underlying this 'economic exercise' is that it makes sense to compare the possible trade benefits of integrating various bundles of transition economies into a common area with the EC. We believe that the results of such a comparison may be meaningful, even though our calculation is based on data of the (recent) past and even though our appraisal does not include the internal costs (restructuring, social, etc.) entailed by a new integration process. The requirements for successful integration are directly derived from the previous analysis, and they may be listed as follows.

1. The number of assembled countries should not be too small, especially if no large national economy is involved into the union; otherwise, only a few gains will accrue to members from economies of scale. This condition ensures a rather wide market likely to attract trade, capital and foreign direct investment into the new economic union.

2. In the future economic union or trade area, one or two countries should be of larger economic size (measured for instance by GDP) than all the other members. This criterion signifies that an economic union is more likely to be sustainable in the long run if it is polarized on a relatively dominant economy (like for example the USA within the NAFTA, the USSR within the former CMEA, Germany within the EC).

3. A rather important trade flow among the would-be members of the new economic union, compared to trade flows with nations left out of the union, usually paves the way for a successful integration. We would normally have compared trade within the new union (for instance former CMEA plus EC) with trade between the new union and the rest of the world. But relevant and coherent data, homogeneous for both CMEA and EC countries, are not available from the detailed Western statistical sources we utilize (OECD and Eurostat). We are therefore compelled to appraise the share of the former CMEA countries in EC trade on the one hand, and the share of EC countries in the former CMEA trade on the other hand. Let us call:

M_{jk} the current value of imports of the good k from the area j to EC countries,
X_{jk} the current value of exports of the good k to the area j from EC countries,
M_j the current value of total imports (for all traded goods) from the area j to EC countries,
X_j the current value of total exports (for all traded goods) to the area j from EC countries,
M_k the current value of total imports of the good k to EC countries (including intra-EC imports),
X_k the current value of total exports of the good k from EC countries (including intra-EC exports),
M the current value of total EC imports (for all goods and all countries),
X the current value of total EC exports (for all goods and all countries).

We define a first index of relative weight as $w_m = M_j / M$. This index shows imports by EC countries from a former CMEA area as a percentage of total EC imports. Obviously, $w_x = X_j / X$ is the percentage of exports by EC countries to a former CMEA area in total EC exports. Symmetrically, $w'_m = M'_j / M'$ and $w'_x = X'_j / X'$ represent, respectively, the percentage of the EC in total former CMEA imports and the percentage of the EC in total former CMEA exports.

4. A fourth criterion is that trade should already be concentrated to a significant degree on one or two future members of the new economic union. Let α denote any EC country and β any country belonging to the former CMEA area (i.e. each β belongs to the set j). One may say that EC exports to an area j is concentrated on the EC country α when the ratio $X_{\alpha j} / X_j$ has a high value, or at least higher than for any other EC country. On the imports side, the corresponding concentration ratio is M_α / M_j. On the other hand, the concen-

tration of EC exports to an area j in a Eastern country β is described by ratios X_β / X_j and M_β / M_j.

5. A fifth criterion is that the sample of would-be members the new union should have a specialization which includes a wide range of competing items in their product structure of trade in order to trigger intra-industry trade and specialization after the union. A link has often been established between successful international economic integration and intra-industry trade and, as has been correctly stressed by van Selm,[23] two partners involved in an economic union "should have some activities in common that allow for an increase in specialization".

The need thus emerges for both an index of product structure of foreign trade and an index showing the degree of similarity in product specialization among economic areas (which will be the springboard for intra-industry trade after the union). For this purpose, we use the index $r_{mjk} = M_{jk} / M_j$ to express the product structure of EC imports from a former CMEA area and we compare it to $r_{mk} = M_k / M$, the product structure of total EC imports. Similar ratios $r_{xjk} = X_{jk} / X_j$ and $r_{xk} = X_k / X$ are utilized on the exports side. A major part of our appraisal relies on a comparison between r_{mjk} and r_{xjk}. We refer to a classical Balassa index[24] in order to specify the quantity of competing items in the product structure of mutual trade between EC countries and various former CMEA areas. This index is defined, for each product k, as $B_{jk} = (X_{jk}-M_{jk}) / (X_{jk}+M_{jk})$, and for all goods as the mean: $B_j = (1/n) \Sigma \mid X_{jk}-M_{jk} \mid / (X_{jk}+M_{jk})$.

6. Some of the possible Eastern members of a new economic union should be market economies or countries well advanced along the road towards a fully-fledged market economy (in order to avoid the reproduction of a CMEA-type integration). This criterion is obviously not quantitative, and it may even be interpreted in a somewhat subjective manner. For this reason we shall not elaborate on it here.

7. Some degree of coordination among national economic policies is required to make the union effective. Hence some collective economic decisions must be centralized at the union level. We have already mentioned that this criterion is not yet satisfied either by the CEECs or the CIS countries, because of the beggar-my-neighbour policies pursued by the former and because of the loss of any central ruling power over the latter. Many countries will probably be unable, in a first phase of independence, to coordinate their trade and economic policies with other members of a free trade area or a payments union, and to follow any kind of (centralized) union regulation. Almost none of them would agree to the almost inevitable (German or Russian) economic leadership in the case of union. However, this last criterion does not discriminate to any significant extent among the different prospective economic areas that we intend to test, and we may therefore omit it.

6. TESTING THE INTEGRATION OF THE FIVE SAMPLES OF EASTERN EUROPEAN COUNTRIES WITH THE EUROPEAN COMMUNITY

We may now briefly utilize the above-listed criteria in order to screen the projects for a new economic union arising out of the disintegration of Eastern Europe. We compare the five above-defined country samples in terms of their potential as a profitable common trade area and, further, in terms of their suitability for economic union with the EC according to the criteria listed above.

1. The first criterion is satisfied for all our five Eastern areas insofar as the countries envisaged as joining a possible new economic union in Europe are of a sufficient number. The smallest new area, i.e. that consisting of the EC and the Vihegrad Channel, comprises sixteen countries. The so-called EC-CEEFTA group would assemble eighteen participants, the EC-European Bridge zone would gather thirty countries given the present state of Yugoslav disintegration and war, the EC-OSEA area thirty-three, once the fifteen former Soviet republics are taken into account, and the EC complemented by Continental Europe (CIS + Bridge) would comprise forty-two members, even without the seven EFTA countries. By its very definition, each possible union is larger than the EC and it will therefore be large enough, in terms of population, national product and wealth, to provide an attractive market for trade and foreign investment. This statement would have been all the more valid had we included the EFTA countries in our analysis and in each of our five integrating areas.

2. The quite large economic size of some would-be members is also a criterion met by all unions including the EC and one of our five country samples. Appraised in terms of gross domestic product (GDP) in 1990 current dollars,[25] the economic size of the former USSR is rather larger than that of any other participant in a possible new Europe. With 2,197 billion dollars, the former USSR's GDP amounts to 79% of the CMEA's total GDP and to about 24% of the total GDP of all the European countries examined below. In the same year, the second largest GDP in Europe was that of unified Germany (1,658.5 billion dollars, i.e. 18% of overall European GDP). The next largest GDPs, those of France and Italy, are both below 1,200 billion dollars and therefore somewhat lag behind. Consequently, two countries were significantly ahead in 1990 insofar as their economic size was concerned, and thus the USSR and Germany might have been regarded as the potential future leaders of any new European economic union. Today, after the disintegration of the USSR, Russia remains among the leaders with 15% of total European GDP in 1990, corresponding to 1,352.3 billion dollars - that is, still ahead of France's GDP. However, the economic crisis has rapidly reduced the size of Russian GDP since 1990, and we may thus conclude that Germany is likely to become the single economic leader (or epicentre, as Steinherr puts it) of any new European economic union. Among its followers, or countervailing economic powers, we should find France, Italy, the UK and Russia. No other Eastern component of a new European

union would have influential economic size; the two biggest of these countries after Russia - Ukraine and Poland - respectively record GDPs of only 356 and 202 billion dollars.

GDP of possible members of a new economic union in Europe (1990, in current dollars)

USSR	2,197.1	UK	979.5	Romania	104.6
of which:		Spain	493.0	Yugoslavia	101.4
Russia	1,352.3	Netherlands	279.9	Hungary	77.9
Ukraine	355.7	Poland	202.0	Greece	66.1
Kazakhstan	97.8	Belgium	193.0	Portugal	59.8
Germany (*)	1,658.5	Turkey	149.3	Bulgaria	52.9
France	1,194.0	Denmark	131.3	Ireland	42.6
Italy	1,093.3	Czechoslovakia	128.8	Luxembourg	8.7

Total European GDP covered: 9,213.7.
(*) Aggregated figure of both FRG's and GDR's GDP.

Source: OECD and World Bank.

3. Now we assess the relative share of each of our five Eastern areas in total EC trade, and the relative weight of the EC in either total former CMEA trade or former USSR trade. We may also draw some conclusions from the evolution, between 1989 and 1991, of the Eastern areas' shares in EC trade, and from the main products involved in it.

There is a pronounced asymmetry between Eastern countries and EC countries: since the former are of relatively lightweight in total EC trade, the latter hold a rather large share of total former CMEA trade:

The percentage of EC exports (to) or imports (from) former CMEA countries is in any case lower than 3%, although it slightly increased in 1991. Half this percentage is accounted for by EC-former USSR trade. In view of the relative share of EC countries in former CMEA or former USSR trade, the percentage appears rather high and in the same range for the CMEA and for the USSR. The EC share is higher in the Eastern countries' exports (27 to 28% in 1990) than in imports (20%). All this reveals that our third criterion is fulfilled much better by Eastern European countries than by EC countries in their mutual trade. The former should gain more than the latter, in terms of trade, from their possible union. This probably explains why former CMEA members are more eager to join the EC than the latter is to accept them.

The calculation of the indexes $w_m = M_j / M$ and $w_x = X_j / X$ (and of $w_{mk} = M_{jk} / M_k$ and $w_{xk} = X_{jk} / X_k$) gives the results set out in Tables 4 and 5 for total trade and for each product (CTCI 10). The share of our five areas in EC trade is, of course, very small, ranging from about 1% for the Viségrad Channel to about 4% for Continental Europe, although it increased between 1989 to 1991. The growing share in EC trade, however, is differentiated among the five areas. For instance, the Viségrad Channel improved its relative share by 50% in EC exports and by 22% in EC imports in 1991, and the CEEFTA countries did so respectively by 40% and 17%. On the other hand, the European Bridge and Continental Europe increased their share in EC exports only by 10 to 15%, and by about 5% in EC imports in the same year. The OSEA performance ranks in between. The Viségrad Channel and the CEEFTA countries, although the smallest of our samples, are therefore less far than the other areas from fulfilling the criterion of already non-negligible trade links with future EC partners in a possible new union. Moreover, on the exports side, each of our five areas maintains almost the same share in EC exports whatever the product may be.

Share of former CMEA countries in EC trade, in percentages

	EC exports to		EC imports from	
	former CMEA	former USSR	former CMEA	former USSR
1989	2.33	1.22	2.54	1.39
1990	2.13	1.01	2.55	1.37
1991	2.84	1.27	2.81	1.43

Source: OECD.

Share of EC countries in former CMEA trade, in percentages

	Exports to EC from		Imports from EC to	
	former CMEA	former USSR	former CMEA	former USSR
1989	18.45	16.14	16.24	18.21
1990	28.16	27.14	20.55	20.05

Source: Eurostat.

The imports side is distorted by the oil trade of EC countries with both OSEA and Continental Europe areas and, to a lesser extent, by trade in food and livestock with the three areas which do not include the former USSR, and by trade in manufactured products (CITC 6 and 8) with all our five Eastern country samples.

4. As regards the fourth criterion, we have calculated indices of import and export concentration on the four main EC countries relative to trade between EC countries and our five Eastern areas: the four EC leading exporters and importers are Germany, France, the United Kingdom and Italy.

Table 4 - Share of each Eastern European economic area in European
Community imports index w_m, 1989-1991, in percentages of total EC
imports (calculated from values in current dollars)

EC imports 91 CITC	Viségrad Channel	CEEFTA	OSEA	European Bridge	Continental Europe
0	1.88	2.04	2.27	3.41	3.63
1	0.39	0.81	0.99	1.77	1.95
2	1.97	2.19	4.52	3.53	5.86
3	0.83	1.03	11.04	1.29	11.29
4	0.98	1.03	1.12	1.26	1.35
5	1.18	1.31	1.86	1.80	2.35
6	1.73	1.93	3.05	3.48	4.59
7	0.54	0.60	0.79	1.16	1.35
8	1.79	2.32	2.41	5.66	5.76
9	0.82	0.93	7.85	1.58	8.50
Total	1.20	1.38	2.81	2.57	4.00

EC imports 90 CITC	Viségrad Channel	CEEFTA	OSEA	European Bridge	Continental Europe
0	1.88	2.00	2.18	3.35	3.52
1	0.31	0.70	0.92	1.71	1.93
2	1.68	1.82	4.30	3.05	5.53
3	0.81	1.18	10.90	1.74	11.46
4	0.64	0.68	0.81	0.88	1.01
5	0.96	1.06	1.62	1.67	2.23
6	1.36	1.58	2.48	3.29	4.19
7	0.39	0.43	0.57	1.00	1.14
8	1.35	1.90	1.99	5.36	5.46
9	0.57	0.65	6.04	1.21	6.60
Total	0.98	1.18	2.55	2.43	3.80

EC imports 89 CITC	Viségrad Channel	CEEFTA	OSEA	European Bridge	Continental Europe
0	1.71	1.90	2.06	3.31	3.47
1	0.28	0.60	0.83	1.45	1.67
2	1.49	1.67	4.23	2.97	5.52
3	0.85	1.83	11.82	2.59	12.57
4	0.85	0.91	1.27	1.09	1.45
5	0.76	0.92	1.54	1.57	2.18
6	1.10	1.40	2.46	3.09	4.15
7	0.34	0.40	0.54	0.87	1.01
8	1.11	1.79	1.89	5.00	5.10
9	0.67	0.77	5.43	1.33	5.99
Total	0.86	1.15	2.54	2.37	3.76

Tot.91/Tot.90	1.22	1.17	1.10	1.06	1.05
Tot.90/Tot.89	1.14	1.03	1.00	1.03	1.01

The definition of each Eastern European economic area is given in the text.

Source: OECD foreign trade statistics.

Table 5 - Share of each Eastern European economic area in European Community exports index w_x, 1989-1991, in percentages of total EC exports (calculated from values in current dollars)

EC exports 91 CITC	Viségrad Channel	CEEFTA	OSEA	European Bridge	Continental Europe
0	1.07	1.39	3.33	1.89	3.82
1	1.34	1.63	2.18	2.23	2.78
2	1.46	1.74	2.13	3.86	4.25
3	1.04	1.26	1.44	2.07	2.25
4	1.17	1.57	3.59	2.82	4.84
5	1.41	1.62	2.99	3.11	4.49
6	1.32	1.55	2.32	3.16	3.94
7	1.49	1.67	3.26	3.05	4.64
8	1.28	1.43	2.33	2.37	3.27
9	1.35	1.69	3.93	7.37	9.61
Total	1.37	1.57	2.84	2.92	4.19

EC exports 90 CITC	Viségrad Channel	CEEFTA	OSEA	European Bridge	Continental Europe
0	0.76	1.09	2.48	1.98	3.38
1	0.69	0.89	1.06	1.53	1.70
2	1.08	1.51	1.91	3.43	3.83
3	0.40	0.51	0.72	0.89	1.10
4	0.97	1.23	2.12	3.53	4.43
5	1.11	1.39	2.58	3.17	4.35
6	0.94	1.16	1.97	2.99	3.80
7	0.98	1.11	2.31	2.68	3.88
8	0.80	0.93	1.65	2.11	2.83
9	1.08	1.55	3.51	4.82	6.78
Total	0.92	1.12	2.13	2.63	3.64

EC exports 89 CITC	Viségrad Channel	CEEFTA	OSEA	European Bridge	Continental Europe
0	0.97	1.17	2.67	1.67	3.17
1	0.61	0.72	0.81	1.21	1.31
2	1.05	1.47	2.08	3.18	3.79
3	0.11	0.17	0.30	0.55	0.68
4	1.13	1.27	2.93	3.97	5.63
5	1.33	1.63	3.33	3.26	4.96
6	0.86	1.14	2.56	2.72	4.14
7	0.90	1.07	2.25	2.33	3.51
8	0.65	0.80	1.63	1.61	2.45
9	1.13	1.28	3.23	3.18	5.13
Total	0.90	1.11	2.33	2.34	3.56

Tot91/Tot90	1.49	1.40	1.33	1.11	1.15
Tot90/Tot89	1.02	1.01	0.91	1.12	1.02

Source : OECD foreign trade statistics.

On the other hand, we have estimated the extent to which EC imports and exports with Eastern areas are concentrated on the four main Eastern countries involved in our five areas: the former USSR, Poland, Yugoslavia and Turkey. Table 6 shows that Germany concentrated, in 1991, more than 40% of EC imports from any of the five Eastern European country samples, and over 50% of exports. These figures reveal a high level of concentration compared with Germany's share of total EC trade, respectively 26% of total imports and 29% of total exports. It appears very clear that Germany is bound to become one of the leading countries - if not the only one - in all schemes integrating Eastern Europe into a new economic Europe. The concentration ratio of German trade is not greatly differentiated between our five Eastern areas, from 42% to 46% for imports and from 51% to 58% for exports.

All the three EC follower-countries - France, the UK and Italy - exhibit a markedly lower level of concentration in their trade with Eastern Europe; in particular, the import and export concentration indices for France and the UK remain generally beneath 10%. It must nevertheless be pointed out that Italy, which only ranks fourth in total EC trade, shows over 10% concentration ratios in its trade with all five Eastern European areas. Italian trade tends to differentiate slightly among our five country samples in favour of the three widest zones: the OSEA, European Bridge and Continental Europe. In some respects, Italian trade thus contradicts the previous conclusion (criterion 3) which advocated the Viségrad Channel and the CEEFTA as the most appealing areas for an integration with the EC.

If we now inspect the five Eastern areas, we find that EC trade is concentrated on a few countries. The share of the former USSR is obviously very big in the OSEA area: the weight of the USSR in EC imports from the OSEA zone is 51% and its weight in exports is 45%. One also notes a predominant position of the USSR in Continental European trade with the EC (import 36%, export 30%). If the USSR had remained integrated as a single economy, it could have claimed to be one of the trade leaders of a new Europe, and the indisputable leader among its Eastern participants. Much lower expectations are open to Russia in today's rather divided CIS. Except for the USSR, the share of Poland, Turkey and former Yugoslavia in EC trade with Continental Europe and with European Bridge is significantly above the average share of other Eastern countries in this trade. Poland, especially, attracts European trade insofar as its weight is 52% in EC exports to the Viségrad Channel and 45% to CEEFTA countries,[26] and respectively 44% and 38% in EC imports. We may therefore conclude that on either the EC side or the Eastern side, most trade is concentrated on a few countries, and one single 'epicentre' emerges - Germany. The concentration criterion is nevertheless met for the EC and for any of our five samples of Eastern European countries.

5. Concerning our specialization criteria, we begin with examination of the product structure of foreign trade between the EC and our five Eastern areas (Table 7). First, it must be stressed that the product structure of total EC imports and total EC exports is somewhat similar: more than 30% of trade, both ways, is made up of machinery and transport equipment (CITC 7), followed by manufactured goods (CITC 6, between 15 and 20%), miscellaneous

manufactured articles (CTCI 8) and chemicals (CTCI 5), again over 10%. As regards the exports side, almost the same product structure prevails in EC trade with any of our five areas. By contrast, the imports side reveals a rather different picture of EC-Eastern European trade compared with total EC trade.

Table 6 - Trade concentration ratios in European Community trade with five Eastern European economic areas, 1991, in percentages (calculated from values in current dollars)

EC 91	Viségrad Channel	CEEFTA	OSEA	European Bridge	Continental Europe
% in EC imports of :					
Germany	44.34	43.51	41.75	46.47	44.18
France	8.15	9.13	11.97	9.43	11.32
UK	5.35	5.44	6.01	5.46	5.85
Italy	11.61	12.56	16.06	16.60	17.62
% in EC exports of :					
Germany	57.17	55.36	58.30	50.96	54.29
France	8.28	9.31	8.89	9.96	9.48
UK	5.67	5.65	4.70	6.80	5.80
Italy	10.07	11.09	12.35	13.47	13.60
EC 91	**Viségrad Channel**	**CEEFTA**	**OSEA**	**European Bridge**	**Continental Europe**
% in imports of each Eastern European economic area of:					
USSR	-	-	50.73	-	35.66
Poland	44.49	38.42	18.93	20.68	13.31
Yugoslavia	-	-	-	24.91	16.02
Turkey	-	-	-	21.05	13.54
% in exports of each Eastern European economic area of:					
USSR	-	-	44.72	-	30.34
Poland	51.92	45.12	24.95	24.89	16.92
Yugoslavia	-	-	-	20.83	14.51
Turkey	-	-	-	24.82	17.29

Source: OECD foreign trade statistics.

Moreover, this imports structure discriminates among our five areas. For this reason we must compare the bilateral trade structure of these areas with the EC in order to assess whether product structures reveal a competing trade or not. In our assessment, we omit products representing a small share (less than 2%) of bilateral trade.

Table 7 - Product structure in trade of European Community countries with five Eastern European economic areas specialization indexes: r_{mjk} and r_{xjk}, 1991, in percentages (calculated from values in current dollars)

EC91	Viségrad Channel		CEEFTA		OSEA		European Bridge		Continental Europe		World	
CITC	Imp.	Exp.	Imp.	Exp.	Imp.	Exp.	Imp.	Exp.	Imp.	Exp.	Imp.	Exp.
0	14.5	6.7	13.6	7.6	7.4	10.1	12.2	5.6	8.4	7.8	9.2	8.6
1	0.4	1.7	0.7	1.8	0.4	1.4	0.8	1.3	0.6	1.2	1.2	1.8
2	7.7	2.7	7.4	2.8	7.5	1.9	6.4	3.4	6.9	2.6	4.7	2.6
3	6.0	2.7	6.5	2.9	34.1	1.8	4.4	2.5	24.5	1.9	8.7	3.6
4	0.3	0.3	0.3	0.4	0.2	0.5	0.2	0.4	0.1	0.4	0.4	0.4
5	9.8	12.7	9.4	12.6	6.6	12.9	7.0	13.07	5.9	13.1	10.0	12.3
6	24.5	17.3	23.7	17.6	18.4	14.7	23.0	19.4	19.5	16.9	17.0	17.9
7	15.4	42.4	14.7	41.1	9.5	44.4	15.3	40.5	11.4	42.9	33.9	38.7
8	20.3	12.0	22.7	11.7	11.7	10.5	29.9	10.42	19.6	10.09	13.6	12.8
9	1.0	1.4	1.0	1.5	4.2	1.9	0.9	3.5	3.2	3.1	1.5	1.4
Total	100	100	100	100	100	100	100	100	100	100	100	100

Source: OECD foreign trade statistics.

A strong asymmetry in the bilateral flow for the same product, according to indexes r_{mjk} and r_{xjk}, basically means that the two partners are not competing, but are in some way complementary. By contrast, when the calculated percentage is not too different for r_{mjk} and r_{xjk}, we may assume that there is a competing trade structure in product k between the EC and the Eastern area j. The above-defined complementarity is very clear in energy trade between the EC and both the OSEA and Continental Europe alone. This would not greatly favour the integration of these two areas with the EC, since energy is the most important import of the EC from the two zones. To a lesser extent, Eastern areas and the EC do not exhibit a competing trade structure for machinery (CITC 7), although this product is the major EC export to each Eastern country sample. This complementarity would again not support integration, but it does not discriminate among the five Eastern areas. A much less significant case of non-discriminatory complementarity in the latters' trade with EC countries is that of raw materials (CITC 2), the share of which is rather smaller than energy or machinery. Food and livestock (CITC 0) and chemicals are interesting to the extent that they draw a dividing line among our five areas. On the one hand, trade in agricultural products with the EC seems more complementary than competitive for the Viségrad Channel, the CEEFTA and the European Bridge, while it seems more competitive than complementary for the OSEA and Continental Europe. On the other hand, trade in chemicals would benefit the integration of the Viségrad Channel and the CEEFTA into the EC because of their rather competitive trade, at least if we compare it to the rather complementary trade in chemicals between the EC and our three remaining Eastern areas.

Trade in manufactured goods (CITC 6 and 8) would be the most profitable to integration of any Eastern European area into the EC because it is the only case of markedly competitive bilateral trade. Manufactured goods might well become the cornerstone of such integration since, when aggregated, they account for about 40% of EC imports from Eastern areas and about 30% of exports. Although not discriminating among our five areas, trade in manufactured goods is a reliable basis on which the Eastern European areas could negotiate a common trade area and, further, an economic union with the EC. Considering, then, the total product structure of mutual trade, it turns out that the Viségrad Channel and the CEEFTA present the two best sets of preconditions for integrating the EC, followed by the OSEA and Continental Europe, where competitive products are partly counter-weighted by complementary items such as energy and raw materials (this is, of course, the outcome of these two areas comprising the former USSR).

We now consider the Balassa indexes B_j and B_{jk}. If the absolute value of these coefficients is low, we may conclude, following Balassa, that intra-industry specialization prevails in trade in the product k (low absolute value for B_{jk}) or in trade in all products (low value for B_j). We must define, somewhat arbitrarily, a threshold below which the indices reflect intra-industry trade. The double threshold will be $B_j \leq 0.3$ and $|B_{jk}| \leq 0.3$. Below this numeric value, we would deduce that competing trade is significant. Looking at the value of B_j (Table 8), one notes that it decreases, between 1989 and 1991, for all our Eastern areas except the OSEA; this is a positive factor for integrating four out of the five areas with the EC. The Viségrad Channel and the CEEFTA show the lowest B_j in each year and its value falls below the threshold in 1991. According to our criterion, these two areas exhibit, on average, competitive trade with the EC in the last year for which OECD data are available.

The value of the average index B_j, however, conceals sharp differences among products. We again find a complementarity in energy and machinery trade $(0.5 \leq |B_{jk}| \leq 0.9)$ between EC countries and the OSEA and Continental Europe. Trade also follows a complementary specialization between the EC and the Viségrad Channel and the CEEFTA for machinery, food and livestock and raw materials, but the value of $|B_{jk}|$ remains within the interval $(0.3; 0.5)$.

Since the Balassa index is lower than 0.3 for all manufactured products in all Eastern areas, this confirms that that EC countries face competitive trade on this item. Additional competitive trade only arises from the Viségrad Channel and the CEEFTA as regards chemicals and animal and vegetable oils and fats (CITC 4). All this empirical evidence again indicates that the two smallest areas we have envisaged would be the most profitably integrated into an economic union with the EC.

Table 8 - Balassa's intra-industry trade ratios in European Community trade with five Eastern European economic areas, 1989-1991 (calculated from values in current dollars)

EC 91 CITC	Viségrad Channel	CEEFTA	OSEA	European Bridge	Continental Europe
0	(-0.33)	(-0.25)	0.13	(-0.34)	(-0.04)
1	0.66	0.47	0.51	0.27	0.33
2	(-0.45)	(-0.42)	(-0.61)	(-0.28)	(-0.46)
3	(-0.34)	(-0.36)	(-0.90)	(-0.23)	(-0.86)
4	0.03	0.15	0.48	0.33	0.52
5	0.16	0.18	0.30	0.33	0.38
6	(-0.14)	(-0.11)	(-0.14)	(-0.05)	(-0.08)
7	0.50	0.50	0.63	0.48	0.58
8	(-0.22)	(-0.29)	(-0.07)	(-0.46)	(-0.33)
9	0.17	0.22	(-0.39)	0.60	(-0.01)
Total trade	0.30	0.30	0.42	0.34	0.36

EC 90 CITC	Viségrad Channel	CEEFTA	OSEA	European Bridge	Continental Europe
0	(-0.47)	(-0.35)	0.01	(-0.31)	(-0.08)
1	0.53	0.30	0.25	0.13	0.12
2	(-0.52)	(-0.42)	(-0.64)	(-0.29)	(-0.49)
3	(-0.67)	(-0.71)	(-0.95)	(-0.66)	(-0.93)
4	0.18	0.26	0.43	0.58	0.61
5	0.15	0.21	0.30	0.38	0.39
6	(-0.18)	(-0.15)	(-0.12)	(-0.05)	(-0.05)
7	0.47	0.48	0.64	0.50	0.58
8	(-0.28)	(-0.36)	(-0.11)	(-0.45)	(-0.33)
9	0.17	0.28	(-0.40)	0.50	(-0.13)
Total trade	0.36	0.35	0.39	0.39	0.37

EC 89 CITC	Viségrad Channel	CEEFTA	OSEA	European Bridge	Continental Europe
0	(-0.32)	(-0.29)	0.08	(-0.37)	(-0.10)
1	0.51	0.26	0.17	0.09	0.06
2	(-0.49)	(-0.41)	(-0.62)	(-0.32)	(-0.50)
3	(-0.90)	(-0.93)	(-0.98)	(-0.85)	(-0.96)
4	0.10	0.12	0.36	0.54	0.56
5	0.35	0.36	0.44	0.43	0.46
6	(-0.11)	(-0.09)	0.03	(-0.06)	0.01
7	0.50	0.51	0.65	0.50	0.59
8	(-0.27)	(-0.39)	(-0.08)	(-0.52)	(-0.36)
9	0.10	0.09	(-0.40)	0.27	(-0.24)
Total trade	0.37	0.35	0.38	0.40	0.38

Source : OECD foreign trade statistics.

6. The last criterion is qualitative in nature. When one seeks to establish which Central and Eastern European economy is furthest along the road towards a fully-fledged market economy, it is difficult to avoid value judgements and to rid oneself of personal views on the dynamics of transition in each of the

countries in our samples. We shall not go very deeply into this topic. The most widespread appraisal in the economic literature is that three or four countries are now leaders in the transition process, namely the Czech Republic, Hungary and Poland and, lagging behind, Slovakia. The qualitative criterion confirms that the Viségrad Channel fulfils to the best extent (or the least worst) almost all the prerequisites for integration with the EC in a new Europe. The second set of economies in transition to a market system is usually considered to comprise Bulgaria, Romania, Slovenia and, to some respect, Croatia and the Baltic States. The second best for a new Europe would thus be the integration of the two former countries and the Viségrad countries (i.e. our CEEFTA, which generally performs as well as the Viségrad Channel according to our above-listed quantitative criteria) with the EC. Had it not been a bad performer on our quantitative criteria, the European Bridge might have been regarded better than third best, insofar as it consists of several partly-achieved market economies: Turkey, the CEEFTA countries, Slovenia, Croatia, the Baltic States, Cyprus and Malta. The two areas including the former USSR do not appear among the best candidates for creating a new Europe once they have been integrated with the EC. The quantitative analysis is reinforced in this regard by the fact that several CIS states are not yet firmly set on the path to a fully-fledged market economy; a statement which may apply to almost all of them today, except Russia. Since it is more heterogeneous than any other area, Continental Europe should even be ranked behind the OSEA in an integration perspective.

7. CONCLUSIONS

The collapse of an economic system brings with it widespread economic uncertainty and non-economic (political, military, ethnic, etc.) events which render the transition process unpredictable as to its path, its pace, its cost and its outcome.[27] The international economic disintegration of the former 'Socialist block' is an integral part of the collapse of 'real Socialism'. Any new integration including Eastern Europe will rely heavily on the unpredictable solution of non-economic problems. Integration perspectives which include all the former Soviet republics together are obviously doomed to failure for both political and ethnic reasons. The Bridge project is vitiated from the outset by the war raging between three former components of Yugoslavia, and to a lesser degree by potential conflict between Turkey and Cyprus. Our conclusions, drawn from an economic 'guesstimate' based on a rough statistical exercise, suggest the political downgrading of those integration prospects that involve either the former USSR republics or the former Yugoslav States. Even in the case of CEECs and the Viségrad group, political or ethnic divergences may slow down the integration drive. Therefore our conclusion that integrating these two bundles of countries into the EC would be more beneficial than the three alternatives we have examined, is to be taken with a pinch of salt. The road to a new integration of Eastern Europe into the West European market economy will remain arduous in the near future, whatever the trade gains and economic benefits suggested by the economic theory of integration. And on a bumpy road, the pace is slower than the drivers want it to be; that is, the willingness of East European political leaders to become full members of the EC.[28]

NOTES

1 As advocated for instance in Csaba, 1990.
2 See, for instance, M. Andreff *et al.*, 1991; W. Andreff, 1991a; Gautron, 1991.
3 As described in Aleksashenko, 1991.
4 See Tinbergen, 1965.
5 Devaluation, however, increases the costs of imports and hence those domestic production costs which depend on imports. Devaluation is thus unlikely to lead to a sustainable level of balance of payments in the long run and will probably keep the devaluating country in a situation of 'high-cost producer'; see Drabek, 1992. Both effects of devaluation hamper the integration of the devaluing country into a new economic union.
6 See Viner, 1950.
7 Especially in Balassa, 1975, and Truman, 1975.
8 See Meade, 1955.
9 As shown, for instance, in W. Andreff, 1991b.
10 This concentration is stressed, for example, in Graziani, 1982, for the CMEA, and in McAuley, 1991, for the USSR.
11 This topic is developed in Caves and Jones, 1981.
12 For one of the first demonstrations of this effect of integration, see Scitovsky, 1956.
13 At least before the country split into an independent Czech Republic and an independent Slovak Republic, the impact on foreign trade of which has not been taken into account by our data.
14 CCE, 1990: translated from the French by W. Andreff. For more detailed discussion of this point, which distinguishes between the level of the internal integration (inter-republican trade) and the external integration (extra-Union trade of republics) of the Soviet economy, see van Selm and Wagener, 1993.
15 An evaluation of this amount is given, for instance, in W. Andreff, 1993b.
16 Such as foodstuffs and agricultural materials, textiles, clothing, iron and steel, and - somewhat less 'sensitive' - apparel and chemicals: see Graziani, 1993.
17 Messerlin, 1993, writes: 'Despite some further liberalization by the EC, the Agreements essentially consolidate the previous EC concessions, and they still maintain a substantial level of protection on crucial CEEC

exports for the next half decade: agriculture, coal, textiles and apparel. More important for the long run, the Agreements contain provisions on export quotas, safeguards and rules of origin which seriously undermine their capacity to be the cornerstone of a CEEC complete integration into an open world trade system'.

18 The opposite view has been developed by Baldwin, 1992, who argues that: (i) if joined by CEECs, EFTA members would multiply their leverage over EC trade policies during accession talks; (ii) joining EFTA would hasten the CEECs' entry into the EC by helping the CEECs to get richer and providing them with the shortest route to the European Economic Area.

19 This name has connotations of the Gorbachev era, when negotiations between the EC and the CMEA were resumed and ended, in 1988, in a EC-CMEA global agreement. Today, this agreement would include the EC members, the CEECs, the Baltic States and the CIS countries. On the other hand, this hypothesis of maintaining all the former CMEA members in the sample may translate into the partial inertia of the strong trade links between the former partners, especially between the former USSR and each CEEC, that a still existing integrated communications network (railways, pipelines, telecommunications and so on) still underlies: on this latter argument, see e.g. van Brabant, 1992.

20 This project is described in B. Horvat, 1992, but with only thirteen countries prior to the break-up of Yugoslavia and the CSFR.

21 See especially Steinherr, 1993. The same sample of countries, called the Continental European Customs Union, is envisaged by Aghion et al., 1992, and called 'a free-trade zone which spans continental Europe' (including the whole of the former Soviet Union).

22 In order to facilitate calculations and the construction of the tables, none of our country samples comprise the EFTA countries. Consequently, our 'Continental Europe' is less continental than that suggested by Steinherr. It aggregates the EC, CEECs, the former USSR and the remaining countries of the Bridge Project (see above). Put otherwise: our Continental Europe = European Bridge (including Baltic States) + the former USSR (excluding Baltic States). The results of the same 'exercise' which also takes the European Economic Area (EC plus EFTA) into account will be published in M. Andreff, 1993; they do not diverge from those presented here.

23 See van Selm, 1993, in this volume.

24 See Balassa, 1975.

25 All the data on GDP in current dollars are from the OECD, except for the three former Soviet republics (source: The World Bank).

26 The theoretical share corresponding to an even distribution of trade - with the economic size of each country not accounted for - is 33% among the three Viségrad participants and 20% among the five CEEFTA countries.

27 The consequences of this line of thought on economic analysis of collapse and of transition are explored in W. Andreff, 1993a.

28 We completed this paper at the beginning of the turmoil affecting the European Monetary System (August 1993). A follow-up paper on our topic might well check whether one can still consider the EC as unified an area as we have assumed here (and in our above 'economic exercise').

BIBLIOGRAPHY

Aghion, P., Burgess, R., Fitoussi, J.P., Messerlin, P.A. (1992), 'Towards the Establishment of a Continental European Customs Union', in Fleming, J., Rollo, J.M.C. (eds), *Trade, Payments and Adjustment in Central and Eastern Europe*, Royal Institute of International Affairs and EBRD, London, pp. 157-79.

Aleksashenko, S.V. (1991), 'The Economic Union of Republics: Federation, Confederation, Community', Stockholm Institute of Soviet and East European Economics, working paper, no. 28, pp. 1-25.

Andreff, M. *et al.* (1991), *Les échanges entre la CEE et les pays de l'ex-CAEM à l'horizon 1992*, Rapport au Commissariat Général du Plan (Paris) for ROSES-CNRS, Grenoble.

Andreff, M. (1993), 'Pour une nouvelle insertion des pays d'Europe centrale et orientale dans l'èconomie europèenne', paper submitted to the *Revue d'Economie Politique*.

Andreff W. (1991a), 'Le rapprochement institutionnel et l'aide des pays de la CEE aux pays de l'ex-CAEM', *Etudes internationales* (Québec), vol. XXII, no. 3, September, pp. 485-96.

Andreff, W. (1991b), 'Soviet Foreign Trade Reforms and the Challenge to East European Economic Relations with the West', in Bertsch, G., Elliott-Gower, S. (eds.), *The Impact of Governments on East-West Economic Relations*, London: Macmillan, pp. 23-46.

Andreff, W. (1993a), *La crise des économies socialistes: la rupture d'un système*, Grenoble: Presses Universitaires de Grenoble.

Andreff, W. (1993b), 'Economic Disintegration and Privatization in Eastern Europe', in Csaba, L. (ed.), *Privatization, Liberalisation and Destruction: Recreating the Market in Eastern Europe*, Aldershot: Dartmouth, pp. 103-30.

Baldwin, R. (1992), 'An Eastern Enlargement of EFTA: Why the East Europeans Should Join and the EFTAns Should Want Them', Centre for Economic Policy Research, London, CEPR Occasional Paper no. 10.

Balassa, B. (1975), 'Trade Creation and Diversion in the European Common Market: An Appraisal of the Evidence', in Balassa, B. (ed.), *European Economic Integration*, Amsterdam: North Holland Publishing Company, pp. 79-118.

Brabant van, J.M. (1992), 'Integrating the New Eastern Europe into the Global Economy', *Structural Change and Economic Dynamics*, vol. 3, 1, pp. 17-35.

Caves, R., Jones, R. (1981), *Economie internationale*, Armand Colin, Paris, vol. 1, Paris: Armand Colin.

CCE (1990), 'Stabilisation, libéralisation et dévolution de compétences: Evaluation de la situation économique et du processes de réforme en Union soviétique', *Economie européenne*, no. 45, December, Commission des Communautés Européennes, Bruxelles.

Csaba, L. (1990), 'The Bumpy Road to the Free Market in Eastern Europe', *Acta Oeconomica*, vol. 42 (3-4), pp. 197-216.

Drabek, Z. (1992), 'Payments Union, Costs of Production and Trade Complementarity in Central and Eastern Europe', NATO Colloquium, Brussels, 7-9 April.

Gautron, J.C. (ed.) (1991), *Les relations Communaut, Européenne - Europe de l'Est*, Paris: Economica.

Graziani, G. (1982), *Comecon, domination et dépendances*, Paris: Maspero.

Graziani, G. (1993), 'Specialization for Eastern Europe and Access to EC Markets', in van Brabant, J.M. (ed.), *The New Eastern Europe and the World Economy*, Boulder: Westview Press, pp. 175-93.

Horvat, B. (1992), 'Economic Integration of Eastern Europe: The Project Bridge', mimeo, Zagreb University, Zagreb, 14 February.

McAuley, A. (1991), 'Costs and Benefits of De-integration in the USSR', MOCT/MOST, no. 2, pp. 51-65.

Meade, J.E. (1955), *The Theory of Customs Unions*, Amsterdam: North Holland Publishing Company.

Messerlin, P.A. (1993), 'Politique commerciale et échanges Est-Ouest', in Mucchielli, J.L., Célimène, F. (eds), *Mondialisation et régionalisation. Un défi pour l'Europe*, Paris: Economica (forthcoming).

Selm van, G. (1993), 'Integration and Disintegration in Europe: EC versus Former USSR', published in this volume.

Selm van, G., Wagener, H.-J. (1993), 'Former Soviet Republics' Economic Interdependence', *Osteuropa-Wirtschaft*, 38, 1, pp. 23-39.

Scitovsky, T. (1956), 'Economies of Scale, Competition and European Integration', *American Economic Review*, March.

Steinherr, A. (1993), 'Emerging Gravity Shifts in International Trade: A Tentative Analysis of the New Europe from the Atlantic to the Urals', in Mucchielli, J.L., Celimene, F. (eds), *Mondialisation et régionalisation. Un défi pour l'Europe*, Paris: Economica (forthcoming).

Tinbergen, J. (1965), *International Economic Integration*, 2nd edition, Amsterdam, Brussels: Elsevier Publishing Company.

Truman, E.M. (1975), 'The Effects of European Economic Integration on the Production and Trade of Manufactured Products', in Balassa, B. (ed.), *European Economic Integration, Amsterdam*: North Holland Publishing Company, pp. 3-40.

Viner, J. (1950), *The Customs Union Issue*, Carnegie Endowment for International Peace, London: Stevens and Jones.

Russia, CIS and the World Economy. Looking for New Structures of Integration, Cooperation and Trade

Horst Brezinski[1]

1. Introduction

The dissolution of the Soviet Union in December 1991 and the foundation of the Community of Independent States (CIS) led to a breakdown in the traditional foreign trade structures of these areas. The collapse was, however, not due solely to the disintegration of the Soviet Union; it also stemmed from a process of economic transformation which began at the end of the 1980s in the Soviet Union and in Eastern Europe.

The break-up of the Soviet empire has curtailed the dominance of ideological aims in international political and economic relations.[2] Most politicians and economists in these areas now favour integration with the world economy. There are, however, no precise guidelines for such integration, and, at the time of writing, at least three possible scenarios can be delineated:[3]

1. **The full economic independence** of the various republics whereby each of them, as a new nation, establishes its own currency, a separate financial system, its own customs regulations and applies for membership of organizations such as the IMF, the World Bank, the General Agreement on Tariffs and Trade (GATT) and, possibly, the European Union (EU). The previous union, with its specific fiscal ties, has become defunct.

2. **Concentric circles of association** in which a core group of republics form a currency union and a common market with which the other republics are associated. The degree of cooperation varies according to the interests of the

individual republic.[4] There may be a second circle of republics which are not members of the currency union but participate in the common market. A third group of republics might be members only of a free trade area, while a fourth group only participates selectively in the free-trade agreement.

3. An **economic union** based on a common market and a currency union controlled by a central bank. This form would provide a limited degree of political independence for the republics.

My analysis begins with the situation in the Soviet Union at the end of the 1980s. It outlines the growth potential of foreign trade, the dependencies created by the old structures, and the reasons for the rapid collapse in foreign economic relations. With regard to earlier attempts at transformation, developments so far will be examined and the various scenarios discussed. Finally, the question will be raised as to the extent to which Western industrial nations can contribute to ongoing development processes and to the success of transformation.

2. BACKGROUND

In order to understand the task of transformation and its magnitude, I shall look first at the general characteristics of the Russian economy and those of the other republics which provide the framework for the transformation process. I shall then examine the specific features of the foreign economic links which in the past determined international economic relations.

The Russian economy, as well as the economies of the other republics, covers a relatively large territory which is well endowed with natural resources. At the moment and in the future, however, these natural resources can only be exploited at increasing costs.[5] Moreover, Russia's infrastructure is totally insufficient, its capital stock is outdated, and large investments are needed to prevent economic growth from declining. To this is added a fundamental misallocation of capital due to systemic characteristics[6] and a neglect of negative externalities in the past. This will make production in certain regions impossible in the future, particularly as regards agriculture.

Apart from these material economic factors, socialism produced patterns of social behaviour and a mentality alien and adverse to those behavioural modes required by a successfully operating market economy. The population lacks the ability to understand the workings of a market-type economy.[7] Monolithic, inefficient bureaucracies have been, and still are, in power. Moreover, the system helped to create social networks within the underground economy which continued to grow as the inefficiencies of the command economy increased. On the one hand, the system impacted positively on economic and social stability; on the other, the social networks of the underground economy collaborated with the political and bureaucratic apparatus and gave rise to Mafia-type organizations. The various republics now lack a democratic structure, and the populace has relatively limited understanding of what constitutes a democratic society. This explains why, after the ousting of the Soviet dictatorship, new and well-functioning institutions and mechanisms able to ensure the peaceful cohabitation of differing nationalities and to form the stable basis for the Community of Independent States did not come into being. National pride, selfishness and nationalism have blinded the population to rational economic argument. Some leaders expect support for a deliberately nationalist policy. There is a belief that continuing membership of the CIS might be an impediment to chances of joining the EC, the group of the Black Sea states, or the Islamic states.

The previous planned economy, with its specific characteristics of foreign trade monopoly, a non-convertible currency, an economic structure centred in Russia, and the particular form of integration within the CMEA, resulted in a volume and structure of Soviet foreign trade which differed fundamentally from that of Western industrial economies. The isolation of its national economy had a negative influence on the Soviet Union. Economic incentives were scant, and access to international technical progress, which could have stimulated structural change, increased productivity and reduced costs, was restricted.[8] The result was declining international competitiveness and an unfavourable structure of exports. Because of its unique character, the Soviet system increased the monopolistic position of domestic producers who, because of the foreign economic monopoly of the state, were excluded from direct participation in the international division of labour.

An analysis undertaken with the help of a gravity model[9] reveals that the former Soviet Union did not use or exhaust all the possibilities of its foreign trade relations (see Graphs 1 and 2), especially as far as trade with the industrialized countries of the West was concerned. As regards trade with Eastern Europe, however, a far greater volume of foreign trade was achieved when compared to a situation in which market-type relations and liberalization of foreign trade prevailed.

After 1986, with the exception of 1989, the value of Soviet exports declined.[10] In 1990 and 1991 this decline continued at a rate of 11.4% and 7.4%. Russia's foreign trade decreased by more than 20% in 1992,[11] amounting to 17% with developed Western economies, 27% with developing countries, and 43% with the other CMEA countries.[12]

It was only in 1993 that foreign trade stagnated. During the first half of 1993, exports increased by 18%, whereas imports declined by 37%.[13] Graphs 3 and 4 illustrate the changes in the regional structure, and the relatively small share of the former republics of the Soviet Union in trade with Russia.

Graph 1 Potential and Actual 1985 USSR Trade (A = Actual, P = Potential)

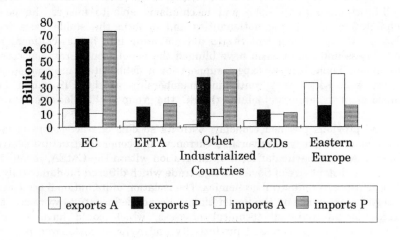

Source: Hamilton and Winters, 1992, p. 85.

*Graph 2 Potential and Actual 1985 USSR Trade with Individual Countries
(A = Actual, P = Potential)*

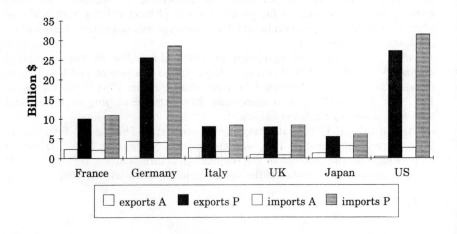

Source: Hamilton and Winters, 1992, p. 86.

Graph 3 Foreign Trade of Russia in 1991 and 1992: Regional Structure

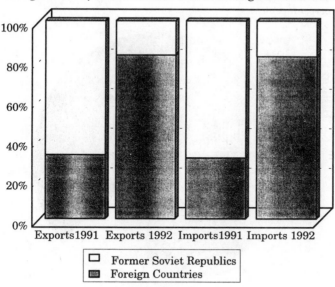

Source: PlanEcon Report, vol. IX, No. 5-6, 1993, p. 34.

Graph 4 Foreign Trade of Russia: Regional Structure in 1992 (without former Republics)

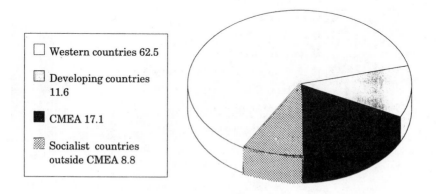

Source: PlanEcon Report, Vol IX, No. 5-6, 1993, p. 35.

*Graph 5 Russian Exports in 1991: Shares of Key Items / Categories Export (in
percentages)*

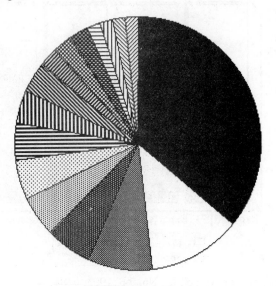

■ Mineral fuels 36.3
□ All other goods 12.2
▨ Precious metals & minerals 8.:
▥ Iron and steel products 6.1
▨ Wood products 5.3
▣ Fertilizers 4.9
⊟ Cars and trucks 4.7
▯ Aluminium 4.2
▨ Non-electrical machinery 4.1
▨ Cotton 2.5
▨ Inorganic chemicals 2.5
▨ Fish and crustaceans 2.4
⊟ Ores 1.7
▥ Organic chemicals 1.7
▨ Nickel 1.6
▨ Copper 1.5

Source: PlanEcon, Report 26, June 1992.

*Graph 6 Russian Imports in 1991: Shares of Key Items / Categories Imports (in
   percentages)*

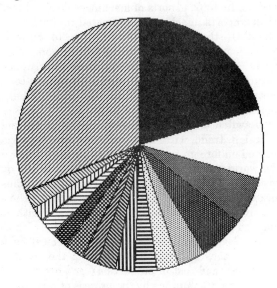

■ Non-electrical machinery 20.7

□ Cereals 9

▨ Sugar 6.1

▦ Electrical machinery 5.8

▨ Railway equipment 3.4

▣ Iron goods 3.2

⊟ Tobacco 2.7

▮ Plastics 2.6

◩ Meat 2.4

▨ Miscellaneous chemicals 2.4

⊠ Iron and steel products 2.3

▨ Pharmaceuticals 2.3

⊟ Footwear 2.2

◫ Non-knitted apparel 2.1

◪ Instruments 2

▨ other goods 30.8

Source: PlanEcon, Report 26, June 1992.

The reasons for this decline lie partly in the structure of Russia's exports and imports (see Graphs 5-6). Exports were dominated by mineral fuels and other raw materials. In 1992, exports of machinery declined by 30%, amounting to only 9.4%.[14] In imports, machinery dominated in 1992 with 39%. However, compared with 1991, they fell by 33%. Owing to difficult conditions in agriculture and inadequate infrastructure, in 1992 imports of grain rose by 37% and of sugar by 14%. The structure of foreign trade clearly shows that Russia's foreign trade structure is more or less that of a developing country, and that it is seriously affected by changes in world market prices. This, in the long run, will lead to a deterioration in the terms of trade.

Moreover, the switch to the use of world market prices and of convertible currencies in foreign trade with Eastern European countries in 1992 has negatively impacted on foreign trade with these countries. The opening of these countries to the world market has led to a reduction in the quality of foreign trade with Russia. The collapse of the East European economies will have to be added to the negative developments. This is illustrated by the example of East and West Germany. While West German foreign trade with Russia remained virtually unchanged in 1992, East Germany's trade with Russia declined dramatically. East German companies now find themselves fully exposed to Western competitors; they suffer in addition from the effects of the currency union (increased prices and cost of production), and are negatively affected by the hard budget constraints imposed by the process of privatization.

On the other hand, the dissolution of the Soviet system increased the transparency of inter-republican relations, which had been concealed for many years. Tables 1, 2, and 3 illustrate these developments, while Table 1 shows Russia's dominant economic position in the Community of Independent States. Table 2 clearly demonstrates that Russia's share in the foreign trade of the former Soviet Union was by far the largest (67.9%). Columns 3, 4, and 5 reveal the close interdependence among the republics, with dependence on mutual deliveries by the different republics in industrial production amounting to between 20 and 55% of consumption by specific republics in 1990.[15] If Russia ever severs her economic relations with the republics, this will be likely to cause a reduction in production of 35%. A decline in the inter-republican trade of most of the other republics by 10% will lead to a similar reduction in national income.[16] According to Granberg, a total halt in inter-republican deliveries will cause total production in the various republics to amount to a mere 15% in the Ukraine, 27% in Kazakhstan, 4% in Belarus, 1% in Moldova and Turkmenistan.[17] Table 3 sets out the commodity structure of Russian inter-republican trade. Sixty-seven per cent of all economic production in Ukraine, 84% in Belarus and 52% in Kazakhstan depend on Russian deliveries.[18]

Most republics depend on Russian energy deliveries. Russia, in turn, imports from the various republics 25% of her requirements of rolled steel, 23% of fertilizers, 31% of tyres, 37-45% of pipes (various types), 47% of tractors, 56% of bulldozers and 95% of cotton, in addition to substantial quantities of food and industrial raw materials.[19] The Soviet command economy created monocultures, especially in the central Asian republics, and established the dependence of these republics on Russia. Consequently, most of the republics are unable abruptly to halt or change their traditional trade relations. In 1992, the republics paid for only a small proportion of Russian deliveries.

Table 1 - Republics of the USSR Economic Potentials 1990 (in percentages)

Republic	Population	GNP	Industrial Production	Agricultural Production
Russia	51.3	58.7	66.4	46.2
Azerbaijan	2.5	1.4	1.7	1.8
Armenia	1.1	1.3	0.8	0.6
Belarus	3.6	3.8	4.1	5.9
Georgia	1.9	1.7	1.2	1.4
Kazakhstan	5.8	5.3	3.5	6.9
Kirgizstan	1.5	0.9	0.5	1.3
Latvia	0.9	1.2	0.8	1.4
Lithuania	1.3	1.6	1.2	2.2
Moldova	1.5	1.2	0.8	2.2
Tajikistan	1.8	0.9	0.4	1.0
Turkmenistan	1.2	0.9	0.4	1.1
Ukraine	18.0	16.5	16.0	22.5
Uzbekistan	7.0	4.0	1.7	4.6

Source: Goskomstat of the USSR, 1990.

The consequence was an unplanned balance of trade in favour of Russia amounting to five billion US$.[20] In addition, the republics benefited from export prices which on average were 70% higher than world market prices. In the first half of 1992, implicit subsidies amounted to at least 8.4 billion US$.[21] According to the IMF, the subsidies disbursed by Russia due to undervalued energy prices, measured by 1992 purchasing power parity, amounted to at least 3% of her GDP. Since the beginning of 1993, most of the republics have paid 50% of current world market prices for oil and one third for gas.[22] Until 1990, most republics, especially the Central Asian ones, benefited from the system of direct transfers and from indirect transfers, which have gradually been dismantled since 1992.[23]

Given the radical changes in foreign trade relations, the impact of transformation, and the considerable burden imposed on Russia in maintaining the Soviet empire, this process of dismantling was a prime necessity. Finding and implementing new international economic structures proved to be an urgent requirement. Analysis of the latest steps in economic transformation and developments immediately after the dissolution of the Soviet Union may provide some indication of the direction that the search for new structures of cooperation, integration and trade might take.

Table 2 - Foreign Trade of the USSR 1990

Republic	Share in Interre-publican Trade	Share in Foreign Trade Turnover	Exports (% of NMP)		Share of Interrepublican Exports in National Income in 1991	Share of Interrepublican Imports in National Income in 1991
			Other Republics	Other Countries		
Russia	37.7	67.9	29.3	7.5	11	16
Azerbaijan	2.8	11.2	58.7	3.7	27	22
Armenia	1.9	0.8	63.7	1.4	20	31
Belarus	8.5	4.2	69.6	6.5	24	26
Georgia	2.8	1.4	53.7	3.9	21	23
Kazakhstan	6.0	2.8	30.9	3.0	15	29
Kirgizstan	1.5	0.8	50.2	1.2	23	25
Latvia	2.6	1.2	64.1	5.7	-	-
Lithuania	3.0	1.2	60.9	5.9	-	-
Moldova	2.9	1.1	62.1	3.4	24	28
Tajikistan	1.5	0.7	41.8	6.9	19	22
Turkmenistan	1.4	0.5	50.7	4.2	23	24
Ukraine	20.5	14.0	39.1	6.7	26	20
Uzbekistan	5.3	2.5	43.2	7.4	19	24

Source: Goskomstat of the USSR 1990; Kossikova, 1993, p. 13.

3. MOST RECENT DEVELOPMENTS

The Soviet Union attempted to avert the threat of economic crisis by integrating into the world economy even before the events of August 1991. Thus, the leadership believed it would be possible to increase competition and to modernize the national economy.

Establishing an open economy entails that domestic consumers and producers may choose goods and services of domestic and foreign suppliers and select them on the basis of relative prices. The same applies to domestic producers offering their goods in the domestic market or abroad at relative prices. Prices and profits determine the flow of capital and labour. World market prices influence relative domestic prices in a truly open national economy. The exchange rate determines the prices. This lesson was learnt by Russia when the Russian government slowly began to take this path and stubbornly adhered to it after Gaidar assumed office.

In 1991, all Soviet enterprises became entitled to participate directly in foreign trade.[24] However, all enterprises engaging in foreign trade had to apply to the authorities for permission to do so. The instrument of export and import quotas was intensively used, because of the balance of payments situation and in order to prevent the uncontrolled drain of domestic resources. The exchange rate system was substantially improved. From November 1990 onwards, the number of exchange rates was reduced and the system of exchange rate coefficients was abandoned. A limited form of internal convertibility was introduced. Enterprises used a commercial exchange rate for their transactions. At first they had to sell 40%, and later 50%, of their revenues in convertible currencies to the state. This in turn led to an increase in barter trade among enterprises,[25] which, except in border regions, is generally illegal and led to an enormous flight of capital, amounting to more than 12 billion US$ in 1991 and 1992 and which may prove to be of the same magnitude in 1993.[26]

In 1992, the Gaidar government attempted to open up the national economy by abolishing export quotas for energy and military goods on 1 July. The aim was to introduce a system of auctions for quotas. At the same time it intended to get rid of the traditional administrative allocation of central imports and to establish current account convertibility. At the time of writing in 1993, there are still export quotas for oil, gas, oil products, non-ferrous metals and chemical products.[27]

These quotas will supposedly be eliminated in 1994. As for imports, a system of tariffs was introduced in order to generate revenues and protect the domestic economy. Despite these liberalization efforts the Russian government still pursues a dirigistic policy. Fewer than 200 enterprises are permitted to export strategic raw materials. Since 18 August 1993, only 14, rather than 246, enterprises have been entitled to export oil and non-ferrous metals.[28] This policy of reducing the number of exporters can be explained by the assumption that small suppliers have extremely limited negotiating power in the world market. In the Russian view the ideal situation would comprise only one company trading in oil, as is the case of the gas industry for instance. This company has to hand over its profits to the various national oil companies.[29] The contradictory behaviour of the Russian government stems from realization that the previous system was not consistent in the implementation of the projected liberalization. Moreover, it has been acknowledged in the meantime that full liberalization will cause substantial problems for various sectors of the Russian industry. It has become obvious that the tax system, the customs system, the inefficient controls of capital flows, and an inflation rate of more than 1000%, impact negatively on the liberalization of foreign trade.

The break-up of the former Soviet Union, accompanied by the continued use of rubles in the various republics, has provoked an uncontrolled rise in the quantity of rubles. At the beginning of 1993, only Kyrgyzstan no longer accepted the ruble as an official means of payment.

The other republics continued to accept the ruble as the only means of payment or as a parallel currency.[30] Yet uncontrolled credit creation by the republican central banks enormously increased the quantity of rubles and 'sent a very strong blast to the ruble zone causing a substantial delineation of purchasing power between the "republican" rubles'.[31]

Table 3 - Interrepublican and International Trade within Russia's External Trade in 1990 (in percentages)

	Total Exports		Total Imports	
	Deliveries to former Soviet Republics	Exports	Deliveries from former Soviet Republics	Imports
All branches of material production	100.0	69	30.9	100.0	46.8	53.2
Industry	100.0	68.9	31.1	100.0	47.2	52.8
Electricity	100.0	83.1	16.9	100.0	99.9	0.1
Oil and gas	100.0	51.6	48.4	100.0	81.5	18.5
Coal	100.0	41.4	58.6	100.0	66.7	33.3
Other fuels	100.0	43.3	56.7	100.0	100.0	0.0
Ferrous metallurgy	100.0	79.2	20.8	100.0	79.5	20.5
Non-ferrous metallurgy	100.0	61.2	38.8	100.0	55.5	44.5
Machine building & metal working	-	70.1	29.9	100.0	41.4	58.6
Chemicals and petrochemicals	100.0	80.8	19.2	100.0	48.1	51.9
Forestry, woodworking & paper	100.0	54.5	45.5	100.0	32.8	67.2
Construction materials	100.0	87.2	12.8	100.0	56.4	43.6
Light industry	100.0	86.7	13.3	100.0	38.3	61.7
Food industry	100.0	59.7	40.3	100.0	54.1	45.9
Other branches of industry	100.0	89.3	10.7	100.0	48.5	51.5
Agriculture	100.0	51.5	48.5	100.0	37.1	62.9
Other types of material production (including payment for transportation services)	100.0	81.0	19.0	100.0	74.2	25.8

Source: Russian Goskomstat Rossiiskaia Federatsia v Tsifrakh, 1992.

Several arguments contributed to the complete dissolution of the ruble zone by the end of 1993:[32]

1. a donor of direct or indirect transfer, such as Russia, is afraid of becoming an importer of inflation;
2. as long as imports from other states of the ruble zone prove not to be highly inelastic, leaving the zone does not appear harmful;
3. leaving the union may function as a shield against repeated hyperinflation and the uncontrollable depreciation of the common ruble against other currencies;
4. a common currency will not function without a uniform and coordinated

monetary and fiscal policy;

5. a ruble zone requires a coordinated programme of transformation (e.g. price liberalization);
6. some republics intend to gain seigniorage (inflation tax to increase government revenues) from printing their own money;
7. privatization programmes are to be based on current net value assessments, and foreign direct investment is to be attracted by a stable currency and a low currency-risk environment;
8. the republics want to gain full political sovereignty and monetary autonomy.

Some of these arguments apply to all the republics. Russia, which seems to support at least the first four arguments, demonstrated her intentions in the first ruble reform of July 1993.[33] Only rubles printed in 1993 are valid in Russia, whereas the other rubles are still valid in the various republics. On September 7, Russia, Belarus, Kazakhstan, Tajikistan and Uzbekistan agreed to form a new ruble zone. This second step in the institution of a new type of ruble zone implied subordination to the Russian central bank, and Russia holds sole jurisdiction over future ruble issues. The five nations must agree to monetary and fiscal goals jointly with Russia and they must bring their economic policies into line with Russia's. Russia has demanded gold and convertible currency in exchange for newly printed rubles and has insisted on the establishment of a gold reserves pool.[34] As a result, the republics has been driven out of the ruble zone.[35] As a statement by Fjodorov proves, this was a deliberate action: "I am principally in favour of integration and the ruble zone, but only with our eyes wide open, with civilised methods, after looking at all the options and after setting up all the needed control and protection mechanisms."[36]

Nonetheless, the dissolution of the Soviet system has not abolished all the economic interdependencies created under the Soviet command economy. Consequently, it appears only logical that since October 1992 Russia should have called for a sustaining of the ruble zone, bilateral clearing of the inter-republican balances of payment, and the formation of an interstate bank to facilitate the payment system. The latest of these attempts was made in Ashabad in December 1993 in an endeavouring to establish an economic union to coordinate fiscal and customs policies.[37] Such attempts constitute nothing more than a return to the former CMEA institutional instruments. As long as they remain merely institutional instruments, they will not prevent the CIS from becoming an association of liquidation attending the civilized funeral of the former Soviet Union.

4. PERSPECTIVES OF THE FUTURE FOREIGN ECONOMIC CONCEPT OF RUSSIA AND THE COMMUNITY OF INDEPENDENT STATES

The first alternative, which envisages the full economic independence of the individual republics with their own monetary, fiscal and currency policies, would mean total rupture of economic and financial relations with the members of the old union. In view of the economic interdependencies, this scenario does not appear realistic. In the recent period of disunion, some republics have attempted to engage in some forms of regional cooperation. Thus, the Central Asian republics were ready to cooperate with countries such as Turkey, Pakistan, India and Iran,[38] while Ukraine favoured closer cooperation with the nations of the Middle East and Austria. Armenia tried closer cooperation with France and the countries of the Middle East. Yet these attempts were not based on economic facts but rather on political considerations. Most republics cannot survive on their own - although, in 1992, Gaidar assumed that in the future the republics could become independent national economies with which normal trade relations could be developed.[39]

Because of strong interdependences and the inability to gain economic independence, the second scenario, which envisages concentric circles of association, cannot be implemented in most of the CIS republics. Only the Baltic states have left the former union, and, because of strong economic interdependence all three of them are interested in establishing a free trade area with the CIS members.

Consequently, there only remains the third scenario, which entails a return to full economic union with a single uniform monetary and fiscal policy. This seems to be a kind of restoration of the old system. There is, however, one main difference. This time the republics participate in the negotiating and engineering of common economic policy.

The currency reform of July 1993 clearly showed that the individual republics do not have functioning currency systems, and the use of parallel currencies has been disastrous. Early in 1993, 'the former Soviet republics predominantly regarded the issuing of a domestic currency as a declaration of political independence'.[40] Russia's July reform, as well as the attempt of September 1993, highlighted the economic and monetary weaknesses of the republics and sought to impose a Russian-dominated and therefore 'designed' ruble zone upon them. The attempt failed. Most of the republics wish to detach their economies from ruble inflation and to pursue fully autonomous stabilization policies which take into account their specific resource endowments and capacities to transform their economies. Moreover, the condition policy of the IMF places additional pressure on them to dismantle the ruble zone.[41] There is a strong desire among the republics to achieve greater autonomy in designing economic policy and an interest in collecting seigniorage revenues from their own money creation. These arguments are stronger than the economic rationale of remaining in the zone because of the short-term inelasticities of trade linkages. As long as these republics pursue the course of introducing new convertible currencies, they will be forced to get rid of monetary excess and to establish truly functioning national markets. "Even partial convertibility is impossible without real domestic convertibility of money into goods, both in the industrial and in consumer goods sectors".[42]

Furthermore, introducing full convertibility entails that the tax, fiscal, and monetary systems, as well as the management of enterprises, will have to meet the conditions of an efficiently operating market economy. Consequently, successful transformation is needed. Also, there must be exportable goods, the step-by-step introduction of foreign trade liberalization and of the means with which to stabilize the national currency.

Only after successful implementation of independent and convertible currencies and the establishment of an effective exchange mechanism can a fresh attempt to create a CIS currency union be made. Then all members will participate in formulating a programme for the coordination of monetary and fiscal policies as well as for the synchronization of privatization and structural adjustment programmes. Creating a union of this kind on the basis of equal membership should ensure long-term stability. Experience acquired during the period of independence will induce all members to compromise and give priority to the economic rationale.

5. SUPPORT BY WESTERN COUNTRIES AND INTERNATIONAL INSTITUTIONS

Successful integration into the world economy and the creation of new foreign trade structures will depend primarily on the decisions and the implementation of Russian policy and on that of the CIS members. Western assistance can only serve as a catalyst in stabilizing and accelerating the process of transformation.

To achieve stabilization, it is necessary to make the investment needed for an improvement of development prospects. Such investment should be targeted at improving the infrastructure and the agricultural sector, and it should assist in the restructuring of the national economy. This, in turn, will facilitate supply and may curb price increases. Investment in energy and the exploitation of raw materials may serve the purpose of earning the necessary currency to finance restructuring and improvement of competitiveness. Moreover, it seems feasible that credits can be granted for technical assistance in order to narrow the technology gap.[43]

Modernizing the national economy of the former Soviet Union, however, does not only entail the granting of financial assistance. A general setting for integration into the world economy can be achieved by the liberalization of imports from CIS members. It has been widely recognized in the West that true integration into the world economy is more useful than mere assistance.[44] The principal opening up of Western markets is still to come. But of even greater importance is Western know-how. It is not enough for business in the CIS countries merely to wish to change; they must also know how to do so.[45] Training and retraining in business will be required, and also the entire educational system will have to be transformed. Curricula must be geared to coping with the operation of market economies and democratic and pluralistic societies. Transformation will be successful only if it starts from both above and below.

NOTES

1 The author has benefited from the helpful and stimulating comments of Hermann Fink.
2 See Bogomolov, 1992, p. 36.
3 See Havrylyshin and Williamson, 1991, p. 13.
4 The cost of exploiting energy and raw materials is estimated to be five to eight times higher in the Eastern regions than in the Western ones.
5 Investment decisions were at first determined by political considerations. Moreover, the evaluation of two equivalent alternatives of investment was biased by an irrational price system.
6 This refers especially to their existence in a market economy.
7 See Smith, 1993, p. 11.
8 See Faude, 1992, p. 80.
9 This methodology and the accuracy of its results are certainly debatable; nevertheless, the analysis helps to illustrate the trend in potential gains. The data are from Hamilton and Winters, 1992, p. 84ff.
10 Commissariat Général du Plan, 1993, p. 47.
11 Foreign trade with former Soviet republics has been excluded. Caution is required cencerning the validity of the most recent empirical data because the various official institutions publish conflicting data. Gutnik reports that statistical data are used as ammunition on the battlefield of domestic policy. See Gutnik, 1993, p. 232.
12 See *Ekonomika i zhizn'*, 1993, no. 4, p. 13ff.
13 *Business Central Europe*, Nov. 1993, p. 73.
14 See *Planecon*, 1993, no. 5/6, p. 36.
15 See Kossikowa, 1993, p. 11.
16 Commissariat Général du Plan, 1993, p. 49.
17 See Granberg, 1991, p. 3.
18 See Kossikova, 1993, p. 11ff.
19 See Kossikova, 1993, p. 14.
20 See *DIW Wochenbercht 1993*, p. 219.
21 See Tiraspolsky, 1994, p. 232.
22 See Institut für Wirtschaftsforschung Halle, 1993, p. 37.
23 See Orlowski, 1992, p. 16; Orlowski, 1993a, p. 15.
24 It was only in November 1991 that all Soviet enterprises were allowed to participate. See Sutela and Kero, 1993, p. 117.
25 The volume of barter trade increased in 1991 by more than 50%. See Sutela and Kero, 1993, p. 119.
26 Russian experts believe that part of this capital returns via joint ventures because of the high interest rate paid on dollar accounts (9-11%). It should be emphasized that this capital is financial capital not invested in the economy and only for short periods.
27 See *Deutsche Bank Research, 1992*, p. 47.
28 See 'A Bleeding Shame', 1993, p. 53ff.

29 See Panasenko, 1993, p. 7.
30 UN ECE, 1993, p. 14.
31 Orlowski, 1993b, p. 12.
32 Orlowski, 1993b, p. 8.
33 There was a general agreement on this move among Yeltsin, finance minister Fjodorov, the governor of the central bank and the other members of the government. Their views differed only on timing and method. The minister of finance was in favour of gradually changing the monetary system.
34 'Rouble Roulette', 1993.
35 This statement was made by the Kazakh president Nasarbajev: *Süddeutsche Zeitung*, 1993a.
36 'Rouble Roulette', 1993.
37 *Süddeutsche Zeitung*, 1993b. This conference, however, did not go into the details of coordinating fiscal and customs policies, nor did it tackle the issue of a payments union.
38 See Granville, 1993, p. 28.
39 Chazan, 1993.
40 This statement was made by Igor Bubnow, member of the special commission on currency of the Russian Central Bank: *Süddeutsche Zeitung*, 1993c.
41 Orlowski, 1993b, p. 26.
42 Dezséri, 1993, p.25.
43 The World Bank grants its credits for these purposes. See *Transition*, 1993, p. 1ff.
44 Höhmann and Meier, 1993.
45 Layard, 1993, p. 360.

BIBLIOGRAPHY

'A Bleeding Shame' (1993), *Business Central Europe,* October 1993, pp. 53-5.
Bogomolov, O. (1992), 'The Collapse of the Soviet Empire: An Avenue to European Civilization', in Keren, M., Ofer, G. (eds.), *Trials of Transition - Economic Reform in the Former Communist Bloc,* Boulder: Westview, 1992, pp. 27-37.
Chazan, G. (1993), 'The Prodigal CIS Sons Come Back to the Russian Folk', *The Moscow Tribune,* 22 September 1993.
'Country Indicators' (1993), *Business Central Europe,* November 1993, p. 73.
Commissariat Général du Plan, *La Transition en Europe,* Paris, 1993.
Dezséri, K. (1993), 'First Practical Steps in Introducing Convertibility in Eastern European Countries', *Working Paper,* no. 22, Institute for World Economics, Budapest.
'Die wirtschaftliche Lage Rußlands', *DIW Wochenbericht 1993,* no. 17, pp. 210-45.

Ekonomika i zizn' (1993), no. 4, pp. 13-15.

Faude, E. (1992), 'Außenwirtschaftsbeziehungen und marktwirtschaftliche Transformation in Osteuropa', in Institut für Internationale Bildung Berlin (ed.), *Marktwirtschaftliche Transformation in Osteuropa,* Berlin, pp. 79-105.

Granberg, A. (1991), 'Chozjajstvennye svjazi i ekonomiceskie interesy Rossii', *Delovoj Mir,* 18 October 1991, p. 3.

Granville, B. (1963), 'Price and Currency Reform in Russia and the CIS', *Russian and East European Finance and Trade,* spring 1993, pp. 3-67.

Gutnik, V., 'Rußlands Weg zur Marktwirtschaft: Konzepte und Resultate', *Osteuropa-Wirtschaft,* vol. 38, no. 3, pp. 230-39.

Hamilton, C., Winters, L. (1992), 'Opening up International Trade with Eastern Europe', *Economic Policy,* April 1992, pp. 77-116.

Havrylyshin, O., Williamson, J. (1991), *From Soviet Disunion to Eastern Economic Community?,* Institute for International Economics, vol. 35, Washington.

Höhmann, H.-H., Meier, C. (1993), 'Hilfsaktivitäten auf Sparflamme? Die Unterstützung für Rußland auf dem Tokioter G7-Gipfel', *Berichte des Bundesinstitutes for ostwissenschaftliche und internationale Studien,* no. 29, Cologne.

Institut für Wirtschaftsforschung Halle (1993), 'Die wirtschaftliche Lage Rußlands', *Forschungsreihe,* no. 7, Halle.

Kossikowa, L. (1993), 'Die Handelsbeziehungen Rußlands mit den ehemaligen Unionsrepubliken: Tendenzen und Probleme', *Berichte des Bundesinstituts für ostwissenschaftliche und internationale Studien,* no. 23, Cologne.

Layard, R., 'The Future of the Russian Reform', *The Economics of Transition,* 1, no. 3, pp. 357-62.

Orlowski, L. (1992), 'Direct Transfers betwen the Former Soviet Union Central Budget and the Republics: Past Evidence and Current Implications', *Kiel Working Paper,* no. 543, Kiel.

Orlowski, L. (1993a), 'Indirect Transfers in Trade Among Former Soviet Union Republics: Sources, Patterns and Policy Responses in the Post-Soviet Period', *Kiel Working Paper,* no. 556, Kiel.

Orlowski, L. (1993b), 'The Disintegration of the Ruble Zone: Driving Forces and Proposals for Policy Change', *Kiel Working Paper,* no. 585, Kiel.

Panasenko, S. (1993), 'The policy of the Ministry of Foreign Relations will not Change', *Moscow News,* 1993, no. 42, p. 7.

'Rouble Roulette', *Business Central Europe,* November 1993, p. 22.

Senik-Leygovnie, C., Hughes, G. (1993), 'Industrial Profitability and Trade among the Former Soviet Republics', *Economic Policy,* vol. 15, pp. 353-86.

Smith, A. (1993), *Russia and the World Economy,* London: Routledge.

Süddeutsche Zeitung (1993a), 'Der stille Tod in der Rubelzone', 9 December 1993.

Süddeutsche Zeitung (1993b), 'Einundzwanzig Dokumente, die wenig bedeuten', 28 December 1993.

Süddeutsche Zeitung (1993c), 'Für gemeinsame Rubel-Zone', 21 September

1993.

Sutela, P., Kero, J. (1993), 'Russian Trade Policies with the West: 1992 and Beyond', in P. Sutela (ed.), *The Russian Economy in Crisis and Transition*, Helsinki: Bank of Finland, pp. 111-41.

Tiraspolsky, A., 'La Russie entre transition et désorganisation', forthcoming in 1994.

Transition (1993), 'Lending to Russia: A New Challenge to the World Bank', vol. 4, no. 6, pp. 1-4.

UN ECE, *East-West Investment News*, 1993, no. 2, p. 14.

Divergent and Convergent Processes in Integrating Europe: Where Are the Balkans?

Rossitsa Rangelova

1. Introduction

Two powerful and inter-related processes are currently reshaping the world economy: regionalism and globalization. Regionalism can be interpreted as the promotion by a government of international economic linkages with states that are geographically proximate. Regionalism in the shape of formal regional trading arrangements began earlier and lasted longer in Europe than elsewhere.[1]

In the 1990s, Europe finds itself in a new political and economic environment. Negative trends have been caused mainly by global recession and the collapse of the East European economies. On the one hand, the slowdown of the world economy which began in 1989 strongly influenced the developed market economies in Europe and has made the present recovery much slower than previous upturns. The economic growth achieved in 1989 is not expected to be reached until 1994. Unemployment is generally on the increase. On the other hand, the political changes in Eastern Europe of 1989 oriented these countries towards market-type economies. However, the transformation process has proved extremely difficult and has been accompanied by steep declines in output and standards of living. Unemployment continues to increase.

The disintegration of the economic ties between the former CMEA member states has led to an unfavourable combination of negative consequences. Up to the end of the 1980s, about 50% on average of the foreign trade of these countries was represented by mutual trade.

Table 1 - The distribution of the population and the economically act
population in Europe (in percentages)

	Population		Economically active population	
	1990	2000	1990	2000
Europe	100.0	100.0	100.0	100.0
of which:				
Western Europe	31.0	30.4	31.0	29.8
Northern Europe	16.7	16.3	17.9	17.7
Southern Europe	29.2	29.8	25.5	25.9
Eastern Europe	23.1	23.5	25.6	26.6
Central East Europe	12.5	13.3	14.3	15.0
Balkan region*	24.9	27.4	24.3	26.7
of which:				
Albania	0.7	0.8	0.7	0.8
Bulgaria	1.6	1.9	1.9	1.9
Greece	2.0	2.0	1.7	1.7
Romania	4.8	5.0	5.1	5.3
Turkey	11.0	12.8	10.2	12.1
Former Yugoslavia**	4.8	4.9	4.7	4.9

Notes:

*   The figures for the Balkan region are not percentage shares but ratios to the
     total population and economically active population in Europe because
     Turkey is added and the other Balkan countries are presented in different
     groups: Bulgaria and Romania in Eastern Europe; Albania, Greece and
     former Yugoslavia in Southern Europe.
** Since disaggregated data on the former Yugoslavia are not yet available,
     only these can be given. In 1991 the population of Croatia was 4.8 million,
     and the labour force percentage of the population was 41.7. For Macedonia
     these figures are respectively 2.03 million and 31.1%; for Slovenia 2.01
     million and 46.1%.[2]

Western Europe includes: Austria, Belgium, France, Germany, Luxembourg,
   Netherlands, Switzerland; in Northern Europe: Denmark, Finland, Iceland,
   Ireland, Norway, Sweden, UK; Southern Europe: Albania, Greece, Italy,
   Malta, Portugal, Spain, former Yugoslavia;
Eastern Europe: Bulgaria, Hungary, the Czech Republic, Slovakia, former East
   Germany, Poland, Romania;
Central Eastern Europe: Hungary, the Czech Republic, Slovakia and Poland.

Source: International Labour Organisation, 1950-2025 Economically Active
   Population. Estimates and Projections, 3rd edition, Geneva, 1986.

Due to disintegration, all the negative phenomena of the transitional period are reinforcing the current economic crisis and are in many respects hindering the process of transition to the market economy.

In the current situation, the European Community is the continent's main integrating centre and aims to consolidate all the economic advantages of such processes for the different countries concerned. The outlook for the 1990s in Europe depends not only on economic but also on political and social changes. On the whole, a trend towards decentralization and wider participation by the population is tempered by concerns over political stability.

However, together with the deterioration of the economic conditions in East Europe, some of the old social values have faded and social problems have greatly increased. The demise of the old political system in these countries has also triggered ethnic and regional changes, which have led to integration in the West (the unification of the two parts of Germany) and disintegration in the East (Czechoslovakia for instance), and also to conflicts such as those in the former USSR and the former Yugoslavia that are currently causing such great human suffering and waste of scarce resources.

In principle, Europe has always been economically considered by international organizations and their respective statistical data to be divided into four regions: Western, Northern, Southern and Eastern. By population these regions are weighted in favour of Western and Southern Europe, whose populations are twice that of Northern Europe (Table 1).

The Balkans are located at the important geographical crossroads of Europe, Asia and Africa. The proportion of their population, including Turkey (of which only part is located on the Balkan peninsula, that is, in Europe) is nearly 25% or similar to that of Eastern Europe. The distribution of the Balkan countries by population is rather uneven: Turkey comprises almost half of the total population and the economically active population, followed by Romania with about one fifth, and then the other countries.

Under present conditions, different divergent and convergent processes are under way in Europe. How do the Balkans fit into this overall picture?

2. TRANSFORMING THE BALKAN COUNTRIES: THE MAIN FEATURES

In the past, political and ideological contradictions divided the Balkan countries because they belonged to different economic, military and political formations. As a result of democratization in Eastern Europe, the Balkans now face more favourable conditions for cooperation in all spheres of the economy and politics. Generally speaking, the present radical political and economic changes provide the basis for a new form of economic interaction: on the one hand among the Balkan countries themselves; on the other, between the Balkans and the rest of Europe.

Together with the historically inherited socio-cultural similarity of the Balkan countries, they are also homogeneous in economic and political features.

The resemblance of these countries concerning their economic backwardness confronts them with another challenge: the increasing disparity of economic level between them and Western Europe. In order to outline the economic 'distance' between Western Europe and the Balkans, the basic indicator for economic development, gross domestic product (GDP) can be used. In the early 1990s the ratio between average per-capita GDP for the countries of Western and Northern Europe and that for the Balkan countries was about 10:1; between the Southern European countries and the Balkan countries it was 5:1.[3]

In addition, Balkan cooperation must be created in parallel with the overall integration process in Europe. These countries' shared problems with respect to their affiliation with Europe could help to establish a common interest centred on regional cooperation.[4]

The Balkan countries can be divided into two basic groups. The first consists of the former centrally planned economies endeavouring to overcome the multi-dimensional crises and hardships of transition to a market economy. It is very difficult to give a general definition of the economic processes under way in these countries. I shall therefore deal with them individually in alphabetical order.[5]

Albania is the poorest country in Europe. After many years of total isolation from the world, the country's present economic situation is extremely tense. There is no other European country whose economy has been so severely affected by the crisis. Stagnation began in the early 1960s, in fact, but at the beginning of the 1990s total output fell by about 40% and industrial production dropped by 42% to the level of the year 1976, even though the population had increased by about 34% during the intervening fifteen years. In this situation, the decisive factor in Albania's transition to a market economy and any further economic progress is helped by the international community in the form of investments and technical assistance.

Bulgaria has made significant progress since it embarked on economic reforms (on 1 February 1991). Much has been achieved in the area of systemic reforms, and macroeconomic stabilization can be regarded as successful. The challenge now is to proceed with the implementation of structural reforms.

Bulgaria faces a particularly difficult situation. As a small country its development depends to a great extent on foreign trade. Close economic interaction in the past with the ex-CMEA and ex-Soviet market has contributed to a large fall in output and it is now necessary to look for other foreign trade partners. In addition, the strict enforcement of the UN resolution regarding the conflict in former Yugoslavia has provoked enormous losses, as well as changing the structure of Bulgaria's foreign trade. For example, in the first half of 1993, 45% of Bulgaria's total exports went to the OECD countries. Germany is the biggest purchaser of Bulgarian goods, followed by Turkey, Italy and Greece. Germany and Italy are the leading exporters to Bulgaria, although they have recently been joined by the UK, Greece and France. Except for Syria, the other Arab countries have lost ground in the Bulgarian market. Exports from Bulgaria to China doubled between January and June 1993.

Imports from the Balkan countries also increased, but the highest increase (13%) was from the ex-Soviet republics, which resumed their role as a primary supplier of raw materials and energy.[6]

The legacy of the 1980s in Romania must be examined in order to gain a true idea of the main processes involved in the transition to a market economy. Romania was in a sense a special case of central planning in the 1980s, and provided an example of shock therapy in balance of payments adjustment. The drastic compression of consumption and the extreme curtailment of hard currency imports of machinery and equipment severely damaged the growth capacity of the country's economy.

The process of transition to a market economy in Romania is currently proceeding at three speeds:

- 'urgent', in order to create the legal and institutional framework;
- 'limited', for trade liberalization within the restrictions imposed by the higher costs resulting from price liberalization;
- 'slow or hardly noticeable', for the privatization process.

In the past, Yugoslavia was regarded as an economic system that had avoided the worst problems associated with the centrally planned economy or capitalist system. In this respect the Yugoslav system was a unique experiment. Its essence was the combination of a market economy with 'social ownership' and the worker self-management of enterprises. It is worth stressing again the well-known feature of the ex-Yugoslav economy: the marked development disparities of its regions.

Since the early 1980s the Yugoslav economy has been in a crisis. In 1991 the military conflicts began to involve most of the ex-republics of the former Yugoslav Federation. The historical roots of the present crisis are of major importance for understanding the reasons for the disintegration of the former Yugoslavia: latent North-South conflicts based mainly on uneven economic levels of development, regional autarchy, economic nationalism, amongst others. The war has destroyed the normal economic relations among the former republics,[7] and the disintegration of the state has grave consequences for the newly created states.

Slovenia, with a population of about two million, was the most developed part of the former Yugoslavia and the biggest exporter. After the downturn in 1991, its economy entered a phase of radical restructuring. However, owing mainly to delays in adopting the legislation on privatization, changes in enterprise structure have only been partially followed by changes in ownership structure. For this reason, the role of the private sector in the national economy is still marginal. Slovenia's loss of the former Yugoslav market forces it to be active and innovative in strengthening its position in Western markets.

Croatia is both a Mid-European and a Mediterranean state with a population of about 4.8 million. After Slovenia's, Croatia's economy was the most developed and advanced in the former Yugoslavia. Since 1990, economic reforms have been under way but they have been hampered by the conflict in the former Yugoslavia. In the summer of 1991, Croatia estimated the damage caused by conflict at twice that suffered during World War II. Croatia is still heavily influenced by the post-war problems.

Croatia's most competitive and developed economic activities are: tourism, agriculture and food production, shipbuilding industry, transport, crude oil and petrochemicals, textiles, pharmaceuticals, machinery and equipment. About 90% of Croatia's economy is still not privately owned. Nearly 60% of its export markets are EC countries, and Italy and Germany are its major trading partners. The principal exports are machines, textiles, chemical products, crude oil, electrical engines, gas.

Macedonia, with a population of about two million, is situated in the southern part of former Yugoslavia. The strategy of this state is to develop an open market-oriented economy. The aim is to activate the latent potential of the state in order to increase the economy's efficiency.

At present, Macedonia's economy is severely affected by the following factors: the disintegration of the former Yugoslavia, the economic blockade imposed by the UN on the latter, as well as the pressure placed by the Greek government on Macedonia by blockading oil supplies.

The other group of countries consists of Greece and Turkey - that is, countries with market-type economies and among the less developed member states of the OECD.

The European integration of Greece as a full member of the EC has had positive effects on the modernization and dynamism of its economy. Greece is an example in the Balkans of the importance of association with the EC in 'opening up' the economy and participating in European economic structures. However, analysis of the performance of the Greek economy during the last decade reveals the problems that this cooperation raises for less developed countries. The figures in Table 2 indicate the widening 'gap' in GDP per capita between Greece and the other member states of the EC during the last decade.

In actual fact, during the 1980s disparities in per capita incomes in the EC increased slightly until 1986 and since then have remained at around the same level. Some of the weakest countries achieved rates of growth above the EC average level, which is the essential precondition for economic convergence. For instance, Spain, Ireland and Portugal showed a tendency towards very gradual convergence to EC average per capita GDP beginning in 1986-1987. At the same time, in Greece, this indicator continued to worsen in relation to that of the rest of the Community throughout the decade (Table 2).[8]

The level of disparities with respect to productivity in the EC member states has developed in a similar way to that of per capita GDP (Table 3). A slight tendency towards a reduction in disparities between the member states began in 1984 following improvements in relative productivity in Portugal and Ireland. However, this trend did not continue after 1987, because increases in economic growth were accompanied by a significant increase in employment. Greece did not share the positive growth in productivity since it has the lowest

GDP per person employed in the EC. This is a result of a relative decline in the rate of investment during the 1980s, in spite of the increasing efforts of the EC.

Table 2 - Gross Domestic Product at current market prices per head of population (PPS; EUR 12 = 100)

	1960	1970	1980	1990	1991	1992	1993
Belgium	97.5	101.1	106.4	104.9	105.9	106.1	106.2
Denmark	115.2	112.2	105.0	105.8	106.0	106.0	107.5
West Germany	124.3	118.6	119.1	117.6	119.4	118.7	116.4
Greece	34.8	46.4	52.3	47.5	47.4	47.4	47.8
Spain	58.3	72.2	71.7	75.4	76.4	76.7	77.2
France	107.7	112.7	113.9	111.0	110.7	111.5	111.9
Ireland	57.2	56.1	60.2	69.0	69.7	70.7	71.6
Italy	86.6	95.5	102.5	102.8	103.2	103.5	104.0
Luxembourg	155.3	138.4	115.6	127.2	128.1	129.1	129.8
Netherlands	116.8	114.1	109.2	102.4	103.0	102.9	102.6
Portugal	37.2	46.9	52.7	53.7	54.2	57.5	58.1
United Kingdom	122.6	103.5	96.4	100.5	97.1	95.3	96.2
Germany (Unified)	:	:	:	:	102.4	102.8	101.7
United States	182.5	158.4	146.0	139.0	134.5	134.9	136.7
Japan	54.1	88.8	96.5	112.7	116.3	116.9	118.1

Notes: Figures for 1992 and 1993 are estimates.

Symbols and abbreviations: PPS = purchasing power standard; EUR 12 = EC member countries, including West Germany; ':' = figures not available.

Source: *European Economy. Annual Economic Report for 1993*, p. 254.

In the past few years, there has been consensus in Greece that priority should be given to the correction of macroeconomic policy, and in particular to reform of the institutional setting and restructuring of the economy. These measures are regarded as the preconditions not only for greater economic growth but also for more rapid restoration of macroeconomic equilibrium.

However, economic performance in the last two years has been rather similar to that of 1991: both domestic and foreign demand has slowed down, business activity has weakened and unemployment has increased further. The main reasons for this situation are the following:[9]

— tight economic policy within the framework of a medium-term fiscal adjustment programme;
— the world economic slow-down;
— delays in structural reform.

*Table 3 - GDP per person employed in the member states of the EC, 1980-1990
(in PPS, EUR 12 = 100)*

Member state	1980	1985	1990
Belgium	110.9	108.8	110.4
Denmark	90.6	90.6	84.3
Germany	106.6	106.0	106.3
Greece	63.4	57.8	56.7
Spain	94.0	98.8	95.3
France	110.3	110.3	111.4
Ireland	75.4	82.6	87.1
Italy	104.9	100.8	102.7
Luxembourg	110.1	107.9	102.6
Netherlands	130.7	130.5	126.1
Portugal	52.9	52.1	59.3
United Kingdom	89.6	93.1	91.7
EUR 3*	60.3	58.4	61.7
EUR 9**	102.9	103.1	102.7
Disparity***	14.4	14.1	13.5

*   Ireland, Portugal and Greece.
** Others.
***Weighted standard deviations.

Source: *The Regions in the 1990s*. Fourth Periodic Report on the Social and
Economic Situation and Development of the Regions of the Community,
1991, pp. 20-2.

The implementation of fiscal adjustment was to a large extent left
incomplete and it was slower than the problems required. For these reasons the
national economy of Greece still faces major challenges.

Turkey could be perceived as one of the few examples of the successful
transition from an inwardly- to an outwardly-oriented economy in the non-
conducive conditions of the 1980s. However, this achievement was at a very
high social cost: decreasing real wages, increasing militarization, internal and
external debt; - that is, 'overheating' the economy. Generally speaking, Turkey
has encountered all the difficulties typical of countries undergoing very fast
development.[10]

The history of Turkey, mainly in recent decades, also shows us that a
traditional society can modernize under market conditions, although repeated
crises are inevitable. Parliamentary democracy can live together with
authoritarian control, as long as this does not upset the majority of the
population.

3. THE PROSPECTS FOR INTRA-BALKAN COOPERATION

In recent decades, economic relations among the Balkan countries have been conducted on a bilateral basis. Current economic trends are conducive to expansion of the bilateral foreign trade of these neighbouring countries. The share of exports and imports among most of them has increased, as we saw in the case of Bulgaria. However, one should bear in mind the extremely serious problem arising from the strict enforcement of UN Security Council Resolution 820 (the so-called 'Yugo-embargo') which brought a dramatic fall in foreign trade with Serbia and Montenegro in favour of other neighbouring countries (and not only these).

On the negative side of these more active bilateral trade relations one must report the invasion by businessmen from some countries. These entrepreneurs exploit the crisis and transition, lack of legislation, and the lack of control in the former centrally planned economies in order to conduct unfair competition. The Bulgarian domestic market has suffered from the uncontrolled invasion of mainly Turkish low-quality goods (legally or illegally imported). In addition, foreign traders have managed, in a period favourable to them, to buy premises for strategically located shops. At the same time, the reverse importing of these kinds of goods is banned. It is unreasonable for Bulgaria, as a country with large productive potential and a high rate of unemployment, to have overstocked markets of imported goods. In other words, these imports entail the exporting of national income.

In 1987 Turkey applied for full membership of the European Community. In 1990 the EC Commission took the position that it was not appropriate to open negotiations with Turkey at that time in view of the economic and political situation of the country. In practice, this meant that Turkey's candidacy had been rejected; in formal terms, it meant that the application would not be processed for the time being. In the meantime, the country must resolve numerous economic, social and institutional problems.[11]

In the present situation, Turkey has expressed its willingness to be an active, leading integrating partner in the Balkans. The disappearance of the Soviet bloc has raised Turkey's hopes of regaining its status as a regional power, and of playing an important role in the restructuring of the newly-established independent states in the Caucasus, Central Asia and the Balkans.

In February 1992 Ankara launched an agreement for cooperation among the countries with an outlet on the Black Sea: Turkey and nine former socialist countries, including Bulgaria, Romania, Moldova, the Ukraine, as well as other countries without such an outlet, Armenia and Azerbaijan, plus Albania and Georgia.

In June 1992, in Istanbul, representatives of the state power of eleven countries signed a declaration for Black Sea economic cooperation, the aim of which is to promote the free inflow of goods, capital, labour force, services and finance in the Black Sea region. The signatory countries were: Albania, Azerbaijan, Armenia, Bulgaria, Georgia, Greece, Moldova, Romania, Russia,

Turkey and the Ukraine, representing a population of about 260 million.[12]

The idea of Black Sea economic cooperation in its essential form is very positive. In general its implementation requires the development of neighbourly relations among the countries involved, and the activation of economic and human capital for the advancement of the people living in the region. However, the proper spheres and nature of cooperation should be defined from the outset, because, bearing in mind that this economic region consists of underdeveloped and transforming countries, many questions arise over their economic strength and competitiveness. Moreover, some of these countries are not yet politically stable, to say nothing of the military conflicts currently in progress in the area.

Apparently, mainly because of these problems, as well as the present underdeveloped infrastructure of the region, the basic intentions of cooperating are addressed to this sector. The founders hope that 'Black seaside cooperation' will lead to the region's further adjustment to European standards. Thus the current trends towards the gradual orientation of the region to the European economic space will be developed on a multilateral basis (the region as a whole).

4. THE EC IN THE DRIVING SEAT OF ECONOMIC INTEGRATION

The EC is the main institution promoting processes of economic integration in Europe. What is the economic development of its member countries? Which pattern should the Balkan countries consider? Which pattern could they be commensurate with? The EC has well-organized statistics which enable us to search for answers to these questions (see Tables 2 to 6).[13]

Considering the long period from 1960 to 1993, one notes immediately that the common turning-point in these countries' economic development came around the beginning of the 1980s. According to the data on the basic indicator of the level of economic development, per capita GDP (Table 2), we can divide all countries observed into three groups: the first consisting of countries with higher development than the average EC level (West Germany, France, Belgium, Netherlands); the second consisting of countries with about the same level of development as the EC as a whole (Italy, the Netherlands, the UK, Luxembourg); and the third including the less developed countries (Portugal, Denmark, Ireland, Spain), all of which with improving positions over time, and Greece which is the least developed state among the EC member countries, with marked economic stagnation in the last years.

The distribution of the EC member states by private consumption per capita is similar to the previous distribution by per capita GDP (Table 4). One notes the worsening positions of Denmark, the UK, Luxembourg, the Netherlands, West Germany, Ireland, and the improving positions of Italy, Portugal, Spain, France, Greece. Belgium maintains a steady position throughout the period under consideration. Naturally, private consumption should not be considered in isolation but in the context of the specificities of each country as well as of the national economic policy pursued.

Table 4 - Private consumption at current prices per head of population (PPS;
   EUR 12 = 100)

	1960	1970	1980	1990	1991	1992	1993
Belgium	108.3	101.1	109.0	106.3	107.8	107.6	108.4
Denmark	114.6	107.5	95.5	89.9	90.3	90.2	91.1
West Germany	118.6	115.6	122.3	116.4	117.5	115.5	113.2
Greece	44.8	53.7	55.0	55.2	54.0	54.1	54.5
Spain	63.1	77.3	76.3	76.6	77.5	78.8	79.5
France	103.3	109.0	109.2	108.6	108.5	108.7	108.7
Ireland	70.3	64.5	64.5	62.9	63.2	64.0	64.3
Italy	83.0	95.0	101.9	103.4	104.1	105.1	105.7
Luxembourg	134.7	116.8	110.5	114.8	119.1	122.4	123.3
Netherlands	108.7	110.4	107.7	97.8	99.4	99.7	98.9
Portugal	43.6	51.7	57.8	55.2	55.7	58.1	59.0
United Kingdom	129.8	106.7	94.3	103.9	100.8	99.9	101.0
Germany (unified)	:	:	:	:	98.2	98.4	98.4
United States	186.8	166.2	149.9	150.5	146.5	147.5	148.5
Japan	50.9	77.5	92.4	105.3	107.2	108.7	110.4

Notes: The figures for 1992 and 1993 are estimates.

Symbols and abbreviations: PPS = purchasing power standard; EUR 12 = EC
   member countries, including West Germany; ':' = figures not available.

Source: *European Economy. Annual Economic Report for 1993*, p. 197.

The data on foreign trade give an idea of the extent to which countries'
economies are open (Table 5 and Table 6). Luxembourg is striking in this
respect, although it can hardly be considered a typical economy. The total
foreign trade balance of the EC has been positive, with the main contribution
being made by West Germany, followed by the Netherlands, Ireland, Denmark,
Belgium. During the period considered, Greece's exports and imports increased
more than twofold. However, its foreign trade balance changed from being
active in the first two decades into passive, and it is still passive at the present
time. Another state in a similar position is Portugal. Of the three less developed
countries, the only one with an active foreign trade balance is Ireland.

In the past few years, there has been consensus in Greece that priority
should be given to the correction of macroeconomic policy, and in particular to
reform of the institutional setting and restructuring of the economy. These
measures are regarded as the preconditions not only for greater economic
growth but also for more rapid restoration of macroeconomic equilibrium.

As regards another basic economic datum, unemployment, it should be
noted that after improving indicators in the EC member countries in the period
1986-1990, they worsened again at the beginning of the 1990s.[14]

The above broad outline of economic performance is intended to give a general view of the EC member countries. Among them there are highly developed countries which play a central, leading role in the Community; there are small countries with relatively successful and stable development; and then there are countries of peripheral importance.

Table 5 - Imports of goods and services at current prices, percentage of GDP at market prices

	1960	1961-1970	1971-1980	1981-1990	1991	1992	1993
Belgium	40.8	46.1	57.4	71.3	69.6	66.4	66.4
Denmark	33.4	30.4	31.4	33.0	30.3	29.1	29.4
West Germany	16.5	17.3	22.0	26.5	27.7	26.5	26.8
Greece	16.7	18.3	24.3	30.6	33.1	32.5	34.2
Spain	7.2	12.4	15.9	20.2	20.4	20.5	21.4
France	12.4	13.1	19.0	22.4	22.3	21.3	21.6
Ireland	37.3	42.5	53.6	55.8	52.9	51.5	51.5
Italy	13.5	14.2	21.2	21.5	19.4	19.3	20.6
Luxembourg	73.7	75.8	83.4	96.4	100.0	98.7	97.0
Netherlands	43.6	41.7	44.8	50.7	48.9	47.7	48.0
Portugal	23.7	28.7	34.9	43.6	41.3	37.9	38.3
United Kingdom	22.3	20.9	26.9	26.5	24.6	25.3	28.2
Germany (unified)	:	:	:	:	25.6	23.8	23.7
EUR12 (ECU)	19.0	19.2	24.9	27.7	26.9	26.3	27.4
United States	4.4	4.7	8.3	10.7	11.0	11.3	11.3
Japan	10.2	9.5	11.5	10.5	8.5	7.6	7.5

Notes: The figures for 1992 and 1993 are estimates.

Symbols and abbreviations: EUR 12 means EC member countries, including West Germany; ':' = figures not available.

Source: *European Economy. Annual Economic Report for 1993*, p. 220.

In the present economic situation, the pace of EC integration is being accelerated, and this has again sparked debate between the supporters and opponents of EC integration. The pro-Market lobby makes great play of the advantages to be gained from taking an active part in the EC. The anti-Market lobby claims that countries can develop their economies much more self-dependently. As good European examples the opponents cite Sweden, Norway, Switzerland and Austria. They estimate the role of the EC as exaggerated, and some of them even assess the integration process as only creating bottlenecks.[15]

The differing economic positions of the individual countries presented above generate different attitudes towards EC agreements. The most recent arguments concern the Maastricht Treaties, in particular the Economic Exchange-Rate Mechanism (ERM), and they delay the process of integration.

The governing circles of the EC have declared it possible for some member states to undertake independent initiatives. This permission mostly concerns the UK, which has attached conditions to its underwriting of the Maastricht Treaties. Official circles in France and Germany have already started to discuss the formation of a central body within the EC, initially consisting of five countries: Germany, France, Belgium, the Netherlands and Luxembourg; that is, the countries that are able to adhere strictly to the integration terms laid down by the Maastricht Treaties. These states fulfil all twelve criteria for realization of currency union: low inflation, small account deficit, active foreign trade balance, and so on. Other countries, like Spain, Portugal, Ireland, Italy and Greece, are viewed as 'undisciplined' and are urged to make efforts to catch up with their partners.[16]

Table 6 - Exports of goods and services at current prices, percentage of GDP at market prices

	1960	1961-1970	1971-1980	1981-1990	1991	1992	1993
Belgium	39.9	46.1	57.8	73.4	72.5	69.5	69.4
Denmark	32.2	28.6	29.2	34.8	36.4	36.6	36.5
West Germany	19.0	19.3	24.2	30.3	34.1	33.6	33.8
Greece	9.1	9.8	16.0	21.7	22.6	23.7	25.2
Spain	9.9	10.5	14.2	19.5	17.3	17.5	18.5
France	14.5	13.5	19.4	22.4	22.6	22.6	22.9
Ireland	31.8	35.7	43.9	57.1	61.7	63.0	63.1
Italy	13.0	14.6	20.8	21.4	19.5	19.5	21.0
Luxembourg	86.7	81.3	89.4	97.2	94.3	90.8	88.8
Netherlands	45.0	40.8	46.0	54.6	54.1	53.0	53.6
Portugal	17.5	23.5	23.7	33.5	31.6	28.9	27.9
United Kingdom	20.9	20.5	26.5	26.0	23.7	23.7	26.1
Germany (unified)	:	:	:	:	25.4	23.9	23.7
EUR12 (ECU)	19.6	19.4	25.2	28.6	28.4	28.3	29.4
United States	5.2	5.3	8.0	8.6	10.5	10.7	10.9
Japan	10.7	9.9	12.2	12.6	10.3	10.3	10.1

Notes: Figures for 1992 and 1993 are estimates.

Symbols and abbreviations: EUR 12 means EC member countries, including West Germany; ':' = figures not available.

Source: *European Economy. Annual Economic Report for 1993*, p. 216.

This means, in fact, that the twelve member states are proceeding with integration at different speeds. In the current complicated international economic situation this process could be defined as converging by diverging.

The EC is a challenge to the Balkan countries in their efforts to achieve faster economic growth in order to reduce the significant disparities with the developed European countries. This is an extremely difficult task, bearing in mind the scale of the disparities as well as the present economic and political situation in the Balkan region, the low self-confidence of the Balkan countries as latecomers to EC integration, and their weaker positions compared with Central European economies in transition. However, for these countries integration into the European market is more than a challenge; it is also a stimulus to adopt the economic trends of today.

5. EUROPE AND THE BALKANS: THE SHORT-TERM OUTLOOK

According to forecasts by the UN Organisation, the growth of world output is not expected to reach the rate of 1989 - that is, the first year of the slow-down until 1994. The developed market economies as a whole are expected to develop at about the same rate in 1993 as in 1992. The trend of Germany's economy will continue to set the pace of growth for the other EC countries, in particular those remaining in the ERM. The social cost of economic stagnation, i.e. the rate of unemployment in the EC countries, is expected to reach 10.5% in 1993 and to remain at the same level in 1994.

For the Central and East European countries, the very nature of their transition to market-type economies makes predictions of their short-term output trend much more difficult than for the other groups of countries. In some of the Central and East European countries, where the reforms began earlier, a certain degree of macroeconomic stabilization has been achieved as well as some progress towards privatization and trade with Western Europe.

In Bulgaria and Romania a continuing and steep fall in output is expected.

For 1994 the UNO predicts that the growth rate will become positive for all the countries in transition, with further shrinkage only in Bulgaria and Slovakia. In most of these countries, however, unemployment is expected to increase in the short term.[17]

The outlook for the 1990s depends not only on economic but also on political and social progress. Economic and social conditions are deteriorating in many countries, but positive trends have emerged in recent years. Reduced international political tensions are expected to accelerate international trade and promote investment. The improved political environment should also facilitate economic coordination at the global and regional level.

According to another forecast by the UNO, economic growth in Eastern Europe and the ex-USSR will increase in the 1990s to 3.6%. This improvement is due mainly to the reallocation of military-related and heavy industry investment to consumer-oriented sectors.[18]

Integrating Europe faces a number of challenges in the future, as well as risks and opportunities. Among the initiatives taken by the European Council to revive economic activity (December 1992), there are actions 'which would boost confidence and promote economic recovery'. More specifically, member countries have been invited to take coordinated action in three main areas:

(i)   exploiting the budgetary area to implement measures to encourage private investment and switch public expenditure towards infrastructure and other growth-supporting priorities;
(ii)   strengthening structural adjustment efforts, measures to enhance competition and market flexibility;
(iii) promoting wage moderation with particular regard to the public sector, given the important demonstrative role it plays and the positive effects on budgetary consolidation.

The economic policy priorities for the medium term are defined as 'generat(ing) greater efficiency in the use of its resources and shift(ing) more of these resources into productive investment so as to improve its industrial base and its competitiveness'. In the long term the structural adjustment efforts must forge ahead.[19] Another important task for the EC is to update the existing convergence programmes taking into account the complicated economic situation both internally to the EC and externally.

The Balkan countries where transition to market type economies is under way - i.e. Albania, Bulgaria, Croatia, Macedonia, Romania, Slovenia - face three main tasks:

(i)   in the short term; stabilizing the economy and economic policy;
(ii)   in the medium term; initiating economic growth;
(iii) in the long term; attaining sustained growth.

In more or less all the Central and Eastern European countries in transition, economic reforms are being carried out according to the traditional IMF model. However, in the view of some analysts the experiences of the past three years and expectations for the next two years are not convincing enough evidence that this is the best way to achieve transition from a centrally planned to a market economy.[20] There are various transitional paths to a market economy; some of them are less painful, some lead to faster recovery, and so on.

IMF analysts have predicted a gradual halt in the East European economic growth slow-down in 1992 and further annual growth of GDP rates for Bulgaria: 0.6% in 1993, 0.8% in 1994 and 3.0% in 1995; Romania: -3.9% in 1993, 2.6% in 1994 and 4.2% in 1995. These trends are very optimistic, but even on a basis of higher rates of growth, calculated GDP per capita indicates the widening gap between the two countries and the developed European countries.[21]

In the light of European integration development, West Europe is expected to provide support for the less developed Balkan region. A widely-shared point of view is that successful consolidation between West Europe and the Balkans requires the involvement of Western capital and assistance from the developed world. This point of view is connected with EC trade policy.

What is the situation in the case of Bulgaria? The macroeconomic restrictive policy imposed by the IMF and the World Bank resulted in a sharp decline in internal demand: consumer, investment and public expenditure. This caused a collapse of economic activity, which can only be stimulated by activating exports.

Given the current economic and political situation in the Balkans, this means that West Europe must allow Bulgaria more free access to its market in compliance with the principles of free trade. However, according to OECD data, the imports share of Western Europe from East Europe and the ex-USSR in its total imports decreased from 4.5% in 1989 to 3.6% in 1992; for the EC these indicators were respectively 4.4% in 1989 and 3.4% in 1992. At the same time exports from West to East increased. Consequently, in a sense, the East helps the West to ensure markets for its goods and services, as well as providing employment for the labour force in the developed countries, to a greater extent than the West does this for the East. This creates additional disequilibrium in the less developed countries of Europe and could have a negative impact on the stability of the Western countries in the medium term[22].

The Balkan countries do not pose a serious threat to EC producers of manufacturing products because of the low price competitiveness of their products. However, the EC carefully protects the interests of its competitive producers, for example those of agricultural products, metals, textiles, whereas it requires the East, in particular Bulgaria, to open its market.[23] The concept of integration implies joint action and requires common effort by both the advanced economies in Europe and the economically weaker Balkan countries in order to approach a unified economic arrangement.

NOTES

1 See Naidenova, Rangelova and Raynova, 1984.

2 See *Emerging Market Economies Report 1993*.

3 The calculations are based on data in *World Tables* 1993.

4 See International Round Table, 1991/92.

5 For detailed data on all these countries see *Emerging Market Economies Report 1993*.

6 For an overview of Bulgaria's economic performance see Bulgarian National Bank, 1992 and 1993.

7 See Cviic, 1991, p. 113.

8 For the period until 1991, the aggregates are defined for member countries as in the ESA (European system of economic accounts), and for the USA and Japan as in the SNA (UN-OECD system of national accounts). Unless otherwise specified, the sources of the data are Eurostat for the EC member countries and OECD for the USA and Japan. Figures for 1992 and 1993 are estimates and forecasts made by Commission staff using the definitions and latest figures available from

national sources. Until 1990 the data for Germany refer to West
Germany, from 1991 onwards data for both unified (D) and West
Germany (WD) are available. PPS stands for purchasing power standard,
and it is calculated by Eurostat methodology. See *European Economy.
Annual Economic Report for 1993*, p. 179.

9 See *European Economy. Annual Economic Report for 1993,* pp. 54-56.

10 See *The Quarterly Economic Information Report. The Turkish Economy
in the Second Quarter of 1993*; 'Turouie: un role de developpement', 1992,
pp. 26-30; Avdasheva, 1992; Yosoldash, 1993.

11 See Hoenekopp, 1993; Josoldash, 1993; Avdasheva, 1992.

12 See 'Turquie: une role de developpement', 1992, pp. 26-30; Radeva, 1992;
Valitova and Vardomskii, 1992.

13 The data for the USA and Japan are included for the purposes of
comparison with the other most developed countries not in the EC.

14 See *European Economy. Annual Economic Report for 1993*, pp. 3-30.

15 See Tether, 1979.

16 See *Duma* (newspaper), 27th July 1993, Sofia; Houbenova-Deliscvkova,
1993.

17 See *World Economic Survey 1993*, pp. 7-34.

18 *Global Outlook 2000*, pp. 43-74.

19 *European Economy. Annual Economic Report for 1993*, pp. 20-21.

20 See *The Bulgarian Economy up to 1995*, 1992.

21 See Rangelova and Raynova, 1990. According to some comprehensive
studies of the world economy, in the future the widening technology gap
between the developed and developing countries may threaten North-
South economic relations much more than disparities in income levels:
see *Global Outlook 1990*, p. 5.

22 See Angelov, 1993; Houbenova-Delisivkova, 1993.

23 *The World Competitiveness Report 1993* and *Emerging Market Economies
Report 1993*.

BIBLIOGRAPHY

Angelov, I. (1993), 'Without Western Import Restraints the East Would Not
Run into Debts', *24 hours* (newspaper), 4 May 1993.

Avdasheva, S. (1992), 'Turkey: National Model of Economic Liberalisation',
Voprosy Ekonomiki, 11 November 1992, pp. 39-41.

Bulgarian National Bank (1992), *Annual Report 1992,* Sofia.

Bulgarian National Bank (1993), *Annual Report 1993*, Sofia.

Cviic, C. (1991), *Remaking the Balkans*, London: Pinter Publishers.

Emerging Market Economies Report 1993, The World Competitiveness Series,
IMD, The World Economic Forum. Lausanne-Geneva, March 1993.

*Global Outlook 2000. An Economic, Social, and Environmental Perspective by
The United Nations*, New York, Geneva: UN Publications, 1990.

Hoenekopp, E. (1993), 'The Effects of Turkish Accession to the EC on Population and Labour Market', *Inter-economics*, vol. 28, no. 2, March/April 1993, pp. 69-73.

Houbenova-Delisivkova, T. (1993), 'The Association of Bulgaria to the European Communities: Problems and Perspectives', *Ikonomicheska misul*, no. 1, pp. 3-16.

International Round Table on 'Market Economies in the Balkan Countries: Problems of Functioning and Mutual Co-operation; papers published in the journal *Economic Thought 91/92*, Sofia.

Josoldash, S. (1993), 'The Relations between the EC and Turkey and some Conclusions and Prognosis for the Bulgarian Association with the EC', *Ikonomicheska misul*, no. 1, pp. 3-16.

Naidenova, P., Rangelova, R., Raynova, M. (1984), 'Problems and Perspectives of the Global Economic Growth', *Ikonomicheska misul*, no. 2.

National Statistical Institute (1993), *Current Economic Business*, 1993, Sofia.

Radeva, J. (1992), 'Bulgaria's Stand on the Black Seaside Economic Co-operation', *Mejdunarodni otnoshenia*, no. 8, pp. 35-8.

Rangelova, R., Mihaylova, Z. (1989), *The CMEA Countries until the End of the Century (Economic Growth and Interaction)*, Sofia: 'Nauka i izkustvo'.

Rangelova, R., Raynova, M. (1990), 'Comparability of the Gross Domestic Product in International Comparisons', *Economic Thought '90*, pp. 42-56.

Tether, C.G. (1979), *The Great Common Market Fraud*, Published by Pentacle Books for the Safeguard Britain Campaign.

European Economy, Annual Economic Report for 1993, Commission of the European Communities, Directorate-General for Economic and Financial Affairs, No. 54, 1993.

The Bulgarian Economy up to 1995, Institute of Economics, Bulgarian Academy of Sciences, Sofia, September 1992.

The Quarterly Economic Information Report. The Turkish Economy in the Second Quarter of 1993, The Central Bank of the Republic of Turkey.

The Regions in the 1990s. Fourth Periodic Report on the Social and Economic Situation and Development of the Regions of the Community, Commission of the European Communities, Directorate-General for Regional Policy, Brussels-Luxembourg, 1991.

The World Competitiveness Report 1993, IMD, The World Economic Forum, Lausanne-Geneva, May 1993.

'Turquie: un role de developpement dans une region troublée', *Problemes économiques*, no. 2305, 1992, pp. 26-30.

Valitova, T., Vardomskii, L. (1992), 'On the Black Seaside Integration', *Vneshnjaja torgovlja*, no. 1, pp. 39-41.

World Economic Survey 1993. Current Trends and Policies in the World Economy, New York: United Nations, 1993.

World Tables 1993, A World Bank Book published for The World Bank, Baltimore and London: The Johns Hopkins University Press, May 1993.

Wage Hikes, Unemployment and Deindustrialization: on Peculiarities in Eastern Germany's Transition

Peter Kalmbach

1. Introduction

There can be little doubt that the transition of the East German economy into a market economy is peculiar and that it cannot be compared with the transformation of the East European countries. East Europeans commonly argue that the former GDR has been in an enviable position: in contrast to their own countries, the 'surgery of stabilisation'[1] was not necessary because a currency was available from the beginning which was not only convertible, but more importantly it had a reputation of stability. Contrary to their own countries' conditions, it was possible to establish legal and economic institutions which had already proven to be successful in promoting economic growth and development. Last, but not least, East Germany can reckon upon a rich uncle, the former FRG, who provides the funding necessary to relieve the hardships of transformation.

The economic development of the former GDR after the German Economic, Monetary, and Social Union (EMSU) which took effect in July 1990 and the German unification on 3 October 1990 requires the question if East Germany's advantages have not been overestimated. Furthermore, we need to ask if the disadvantages characteristic of the former GDR's transition will not prove to become an obstacle to economic development.

As is well-known, a dramatic and unprecedented decline in production - particularly in industrial production - took place immediately after the currency union was established:[2] in July 1990 industrial production had already dropped to about 60% of its pre-unification level and at the end of the year it had been halved (Figure 1). Even during the Great Depression neither Germany nor the United States had experienced such a fast decline.[3]

Figure 1 East German manufacturing industry index of net production seasonally adjusted (2nd half 1990 = 100)

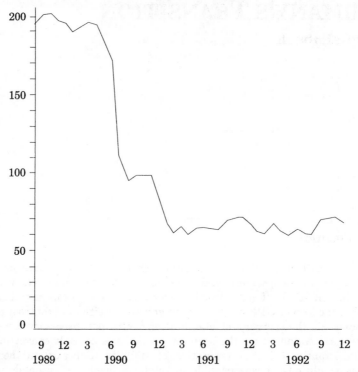

Source: Statistisches Bundesamt, DIW computation and estimation (DIW 1992).

Compared to the tremendous decline in real production the official figures for unemployment where relatively low in the early months after the EMSU although the rate of growth of unemployment was considerable. The main reason explaining this development have been the various programmes which were introduced and which have kept the number of openly unemployed considerably below the total reduction of the pre-unification labour force. Continued migration, an increasing number of commuters and a substantial number of people (predominantly women) who left the labour force, have been additional factors.

Table 1 - Employment and Unemployment in East Germany (Numbers in thousands)

	1990				1991				1992			
	1	2	3	4	1	2	3	4	1	2	3	4
Total employment (including work programmes)	9568	9130	8672	8102	7773	7311	6907	6726	6485	6411	6312	6297
Employment in industry	4266	4097	3965	3649	3443	3181	2785	2584	2362	2312	2238	2225
Unemployed persons (registered)	13	83	309	565	757	835	1022	1038	1254	1172	1158	1097
Short time workers					1926	1962	1464	1113	511	440	292	275
Work programmes	0	0	0	12	41	101	234	357	396	404	386	366
Education (full time only)	0	0	20	35	105	170	245	305	355	390	385	385
Early retired	45	235	270	305	316	375	359	328	324	305	285	245
Migrants (members of labour force)	129	166	221	299	352	384	416	448	480	512	544	576
Commuters (on balance)	14	28	101	175	222	278	308	352	343	351	353	351
Open and hidden unemployment (sum of 3 - 7; short-time workers multiplied by estimated labour hours)				1720	2321	2715	2893	2977	3069	2982	2918	2823

Sources: Sachverständigenrat, 1991, 1992; DIW, 1992a, 1992c, 1993c.

Hence, the decline of the labour force, especially in manufacturing, is a more adequate measure for the decline in employment than the development of the official unemployment (Table 1). In particular, the decline of industrial production and employment comes close to a process of rapid deindustrialization in the new *Bundesländer*.

For economic theoreticians one of the most astonishing facts regarding the German unification process are wage-hikes which took place despite rising unemployment. To name only two representatives of a long tradition of economists who argued that a deterioration in production and employment will be accompanied by declining real wage rates: Marx[4] and Goodwin.[5] One of the puzzling facts of the unification process is that exactly the opposite happened. In the following I will try to give a description and some explanations for a development which in the light of traditional views may be christened 'the east German wage paradox'.

2. SETTING THE STAGE: SOME REMARKS ON THE DEVELOPMENTS PRIOR TO THE EMSU

In order to understand what happened in Germany we should remember three important events: the fall of the Wall on 9 November, 1989, the effectiveness of the EMSU on 1 July, 1990 and the German unification on 3 October, 1990. From an economic perspective the latter is least important, for major economic decisions had been anticipated by the EMSU. This has been well-understood by the majority of analysts, however, there are disagreements as far as the importance of the first date is concerned. What happened after 1 July, 1990 cannot be separated from the pre-unification developments which can be understood by the historic event of the fall of the Wall.

The main reason to erect the Wall in 1961 had been the economic superiority of West Germany and the resulting incentives for East Germans to migrate to the west. The developments on both sides of the Wall between 1961 and 1989 have not weakened but rather strengthened economic motives for migration. Hence, after the Wall came down the GDR had to face exactly the same problem which it once had tried to solve by building the Wall. As soon as the artificial segmentation of labour markets had been abolished, the economic perspectives for the GDR became gloomy. A standard of living comparable to West Germany's was not compatible with existing levels of productivity: a much lower standard of living in combination with high uncertainty about future developments would have stimulated migration - particularly of trained labour who could expect to get a job in West Germany. In light of this scenario, the GDR's government could not refuse West Germany's offer to negotiate an EMSU, especially considering the slogans on the banners of the ongoing demonstrations: *'Wenn die DM nicht zu uns kommt, kommen wir zur DM'* (i.e. East Germans demanded the introduction of the DM by threatening to migrate).

However, it was well-understood that the promise to introduce the DM was a necessary but not a sufficient measure to change the expectations of East Germans and thereby to reduce migration. The concrete conditions of the union and its prospects with regard to the development of East Germany were of equal importance. The fight over the conditions evolved predominantly around the conversion rate. While in the new *Länder* it was claimed unanimously that the conversion rate had to be 1:1 ('One people, 1:1'), West Germans warned to adopt this rate which they thought to be too generous. On the one hand, they were afraid of an inflationary push. On the other hand, the opponents predicted that a 1:1 conversion rate would inevitably result in most eastern firms facing a hopeless competitive situation due to the existing productivity and quality gap between the two economies.

Finally, it was decided that stock variables in general were converted by 2:1 (except for saving deposits which could be converted 1:1 up to a certain amount depending on the age of the person involved), and flow variables, especially wages and salaries, were converted at a rate of 1:1. Trusting the data of the Federal Statistical Office which should still be taken with caution, this was equivalent to an average gross wage of a fully employed East German of approximately one third of the western level immediately after the EMSU.

The fear of an accelerating inflation has proven to be insubstantial. West Germany's often criticized policy to run a huge surplus in the current account was very beneficial in this historical situation because the surplus reduction in 1990 which turned into a deficit in 1991 and 1992 facilitated an adaptation of supply to the increased demand which otherwise would not have been possible. The expectation, on the other hand, that the majority of East German firms would not be able to handle the new situation is being confirmed. Indeed, a worsening of the situation is expected and it might turn out to be more disastrous than even pessimists have anticipated.[6]

At the same time the remaining wage gap was substantial and posed a major problem for the unified economic region. No practitioner could assume that the problem of migration which to prevent was the main objective of the EMSU could be solved facing the wage gap. In order to stop an unhindered migration from east to west it was necessary to convince East Germans to stay, notwithstanding the existing difference in wages.

West Germany's chancellor had already promised during the election campaign for the first freely elected parliament that 'nobody will be worse off and many will be better off' after the EMSU. Economists have appropriately characterized it as a Paretian promise.[7] East Germans were probably more impressed by the additional promise that within a three or four year period the still existing differences in income levels between the western and the eastern parts of Germany will have disappeared. At the same time the citizens of the old *Länder* were assured that unification would be possible without any loss for them.

These promises served their short-run purposes very well. The eastern Christian Democrats, junior partner of the chancellor's party, achieved an overwhelming victory in the March 1990 election. And in January 1991, when the first election of the united Germany was held, the Christian Democrats were again successful. However, these campaign promises have strong socio-economic implications:

- Due to the existing wage gap between east and west, the promise of a rapid catching-up lead inevitably to wage-hikes the following years. Assuming e.g. that the wage rate increases at an annual rate of 6% in West Germany, a full catching-up within a four-year period requires an annual increase of eastern wages at a rate of 49% starting from a 33.7% ratio in July 1990. Nobody could presume that productivity growth rates would be of a similar order.[8]
- The situation of eastern firms which was already difficult immediately after the introduction of the EMSU had to become even more severe with rising unit labour costs which contribute directly and indirectly to rising unemployment. They contribute directly, because with declining production and eroding producer prices increasing unit labour costs require lay-offs. The indirect effect is that loss-making firms are not able to restructure their capacities and improve the quality of their products and this way they sooner or later have to close down.
- With increasing unemployment the problem of a high migration rate would again be on the agenda. According to labour market research, unemployment is a stronger incentive for migration than wage rate differentials. Hence, when high wage increases are at least partially responsible for higher rates of unemployment they can hardly be defended on the grounds that they are necessary to prevent migration.
- Rising unemployment - open or hidden - requires considerable transfer payments provided by the Federal Budget. This was the consequence of the Social Union which basically established the extension of the social security system to East Germany. In addition to these transfers for consumption, the rotten state of the capital stock in the new *Länder* also required huge amounts of transfers which can only be realized by way of substantial tax increases. Hence, it could have been anticipated that the campaign promise of no tax increases in the former West Germany could not be kept.
- Finally, the unrealistic expectations which already existed about the economic effects of the introduction of 'Mark and market' were reinforced by the promises. Nobody told East Germans that historical experiences with catching-up processes are different. As Barro and Sala-i-Martin[9] have shown, indeed convergence in productivity did often take place, but normally it has been very slow. Applying the results to East Germany, Barro concludes: "Eastern Germany will eventually catch up to the West, but in a couple of generations rather than a couple of years or a couple of decades".[10] Even if the special circumstances are taken into account which will perhaps speed up the process[11] it is still a long haul for East Germany - contrary to their own expectations and the promises which encouraged

them.

These aspects of the recent developments are not negligible for an understanding of the wage increases after the EMSU which will be addressed in the following.

3. PECULIAR SITUATION: ASYMMETRY OF POWER IN FAVOUR OF UNIONS

The wage negotiations which took place in the period immediately after the establishment of the EMSU were unusual. In the former GDR a trade union existed, but it could not be compared to a western trade union. In contrast, it was part of the communist party and therefore totally discredited. Moreover, it had no experience in the day to day business of every western trade union, i.e. to negotiate wages. Thus, it immediately became the task of West Germany's trade unions to participate directly or indirectly in the negotiations; not surprisingly this led to high wage demands for East Germany. The trade unions believed that higher wages would equally serve the interests of both the workers in the east and the west.

- They argued that considerable and lasting wage differences would trigger migration and thereby weaken their position in wage negotiations in the west. Consequently, workers in the west would have to pay the bill in future wage negotiations. Moreover, their economic situation would be further aggravated through rising rents caused by substantial migration.
- A low wage region in the east appeared to comprise the danger that only labour-intensive and technologically inferior sites would be established in East Germany. Therefore, to press for a rapid adoption of western wage levels was believed to be in accordance with the interests of the East Germans, i.e. their expectations would be fulfilled and the formation of a dual economy could be prevented.
- Apart from the supposed mutual interests of eastern and western workers with respect to a fast convergence of wages this objective was in accordance with the German trade union's legacy: high regional wage differentials contradict their sense of fairness.

In general, German trade unions have the reputation to be realistic and they are known to act according to the principle 'we must not starve the goose that lays the golden eggs'. That's why we have to ask whether under these special circumstances they completely failed to notice the negative implications of their strategy. In principle these implications were previously known: on the one hand, a fast convergence in wages would be beneficial only to a rapidly declining number of workers in the new *Länder*. On the other hand, the huge transfer payments necessary because of rising unemployment (open or hidden) and because of subsidies to otherwise collapsing firms will mainly have to be paid for by western employees.

Of course, we can only speculate about the trade union's awareness regarding these problems. It is most probable that they were aware of these possible developments, but they seemingly underestimated their significance. Moreover, they argued that high unit labour costs are not the main problem of eastern firms but the quality of their products and their lack of experience in marketing them. According to the unions the emergence of unemployment had to be expected in any case, therefore moderate wage increases would not make much of a difference with respect to employment opportunities.

In my opinion this is not conclusive. Even when quality problems have been more significant than high unit labour costs these two problems are not independent. Firms which are overtaxed due to high labour costs obviously have a much lower chance to overcome their fundamental problem because retained profits are an important prerequisite for improving quality.

The willingness of the trade unions' antagonists to accept their demands was more surprising than the trade unions' strategy to press for fast convergence in wage rates. Wage negotiations in the west are characterized by opposing interests of the parties.

Collective bargaining has always been understood as a successful method to reach an agreement. Employers will not accept demands which they cannot afford. Trade unions' main objective is to improve the incomes of their members, but finally accept the constraints set by the conditions necessary for the viability of the average firm.

The implicit preconditions for collective bargaining were not present in the wage negotiations which took place immediately after the EMSU. In fact, it was a peculiar situation which was characterized by an asymmetry of power in favour of trade unions. Whereas West Germany's unions started very early to transfer their organizational structures to the East and to support the eastern unions with material and human resources, employers' associations in the west acted reluctantly. Hence, during the early negotiations the employers' interests were predominantly represented by previous managers of eastern firms. They were not only inexperienced in wage negotiations, but they were often interested in significant wage increases themselves facing jobloss due to the privatization policies. Since they could not expect to keep their jobs they would at least increase higher unemployment benefits (which according to German law is a certain percentage of the latest wage earned).

But even during the second round of wage negotiations when western employers' associations had taken command, wage increases did not slow down. One reason was that the extensive protection of employees against rationalization which was partly agreed upon before the EMSU appeared to be the greater evil. In order to reverse the existing agreements the following deal was offered: higher wage increases for the repeal of these agreements.

Another and probably even more important incentive to accept rapid wage increases was the self-interest of western entrepreneurs. A considerable wage gap between east and west would give at least the most advanced eastern firms a chance to become competitive. Hence, the potential advantage of lower wages for investors in the east was weighted against the above mentioned threat.

The entrepreneurs' position regarding this question was hardly unanimous but could be expected to differ according to their respective situations. In short, the employers' interests were not as unified as those of the unions.

Maybe the asymmetry of power in favour of unions and the heterogeneous interests of employers are only partial explanations for the huge wage increases and for the agreements which scheduled a gradual but rapid convergence of wage rates (discussed in the following chapter). It has to be added that both parties had the common interest to play against a third participant who was not involved in the wage negotiations but was nevertheless in charge of their outcome: the state, or, in the last instance, the tax payer. Both employers' associations and unions had reason to assume that in the end politicians would be willing to bear the consequences of their arrangements. These circumstances under which both sides were not willing to take responsibility for the outcomes led to the peculiarity of collective bargaining in East Germany and certainly contributes to an understanding of its results. However, we should keep in mind that politicians were mainly responsible for the emergence of these peculiar circumstances.

4. THE HIKES IN LIGHT OF HIGH AND RISING UNEMPLOYMENT

Now we attempt to look more closely at the wage increases which occurred in East Germany. Because statistics are still uncertain, insufficient, and sometimes they are not updated, it is possible that quite substantial revisions have to be made when further information becomes available. Nevertheless, it seems worthwhile to give an account on the basis of available evidence.

As far as wages and salaries negotiated by collective bargaining are concerned the following figure (Figure 2) gives some insight into the situation two years after the EMSU. It shows that there are considerable differences in the convergence of negotiated wages with respect to different sectors, however, at the same time it is apparent that even the least successful sectors have converged.

Ignoring the data problem for the moment, we assume that the ratio derived from the income statistics of July 1990 (33.7%) also exists for standard wages in all sectors at the end of June. Under this assumption we conclude that the laggard in our table realized an annual growth rate of 35.8% [12] compared to the leader with an impressing annual rate of 84.9%. Albeit these figures are based on an assumption, actual rates of growth in standard wages were probably in the above mentioned range.

The catching-up of effective wages for fully employed was not as fast as that of negotiated wages but nevertheless considerable. Unfortunately, data of the income statistics of the Federal Office of Statistics are only available until October 1991. As the following table (Table 2) shows, the relation which was

33.7% in July 1990, the first month of the EMSU, climbed to 44.8% in October 1991. The table also gives estimates for more recent periods which show substantially higher relations. The first of these relations for the third quarter of 1992 was estimated by the German Institute for Economic Research,[13] the second by the German Council of Economic Experts.[14] Although the latter probably overestimates the relation, there can be little doubt that the growth rate of effective wages in the east by far exceeded that of western wages.

Figure 2 Achieved negotiated standard wage level in selected East German industries mid 1992 (in % of West German negotiated standard wage rates)

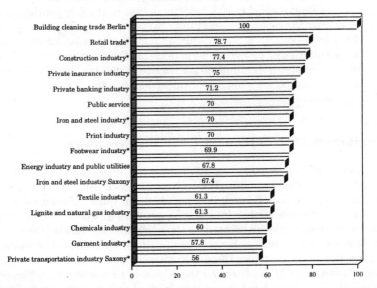

* wages only.

Source: WSI-archives for pay scale, as of June 30, 1992.

However, especially trade unions have argued that the convergence of real wages has been much more moderate. A recent paper of the metal workers' union,[15] for example, computed for the fourth quarter of 1991 that the relation of real wages in the metal-processing industry was only 32.9% compared to 30% for the first quarter of 1990.

This argument has to be scrutinized. It is true that after EMSU the cost of living index in East Germany rose at a greater rate than it did in the west. Reduction or abolition of subsidies for basic goods and a considerable increase in rents which took place on 1 October, 1991 are the main reasons. But immediately after EMSU these specific prices had not changed very much in comparison to the previous situation whereas consumer durables became much cheaper and were available without restrictions.

Table 2 - Average monthly earnings of fully employed persons in East and West Germany's manufacturing industry (in DM)

	East	West	Relation (in per cent)
April 1990	1140	3858	29.5
July 1990	1341	3977	33.7
October 1990	1498	4019	37.3
January 1991	1584	4023	39.4
April 1991	1789	4065	44.0
July 1991	1842	4205	43.8
October 1991	1902	4243	44.8
March 92[1]	2605	4381	59.5
End of 92[2]			67.5
Increase July 1990 - March 92	94.3	11.5	76.6

(1) Estimate DIW (2) Estimate *Sachverständigenrat*.

Sources: Statistisches Bundesamt, 1991/92; DIW 1993b; Sachverständigenrat, 1992.

Accepting estimates of purchasing power parities of roughly 1:1 between GDR and FRG[16] - much lower prices for basic goods, energy and rents in the GDR compensated higher prices of consumer durables - the immediate effect of the EMSU was that the real wage relation in the beginning was higher than the relation of nominal wages. The *IG-Metall* computations do not take this into account. It is true that real wage convergence was slower than the nominal wage convergence, however, it is wrong of the *IG-Metall* to insinuate that real wage adjustments lag hopelessly behind nominal wage adjustments. The truth is that the real wage relation had been higher in the beginning than the nominal wage relation (taking the previous situation (1989) as point of departure) and that after the establishment of the EMSU the former had improved with a considerable slower rate than the latter. As an aside, it should be mentioned that things have changed in the meantime. While the increase in the eastern cost of living index has been mainly due to the substantial increase in rents on 1 October, 1991, the cost of living index for West Germany increased at a higher rate than the respective index for East Germany in October/November 1992. The main reason is that rents in East Germany after 1 October, 1991 had been fairly stable whereas they had risen substantially in West Germany.

Most spectacular of the wage negotiations in East Germany was the agreement in the metal-processing industry in spring 1991 which included a stepwise convergence of basic wages until 1994. In the following table (Table 3) the implications for standard wages are shown assuming fairly moderate wage increases in 1993 and 1994 for Schleswig-Holstein, the western *Land* which is compared with Mecklenburg-Vorpommern here, one of the new *Länder* where this agreement was first signed.

As can be seen the relation reached in February 1992 amounted to 67.4% and would have been about 80% when the next step of the agreement would have occurred in April 1993. Employers declared to be unable to accept wage increases which in fact would have amounted to about 26% (side payments included). They insisted on a revision of the agreement - a breach of contract, according to union's view.

Table 3 - Adjustment of negotiated standard wages in East Germany's metal-working industry 1990-1994 (model calculation)

Quarter	Monthly standard wage rate Schleswig-Holstein		Monthly standard wage rate Mecklenburg-Vorpommern		Standard wage level
	in DM (1)	% change on the previous year	in DM (2)	% change on the previous year	east to west in % (2) / (1)
1/90	2,194	-	799	-	26.4
1/91	2,326	+6.0	1,099 [3]	+37.5	47.2
2/91	2,482	+6.7	1,455	+82.1	58.6
2/92	2,615	+5.4	1,762	+22.1	67.4
2/93	2,693	+3.0	2,144	+21.7	79.6
1/94	2,693 [1]	+3.0	2,208	+25.3	82.0
2/94	2,693 [1]	0.0	2,693	+25.6	100.0 [2]

[1] excluding increase of negotiated standard wage rate west by 1 January, 1994.

[2] including increase of negotiated standard wage rate by 1 January, 1994.

[3] + DM 250 since 1 July, 1990; + DM 50 since 1 October, 1990.

Source: IG Metall 1993.

The conflict resulted in a strike in May 1993 in eastern Germany's metalworking industry (the first strike after more than 60 years because industrial disputes were forbidden in both Nazi Germany and the former GDR). The compromise which was finally reached implies that at the end of 1993 standard wages in eastern Germany's metalworking industry will be 80% of western wages but the period of complete adaption will be extended until 1996. Hence, further substantial wage increases will take place in 1993. Whether and to what extent the prolongation of the period of adaption will contribute to prevent a further decline in metalworking industry's employment level is an open question.

When the wage contract was signed nobody could assume that labour productivity increases in East Germany could match the huge wage increases. This is not only true for the metal-processing industry but also for the whole economy. This caused an increase in unit labour costs which were already much higher than in West Germany after the EMSU. Since data on levels and growth rates of labour productivity since the EMSU are still unreliable there is some dispute about the east/west relation. For example, the employers' institute has estimated that in January 1992 unit labour costs were 116% above those of West Germany. In contrast, the estimates of the metal workers' union show a 73% higher level in February 1992, and moreover that they had fallen between January 1991 and February 1992. Further investigations of these developments will have to be based on more reliable data. The most recent information which was available when the final version of this article was written (May 1993) is shown in the following figure.

Figure 3 Unit labour cost[1]- East Germany in % of West Germany

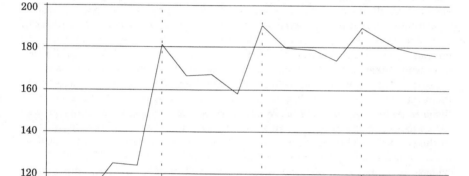

(1) Gross wage and salary income over real GDP (at 1991 prices). 1993 figures estimated.

Source: DIW, 1993d.

It exhibits that a reduction in the relation of eastern and western labour unit costs took place between the first and forth quarter of 1991 as well as 1992. But that was compensated by increases at the end of these respective years with the result that eastern Germany's unit labour costs still exceeded western Germany's by more than 80% at the beginning of 1993.

In summary, it has to be emphasized that a fast convergence of wages went hand in hand with a drastic decline in employment. At the end of 1992 employment in East Germany was more than one third lower than 1990.[17] The decline of industrial employment was even more dramatic and it is no exaggeration to say that a process of deindustrialization took place at an unprecedented scale and speed.

The preceding discussion was mainly concerned with the influence of employment on wage increases. As it should have become obvious, the development in the new *Länder* can be considered as an unambiguous counter-example to the familiar hypothesis stipulating that high unemployment will prevent (huge) wage increases.

But the relationship between the rate of employment and the wage rate is a mutual one. In fact, the attention of theoreticians normally was devoted to the reverse causal relationship which views the wage rate as the independent and employment as the dependent variable. The answer of traditional theory with regard to this relation is well-known: there is an inverse relation between the real wage rate and employment. From this perspective there doesn't exist an eastern German wage paradox at all: the rapid decline in employment is in this view the result of wage increases which outstripped productivity growth.

Although our interest rested mainly on the question of why the decline in employment did not prevent wage hikes in this peculiar case at hand, we could not get around the discussion of whether conventional wisdom is confirmed: have wage hikes in East Germany contributed to the decline in employment?

In principle, the inverse relationship between the wage rate and employ-ment can be annulled on two routes. The first consists in the acceptance of firms to reduce profit margins. Wage increases exceeding productivity growth can in this case be compatible with constant or even rising employment, at least in the short run. The second and more important case is that which has always been emphasized by the purchasing power argument: Wage increases can trigger an increase in demand which in turn stimulates output, employment and capacity utilization. In the last mentioned case it is quite possible that an increase in the rate of profits goes hand in hand with an increase in wage rates.

However, there is no evidence at all that one of these cases is relevant for the new *Länder*. According to the still insecure national accounts for eastern Germany[18] the wage share was 108.6% in 1991 and 104.1% in 1992! Although the peculiarities of the situation demand a cautious interpretation of these results, they nevertheless indicate that there has been no room for a reduction of profit margins. Additionally, a situation in which the purchasing power argument can attain plausibility looks very different to that existing in eastern Germany. In 1991 private consumption exceeded gross domestic product (100.8%) and in 1992 it was still 91.8% of the latter. The comparative shares of West Germany were 54.4 and 53.8%, respectively. These differences reflect the huge deficit in the current account of eastern Germany (1991: DM -172.3 bn, 1992: DM -196.0 bn) and at the same time the requirements of transfer payments which had to be satisfied by western Germany. In all probability, further wage hikes without corresponding productivity increases will stimulate imports primarily and production only to a minor extent. Additionally, a further increase in transfer payments for consumption purposes will become necessary. In face of the already existing huge fiscal deficit of the Federal Government a reduction of transfers for investment purposes probably will become unavoidable. The detrimental effects of such a course of things for East Germany's further development (and especially productivity) are quite obvious. Hence, we come to the conclusion that the purchasing power argument cannot claim to be valid for eastern Germany's special situation.

We cannot offer own quantitative results with regard to the effects of a slower increase in eastern Germany's wage rates. But our conjuncture that a slower growth in wages will contribute to eastern Germany's development and to an acceleration in the catching-up of its productivity is substantiated by simulation experiments with International Monetary Fund's MULTIMOD.[19] One of the results obtained is that a 1% slower wage increase in eastern Germany than in the reference scenario will increase the share of investment in GDP, the rate of growth and decrease the rate of inflation (in fact, the inflation problem is offset). Moreoever, productivity catch-up is accelerated but still slow: whereas in the reference scenario eastern productivity moves until 2005 to around 50% of western, in the slower wages growth scenario it reaches 62%.

5. ON WINNERS AND LOSERS

Since the enthusiastic reactions on the fall of the Wall the mood has changed considerably in both parts of Germany. Statements of West and East Germans must give the foreign observer the impression that unification has been a negative-sum game with only losers. East Germans complain that their situation does not at all match their high expectations. Western Germans complain about their new fellow-citizens' high demands and their inability to adapt to the new rules of the game. Furthermore, West Germans complain about the burden which they already have to bear and which will become even more pronounced in the next years.[20]

Reality is different. The immediate impact of EMSU and German unification provided West Germany in 1990 with the highest real rate of growth since 1976 and prevented the West German economy from being affected by the world-wide recession. Profits and wages rose considerably. At the same time East German incomes exhibited remarkable increases.

However, highly different cases are hidden behind those generalized data. Those East Germans who lost their jobs soon after the EMSU could only claim very low unemployment benefits, and moreover, the following wage increases had no positive effects for them. Naturally, in West Germany the economic effects of unification were also extremely diverse. Whereas, for example, some lawyers were able to multiply their income, pensioners did not immediately benefit.

The fact that different social groups in east and west have been affected differently by unification (some big winners, some losers) is too important to be ignored in the discussion. The other one is more subtle. It concerns the relation of gains (or loses) of stocks and flows.

The state treaty and the unification treaty have been predominantly interpreted as an act of solidarity on the part of West Germany in which political motives dominated economic ones. In contrast, Schrettl[21] especially emphasized the fact that the treaties should be understood as an insurance contract with West Germany as the insurer and East Germany as the insured. The implication of this interpretation is that the generous financial assistance of West Germany was not entirely free of charge. The insurance premium paid for the availability of a respectable currency and a transition without falling real wage rates consisted essentially of East Germany's agreement that its endowment, capital as well as land, would be available for two purposes. Those state-owned assets which resulted from the expropriations between 1945 and 1949 were excluded from restitution claims and should become property of the *Treuhandanstalt*, the agency responsible for privatization. Assets which had been expropriated after 1949 should be restored.

At first glance only the latter appears to be 'an insurance premium', for the beneficiaries of the restitution principle were mainly citizens of West Germany. Since it was agreed that revenues arising from privatization should exclusively be used for the development of East Germany's economy this aspect of the agreement seemed only fair. Moreover, the interpretation that this is an additional fee to be paid by East Germany appears to be inadmissible.

The privatization policy of the *Treuhandanstalt* in retrospect gives reason to fundamentally change this view. The inevitable outcome of its policy to privatize as fast as possible resulted in extremely low prices for their assets. And it was changed to the worse by its intentions to favour those buyers who gave investment and employment guarantees.[22] Since through these special rules of the game western firms predominantly got a contract, a further fee was levied on East Germany in retrospect. By this way privatization clearly could not generate a surplus for the *Treuhandanstalt* to be used for East Germany's development. Instead, it will end up with a tremendous deficit of which the Federal Government has to take care. But it is apparent that after privatization no property will be available to be distributed among East Germans. Moreover, in the end East Germany's endowment will be owned to a large extent by West Germans.

On the one hand, it is indeed admissible to interpret the state and the unification treaty as an insurance contract with West Germany guaranteeing wages and social security payments which in real terms are high enough that nobody will be worse off (the Paretian promise) moreover they will reach western levels in due time. East Germany, on the other hand, accepted regulations which factually (whether intentionally, we do not discuss this here as well) provided West Germans with easy access to East Germany's property. It is hardly exaggerated when we conclude that claims on stocks were offered for flows.

Since the ratification of the treaties distributive conflicts in Germany have become much more pronounced. East Germans are often outraged that the so-called 'people's property' is restored or sold for a fraction of its value to western firms. West Germans groan about increasing taxes and social security contributions, at times attributed to East Germans' high demands. Since indeed the vast majority of West Germans have not acquired eastern property, the 'payment' made by the East is unknown, and even if it was known it would be irrelevant for them. While the financial burden of unification predominantly rests on the lower income groups, the upper income groups have proportionally contributed little. The majority feels that there exists a 'gap in justice' or what Germans call '*Gerechtigkeitslücke*'. In fact, this gap is greater than generally perceived because unification offered a small percentage of West Germans the unique opportunity to increase their incomes or to acquire property at extremely low prices (or both). Hence, only a few benefited from the insurer's fee, while the insurer's payments have to be paid by all and unproportionally by those who don't benefit from the insurer's fee.

NOTES

1 Kornai, 1990.
2 See eg. Akerlof *et al.*, 1991.
3 Sinn and Sinn 1991, p. 125.
4 Marx, 1976.
5 Goodwin, 1967.
6 Cf. Kalmbach, 1993a.
7 Cf. Schrettl, 1992.
8 For some computations see Kalmbach, 1993b.
9 Barro and Sala-i-Martin, 1991.
10 Barro, 1991.
11 Cf. Dornbusch and Wolf, 1992; Alexander, 1992.
12 This calculation is based on the stimate that negotiated wages in West Germany in the respective two-year-period rose by 11%.
13 DIW, 1993b.
14 *Sachverständigenrat*, 1992.
15 *IG Metall*, 1993.
16 Cf. Sinn and Sinn, 1991, p. 36.
17 See table 1 and *DIW-Wochenbericht*, various issues.
18 DIW, 1993c, p.270.
19 Hughes Hallett and Ma, 1993.
20 See e.g. Collier, 1991.
21 Schrettl, 1992.
22 Sinn and Sinn, 1991.

BIBLIOGRAPHY

Akerlof, G.A., Rose, A.K., Yellen, J.N., Hessenius, H. (1991), East Germany in from the Cold: The Economic Aftermath of Currency Union, *Brooking Papers on Economic Activity*, 1, pp. 1-105.

Alexander, L. (1992), Comment on Dornbusch, R. and Wolf, H., Economic Transition in Eastern Germany, *Brooking Papers on Economic Activity*, 1, pp. 262-268.

Barro, R. (1991), Eastern Germany's Long Haul, *The Wall Street Journal*, May 3, A 10.

Barro, R. and Sala-i-Martin, X. (1991), Convergence across States and Regions, *Brooking Papers on Economic Activity*, 1, pp. 107-158.

Collier jr., I.R. (1991), On the First Year of German Monetary, Economic and Social Union, *Journal of Economic Perspectives*, 5, no. 4, pp. 179-186.

DIW (1992a), Gesamtwirtschaftliche und unternehmerische Anpassungsprozesse in Ostdeutschland, Sechster Bericht, *DIW-Wochenbericht*, 39, pp. 467-492.

DIW (1992b), Ausgeprägte gesamtwirtschaftliche Verlangsamung, *DIW-Wochenbericht*, 47, pp. 623-633.

DIW (1992c), Strukturwandel im Prozeß der deutschen Vereinigung, *DIW-Wochenbericht*, 48, pp. 641-652.

DIW (1992d), Gesamtwirtschaftliche und unternehmerische Anpassungsprozesse, Siebter Bericht, *DIW-Wochenbericht*, 52, pp. 709-738.

DIW (1993a), Grundlinien der Wirtschaftsentwicklung 1993, *DIW-Wochenbericht*, 1-2, pp. 1-13.

DIW (1993b) Sinkende Beschäftigung und steigende Arbeitslosigkeit in Deutschland, *DIW-Wochenbericht*, 4, pp. 35-42.

DIW (1993c) Gesamtwirtschaftliche und unternehmerische Anpassungsprozesse, Achter Bericht, *DIW-Wochenbericht*, 13, pp. 131-158.

DIW (1993d) Die Lage der Weltwirtschaft und der deutschen Wirtschaft im Frühjahr 1993, *DIW-Wochenbericht*, 18-19, pp. 237-274.

Dornbusch, R. and Wolf, H. (1992), Economic Transition in Eastern Germany, *Brooking Papers on Economic Activity*, 1, pp. 235-261.

Goodwin, R.M. (1967), Growth Cycles, in: C.H. Feinstein (ed.), *Socialism, Capitalism and Economic Growth*, Cambridge, pp. 54-58.

Hughes Hallet, A.J. and Ma, Y. (1993), East Germany, West Germany, and Their Mezzogiorno Problem: A Parable for European Economic Integration, *The Economic Journal*, 103, pp. 416-428.

IG Metall (1993), Wirtschaftliche und soziale Gründe gegen eine Revision der tariflichen Stufenvereinbarungen in der ostdeutschen Metallindustrie, Frankfurt, mimeo.

Kalmbach, P. (1993a), Two Years After the German Monetary Union: The Transition to a Market Economy with the Help of a Rich Uncle, *Annali Scientifici del Dipartimento di Economia dell'Università degli Studi di Trento,* supplemento annuale a Economia e Banca, no. 5-6, 1992-1993,

Banca di Trento e Bolzano, Trento, pp. 39-68.

Kalmbach, P. (1993b), Alternative Strategies of Wage Policy in East Germany, in: H.D. Kurz (ed.), *United Germany and the New Europe*, Aldershot, pp. 119-133.

Kornai, J. (1990), *The Road to a Free Economy, Shifting from a Socialist Economy: The Example of Hungary*, New York and London.

Marx, K. (1976), *Capital*, vol. I, Harmondsworth.

Sachverständigenrat zur Begutachtung der gesamtwirtschaftlichen Entwicklung (1991), *Jahresgutachten 1991/92*, Bonn.

Sachverständigenrat zur Begutachtung der gesamtwirtschaftlichen Entwicklung (1992), *Jahresgutachten 1992/93*, Bonn.

Schrettl, W. (1992), Transition with Insurance: German Unification Reconsidered, *Oxford Review of Economic Policy*, 8, No. 1, pp. 144-155.

Sinn, G. and Sinn, H.W. (1991), *Kaltstart*, Volkswirtschaftliche Aspekte der deutschen Vereinigung, Tübingen.

Statistisches Bundesamt (1991-1992), *Fachserie 16*, Reihe 2.1 and 2.2, various issues.

Statistisches Bundesamt (1993), Bruttoinlandsprodukt 1992, *Wirtschaft und Statistik*, 1, pp. 11-24.

PART THREE

FROM THE SOVIET RUBLE TO NATIONAL RUBLES AND INDEPENDENT CURRENCIES: THE EVOLUTION OF THE RUBLE AREA IN 1991-1993[1]

Marek Dabrowski

1. INTRODUCTION

As Western Europe attempts to strengthen its economic and political integration, including the establishment of a monetary union with a common currency unit in the coming decade, one can observe the opposite process taking place in the Eastern, post-communist part of the continent. Former Yugoslavia, Czechoslovakia and the Soviet Union represent three, more or less dramatic, examples of political and economic disintegration. The Soviet case is probably the most interesting, given both the size of the country and the specific features of its transformation.[2]

The process of political and economic disintegration of the former USSR also has its monetary aspect. The former Soviet currency - the ruble - was inherited in the first stage of transformation by all post-Soviet states. This is true both for the nations that became members of the CIS in December 1991 and for those which chose to go the way of full political separation (i.e. the Baltic states). However, strong disintegration factors began to influence the functioning of the monetary system, and they very soon led to the almost total collapse of the monetary union in the second half of 1992 and in the first half of 1993.

The situation at the end of May 1993 is still unclear. Some post-Soviet states (such as Ukraine, Kyrgyzstan and the Baltic states) have definitively left the ruble area. Others still maintain the ruble as a currency unit but use, in most cases, parallel currencies (coupons). The ruble area therefore seems to have come to the end of its life as a monetary union. Some influential politicians, for instance Nursultan Nazarbaev, the President of Kazakhstan, continue to call for the restitution of a common currency, although it is doubtful whether this is still a realistic political goal.

The final shape of the monetary system of the CIS countries has not yet been defined. There are a number of proposals under discussion and other variants are to be taken into consideration. The final outcome also depends to a significant extent on the results of macroeconomic stabilization and of political and systemic transformation in individual countries.

2. THE ECONOMIC LEGACY OF THE USSR: REPRESSED HYPERINFLATION

The starting-point for the economic policy of all the post-Soviet states was a situation of formidable difficulty. The last stage of the economic history of the USSR was characterized by hyperinflation, mainly in its hidden (repressed) form. Thus, at the beginning of 1992, all the successors to the USSR were faced by the necessity of achieving monetary stabilization, liberalizing prices, and initiating the process of market-oriented institutional and ownership reforms.

This situation seemed to be common to most of the post-communist countries in Central and Eastern Europe. Although in these economies the central planning system no longer worked as a mechanism for microeconomic discipline and macroeconomic coordination, the newly-introduced market mechanism had yet to prove itself able to perform this role. Thus the typical syndrome arose of a non-planned and non-market economy which lacked sufficient microeconomic motivation and was unable to achieve elementary macroeconomic equilibrium.

Moreover, weak governments (in the sense that they lacked political support in society) were ready to buy temporary social peace in exchange for inflationary money. This was not only the case of the former USSR in 1989-1991 but also of Poland in 1987-1989, Romania after the collapse of Nicolae Ceauçescu's dictatorship, Bulgaria and Albania. Only East Germany, Hungary and Czechoslovakia have been able to avoid inflationary chaos during the transition period.

The two last years of the former USSR were distinguished by a continuous decline in output and an uncontrolled increase in monetary overhang. In the past, the money supply in the Soviet economy (as in the other countries with a traditional command economy) had been constantly excessive from the point of view of normal market economy standards. For example, the average annual rate of growth of M2 in 1981-5 amounted to 7.5%.[3] This factor plus total price control contributed to the repressed inflation and the forced savings that seem to be normal phenomena in a traditional command economy (although in the former USSR the level of repressed inflation was probably higher than in other socialist countries such as the GDR, Czechoslovakia and Hungary). Monetary overhang was also neutralized to some extent by the commodity nonconvertibility[4] of the ruble, especially at the enterprise level. I refer here to the total rationing system (administrative allocation of material resources and investment goods) and the rigid control of different types of expenditure in state-owned enterprises (wage fund, investment money, etc.).[5]

The second half of the 1980s saw a gradual worsening of monetary equilibrium. The discipline imposed by the central plan began to evaporate as a result of the partial political and economic liberalization of the *perestroika* period. The money supply also increased. According to IMF estimates, the M2 annual rate of growth was 8.5% in 1986, 14.7% in 1987, 14.1% in 1988, 14.8% in 1989, and 15.3% in 1990.[6] Increasing fiscal deficit was the main factor responsible for this monetary expansion: according to the same estimates it amounted to: 2.4% of GDP in 1985, 6.2% in 1986, 8.4% in 1987, 9.2% in 1988, 8.5% in 1989.[7]

Moreover, the above-mentioned partial economic liberalization increased the commodity convertibility of the ruble (that is, it gave enterprises more flexibility in the use of their financial assets) and thus increased money velocity. This is also a standard effect of the deregulation of the traditional socialist economic system.[8]

The latter years of the 1980s were also a period of significant decreases in external balances. The current account balance in convertible currencies, which was positive until 1988 (+US$ 2.3 bn in 1986, +US$ 6.7 bn in 1987 and +US$ 1.6 bn in 1988) dramatically deteriorated in 1989 (-US$ 3.8 bn) and in 1990 (-US$ 10.7 bn).[9] Consequently, the external debt rose from US$ 28.9 bn in 1985 to US$ 54.0 bn in 1989. These developments derived both from the growing level of internal macroeconomic disequilibrium (budget deficit and monetary expansion) and from sharply deteriorating terms of trade, especially in the oil market.[10] Declining oil export revenues and profitability also contributed to fiscal difficulties (oil exports had previously been a significant source of budget revenues).

The level of this repressed inflation increased further because of monetary expansion, decreasing demand for money and continuing price control. Until the beginning of 1991, the official consumer price index was not high. CPI in the state-owned retail trade amounted to 2.4% in 1989 and 5.2% in 1990. The retail price increase in so-called cooperative trade[11] was 0.5% in 1989 and 5.2% in 1990. The same indicators for the *kolkhoz* market were 7.4% in 1989 and 34.3% in 1990.[12]

These figures indirectly illustrate the increasing level of repressed inflation and forced savings. Cottarelli and Blejer estimate that "... at the end of 1990 the amount of wealth accumulated in monetary form by Soviet households as a result of forced savings was around 170-190 billion rubles, close to 20% of GDP and around one third of the existing financial assets".[13] One may add that monetary overhang was equal to two-thirds of private consumption.

After 1 April 1991, in connection with the price reform implemented by the Valentin Pavlov government,[14] inflation started to take a more overt form. In 1991, CPI in the state retail trade amounted to 89.5% (average level of 1991 to

average level of 1990) and 146.1% (December 1990 to December 1991).
Consolidated CPI amounted to 90.4% and 152.1%, the price index of the *kolkhoz*
market to 132.1% and 281.2%.[15] Inflation (and later hyperinflation) had a
mixed character in the second half of 1991, taking partly the form of open price
increases and partly the form of growing market shortages.

The increasing budget deficit, financed exclusively by credit from the state
bank (*Gosbank*) of the USSR, was the main cause of the high inflation in 1991.
According to IMF estimates, the total budget deficit of the Russian Federation
in 1991 (including the consequences of assuming responsibility for the entire
budget of the former USSR) reached a level of 31% of GDP.[16] Increasing state
subsidies for administratively controlled prices, the decrease in output, and
weak tax discipline were the sources of this huge fiscal deficit.

The above-mentioned weakening of financial discipline at the micro level led
to the rapid growth of nominal and 'real' wages[17] in the second half of 1991. In
the last quarter of 1991, 'real' wages in industry were 33% higher than their
average level in 1990,[18] and they also contributed to the significant decrease in
the real profits of enterprises.

In the years of *perestroika*, economic growth in the USSR and the Russian
Federation was lower than in the preceding decades and gradually decreased.
Russia's net material product (NMP) increased only by 2.4% in 1986, 0.7% in
1987, 4.5% in 1988 and 1.9% in 1989. From 1990 onwards NMP decreased by
3.6% in 1990 and by 11.0% in 1991 (preliminary estimates).[19] At the same time,
the index of gross industrial output amounted to +4.5% in 1986, +3.5% in 1987,
+3.8% in 1988, +1.4% in 1989, -0.1% in 1990 and -8.0% in 1991.[20]

The main reasons for the 1990-1991 recession were the breakdown of the
central planning system, the motivational crisis in state-owned enterprises, the
disintegration of trade relations between East European countries after the
collapse of CMEA, and the gradual weakening of trade links among the former
USSR republics.

After political dictatorship and the rule of terror had been gradually
dismantled under *perestroika*, the system of central planning lost its capacity to
mobilize resources for production. For example, the rate of investment
decreased in the second half of the 1980s. Also lost was the ability to guarantee
elementary macroeconomic equilibrium and microeconomic discipline. The
severe recession suffered by the former USSR supports the hypothesis that a
steep fall in output is inevitable in post-communist economies before the onset
of real stabilization and liberalization - unless this stabilization occurs almost
simultaneously with the collapse of communism.

3. MONETARY UNION WITH FIFTEEN INDEPENDENT CENTRAL BANKS

The specific monetary system of the ruble area can be seen as the second major
barrier (apart from macroeconomic disequilibrium) against radical market
reforms. The co-existence of one currency and fifteen fully independent central

banks was the essence of this system in the first half of 1992. Political factors such as newly-achieved national independence prevented the effective coordination of macroeconomic policy between governments and central banks in the ruble area. Earlier, political agreements like the Economic Union signed in Novo-Ogarevo in October 1991, or the economic and monetary components of the treaty that created the CIS (signed by the presidents of Russia, the Ukraine and Belorussia at the beginning of December 1991 in the Belovezha Forests) had never worked effectively. The 'nationalization' of the former *Gosbank* of the USSR by Russia and the decision to assign the Central Bank of the Russian Federation (CBRF) the role of central monetary authority in the ruble area taken in December 1991 did not solve the problems.

Most of the central banks of the republics were reluctant to subordinate themselves to the CBRF. In fact, this situation had already arisen previously - in 1991, maybe even in 1990. The central banks of the republics found themselves freed from effective control by *Gosbank*. They were quite independent in issuing refinancing credit for commercial banks and in covering budget deficits. *Gosbank* only maintained 'monopoly' in the inflationary financing of the former USSR budget deficit, while *Gosznak* (the banknote printers controlled by the Ministry of Finance of the USSR) preserved technical monopoly over the issue of banknotes and coins.

The system described above created total anarchy in monetary policy. One must agree with Sachs and Lipton that "... there is no realistic possibility of controlling credit in a system in which several independent central banks each have the independent authority to issue credit. The reason is simple. There is an overwhelming pressure in each of the states to 'free ride' by issuing ruble credits at the expense of the rest of the system".[21] The effect was similar to that of banknote forgery - it may even have been more serious - because additional credit money was technically far easier to issue than cash money.

In the short run, countries with the most expansionary credit policy benefited from an additional inflow of goods, services and foreign reserves from countries trying to control credit expansion. In the medium and long run, the entire system suffered from hyperinflation.

Control of the cash money supply to other post-Soviet states was the first instrument resorted to by the Russian government in order to halt the inflow of credit money from those countries. Cash rationing also became necessary because of the technical cash crisis in the first half of 1992 caused by general credit expansion as well as by technical and organizational mistakes (the reluctance of the Supreme Soviet of the Russian Federation to print higher-denomination banknotes at the end of 1991).

The Russian government rationed cash between the CIS states and regions of Russian Federation. Rationing became an instrument for political bargaining and pressure, and the cash shortage had a disastrous effect on monetary settlements.

The other CIS states, such as the Ukraine, Azerbaijan and Belorussia, introduced coupons as a parallel cash currency, thereby contributing to the monetary and trade disintegration of the former USSR. The Russian government also had to pay special compensation to employees in Russia who had not received their wages and salaries on time.

4. THE GRADUAL DISINTEGRATION OF THE RUBLE AREA

Cash rationing did not solve the problem of monetary control in the ruble area, and the Russian authorities had to look for other, more effective, instruments. At the end of June 1992, President Yeltsin promulgated a special decree concerning the protection of the ruble. In compliance with this decree, in July 1992 the CBRF halted automatic and unlimited settlements with other states in the ruble area. Ruble payments from outside (especially from the Ukraine) to Russia could be realised only to the extent determined by payments from Russia to the corresponding states. This decision created a system of daily bilateral clearing. Simultaneously, the CBRF allowed decentralized settlements through correspondent accounts in the Russian commercial banks.

From 5 November 1992 onwards, the CBRF forbade the purchase of convertible currencies in the Russian foreign exchange market by financial and commercial institutions in other post-Soviet states. This decision precluded the possibility of using rubles from accounts in Russian commercial banks for direct and portfolio investment in Russia.[22]

This new mechanism effectively marked the end of the ruble as a single currency, although ruble banknotes and coins were still used by most of the post-Soviet countries as cash money. The separation of credit activity by non-Russian central banks from the CBRF led to the creation of independent national rubles outside Russia. Because of the daily bilateral clearing mechanism described above, these new rubles are only partly convertible one to another. In most of the CIS countries (see Table 1) coupons have been gradually introduced as a parallel currency to ruble banknotes.

A number of states decided to leave the ruble area. Estonia began the process when it introduced its own currency on 20 June 1992.[23] The Estonian crown was established as a convertible currency on the basis of a money board with extensive powers.[24] Its fixed rate of eight crowns per one German mark has been successfully maintained since then.

Full monetary separation was also introduced on 20 July 1992 by Latvia. The Latvian ruble (*rublis*) previously functioned as a cash currency (coupon) parallel to the Russian ruble. After the withdrawal of Russian rubles, the *rublis* became a transitional currency in Latvia. The Latvian authorities plan to introduce a new, convertible currency bearing the historical name *lat*.[25] This process started in March 1993, when the Latvian central bank began to issue banknotes with a nominal value of 5 *lat*. However, the *rublis* is already convertible in current account transactions, with a floating exchange rate in relation to both Western currencies and the Russian ruble. The Latvian government and central bank managed to maintain the exchange rate at the level of around 170 *rublis* per 1 USD for eight months.[26] In April and May 1993 the *rublis* even appreciated against the US dollar and other convertible currencies (134 *rublis* per 1 USD on 21 April 1993 - see Table 5).

Lithuania was the third country to introduce its own currency, on 1 October 1992. The Lithuanian *talon* (which had earlier circulated as a parallel cash currency) also acts as a transitional currency until a convertible *lit* (the Lithuanian currency prior to World War II) is introduced. Unfortunately, in contrast to Latvian experience, the Lithuanian authorities were unable to stabilize the *talon* and make it convertible. The *talon* depreciated very quickly against the major convertible currencies, but more slowly than the Russian ruble.

A similar decision was taken by the Ukrainian government on 11 November 1992 when it introduced the Ukrainian non-cash ruble, the *karbovanets*, which at that time was already separate and only partly convertible to the Russian ruble (see above). All remaining cash rubles were converted into Ukrainian coupons which, from 1 January 1992, were used as a parallel cash currency. The *karbovanets*, too, is a transitional currency and should be replaced in the future by the *hryvna*. The *karbovanets* is a non-convertible currency and is probably the weakest of all the 'national' rubles. It depreciated rapidly against both Western currencies and Russian ruble as a result of the highly expansionary macroeconomic policy pursued by the Ukraine.

In May 1993, the government and parliament of Kyrgyzstan took the decision to separate the Kirgiz ruble (*som*) from the Russian ruble. This decision came into effect on 15 May 1993 together with complete withdrawal of Russian cash rubles.

At least six countries - Azerbaijan, Belorussia, Moldova, Georgia, Turkmenistan and Uzbekistan - seem to be on the verge of leaving the ruble area. They use both Russian cash rubles and local coupons (parallel cash currencies). Non-cash settlements are made in 'national' rubles which are only partly convertible to the Russian ruble and other currencies.

In Belorussia and Azerbaijan this transitional situation has lasted for many months. The Belorussian coupon[27] was introduced as a parallel cash currency in September 1992. After 11 November 1992, when the Ukraine withdrew Russian cash rubles, Belorussia extended the area of use for its coupons in an attempt to protect its domestic market against a massive inflow of rubles from its southern neighbour. During the next few months, Belorussia endeavoured to be both in and out of the ruble zone. In May 1993, however, it again extended the area of Russian cash rubles - probably for technical reasons, i.e. the shortage of coupons.

Similar circumstances (the withdrawal of Russian cash rubles in Kyrgyzstan) prompted Uzbekistan to introduce its own coupon on 10 May 1993. This parallel cash currency is the only legal tender for the purchase of most of the basic consumption products in the country's retail trade. Transactions over 10,000 rubles must be conducted using special cheques.

A further three post-Soviet countries - Kazakhstan and probably Tajikistan and Armenia[28] - still use Russian rubles in cash settlements and their 'national' rubles in non-cash settlements. Bearing in mind that Kazakhstan has unlimited access to technical credit from the CBFR (see Table 2), this means that the country still maintains monetary union with Russia.

Table 1 gives a general picture of the evolution of the ruble area.

Table 1 - Monetary systems in post-Soviet states: the situation in May 1993

Variant of monetary system	Country - currency
Convertibility on the basis of *high powered money board* (fixed exchange rate)	Estonia - crown
Current account convertibility - floating exchange rate, but *de facto* stabilized	Latvia - rublis
Partial current account convertibility - floating exchange rate	Russia - rubel
Transitional currencies, partly convertible to Western currencies and to Russian ruble	Lithuania - talon
	Ukraine - karbovanets
	Kirgistan - som
Cash payments - Russian rubles and coupons (parallel currency)	Azerbaijan - manat
	Belorussia
Non-cash payments - 'national' rubles, partly convertible to Russian ruble	Moldova
	Georgia
	Uzbekistan
	Turkmenistan - manat
Cash payments - Russian rubles	Armenia
Non-cash payments -'national' rubles, partly convertible to Russian ruble	Tajikistan
Monetary union with Russia (*de facto*)	Kazakhstan

5. THE ECONOMIC CONSEQUENCES OF PARTIAL MONETARY DISINTEGRATION

5.1. CONTROLLING THE IMPORTING OF INFLATION TO RUSSIA

Decisions taken at the end of June 1992 gave the CBRF the technical means to control the importing of inflation from the other CIS states. These new instruments, however, were only used to a limited extent. In August 1992, when Victor Gerashchenko became Acting Governor of the Central Bank, the policy of the intensive crediting of Russian exports to other CIS states was reintroduced. Two technical instruments were used: first, the granting by the Russian government and the CBRF of technical credit to other countries; second, the acceptance by the CBRF of overdrafts on inter-republic correspondent accounts.

Table 2 shows the results achieved by the new mechanism of settlements among republics during its first nine months of operation. Column 2 illustrates the balance of correspondent accounts between Russia and other post-Soviet states on 31 December 1992; column 3 the corresponding data on 31 March 1993, but only as regards trade settlements. Column 5 gives the balance of correspondent accounts connected with the supply of cash rubles from Russia to other states in 1993, while column 6 lists inter-enterprise arrears among republics. Column 4 shows the amounts of technical credit granted to individual CIS countries in 1993. The sign (+) denotes Russia's debt to the other country, the sign (-) the debt of the other country to Russia.

Table 2 - Correspondent accounts of CBRF with central banks of post-Soviet states in millions of rubles

Country	Balance of correspondent account 31.12.1992	Balance of correspondent account - trade payments 31.03.1993	Limit of technical credit for 1993	Balance of correspondent account - ruble cash supply 31.03.1993	Balance of correspondent account - inter-enterprise arrears 31.03.1993
Ukraine	-293343.60	-122398.9	250000[b]	0	-408605.2
Belorussia	-75223.80	-36839.3	150000[c]	0	70.3
Kazakhstan	-343549.9[a]	-183407.2	unlimited	-50400	8.1
Uzbekistan	-263522.7[a]	-98774.5	180000[c]	-49585	-374.7
Tadzhikistan	-31869.2[a]	-24099.7	30000[d]	0	1.1
Turkmenistan	-116181.9[a]	-18994.2	20000[d]	-22000	-6377.8
Kyrghyzstan	-34917.8[a]	-18424.8	30000[c]	0	3.5
Moldova	-22270.1[a]	-18750.6	19000[d]	-1001	0.5
Armenia	-33344.8[a]	-3126.8	50000[d]	0	2.4
Azerbaijan	-32818.1[a]	-4713.1	5000[d]	0	0.0
Georgia	-54200.2[a]	575.7	0.0	0	0.0
Latvia	-37.80	979.6	0,0	0	0.0
Lithuania	9134.10	-2869.1	0.0	0	0.0
TOTAL	-1292145.80	-530.832.9	734000.0	122986.0	-415222.0

a - together with cash supplied by Russia
b - limit for the first quarter of 1993
c - limit for the first half of 1993
d - limit for all of 1993.

Source: Data from CBRF.

Five countries - Kazakhstan, Ukraine, Uzbekistan, Turkmenistan and Belorussia - are the leading debtors to the CBRF. At the same time, Ukrainian enterprises are huge debtors to Russian firms.

Tables 2 and 3 confirm that the inflow of inflationary money to Russia has continued. Credits to other post-Soviet states effectively constitute grants because they are never likely to be repaid. Table 3 illustrates the size of these credits in 1992 and the first quarter of 1993. Almost 11% of Russian GDP was 'exported' to other CIS countries in 1992 solely by means of centralized settlements.

Table 3 - Net credit of CBRF to central banks of other states in the ruble area

	Net credit to central banks in the ruble area		
Month	Balance	Increase in last month	
	in bn rubles	in bn rubles	% of Russian GDP[a]
A.			
1.02.1992	0.0	x	x
1.03.1992	6140.4	6140.4	1.3
1.04.1992	61889.6	55749.2	10.0
1.05.1992	110695.2	48805.6	7.6
1.06.1992	178752.6	68057.4	9.2
1.07.1992	312390.5	133637.9	15.7
1.08.1992	309098.9	-3291.6	-0.3
1.09.1992	609589.4	300490.5	21.7
1.10.1992	1177976.9	568387.5	25.8
1.11.1992	1212203.1	34226.2	1.7
1.12.1992	1370000.0	157796.9	7.2
1.01.1993	1532000.0	162000.0	6.3
Total increase in 1992	x	1532000.0	10.9
B.			
31.12.1992[b]	1292145.8	1292145.8	8.6
31.03.1993[c]	2149131.8	856986.0	*

a - GDP data from: *Russian Economic Trends*, vol. 2, no. 1, table A15.
b - balance of correspondent account, confirmed by other central banks in the ruble area.
c - sum of balances of correspondent accounts connected with trade settlements and with ruble cash supply (see Table 2).
* - no data.

Sources:A - Monthly balance sheets of CBFR - item 'Inter-state settlements' data from Russian Economic Trends, vol. 2, no. 1, Table 5 and A16.
        B - current reports of CBFR.

Price relations in trade among republics (mainly underpriced energy factors and other raw materials imported by the CIS states from Russia) are the next important source of the transfer of Russian GDP to other post-Soviet states. This is shown in Table 4, which is based on very rough estimates made by Russian experts working at the Institute of Economy in Transition in Moscow.

Havlik and Boss[29] quote figures very similar to those announced publicly by Peter Aven, the former Minister of Foreign Economic Cooperation in the Gaidar government.

Table 4 - Price subsidies by Russia for other post-Soviet states in 1992 (in millions of US dollars)

Country	All year	Second half
All countries	10029.3	2942.0
Of which:		
Ukraine	7492.1	3651.2
Belorussia	3623.9	1889.5
Latvia	187.9	122.0
Estonia	94.9	37.0

Source: Estimation by Institute of Economy in Transition, Moscow.

Taken together, these figures paint a general picture of the problem rather than setting out detailed calculations. First of all, it is very difficult to estimate the real volume of Russian exports and imports to and from CIS countries (see below).

Secondly, the level of underpricing of Russian exports also raises a number of problems for measurement. Even in the case of a commodity like oil, it is unclear how the subsidy is to be calculated. If Russia sells oil below the Rotterdam price, for example, is this a subsidy, or does it simply reflect the true market price for Russian oil exports (given limited pipelines and port capacities for shipping to Western markets)?[30]

The positive balance of inter-republic correspondent accounts became one of the three main sources of monetary expansion in Russia in 1992: domestic credit expansion and a huge budget deficit financed by the central bank were the two other inflationary factors.[31] This inflationary policy resulted in the fresh round of high inflation that began at the end of 1992.

An interesting question is why the Russian government and the CBRF accept this burgeoning credit *vis-à-vis* the other post-Soviet states. The CBRF leadership's bureaucratic 'conservatism' and lack of professional expertise may be an explanation, but these features cannot account for the problem in its entirety. In my view, at least two other factors play an important role.

The first factor, which is mainly political in character, is closely connected with Russian foreign policy, which concentrates on relations with the former Soviet republics now called in official Russian terminology 'nearest foreign countries' (*blizhnee zarubezhie*). Russia has numerous reasons for maintaining special relations with this area. The situation of the Russian population in these countries, the future of Russian military troops located on their territories, the unsolved problem of strategic military forces, including nuclear weapons, mutual economic dependence, sometimes the imperialistic ambitions of Russian policy - all these play an important role. Economic assistance in the form of 'technical' credit or the acceptance of overdrafts, as well as the privileged export of energy inputs, is the price of this policy. There are very clear analogies with the policy of the former USSR towards the CMEA countries and various developing countries with a pro-Soviet orientation.

The second reason is the pressure applied by Russian enterprises, which are extremely interested in the relatively easy exports to former Soviet republics (with their hyperinflationary, unlimited demand for many goods). It is likely that the tightening of monetary and fiscal policy in Russia will step up this pressure in the future.

5.2. THE BEGINNINGS OF AN EXCHANGE MARKET FOR NEW CURRENCIES

The separation of the new currencies or quasi-currencies from the Russian ruble created room for a foreign exchange market. The transfer of payments with some sort of premium or discount among republics was the earliest form of exchange operation, which began in August 1992. These premiums or discounts functioned as an exchange rate and an interest rate (in the case of transactions with delayed payments).

The next stage in the formation of a market for post-Soviet currencies was the quotation of market-based exchange rates by the commercial banks and other financial institutions. Subsequently, a number of central banks in the republics began the regular publication (every day or every week) of average exchange rates based on commercial rates. The Latvian Central Bank was the first, followed by the central banks of Lithuania, the Ukraine and Belorussia. In Russia and Estonia the exchange rates of 'soft' currencies were fixed only on the commercial market.

Table 5 illustrates the exchange rates among Estonian, Latvian, Lithuanian, Ukrainian, Belorussian and Russian currencies, on the one hand, and the US dollar on the other, at the end of April 1993. These rates are the principal but not the only determinants of mutual exchange rates between individual currencies. Indirectly, the monetary and fiscal policies in individual countries played a crucial role.

Two countries (Estonia and Latvia) successfully stabilized their currencies against Western convertible currencies. Latvia, indeed, even managed to push up the nominal exchange rate of its *rublis*. The exchange rate of the Russian ruble with these currencies consequently fell as a result of the huge depreciation of the ruble in relation to the US dollar. However, one should bear in mind that the bilateral balance of payments (between Russia and both the above-mentioned Baltic states) was influenced by price subsidizing in Russian raw material exports.

The Lithuanian example provides the best evidence for this phenomenon. The Lithuanian *talon* appreciated against the Russian ruble from September to late November 1992. At the beginning of December 1992, this trend was reversed as a result of dramatic changes in the terms of trade. In the fourth quarter of 1992, Russia began to deliver oil and natural gas to Lithuania at world prices (earlier Lithuania bought energy factors at Russian, that is, domestic prices). In the first and second quarter of 1993 the *talon* again appreciated in relation to the Russian ruble.

Table 5 - Exchange rate of national currencies against the US dollar on 21 April 1993

Country	Currency	Exchange rate of central bank (average)	Market exchange rate-buying/selling rate in cash transactions
Estonia	crown	12.7272	12.58/13.0
Latvia	rublis	134.05	130/143
Lithuania	talon	507.43	501/509
Ukraine	karbovanets	3002	2800/2950
Belorussia	ruble	1023	780/800
Russia	ruble	786	750/800

Source: Rzeczpospolita, 22.04.1993.

The Ukraine represents the opposite case. Monetary and fiscal policy in the Ukraine was, in 1992 and at the beginning of 1993, far more expansionary than in Russia, and this factor determined the decreasing exchange rate of the *karbovanets* in relation to the Russian ruble. This trend deteriorated even further after the partial price liberalization introduced by the Ukrainian government on 26 December 1992. At the beginning of January 1993, more than 2 *karbovanets* were being paid for one Russian ruble.[32] At the end of January 1993 the *karbovanets*/ruble exchange rate returned to almost its previous level (1.64)[33] because of the substantial depreciation of the ruble in relation to the US dollar. In the second half of March 1993, the Ukrainian currency again depreciated to a level of around three *karbovanets* per one Russian ruble - and in April even to four (in non-cash settlements). In May 1993 the *karbovanets*/ruble exchange rate returned to the level of three. From time to time the gap between official and market rate (in relation to USD) appeared.

Other non-cash national rubles, as well as parallel cash currencies, are quoted on the commercial market. This concerns all 'national' non-cash rubles. At the end of January 1993, the Belorussian non-cash ruble was quoted in Minsk at the rate of 1.21 per one Russian ruble. At the same time, in Moscow one Russian ruble was equal to 0.8-0.9 Uzbek non-cash rubles[34]

5.3. THE IMPACT ON CIS TRADE

Because of seventy years of a central planning system, production in the ex-Soviet economy was highly specialized (especially in industry). This rendered each Soviet republic heavily dependent on inter-republic trade. According to Dornbusch, "intra-union trade accounts for 71% of total trade, on average, far more than trade among Canadian provinces or intra-European trade in the case of the European Community".[35] Tables 6 and 7 illustrate this problem in more detail and disaggregate the figure given by Dornbusch. As Table 7 shows, Russia's share of inter-republican trade in total trade of 'only' 57.8% reduced the average Soviet figure. Most of the republics had shares between 85% and 87%; the highest shares being those of Armenia and Turkmenistan (89.1%).

Table 6 - Trade Dependence of former Soviet Republics in 1988

Republic	Republic share in USSR GDP (in %)	Intra-Union trade to GNP (in %)	Extra-Union trade to GNP (in %)	Total trade to GNP (in %)
Russian Federation	61.08	12.92	9.37	22.29
Ukraine	16.24	26.89	7.14	34.03
Belorussia	4.15	44.54	7.38	51.93
Uzbekistan	3.28	34.08	5.62	39.70
Kazakhstan	4.26	29.47	4.69	34.15
Georgia	1.62	37.87	5.90	43.77
Azerbaijan	1.73	35.37	5.95	41.32
Lithuania	1.41	47.24	7.21	54.45
Moldova	1.22	45.86	6.36	52.22
Latvia	1.11	46.84	7.21	54.05
Kyrghyzstan	0.79	39.63	5.98	45.61
Tadzhikistan	0.79	36.17	5.76	41.94
Armenia	0.92	47.83	5.84	53.67
Turkmenistan	0.74	37.56	4.60	42.16
Estonia	0.65	50.09	8.79	58.88
USRR	**100.00**	**21.10**	**8.27**	**29.37**

Source: Selm and Wagener, 1992, table 1.

Table 6 shows that in 1988 Estonia had the highest dependence of GNP on inter-republican trade (a trade/GNP ratio of 50.09%). Most of the other republics ranged between 34 and 48%. The two biggest republics (Russia and Ukraine) were far less dependent, although Ukraine's ratios still exceeded the USSR average (21.1%).

The spontaneous disintegration of the ruble area probably had a negative effect on inter-republic trade and therefore on the economic activity of all the post-Soviet states. Unfortunately, no credible statistical information is available as yet; consequently, any quantitative estimation of the trade collapse is a highly risky undertaking.

However, there are alarming reports of a total shortage of Russian oil and natural gas in the Ukraine, Lithuania and some other post-Soviet states. In the case of Estonia, Russia has lost its position as first trading partner to Finland.

Table 7 - Share of inter-republican trade in total trade of the former USSR republics in 1988

Republic	Share of Inter-Republican Trade in Total Trade (%)
Russian Federation	57.8
Ukraine	79.0
Belorussia	85.8
Uzbekistan	85.8
Kazakhstan	86.3
Georgia	86.5
Azerbaijan	85.6
Lithuania	86.8
Moldova	87.8
Latvia	86.7
Kyrghyzstan	86.9
Tadzhikistan	86.3
Armenia	89.1
Turkmenistan	89.1
Estonia	85.1
USRR	**71.8**

Source: IMF, 1992b, p. 37, table 1.

Havlik and Boss[36] give some very rough estimates of inter-republican trade, especially between Russia and the Ukraine. They calculate[37] that total Russian exports in real terms declined in 1992 (compared with 1991) by 23%, of which exports to former USSR republics fell by only 7%. The corresponding figures on the imports side amounted to minus 20% and minus 12%. Havlik and Boss maintain that this "... would imply that Russian trade with the CIS has so far dropped less than foreign trade, despite all the payments problems and the new tariff and non-tariff barriers". The above estimations are plausible because of the hyperinflationary financing of Russian exports to other post-Soviet states, and because the process of real disintegration of the ruble area only started in the second half of 1992.

As far as the Ukraine is concerned, the decrease in inter-republican exports and imports in 1992 seems to have been more serious than in Russia, although detailed and reliable statistics are not available.

Apart from monetary disintegration and technical payment problems (very long transfers in terms of hyperinflation), other factors have exerted a negative influence on inter-republic trade relations:

First, the former Soviet republics have begun to raise reciprocal trade barriers such as tariffs, export quotas, and so on. Although barriers existed earlier under the central planning system (in the form of the command allocation of production and the administrative rationing of inputs), in the second half of 1992 they started to increase. In October 1992, Russia decided to establish custom borders with the Ukraine, the Baltic states, Georgia and Azerbaijan. In February 1993, the Russian government announced the increase of tariffs with Latvia. There are no free trade agreements among most of the post-Soviet states, nor even any most-favoured-nation clauses.

Export controls are a specific feature of new post-Soviet protectionism. There are several reasons for this phenomenon, including major shortages of many goods on the domestic market and the attempt to stop the profitable re-exporting (especially through the Baltic states) of underpriced energy factors and raw materials. To solve this latter problem, President Yeltsin announced in November 1992 that all countries leaving the ruble area would have to pay world prices for Russian oil, gas and other raw materials. The practical implementation of this declaration, however, is proceeding only gradually.

Second, regional political conflicts as well as nationalism[38] prevent effective trade contacts.

Third, different levels of price liberalization, the lack of effective legal protection of trade contracts,[39] and so on, should also be taken into consideration.

One must agree with Havlik and Boss that "... one cannot say that the 'real' interstate trade collapse is behind the two republics[40]; it may still lie ahead".[41] This statement seems to apply to all trade contacts between post-Soviet states.

6. ATTEMPTS TO BUILD A NEW MONETARY REGIME

The present bilateral clearing between 'soft' currencies and parallel currencies must be counterproductive with respect to inter-republic trade. Payment surpluses achieved with one country cannot be used to finance payment deficits with another. In theory this mechanism allows Russia to control the importing of inflation from other CIS states. However, as previously mentioned, external and internal political pressures prevent the achievement of this goal. The existing system of settlements cannot be viewed as a final monetary regime on the former USSR territory.

The need to find a more sustainable model led to the Bishkek Agreement signed at the CIS summit on 9 October 1992 by representatives from eight states - Russia, Armenia, Belorussia, Kazakhstan, Kyrgyzstan, Moldova, Tadzhikistan and Uzbekistan.[42] This agreement contained the following main points:

- acceptance of the ruble as the legal currency unit, but with the possibility of issuing parallel money substitutes as well as national currencies in the future;
- a multilateral settlement system;

- the bilateral regulation of debt accumulated on central bank correspondent accounts;
- monopoly by the CBRF in issuing ruble cash and its leading role in issuing credit; the latter to be decided by the Interbank Coordination Council created by representatives of the central banks of the republics and affiliated to the CBRF;
- an undertaking to introduce the full convertibility of the ruble;
- the coordination of monetary and fiscal policy;
- common responsibility for the assets and liabilities of the former *Gosbank* of the USSR;
- the creation of the Inter-State Bank (ISB) or *Mezhgosudarstvennyi Bank*.

Most of the points in the Bishkek Agreement, however, were made very ambiguous by political compromise. For example, the document did not define what role the ISB should play: whether it should be the common central bank of the ruble area or only the bank for multilateral clearing. Moreover, the system of decision-making by the board of ISB was not specified. Almost all other points, like common macroeconomic policy, remained without effective policy instruments.

All these questions were negotiated during the next three and half months by politicians and experts. Finally, in January 1993, the CIS summit in Minsk accepted regulations concerning the ISB, but only as a bank of multilateral clearing.[43] The Russian ruble will be the currency of multilateral settlements. Russia will have 50% of votes on the ISB board, although decisions will require a qualified majority of 75% of votes.

By May 1993, neither the Bishkek nor Minsk agreements have been implemented. On the contrary, as mentioned earlier, the process of monetary and trade disintegration has continued, and may even have accelerated. These facts did not stop CIS countries from signing, in Moscow on 14 May 1993, a new document: the treaty on economic union which established, among other things, the free trade regime.

7. POSSIBLE FUTURE DEVELOPMENTS

It is hard to accept the current monetary system on the former Soviet territory as a final solution. I discussed earlier the weaknesses in the existing arrangements, which will probably evolve into one of the following models:

1. The most probable solution is, unfortunately, that of 'soft' currencies or parallel cash currencies in each country with only limited convertibility among them. Bilateral clearing and barter transactions seem to be the dominant payment arrangements in this model.
2. The current account convertibility of each post-Soviet currency in relation to Western currencies and therefore their mutual cross-convertibility (as

between the Polish zloty, the Hungarian forint and Czech crown) is another, although not very probable, variant. It is likely that only the Baltic states will be able to create such monetary arrangements in the near future.

3. A payment union is recommended by some Western experts.[44] The Bishkek and Minsk agreements creating the ISB give this opportunity to at least some of the CIS member-countries. It should be stressed that two sub-variants of this model are possible: one modelled on the post-war European Payment Union, which was based mainly on decentralized transactions by autonomous enterprises; the other organized on a more centralized pattern and to some extent similar to the former CMEA.

4. Ruble monetary union still seems to be a possible solution for those countries that have not introduced their own currencies. However, each month that passes of hyperinflation and monetary mismanagement renders this variant less and less likely. Countries using Russian cash rubles find themselves in a very difficult position. They must suffer the importing of Russian hyperinflation and they must pay permanent high seignorage to Russia. From this point of view, these countries may see increasing debt in settlements to Russia, as well as underpricing in imports from Russia, as a form of compensation. It may be that for some countries with even higher macroeconomic disequilibria than Russia's - e.g. Georgia, Armenia, Azerbaijan and Tadzhikistan, presently torn by civil war - this situation is convenient in the short run. However, it is difficult to imagine an indefinite continuation of the status quo.

The continuation of ruble monetary union requires, on the one hand, a serious attempt at stabilization in Russia;[45] on the other, the far-reaching coordination of monetary, fiscal and trade policies, as well as numerous institutional arrangements (e.g. banking regulations) among member countries. Non-Russian states must above all abandon their independent central banks in favour of the CBRF.

All these measures will depend on political circumstances in individual countries. Most of them still lack the political determination to start radical market-oriented reforms, and they are reluctant to surrender part of their newly-achieved national sovereignty to external authorities, especially ones controlled by Russia. The question is whether it is realistic to expect a radical change in this attitude before the final disintegration of the ruble area occurs.

POST SCRIPTUM

In May 1993, the situation gradually began to change towards the first variant discussed above; that is, towards the full separation among the monetary systems of each of the post-Soviet countries in their creation of 'soft', non-convertible currencies. Russia stimulated this process by exchanging old ruble banknotes issued before 1993 on its territory. This operation, implemented on

26 July 1993, left the other post-Soviet states still using Russian cash rubles with banknotes that were invalid within Russia. Although the next attempt to rebuild the ruble area was made in September (the Moscow agreement on economic union and monetary union of a 'new type'), the process of final disintegration was by now unstoppable. Moldova introduced the *leu* in September, Turkmenistan introduced the *manat* in October. Belorussia, Georgia and Azerbaijan extended the circulation of their coupons (temporary cash currency). Finally, Kazakhstan and Uzbekistan left the ruble area on 15 November, 1993. Kazakhstan introduced the *teng*, and Uzbekistan the temporary currency *som*. Two last states, Armenia and Tajikistan are expected to introduce their own currencies soon.

NOTES

1 I am very grateful to Jacek Rostowski of the London School of Slavonic and East European Studies, University of London, Ardo H. Hansson of the Stockholm Institute of East European Economics, Hans-Jürgen Wagener and Bert van Selm of the University of Groeningen, and Pekka Sutela of the National Bank of Finland for their helpful comments and suggestions. However, I alone am responsible for the contents of this paper and its shortcomings.

2 Aslund, 1992.

3 IMF *et al.*, 1990, p. 49.

4 I have in mind the situation where money is not enough to buy rationed goods and services.

5 McKinnon, 1991.

6 IMF *et al.*, 1990, p. 49.

7 IMF *et al.*, 1990, p. 10.

8 McKinnon, 1991.

9 IMF *et al.*, 1990, p. 10.

10 IMF *et al.*, 1990, p. 50.

11 Shops formally owned by trade cooperatives with prices controlled by the state, far more flexible than in the case of typical administrative prices and usually not subsidized.

12 IMF, 1992, table 11.

13 Cottarelli and Blejer, 1991.

14 This was, in principle, a typical administrative price reform. However, it included elements of liberalization, especially in the producer goods sphere. In the following months, effective price control weakened due to the political break-up of the all-union government.

15 IMF, 1992, table 11.

16 IMF, 1992, p. 12.

17 I place the word 'real' in quotation marks in order to stress its merely formal, statistical sense. In reality the increase in 'real' wages does not

have a market equivalent because of increasing market shortages.

18 IMF, 1992, p. 11.
19 IMF, 1992, table 4.
20 IMF, 1992, table 5.
21 Sachs and Lipton, 1992.
22 Kirichenko and Shpagina, 1992.
23 Hansson, 1992.
23 Rostowski, 1993.
24 Rostowski, 1992.
26 Lainela and Sutela, 1993.
27 Colloquially called the *zaichik* (leveret) because of the picture on the banknote.
28 I do not possess reliable information on Tajikistan and Armenia.
29 Havlik and Boss, 1993.
30 I am grateful to Ardo H. Hansson for this latter point.
31 Dabrowski, 1993; Sachs, 1993.
32 Obzor, 1993.
33 Sud'ba, 1993.
34 Sud'ba, 1993.
35 Dornbusch, 1993, p. 46.
36 Havlik and Boss, 1993.
37 Havlik and Boss, 1993, table 2.
38 Dornbusch, 1993.
39 Dornbusch, 1993
40 That is, Russia and the Ukraine.
41 Havlik and Boss, 1993.
42 Gurevich, 1992.
43 Zhagel', 1993; Seninskii, 1993; SNG, 1993.
44 See Dornbusch, 1993.
45 Dabrowski, 1993.

BIBLIOGRAPHY

Aslund, A. (1992), 'Prospects for a Successful Change of Economic System in Russia', Stockholm Institute of East European Economics, Working Paper no. 60.

Cottarelli, C., Blejer M.I. (1991), 'Forced Savings and Repressed Inflation in the Soviet Union: Some Empirical Results', IMF Working Paper, Washington D.C.

Dabrowski, M. (1993), 'Itogi deyatel'nosti komandy Gaidara', *Evraziya*, forthcoming.

Dornbusch, R. (1993), 'Payments Arrangements among the Republics', in *Post-communist Reform: Pain and Progress*, WIDER 3 Report, Helsinki, forthcoming.

Gurevich, V. (1992), 'Izgnanie iz rublya', *Moskovskie Novosti*, 1992, no. 42.

Hansson, A. (1992), 'Transforming an Economy While Building a Nation: The Case of Estonia', Stockholm Institute of East European Economics, Working Paper no. 62.

Havlik, P., Boss H. (1993), 'Disintegration of the USSR: Structural Consequences for Russia and Ukraine', mimeo, WIIW, Vienna, April 15.

IMF, The World Bank, OECD and EBRD (1990), 'The Economy of the USSR. Summary and Recommendation (A Study Undertaken in Response to a Request by the Houston Summit)', 19 December 1990.

IMF (1992a), *Economic Review. Russian Federation*, Washington D.C., April.

IMF (1992b), *Common Issues and Interrepublican Relation in the Former USSR*, Washington D.C., April.

Kirichenko, N., Shpagina M. (1992), 'Rublevoe prostranstvo kupirovano', *Kommersant*, no. 42.

Lainela, S., Sutela P. (1993), 'Escaping from the Rouble: Estonia and Latvia Compared', paper presented at The Third EACES Workshop on *Integration and Disintegration in European Economies: Divergent or Convergent Processes?*, Trento, 4-5 March 1993.

McKinnon, R.I. (1991), 'Financial Control in the Transition from Classical Socialism to a Market Economy', paper prepared for the IPR-IRIS Conference *The Transition to a Market Economy - Institutional Aspects*, Prague, 24-27 March 1991.

Obzor (1993), Obzor valyutnykh rynkov, *Kommersant*, no. 1, 4-10 January 1993.

Rostowski, J. (1992), 'A Proposal on How to Introduce a Currency Board Based Monetary System in the Republic of Latvia', Centre for Economic Performance Discussion Paper, CEP London School of Economics.

Rostowski, J. (1993), 'Creating Stable Monetary Systems in Post-Communist Economies', mimeo, London.

Sachs, J. (1993), 'Achieving Monetary Stabilization in Russia in 1993', unpublished memo, March 7.

Sachs, J., Lipton, D. (1992), 'Remaining Steps to Achieve a Market-Based Monetary System', unpublished memo, May 1.

Selm, G. Van, Wagener, H.-J. (1992), 'Former Soviet Republics' Economic Interdependence', mimeo.

Seninskii, S. (1993), 'Rubl' Central'nogo banka Rossii stanet EKYU SNG', Moskovskie Novosti, no. 5.

SNG (1993), 'SNG posle Minska: chto budet s ekonomikoi?', *Kommersant*, no. 3.

Sud'ba (1993), 'Sud'ba rossiiskovo rublya v stranakh Baltii i Sodruzhestva reshaetsya na moskovskikh torgakh', *Kommersant-Daily*, no. 15, 29 January 1993.

Zhagel', I. (1993), 'Rublevogo prostranstva uzhe net, a est' rublevaya zona', *Izvestiya*, no. 14, 26 January 1993.

ESCAPING FROM THE RUBLE: ESTONIA AND LATVIA COMPARED[1]

Seija Lainela and Pekka Sutela

1. THE BALTIC STATES INTRODUCE THEIR OWN CURRENCIES

The Baltic states introduced new currencies in the summer and autumn of 1992. Estonia was the first state to do so by introducing the kroon, followed by Latvia and Lithuania, which left the ruble zone a little later when they declared the supplementary currencies that had been circulating alongside the Russian ruble to be the sole legal tender. Latvia's official currency is currently the lats, together with the Latvian ruble, while Lithuania's is the coupon. These interim currencies will eventually be replaced by the lats in Latvia and the litas in Lithuania. The introduction of the lats began in March 1993. This should be largely a technical operation involving the exchange of banknotes and with no fundamental change to the monetary system, since this already took place when the Russian ruble was abandoned. As the Estonian experience shows, however, one should not underestimate the socio-psychological importance of at last having the 'real' national currency in circulation.

As nationals of the Baltic states would be the first to emphasise, these currencies are not entirely new, since all three states had their sovereign currencies between the World Wars. In Estonia the currency was initially the markka and subsequently the kroon, in Latvia it was the lats, and in Lithuania the litas.

There are several valid economic arguments for introducing national currencies in the countries which formerly belonged to the ruble zone:[2]
1. A national currency allows a more independent economic policy to be

pursued, while at the same time emphasising that national decision-makers are responsible for the development of their own economies.

2. There is no reason why the ruble zone should be considered an optimal currency area: the resource endowments, probable exogenous shocks, institutions, and policy goals of the former Soviet republics vary enormously.

3. The rapid depreciation of the ruble has made it necessary for these countries to buffer themselves against the crisis of the ruble.

4. During the early months of 1992, in particular, the ruble zone suffered simultaneously from an excess supply of deposit rubles and a shortage of cash rubles. Supplementary currencies were duly introduced in several of the former Soviet republics for transactions purposes. There was a probability that regional or enterprise-based monies (witness the Estonian *Tartu* money of Spring 1992!) would have appeared in the Baltic countries if sovereign currencies had not been introduced.

5. The existence of a national currency also means that government revenue can be garnered in the form of seigniorage.

Apart from these legitimate economic considerations, Baltic currencies were also viewed from within a wider perspective. A national currency is of great importance as a symbol of national independence. The enthusiasm shown by the Baltic states for their own currencies is easy to understand from this point of view, and should be respected.

Nevertheless, international understanding of the Baltic currency plans was rather less than complete in 1992. The International Monetary Fund (IMF) and the European Community (EC) apparently urged the Baltic states to be prudent in introducing their own currencies. This was widely, even if incorrectly, interpreted in the Baltic states as constituting opposition in principle to national currencies. Hansson and Sachs[3] maintain that the IMF "tried at first to delay the introduction of Estonia's currency, arguing that the country was not yet ready". Only after the IMF had seen that the Estonian authorities "proceeded on their own" did it "provide them with some last-minute technical support". Hansson and Sachs would seem to be well placed to make this comment, given that Hansson (a Canadian economist with Estonian origins now resident in Sweden) was a member of the official three-person Estonian Currency Reform Committee when the kroon was introduced.

The IMF, for its part, has vehemently protested against this interpretation.[4] The Fund does not deny that - as evidenced by Hernandez-Cata[5] - it was originally very sceptical about the introduction of national currencies in the former Soviet Union. In the Fund's view, "certain key elements would need to be in place to improve the chances for success, including, *inter alia*, completion of the price liberalization process and a balanced budget". In spite of IMF protestations, however, the fact remains that not all such preconditions were present when the kroon was introduced. The difference in the monetary reform schedules thereby implied partly stemmed from the fact that the Fund was apparently considering the establishment of fully-fledged central banking, while Estonia chose to set off along the shorter and narrower road of a currency board. The IMF, of course, never questioned Estonia's sovereign right to make its own decisions: the introduction of a national currency is a matter for sovereign decision-making in every independent country. What has changed, though, is the emphasis apparently given to national currencies as policy instruments. Whereas in early 1992 the IMF was recommending caution to the Baltic countries, in early 1993 it appeared to be pushing such unwilling former Soviet republics as Belorussia and Kazakhstan towards the introduction of national currencies as a condition for full-scale Fund support. Once it is technically feasible to print banknotes, there is no economically acceptable reason why a national currency should not be introduced in any of the countries of the former ruble zone.

The Baltic states have only now begun the process of developing institutions and instruments for the pursuit of monetary and foreign exchange policies. The assistance of the IMF and other international organizations is available and is being utilised; nevertheless this process will inevitably take a long time.

The IMF also stressed that payment arrangements should be negotiated with the ruble zone countries before national currencies were introduced, in order to prevent the dislocation of trade among these countries. In negotiations, Russia was forthcoming concerning the technical issues of exchanging kroons for rubles, but trade issues proper were bogged down by various economic and political conflicts of interest. All the Baltic states have seen a collapse in their trade with the ruble zone countries, especially Russia, although trade had already started to decline before these countries left the ruble zone. Thus the Baltic states' own currencies were not a decisive factor in this regard, although they did give rise to some technical difficulties and payment delays.

Opinions differ in the Baltic states concerning the pace at which foreign trade could and should change from almost complete dependence on Russia to a more balanced geographical distribution. It is generally accepted, however, that there is a need to continue trading with Russia and other CIS states. Payment arrangements between these countries have been agreed or are still being negotiated. They are probably least advanced in Lithuania, partly because Lithuania was forced to introduce an interim currency very rapidly. Negotiations between the Baltic states and Russia have been hampered by political disputes and problems relating to, for example, the servicing of outstanding debt commitments.

It is widely believed in the Baltic states that the decline in trade with Russia is due mainly to the serious economic situation in Russia, as well as to political measures implemented by Russia which are regarded as being anti-Baltic. On the other hand, the outcome of the parliamentary elections in Lithuania in the autumn of 1992 demonstrated that, at least in that country, people feel that their government could do more to maintain and develop traditional trade relations.

The introduction of national currencies and the consolidation of their position have been most successful in Estonia, where the kroon seems to have replaced practically all the rubles and convertible currencies in circulation. That the Estonian kroon enjoys the confidence of the population is evidenced by the extensive exchange of cash convertible currencies for kroons, and by the increase in kroon deposits since the currency reform.

The reform in Lithuania has taken place more recently. Since little information on Lithuanian currency developments is available, they are not considered in this paper. They would, however, be interesting from a comparative perspective. Unlike Estonia and Latvia, Lithuania has so far been unable to stabilise its inflation and currency. Nevertheless, the decline of the ruble has been such that even the Lithuanian coupon has appreciated relative to it.

Convertible currencies can still be used - and are widely so - in Latvia. At the end of 1992, half of transactions in the country were reportedly conducted in hard currencies, and Russian rubles were also in circulation. The Latvian monetary authorities deny that this is a problem: in Hayekian vein, they argue that there should be a choice of monies.

The stability of the new currencies in the longer term is difficult to assess at this point. The Estonian kroon has been pegged to the German mark since its introduction, and has strengthened in parallel with it as a result of general turmoil in European currencies.

The Latvian ruble floats. This may have been a deliberate policy choice as regards the exchange rate regime, or it may have been due to such technical reasons as the absence in the country of the conditions appropriate for adopting a fixed exchange rate and conducting foreign exchange policy in general. Nevertheless, to date Latvian exchange rates have been fairly stable.

Against the background of Russia's monetary chaos, the introduction of the Baltic currencies stands out as a major achievement. In late 1992 and early 1993 the inflation rates of Estonia and Latvia were just one-tenth of Russia's. Whatever the outcome, monetary reform could hardly have made the situation in the Baltic states worse than it was in Russia. That leaving the ruble zone was the wisest option became increasingly evident in the course of 1992. The uphill struggle to stability and onwards to prosperity, however, has only just begun. The Baltic states suffer from a severe lack of effective instruments for macroeconomic management as well as expertise in such areas as monetary and fiscal policies; a deficiency that may still undermine the credibility of the new currencies.

In Estonia, economic policy is now decided by a right-wing government accountable to a parliament elected in September 1992. The government remains committed to stringent economic policies. The Lithuanian elections held in October resulted in a shift of power to the left. According to statements by Algirdas Brazauskas, the leader of the victorious Democratic Labour Party, some changes must be made to the economic programme agreed on with the IMF, although what form these changes should take is still unclear.[6] Latvia has been the last of the Baltic states to hold parliamentary elections, which are

circulation at a particular time involves very complex logistics. In the practical exchange of one currency for another, a large number of volunteer workers assisted at conversion points in different parts of the country. The aim was to ensure that the rules and arrangements were as unambiguous as possible so that opportunities for discretionary decisions and abuse could be reduced to the minimum.

In carrying out the currency reform there was the risk that large sums of rubles might flow into the country from Russia for conversion. This danger was averted by restricting the amount of cash that each inhabitant could exchange and by separately investigating all unusually large transfers made between bank accounts prior to the conversion. It may also be that, in the end, the possessors of large amounts of ruble notes decided not to trust in the new currency of a small nation.

The currency reform was carried out between 20 and 22 June 1992. The ruble ceased to be legal tender in Estonia with immediate effect on 20 June, and the only legal tender since then has been the kroon. The kroon (abbreviation EEK) is divided into 100 senti. All persons resident in Estonia who had registered their names for conversion were allowed to exchange 1,500 rubles at a rate of one kroon per 10 rubles in the period from 20 to 22 June. This amount was equivalent to about 12 dollars; larger amounts of rubles could be converted into kroons at a rate of one kroon to 50 rubles in the period from 26 to 30 June, after which date the rubles could no longer be converted into kroons. Apparently, the Tallinn authorities believed that Estonians would use any remaining rubles for shopping in Russia. The central bank of Russia has, on the other hand, forbidden the import of rubles from Estonia to Russia after the currency reform. The non-implementability of such restrictions is not a major problem in the case of such a small former Soviet republic as Estonia; a circumstance which made reaching agreement between Tallinn and Moscow authorities easier than would have been the case of, for instance, Ukraine.

Bank deposits made by residents were also converted into kroons at the rate of 1:10, the only exception being deposits of more than 50,000 rubles made after the beginning of May. The conversion of such deposits was decided on a discretionary basis. Rubles held by enterprises were also converted into kroons at the rate of 1:10. As soon as the currency reform began, stores marked their prices in kroons and, for example, all hard currency stores started to sell their goods in kroons only. Today, the only person in Tallinn to ask for payment in foreign currency will be the occasional Russian taxi driver.

Foreign currency accounts held by enterprises or individuals remained valid, and foreign currencies in such accounts could be used until the end of 1992. The accounts were, however, closed as regards new foreign currency entries, which must be converted into kroons.[17] After 1 March, 1993, Estonian firms were again allowed to open settlement accounts in foreign currencies in authorised Estonian banks. According to the governor of the Bank of Estonia, Siim Kallas, this measure was made possible by the strengthened position of the kroon.

Since the introduction of the kroon, the official exchange rate quoted by the Bank of Estonia has been one German mark = eight kroons. The exchange rate between the kroon and the German mark was set at the level of the so-called market rate of the ruble at the time of the currency reform, which meant that the kroon was undoubtedly undervalued to some extent. The ruble's market rate was determined in interbank auctions and, because of the scarcity of the currencies offered and the abundance of rubles, the ruble's rate was undervalued. The undervaluation of the kroon should facilitate economic development by promoting exports and protecting home markets from import competition. On the other hand, it is one of the possible explanations for the continuation of Estonian inflation.

A crude way of assessing the feasibility of the current exchange rate over the longer term is to look at Estonian competitiveness in terms of wage levels. Currently, average Estonian wages are approximately 60 US$ per month. Taking the Polish level of 150 US$ per month as the benchmark, Estonia could at least double its cost level while maintaining the current exchange rate.

Altogether, about 2.2 billion cash rubles were converted into kroons.[18] This amount was about the same as estimates of the amount of rubles in circulation in Estonia made at the time, for which no accurate data were available. It seems that only small amounts of rubles were converted into kroons at the more unfavourable rate of the second stage of the conversion.

Implementing the currency reform required prior discussions with Russia on practical matters relating to the issue of the kroon. The Bank of Estonia has agreed to return the rubles collected during the conversion to the central bank of Russia without compensation. Because of problems connected with payment arrangements, however, this has not yet been done.

2.4. AFTER THE REFORM

The currency reform also seems to have succeeded rather well in achieving goals other than technical ones, as indicated by the fact that the kroon immediately became the only currency in circulation. Since the currency reform, significant amounts of foreign exchange have flowed into the Bank of Estonia. During the first months after the currency reform the foreign currency converted into kroons consisted mainly of cash held by residents, and the magnitude of these sums came as a surprise to the authorities.

Subsequently, enterprises, too, started to repatriate their foreign exchange funds. In July, the Ministry of Economy estimated that the foreign exchange held by Estonian companies in foreign bank accounts amounted to the equivalent of 65 million US$,[19] while other estimates put the sum as high as 100 million US$. Currency had evidently been transferred abroad at an accelerating pace prior to the currency reform because companies were uncertain as to how foreign currency holdings would be treated.[20]

On 16 July 1992, the Bank of Estonia published its first balance sheet, which showed foreign exchange reserves of 98 million US$. By early April 1993, the reserves had already increased to 237 million US\$. The relevant developments in the Bank's balance sheet are shown in Figure 1. As will be seen, the kroon is overbacked relative to the currency board principle adopted.

Figure 1 Balance sheet of the Bank of Estonia

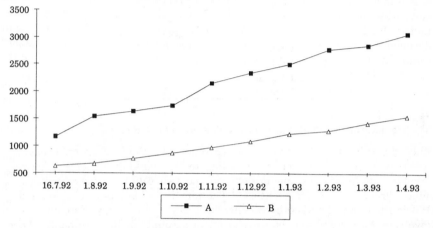

A   Gold and convertible foreign currency claims.
B   Notes and coin circulation.

Criticism of Estonia's currency reform has come mainly from economists and spokesmen for the business sector. The level at which the kroon's exchange rate was fixed has been targeted in particular, the argument being that the undervaluation of the kroon makes imports too expensive, with the result that a large part of production has become unprofitable.[21] It should be noted, however, that this criticism has not been levelled at the choice of a currency board as such.

The grievances of enterprises and banks centre on the problems created by the practical arrangements associated with the conversion and the new exchange rate system. Large companies trading with Russia complain that they are hampered by the obligation to convert all of their rubles. Altogether, companies exchanged 700 million cash rubles into kroons when the reform came into force.

As regards commercial banks, problems have been caused by the central bank's practice of operating only in the German mark and not in other foreign currencies. The commercial banks are obliged to convert other currencies deposited in accounts with them into German marks before presenting them to the Bank of Estonia for conversion into kroons. This operation is time-consuming and weakens the banks' liquidity, since they still have to pay the corresponding amounts in kroons immediately to their customers.[22]

Bank of Estonia's foreign exchange quotations

	US$ exchange rate
14 July 1992	11.8824
1 Aug	11.8320
1 Sept	11.2776
1 Oct	11.2744
3 Nov	12.3824
1 Dec	12.8120
1 Jan 1993	12.9120
1 Feb	12.6104
1 March	13.1440
1 Apr	12.9144

2.5. THE IMPACT OF THE REFORM ON THE FOREIGN TRADE SECTOR

Since the ruble is not a convertible currency, the Bank of Estonia does not quote an exchange rate for it. According to the banking agreement between Estonia and Russia, payments between the two countries may be made in rubles, kroons or other currencies.[23] The aim is to have payments related to trade with Russia handled by commercial banks. Accordingly, Estonian banks have been authorized to open correspondent accounts in Russian banks. There are three ways in which companies trading with Russia can spend the rubles they have earned: they can keep them in the Estonian banks' correspondent accounts in Russia, exchange them for convertible currencies in the Russian currency auctions, or find a buyer on Estonia's currency exchange.[24] Even after the reform, there are still currency exchanges operating in Estonia where banks, acting on the instructions of companies, buy and sell kroons, convertible currencies and rubles.

Estonia and Russia have opened accounts in each other's central banks in order to effect payments between the two governments. Estonia has transferred 50 million kroons and Russia 500 million rubles to these accounts. Russia has used its account for the maintenance of Russian military units in Estonia, whereas Estonia intends to use its account for energy imports from Russia.

Trade between Estonia and Russia has declined sharply over the past two years or so. Difficulties have been encountered in importing goods from Russia and also in receiving payments for export deliveries. Hence the introduction of Estonia's own currency has not been crucial for trade with Russia, although the new payment arrangements apparently still do not function smoothly. It is obvious that a substantial part of trade between Estonia and Russia omitted from official statistics is based either on barter or on convertible currencies.

Payments to other CIS states will be effected through correspondent accounts kept in the central banks and commercial banks. In practice, trade is now partly conducted in cash convertible currencies as well. It has been agreed that payments among the Baltic states should take place mainly in convertible currencies.[25]

2.6. THE IMPLICATIONS OF THE REFORM FOR OTHER SECTORS

In concomitance with the currency reform, turnover tax in Estonia was raised from 8% to 18%, and corporate income tax was raised by 10 percentage points to 35%. Personal taxation was increased, and wage rises were restricted. These measures were part of the economic stabilization programme drawn up by the Estonian authorities jointly with IMF experts. The stabilization programme was based on a restrictive monetary policy and a tight fiscal policy aimed at improving a budget balance which had started to move into deficit.

As a result of these measures, living costs rose by almost a quarter between June and July 1992. The rate of increase was still 18% in August and 7% in September of that year. Inflation only slowed down to 3.4% in December, and remained at the same or an even lower level in early 1993. There are several possible explanations for why the currency board did not immediately bring about stable price levels. One factor contributing to the steep rise in inflation after currency reform was the larger-than-expected inflow of currencies into the Bank of Estonia, which turned into a rapid increase in the amount of currency in circulation. These currencies came both from larger-than-expected original cash reserves and from exports, including the reportedly very profitable retrading of metals and other commodities from Russia.[26] The share of exports in the economy has thus, temporarily at least, been larger than expected. Performance on the real side of the economy has, however, remained poor, and output has fallen constantly. The rapid rate of inflation has reduced the considerable original undervaluation of the kroon, and this has also generated inflation. Finally, one should note that Estonian price liberalization has been to some degree step-by-step, which has also fuelled inflation in spite of a balanced budget.

The commercial banks are free to set interest rates, and those on loans have been high, with annual rates averaging 50% in the autumn. However, when inflation is taken into account, real interest rates have been clearly negative. Bank-specific variation in interest rates has recently ranged from less than 30 to almost 200% annually. The Bank of Estonia does not quote a interest rate that could be taken as an official policy guideline.

Problems may arise in the near future on account of the fact that part of the population expected economic conditions to improve following the introduction of the kroon; expectations which have recently been running high. Merely changing the currency unit, however, cannot solve the basic problems of a weak economy: namely, the need for structural change and the introduction of market economy methods. The true significance of the strict requirements of the economic programme drawn up with the IMF will only gradually become apparent. The increase in unemployment is expected to accelerate and real incomes to continue to decline. International support will remain crucial.

The application of the currency board system in Estonian conditions over the longer term will raise special problems. As already mentioned, foreign currency reserves have grown faster than expected both because the size of domestic foreign currency cash funds was larger than expected and because export earnings had been boosted by receipts from retrading. In theory, export earnings may continue to increase at a faster rate than domestic production in the future, in which case the currency board system could turn into a mechanism sustaining inflation.[27] Perhaps partly in recognition of this danger, the central bank, which is responsible for the currency board's functions in Estonia, has also retained monetary instruments at its disposal. It is not known exactly to what extent these might be used. In principle, however, a potentially unstable combination of a currency board and a central bank pursuing monetary policy might emerge.

An outcome more probable than oversized export revenue will be the drying up of incomes from retrading Russian commodities. In this case, adherence to the currency board would give rise to a contraction of the money supply in an economy which has already undergone a statistical downturn of some 50% in production. This might be the occasion for the Tallinn authorities to abandon the currency board, which at least some of them have always viewed as a temporary instrument with which to create credibility and to borrow time for the development of central banking policies proper.

The Banking Department of the Bank of Estonia has already intervened vigorously in the banking system. In a first round of post-socialist banking crisis, several banks, including three of the largest, had to be liquidated or consolidated.[28] These moratoria consequent on insolvency translated into illiquidity were due to general incompetence, too high inflationary expectations and the loss of currencies in the Moscow VEB debacle. It was not yet a case of bank crisis induced primarily by bad loans, although this is still waiting in the wings.

Hanke, Jonung and Schuler[29] give three criteria for a genuine currency board: the monetary base must be fully backed by foreign reserves: the currency must be fully convertible: and the exchange rate must be fixed. In their view, the Estonian case fails on two counts. The kroon convertibility is not complete even for current-account transactions, and the kroon is not convertible for capital-account purchases by Estonians. Also, the kroon exchange rate is not fixed but pegged. It can, therefore, be changed.

There is no doubt that the Estonian case is not that of a pure currency board. But, as Fieleke[30] argues, it seems that a pure currency board is impossible to find anywhere. Also, it seems that Hanke et al. may exaggerate the ease with which the kroon exchange rate can be altered.[31] Finally, their case is weakened by their insistence that "when the pegged exchange rate of the Estonian monetary system is altered, as we believe will occur in the near future, the currency board system should not be blamed, since Estonia does not have that". As all good Utopians know, the only way that any system can be made immune to failures is to define it in such a way that it will never be subjected to empirical judgement.

Nevertheless, as the above discussion should have made clear, Hanke et al. are very probably right to view current Estonian monetary arrangements - whatever one decides to call them - as temporary.

Fieleke[32] tends to judge the adoption of a currency board by economies in transition as in some sense superfluous. If the authorities were able to commit themselves to reform, why would they require so drastic a remedy? If they were inclined to inflate, why would they agree to a currency board?

Surely, however, the alternatives are not that simple. First of all, the Baltic countries are obviously cases in which the authorities have not reformed themselves. What is required are genuinely new authorities, quite possibly with genuinely new frames of mind.

Second, and more importantly, the most significant lesson to be learnt from the Estonian case seems to be that money is not just money, it is also a crucial symbol of nationhood. It is highly unlikely that the Estonians would have accepted the policies of a balanced budget so stoically, had it not been for the sake of maintaining the value of the kroon. The currency board principle made 'the only stable currency in the North of Europe' possible, and national pride helped to make drastic stabilization policies feasible.

3. THE LATVIAN RUBLE

3.1. IMPLEMENTATION OF THE CURRENCY REFORM

Latvia's intention to introduce its own currency was first made public by the government's first economic reform programme drawn up in 1990.

Latvian currency reform is not as well known abroad as Estonia's, perhaps because rubles were gradually replaced by the national currency, and initially through the introduction of an interim currency. In Latvia, there was no single conversion operation to attract the glare of publicity. Unlike the Estonians, the Latvians have opted for a step-by-step reform. The introduction of Latvia's true national currency, the lats (divided into 100 santimi), only got under way in March 1993.

The issuing of the interim currency, the Latvian ruble, began in May 1992. Latvian rubles were introduced alongside rubles at the exchange rate of 1:1. The immediate reason for the introduction of Latvia's own currency was a severe shortage of ruble notes; a shortage which was felt throughout the entire ruble zone, especially in the early part of 1992.

Since May 1992, wages have been paid in Latvian rubles. The position of the Latvian ruble gradually strengthened during the summer of that year. In July, retail stores started to give change in Latvian rubles only, and the Savings Bank of Latvia started to accept deposits from individuals solely in Latvian rubles. Russian rubles could still be withdrawn from savings accounts, however. The Bank of Latvia exchanged cash rubles for Latvian rubles until mid-July at the rate of 1:1.

On 20 July, the Latvian ruble became the only legal tender in Latvia. Bank deposits of both enterprises and individuals were automatically converted into Latvian rubles at the rate of 1:1. Simultaneously, the Russian ruble became a foreign currency, and regulations regarding foreign currencies now apply to it. The use of foreign currencies within the country is not wholly forbidden, but all prices must be given in Latvian rubles and, because of their legal tender status, Latvian rubles must be accepted for payment. Wages may still be paid in foreign currencies. According to the sparse information available, enterprises - particularly the all-Union ones formerly subordinated to Moscow - are still using Russian rubles to a large extent in their payments. Accurate data on the scope of the use of Russian rubles and convertible currencies are not forthcoming, but the Riga authorities have recently cited figures which claim that, at least at the end of 1992, half of all transactions were still being conducted in convertible currencies, and perhaps some 15% in rubles.

Numerous hard currency shops were obliged to start selling their goods in Latvian rubles as well. However, shops effectively circumvent this obligation by pricing their products so high in Latvian rubles that it pays customers to exchange their rubles for foreign currency in exchange offices and pay for their purchases in foreign currency. Exchange offices - Polish-style *kontors* - are plentiful and competitive. Central Bank officials refer to the freedom of markets and claim ignorance of the volume of Riga cash market, which is believed to be the largest in the former Soviet Union.

The practical implementation of currency reform in Latvia was successful, although for reasons different from those in Estonia. Latvia chose a very simple method whereby Russian rubles were gradually replaced with the new currency. This method, however, is not without its dangers: had Latvia been unlucky, it would have been flooded by rubles from Russia and other former Soviet republics. The value of the new currency would then have collapsed. Fortunately for Latvia, there was little confidence in the new Latvian currency outside the country, and foreigners were uninterested in acquiring Latvian rubles.

The Latvian ruble was always intended to be an interim currency before the lats was introduced. According to the authorities, the lats should have been issued as soon as inflation had been brought under control and the exchange rate stabilized. In the autumn of 1992, according to the governor of the central bank, this was expected to happen in the latter part of 1993. Considering that the original plan was to introduce the lats in 1992,[33] it is evident that, unexpectedly, the Latvian rubles temporarily lost their interim nature and became relatively permanent. This also created a technical problem, since the existing Latvian ruble notes are easy to forge.

The announcement of the gradual introduction of the lats was made - after much speculation - in early March 1993. The official reason given was that as the economy had been stabilized, the time for the lats had now come. Bearing in mind what was said above about the socio-psychological importance of the kroon in Estonia, there is some reason to believe that the June 1993 elections were a contributing factor. Finally it seems clear that the flow of forged Latvian ruble notes was much greater than expected.

Latvian rubles are convertible into lats at a rate of 200:1. The first lats-denominated banknotes, placed in circulation on March 5, were five-lats notes. Latvian rubles will be gradually phased out with the further issue of lats notes. According to various official statements the conversion process should be complete by summer 1993, although it seems that this deadline may not be met.[34]

The Latvian and Russian authorities have apparently not yet reached final agreement regarding the Russian rubles that have accumulated in the Latvian central bank as a result of currency reform, and which Latvia has agreed to keep in its custody. There are still some unresolved issues between the countries regarding debts, and Latvia may be interested in linking them to the return of the rubles to Russia.[35]

Latvia has also recovered the gold reserves it deposited with Western central banks before 1940. The gold reserves were in late 1992 estimated to amount to a meagre seven tonnes.[36]

Despite heavy criticism, the Bank of Latvia is trying to pursue a tight monetary policy. Inflation was running at a rate of 11% a month at the end of August 1992, accelerated thereafter to 15%, but finally fell to 3-4% in December, remaining at that level for the first months of 1993. In the run-up to the June 1993 parliamentary elections, these achievements were in jeopardy, since as the Bank of Latvia seemed to be almost the sole domestic defender of stabilization policies.

3.2. THE EXCHANGE RATE SYSTEM

The exchange system in Latvia is very liberal. This is at least partly due to incomplete foreign exchange legislation and the undeveloped state of monetary institutions and instruments. In practice, the Latvian ruble is freely convertible as regards current transactions. Convertibility is wider than in Estonia, since it is not restricted to Latvian citizens only, nor is it necessary to present documentary evidence when purchasing foreign exchange.[37] Enterprises are not obliged to repatriate foreign currency earned abroad, but the state taxes foreign exchange earned by enterprises and individuals. There are no restrictions on the repatriation of either capital or dividends by non-residents.

The exchange rate of the Latvian ruble floats against both convertible currencies and the Russian ruble. In principle, exchange rates are determined freely in the market. A special feature of Latvia is the existence of private foreign exchange offices, which have been set up in large numbers in a short period of time. The best known of them is Parex, which controls the major part of the market. Officially at least, neither the banks nor the central bank are very active in the foreign exchange market. This is mainly due to the undeveloped state of the banking sector and lack of resources.

Figure 2 - Currency rates for US-dollars in the Baltic countries

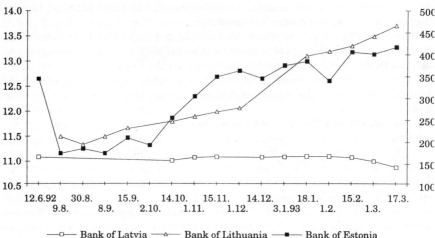

─□─ Bank of Latvia ─△─ Bank of Lithuania ─■─ Bank of Estonia

Left scale: Bank of Estonia.
Right scale: Bank of Latvia, Bank of Lithuania.

In actual fact, however, it seems that the floating of the Latvian ruble is not 'clean' at all. During the latter half of 1992, the Latvian ruble was notably stable against the dollar (see Figure 2). It is unlikely that this stability could have existed without central bank intervention in the currency market. *'De facto* pegging, officially called "floating", in the face of uncertainty concerning the authorities' ability to defend the rate of exchange originally chosen', may be the aptest description of Latvian policies.

During the first months after declaration of the Latvian ruble as the only legal tender, its rate against the dollar in fact strengthened. In late August, dollars were being sold at Parex at the rate of 200 Latvian rubles per dollar while in November the corresponding rate was 177 Latvian rubles per dollar. After that the rate of the Latvian ruble remained relatively stable until February 1993. In February the Latvian ruble again appreciated relative to the dollar, from the level of 170 to that of 155 or less. This may have reflected continued stringent money supply in Latvia. On the other hand, February was a time of rumours concerning the impending introduction of the lats, and many holders of 'Russian' rubles and other currencies may have wanted to convert their balances into Latvian rubles in case there was an Estonian-type sudden exchange of (only) Latvian rubles into the lats.

According to a semi-official estimate, the Riga markets for cash rubles and convertible currencies are the biggest in the area of the former Soviet Union. Latvia is considered to be the only former Soviet republic in which obstacles to the exchange of non-cash rubles for cash and vice versa have in principle been removed. According to the authorities, the size of the ruble/foreign currency market is unknown, nor is any attempt being made to determine the origin of the convertible currencies traded on it. Despite efforts to develop Riga into the biggest money market centre in the Baltic region, the complete lack of control that is claimed to exist in the market, especially regarding the origin of the currencies traded on it, could prove to be a major problem. The authorities may not be sufficiently sensitive to the magnitude of the question.

In early 1993, the Bank of Latvia stopped exchanging CIS currencies for Latvian rubles. It continued to quote their rates of exchange but now wanted banks and exchange offices to do the trading. It is understood that this decision was prompted by the accumulation of ruble assets in the central bank.

3.3. THE IMPACT OF THE REFORM ON THE FOREIGN TRADE SECTOR

Prior to withdrawal from the ruble zone, Latvia held negotiations with Russia on new arrangements for payments and settlements between the two countries. Accounts have been opened in the central banks of both countries, through which payments are made. Latvian commercial banks may open correspondent accounts in Russian banks and transfer companies' payments through them.

In order to protect its economy against a possible flood of rubles from the former Soviet republics, the Bank of Latvia introduced differentiated exchange rates for non-cash rubles transferred from different republics. According to the first quotation, rubles originating from Ukraine have the lowest value, with a buying rate of 0.3 Latvian rubles. The highest rates were for rubles originating from, *inter alia*, Russia and Lithuania, with a buying rate of 0.9 Latvian rubles.[38] Commercial banks may set their rates freely, as long as buying rates do not exceed the central bank quotations.

The Bank of Latvia quotes exchange rates daily on the basis of the balance of trade between Latvia and each republic, and the monetary and credit policy pursued in each republic. Thus the rates quoted by the central bank are administratively determined. Since markets among the rubles of different republics do not seem to have emerged yet, the central bank quotations regulate the market and divide it into segments according to republics. These can be circumvented, in particular through convertible currencies. It seems, however, that this rarely occurs, and enterprises trading with the former Soviet Union therefore have to be able to balance their transactions bilaterally with each of the former republics. This is a major impediment to trade. The central bank has emphasized that its quotations are only meant to serve as guidelines for transactions between banks and enterprises. Latvian enterprises have been highly critical of the central bank's new system, since their export earnings have been significantly reduced by the new rates.

4. CONCLUDING REMARKS

The withdrawal of the Baltic states from the ruble zone and the introduction by these countries of their own currencies proceeded smoothly. The process, in fact, was much easier than many foreign experts expected. The sharp depreciation of the ruble since summer 1992 shows that the Baltic countries were correct to uncouple their currencies from the ruble and to issue their own currencies, which are already partly convertible, whereas the aim of a convertible ruble seems to have been postponed indefinitely.

The example of the Baltic countries shows that a national currency and an independent monetary policy can be introduced under very different principles and procedures. However, given the rather sparse information available, it is difficult to assess how the systems work in practice.

The Baltic countries have successfully passed through the first stage of the introduction of their own currency units; that is, they have left the ruble zone. However, greater problems lie ahead because these countries will have to secure the long-term stability of their currencies. This calls for tight monetary and fiscal policies together with the restructuring of the economy, which, initially, will lead to a declining standard of living. Foreign trade plays a crucial role in the small Baltic economies, and the countries' capacity to earn foreign currency through exports is a key factor in the stability of their currencies. Finally, the availability of international financial support for the changes in these economies will be important.

NOTES

1 The opinions expressed in this paper are those of the authors and do not necessarily reflect the views of the Bank of Finland. The comments by Tapio Aho and Ardo Hansson are gratefully acknowledged.

2 See, for instance, Fieleke, 1992; Hansson, 1993.

3 Hansson and Sachs, 1992, pp. 1-3.

4 Odling-Smee, 1992, p. 9.

5 Hernandez-Cata, 1992.

6 In 1992, Lithuania was generally characterized by strict fiscal and loose monetary policies. There are signs that this may change in the opposite direction.

7 For the political and economic background to Estonia and Latvia, see Misiunas and Taagepera, 1983; Van Arkadie and Karlsson, 1992. For recent Estonian economic policies, see Hansson, 1992a. An authoritative account of the Estonian currency reform is provided by Kallas and Sörg, 1993.

8 Osband and Villeneuva, 1992; Walters, 1987, pp. 740-2.

9 Paradoxically, however, a currency board system may lead to the abandonment of balanced budgets because it may enhance the credibility of the government so that market-based deficit finance becomes feasible. In the Estonian case, this phase may already have been reached.

10 Fieleke, 1992, pp. 20-1.

11 See 'Argentina, History in the Making', *Euromoney Supplement*, February 1992.

12 See Eesti Pank, 1992.

13 Bennett, 1992.

14 Hanke, Jonung and Schuler, 1993.

15 Fieleke, 1992, pp. 14-24.

16 See *Äripäev*, 18 August 1992 for the relevant regulations.

17 See *Äripäev*, 20 June 1992.

18 Hansson, 1992b.

19 Baltic News Service, 24 July 1992.

20 *Äripäev*, 4 August 1992.

21 Rajasalu, 1992.

22 Otsason, 1992.

23 'Estoniya: Novyi poryadok rasschetov', *Ekonomicheskaya Gazeta*, no. 29., 1992.

24 *Äripäev*, 13 August 1992.

25 *Äripäev*, 12 September 1992.

26 The shares of such re-exports reported to the authorities and of currency revenue repatriated remains a mystery.

27 Of course, the currency board principle only sets the upper limit on money supply, leaving it to the discretion of the monetary authority to decide what share of currency revenue should be 'activated' in momey supply. As Figure 1 shows, the Bank of Estonia has not issued money up to the limit set by currency inflow. The accumulation of reserves - in the case, say, of a banking crisis - might however become politically difficult to sustain in some circumstances.

28 In particular, it was decided to liquidate *Tartu Kommertsbank*, the first commerical bank in the former Soviet Union. Two other banks will be merged and restructured, using the existing surplus reserves of the Banking Department.

29 Hanke, Jonung and Schuler, 1993, p. 12.

30 Fieleke, 1992.

31 "... the governor of the central bank has warned that he would have to devalue the kroon if the Estonian parliament approved a high minimum exchange rate": Hanke, Jonung and Schuler, 1993, p. 12. According to existing legislation, he can do no such thing. Changing the rate of exchange is under the jurisdiction of parliament, since the current rate is stipulated by law.

32 Fieleke, 1992.

33 As reported in *Estoniya*, 9 September 1992.

34 *Baltic Observer*, 9/93.

35 A total of 1.5 billion rubles accumulated in the central bank of Latvia during the currency conversion, according to *Baltic News Service*, 9 October 1992.

36 *Financial Times*, 19 December 1992.

37 'Valyutnoe chudo Latvii', *Ekonomicheskaya Gazeta*, no. 26, 1992.
38 *Baltic News Service*, 14 August 1992; 16 August 1992.

BIBLIOGRAPHY

Bennett, A.G.G. (1992), 'The Operation of the Estonian Currency Board', IMF Paper on Policy Analysis and Assessment 92/3.
Eesti Pank (1992), *The Monetary Reform in Estonia 1992*, Tallinn.
Fieleke, N.S. (1992), 'The Quest for Sound Money: Currency Boards to the Rescue?', *New England Economic Review*, November-December.
Hanke, S.H., Jonung, L., Schuler, K. (1992), *Monetary Reform for a Free Estonia*, Stockholm.
Hanke, S.H., Jonung, L., Schuler, K. (1993), 'Estonia: It's not a Currency Board System!' *Transition*, no. 1.
Hansson, A. (1992a), 'Transforming an Economy while Building a Nation; The Case of Estonia', Stockholm Institute of East European Economics Working Paper 62.
Hansson, A. (1992b), 'Estonian Currency Reform: Overview, Progress Report and Future Policies', Östekonomiska Institutet, Stockholm, Memorandum, 7 August.
Hansson, A., 'The Trouble with the Ruble: Monetary Reform in the Former Soviet Union', in Åslund, A. and R. Layard, (eds), *Changing the Economic System in Russia*, London 1993, pp. 163-182.
Hansson, A., Sachs, J. (1992), 'The Crowning of the Estonian Kroon', *Transition*, no. 9.
Hernandez-Cata, E., 'Introduction of a National Currency', in Gros, D., Pisani-Ferry, J., Sapir, A. (eds), *Inter-State Economic Relations in the Former Soviet Union*, CEPS Working Document no. 63, 1992, pp. 63-71.
Kallas, S., Sörg, M. (1993), 'Estonia's Currency Reform of 1992', *Bank of Finland Bulletin 67*, no. 3, 1993, pp. 3-7.
Misiunas, R.J., Taagepera, R. (1983), *The Baltic States: Years of Dependence 1940-1980*, Los Angeles.
Odling-Smee, J., 'Letter to the Editor', *Transition*, no. 10, 1992.
Osband, K., Villeneuva, D. (1992), 'Independent Currency Authorities: An Analytic Primer', IMF Working Paper 92/50.
Otsason, R. (1992), 'Eesti krediittturg on täiesti tühi', *Äripäev*, 30 July 1992.
Rajasalu, T. (1992), 'Rahareformist, valuutakursist ja selle võimalikust järelmõjust', *Äripäev*, 9 July 1992.
'Valyutnoe chudo Latvii', *Ekonomicheskaya Gazeta*, no. 26, 1992.
Walters, A., 'Currency Boards' in Eatwell, J., Milgate, M., Newman, P. (eds), *The New Palgrave*, London 1987, vol. 1.
Van Arkadie, B., Karlsson, M. (1992), *Economic Survey of the Baltic States*, London.

Intermediate and Final Objectives in the Process of EMU

Ferdinando Targetti

1. The Relationship Between the EMS and Bretton Woods

In March 1979, eight years after abandonment of the Bretton Woods system (BW), the EMS was born as an agreement among the central banks of the countries belonging to the European Community; six years later, this agreement became an integral part of the Treaty of Rome. The crisis of the BW system led to the creation of a system of fixed exchange rates different from its predecessor, but which recent experience has shown was insufficiently innovative.

The weakness of the BW system was due to three factors:

1. The increasing freedom of capital movements, which increased speculative attacks against individual currencies in the absence of sufficient intervention capacity on the part of the institutions to defend them (the 'gold tranches' that the countries belonging to the agreement had available in the IMF, and the so-called 'stand-by' financing that the IMF could grant, were largely inadequate);
2. the lack of a code of behaviour regulating realignments (fundamental disequilibrium was too vague a concept);
3. the asymmetric position of the dollar *vis-à-vis* the other currencies in the system.

This latter factor, as is widely known, meant that n-1 countries were obliged to set their fiscal and monetary policies in such a way that they produced an interest rate which, in a system of free capital movement, determined a pre-fixed exchange rate between their own currencies and the n-th one, while the n-th country was free to decide its economic policy independently of those of the other countries. The dollar was this n-th currency.

The United States was therefore free to establish its own economic policy. The other countries either adjusted their policies to that of the United States or altered their exchange rates with respect to the dollar.

When the EMS was set up, care was taken to modify the first two of the above factors, but not the third one. The central pillars of the EMS, in fact, were the following:[1]

1. Identifying the intervention rules which the central banks of the member countries had to comply with - changes in parity should therefore have stemmed not from unilateral decisions, but from collective ones;
2. Identifying forms of financing for these interventions which were of a magnitude sufficient to discourage international speculation which did not believe in the resilience of the exchange agreements.

2. THE MECHANISMS OF THE EMS: 'INTERVENTION RULES' AND 'FINANCING RULES'

Unlike the BW system, the EMS created a unit of account for the countries beloging to the agreement: the ECU. This was a bundle of currencies present in various units. These units were fixed, but the weights of the various currencies varied with variations in the exchange rate. In the absence of realignments, each currency had a central parity with the ECU. Each pair of currencies had a bilateral central parity, and all the pairs of parities formed the parity grid. Each exchange rate could only fluctuate by +/- 2.5% with respect to the other currencies.

Intervention by the central banks belonging to the arrangement could take three forms:

a. interventions in non-EC currencies (the dollar or the yen);
b. interventions in infra-marginal EC currencies; undertaken, that is, by a country's central bank before its currency reached one of the two limits set on its bilateral band with another currency in the system;
c. interventions at the margin in EC currencies undertaken by the central bank of a member country when its currency reached one of the band limits.

Only the third kind of intervention was compulsory, and had to be implemented by both the central banks of the countries whose currencies stood at the extremes of the band. If one adds that changes in the central parities were the outcome of collective rather than single-member decisions, what was meant by 'intervention rules' becomes clear.

The 'financing rules' were connected with these 'intervention rules'. The central banks belonging to the EMS had access to three forms of financing: the very short term financing facility, short term monetary support, and medium term financial assistance. The first of these was of major importance and consisted of a line of credit which the central banks made reciprocally available to each other. The aim was to ensure unlimited and automatic financing for interventions at the margin, and gave rise to a system in which the central bank of the country whose currency was weak, and might therefore be susceptible to speculative attacks, had unlimited and automatic access to the lines of credit offered by the central bank of the country with the strongest currency. It seemed, therefore, that the exchange parities decided by the various countries could be accepted by the markets, that parities could be defended against speculative attacks, and that the BW problem of the lack of international institutions able to intervene in defence of weak currencies had been overcome.

3. ASYMMETRIES ALSO IN THE EMS AND THE BOGUS DOCTRINE OF 'CREDIBILITY'

Compared with the BW, therefore, the EMS had two innovative features: its creation of 'intervention rules' and its creation of 'financing rules'. However, like the BW, the EMS also operated as an asymmetric system. In an asymmetric system, n-1 countries adjust to the fiscal and monetary policy of the n-th country if they wish to keep the exchange rate pegged to the n-th currency; otherwise, if they do not adjust, they are obliged to change the parities. This was the case of the dollar in the BW system and of the mark in the EMS.[2] The weakness of an asymmetric system is greater the less the economic policy of the n-th is accepted by or acceptable to the other countries: indeed, the more frequently realignments take place, the less credible the fixed parities system becomes and the greater the likelihood of speculative attacks.[3]

Prior to the summer of 1992 a thesis was advanced which proved to be mistaken; a thesis based on three cardinal points:

a. the autonomy of the n-th country in setting its money supply policy;
b. the asymmetry of the position of the dollar rendered the BW system fragile during the 1960s because American monetary policy was inflationary (because of the monetary rather than fiscal financing of the Viet Nam War), whereas the the asymmetry of the mark strengthened the EMS because the Bundesbank was independent of the government and was obliged by statute to set anti-inflationary policy as its priority;
c. there was a strong incentive to join the EMS for countries with low-credibility central banks, who therefore 'imported credibility' from the

Bundesbank.[4]

The erroneous nature of these three propositions, I believe, lies in the following facts:

a. the autonomy of the n-th country and the dependence of the n-1 countries did not manifest itself in the money supply, but in its policy of financing public spending and the public debt; it was this policy that determined the interest rate and hence the exchange rate;
b. autonomy in the sense of the independence of the monetary policy of the central bank of the n-th country from the fiscal policy of the government of that country, in the presence of an exceptional amount of public spending, applied pressure on internal interest rates which pushed the n-th currency away from the central parity and upwards in its oscillation band, while simultaneously pushing one or more of the n-1 currencies downwards;
c. inflation in the EMS countries comprises a component based on expectations (which are greater the stronger the inflationary process) and a hard core of structural and distributive inflation which has nothing to do with either the money supply or the credibility of the monetary policy pursued by its central bank - the institutional structure of which, therefore, does not influence the inflationary process itself;
d. financing for 'interventions at the margin' is by no means unlimited: given that the use by the central bank of the weak-currency country of the line of credit granted to it by the central bank of the strong-currency country increases the money supply of that country, the goal of maintaining the central parity conflicts with the internal monetary policy goals of the strong-currency country - even more so when the strong-currency country has an autonomous central bank with a priority anti-inflationary commitment.

The persistence of structural inflation differentials over a number of years, combined with the quasi-fixed nominal exchange rates and the autonomous economic policy pursued by the n-th country that pushed up interest rates in Germany, have been responsible for the breakdown in the EMS.

4. THE FRAGILITY AND BREAKDOWN OF THE EMS

Events between September 1992 and the end of that year proved that, in the long period (that is, over a time-span of some years), there is a crucial fragility in a system, like the EMS, which possesses the following four features:

a. the countries belonging to the arrangement have divergent economies in both real terms (production, employment and geographical homogeneity) and monetary and financial ones (inflation, deficits and public debt);
b. free capital movement;
c. oscillations in exchange rates are restricted by narrow bands;

d. the system exhibits an asymmetry in favour of the n-th country, which gives priority to internal economic policy objectives at the expense of the system's cohesion.

What was responsible for the breakdown in the EMS? Four fundamental factors, which must be distinguished from contingent causes, and which consist of the reasons why the weak currencies like the lira, the pound and the peseta were cut adrift from the mark. Even if the Italian *Consiglio dei Ministri* had passed stringent financial measures, the storm would broken out in any case, perhaps later and perhaps not beginning with the lira, but inevitably nevertheless. Nor could any kind of foreign loan, in September 1992, have stemmed the flood of speculation against the weak countries, as demonstrated by immediate burn-off of the enormous loan obtained by the Bank of England to defend sterling a week after the drastic realignment of the lira. It would be more appropriate, in fact, to speak of devaluation rather than of realignment of the lira, first, and then sterling, because the delayed attempt by the European monetary authorities to contain the realignment of the parities of these currencies within margins deemed too narrow by the market proved to be a failure - to the extent that one can state that the markets 'forced' these currencies out of the EMS.

The contingent causes of the EMS breakdown were a series of factors: the Danish referendum, uncertainty over the French one, and the message implicit in the Maastricht Treaty that only realignments by a certain date were possible and, for this selfsame reason, probable. Finally, one should add that the realignment of the lira on Sunday 13 September 1992 showed, if anything, that the defences raised by the EMS against speculation on the official currency parities were unable to withstand trial by speculative fire, once the opinion that the other currencies would also be realigned became firmly established. The Governor of the Bank of Italy, Ciampi, had done well before the summer to insist on a general and substantial realignment of all the currencies, which would have led to depreciation of the lira and the pound against the central parity - albeit to a lesser extent than the depreciation that actually ensued in the free markets - and an appreciation of the mark against the French franc. It was short-sighted, though, of the other governors to believe that realignment would only have involved the lira. What is certain is that when the explosion came and the chain disintegrated, the first link to snap was obviously the weakest one.

5. THE WEAKEST LINK: THE ITALIAN LIRA

Italy was only the first link to break. In an overall system unable to withstand the pressure, twenty-four hours later sterling also succumbed - the currency of a sick economy but with healthy public finance - and then the infection spread to Spain, a country with some problems of inflation and public finance but with a dynamic economy. It was thus the system that displayed its weakness of being 'centred on the mark'; a weakness also manifest by the fact that a certain tension on the markets between France and Germany still persists in favour of the mark, although it is France which is the most financially virtuous of the two.

Italy should have realized earlier that the real appreciation of the lira, which had occurred in a three-year period of fixed exchange rates and a positive inflation differential, brought with it an indefensible exchange rate (from spring onwards there had been vicious skirmishes on the exchange markets). It should have devalued earlier (unilaterally if Great Britain, France and Spain were so short-sighted as to feel themselves protected against speculation and to refuse a downwards realignment of their currencies against the mark), and to an extent that market expectations changed. By so doing, Italy would not have lost those reserves in the absence of which it is now impeded from undertaking any manoeuvre aimed temporarily to maintain the exchange rate at a 'realistic' value protected against speculative bubbles, and with the long-term objective of re-entry into the EMS.

6. The Strongest Link: the German Mark

Although the weaker countries had their own responsibilities for the breakdown in the EMS arrangement, because of economies weak in financial terms (Italy) and real ones (Great Britain), most blame attaches to the strongest link in the system, Germany, although France was also to some extent responsible. Germany did not wish to finance German unification out of an increased tax burden on its citizens, and it failed (mainly because of France) to revalue the mark through an overall realignment agreement. Hence its only option was to increase its interest rates in order to dampen the inflationary tensions exerted by the surplus of demand created by German unification and the absurd political exchange rate of one East mark for one West mark. It was this persistence of high rates, combined with the constant declarations of the Bundesbank (declarations which still continue) that it would sternly resist any deflection from its traditional anti-inflationary policy, that convinced the markets in September that they had won their 'match' against the European central banks, and still convinces the markets today that they can profitably speculate on a rise of the German mark against the European currencies, whether the lira, the peseta or before long, I suspect, the French franc. One should remember that it is of little importance that, today, German real interest rates stand only a little higher than they did in the 1960s (although they are higher than they were in the 1970s and 1980s), since financial capital movements are governed by relative nominal interest rates among countries, weighted by a vague idea of changes, in a highly uncertain future, in exchange rates. I must insist on this point. As we saw in section 2, the founders of the EMS believed that the "speculation with loaded dice" of the BW era (summed up by the dictum "if I speculate against a weak currency and in favour of a strong one, either I win or I don't lose", which implied an asymmetry in favour of the market and against the central bank of the weak-currency country) could not occur again because both the central bank of the weak-currency country *and* that of the strong-currency country were committed to maintaining parities. This belief, however, proved illusory. In order to maintain the parity of the lira with the mark, the Bundesbank would have had to create a supply of marks on the international markets which conflicted with a money supply policy which, by statute, it was free to determine in function of the internal stability its own currency. The conclusion to be drawn is that the desirability of the EMS as a fixed and n-th currency exchange rate system was based on the anti-inflationary 'reputation' of the Bundesbank; a reputation stemming from its independence but which undermined the stability of the EMS in a world of free capital movements.

As a marginal note to the present discussion, I must make brief mention of the long-term costs of a combination *à la* Mundell-Fleming of expansionary fiscal policy and restrictive monetary policy. This was the policy of Republican administrations in the United States, the unwitting result in Italy of the budgetary laxity of its four-party governments combined with the institutional 'divorce' between the Treasury and the Bank of Italy, and the policy of unification pursued by the German Christian Democrats without an increase in taxes and in the presence of an autonomous central bank with monetarist goals. The short-term effect of these policies was positive, with strong exchange rates and low inflation, but harmful in the long run in that it produced weak exchange rates and/or sky-high interest rates. Both the countries to have adopted these policies for any length of time, the United States and Italy, have found themselves faced by a severe 'twin deficit' financial crisis. The costs to Germany were the breakdown of the EMS and the postponement of the goal of monetary union.

7. THE GOAL OF MONETARY UNION

Monetary union is the principal component of the Maastricht Treaty, which gives it excessive emphasis (especially in terms of the virtuous paths that each country must individually follow to achieve it) compared with other objectives which should be accorded equal status in the process of monetary unification. Objectives which range from strengthening the community's institutions, e.g. the setting up of a European Executive as an expression of the European Parliament as opposed to national governments, to the coordination of budgetary policies, from the harmonization of tax systems to strengthening the community budget in compensation for the drops in income and employment that derive from the inability of individual countries to use monetary and exchange rate policy, to other measures examined below.

The principal stages in monetary union envisaged by the Treaty are the following:

Phase 1 (1/7/90 - 31/12/93): decision on the headquarters of the European Monetary Institute (EMI) and the European Central Bank (ECB) to be instituted in phases 2 and 3 below, respectively; ratification of the Treaty by the member states before it comes into force on 1/1/93; acceptance of the ban on financing national deficits by the national central banks.

Phase 2 (1/1/94 - 31/12/98): creation of the EMI coordinating the monetary policies of the member states; creation of a Monetary Committee with the task of monitoring payment balances; monitoring the public deficits and public debts of member states with the objective of keeping them below 3% and 60% of GDP respectively; independence, on the German model, of the national central banks from the Treasury; examination of the member states' convergence on objective values (convergence towards the country with lowest inflation, convergence of low-value interest rates, exchange rate stability for two years, convergence to deficit and debt values compared with GDP, as above) and identification of repealing countries remaining outside monetary union, but with a two-yearly review.

Phase 3 (from 1/1/99): winding up of the EMI and constitution of the ECB with immediate powers and the specific objective, on the Bundesbank pattern, of stabilizing prices; the irrevocable pegging of exchange rates and implementation of the measures necessary to convert national currencies into ECU; replacement of the Monetary Committee with an Economic and Financial Committee with the task of advising on and monitoring the economic-financial situations and the payments balances of the member states; sanctions applied to countries with excessive public deficits.

The Treaty evidently envisages monetary union as the long-term goal (post 1999) with intermediate objectives of economic convergence to be fulfilled by the countries that, by signing the Treaty, committed themselves to monetary unification with their fellow signatories.

For some, those whom I call institutional monetarists, monetary union is of secondary importance; what matters is the financial rigour to which countries must submit if they are to achieve monetary union; a rigour which their political institutions - too democratic and hence incapable of taking 'impolitic' decisions - cannot enforce. For others, including numerous Keynesians, Europe can unite without a single currency; and among these there are advocates of increased cooperation among European states over large-scale technological, industrial and infrastructure programmes, but who leave it up to individual countries to decide their macroeconomic policies, and exchange rate policy in particular. For yet others, and I include myself in this category, the single currency is an objective to be achieved in itself, although it is one which conflicts with the Maastricht design that obliges countries to set themselves intermediate objectives - the which, as the experience of these months has shown, postpone the final outcome rather than bringing it closer.

To be an objective in itself (irrespective, that is, of the path to follow in achieving it), monetary union must yield greater benefits than costs. This, I believe, can be asserted concerning EMU even though it is a proposition which depends closely on the fulfilment of certain institutional conditions. The first argument in favour of EMU is extra-economic: a common currency provides a social cement for the European peoples who, as the end of the century approaches feel themselves, more than at any other time during the modern history of the continent, part of a single historical, cultural and political entity. Passing to economic factors, a powerful argument in favour of monetary union derives from the shortcomings of both a system of fixed exchange rates and one of flexible rates. In economies in which prices and wages are not flexible, maintenance of a fixed exchange rate system entails a mix of restrictive fiscal policies and high interest rates in order to: (a) restrict internal absorption; (b) counteract inflation (and therefore the real revaluation of the currency); (c) attract capital flows. If only restrictive monetary and expansionary fiscal policies are implemented, after a certain period of time the country will be forced to deal with a financial crisis such as the one currently afflicting Italy. Virtuous behaviour which gives long-term stability to an economy in a system of fixed exchange rates therefore entails a deflationary propensity of the economy. A flexible exchange rate system, on the other hand, gives rise, especially in index-linked economies, to an inflationary propensity, given that for all countries the deflationary effects of revaluation are less marked than the inflationary effects of devaluation. In flexible exchange rate regimes, moreover, the additional uncertainty over future effective demand provoked by the variability of exchange rates is hardly dispelled by the diffusion of forward markets and forward hedging, and this depresses the propensity to save (even though the literature is admittedly far from offering conclusive empirical evidence on the matter). Finally, in a fixed exchange rate system, the market may be 'disoriented' by speculative bubbles, like those that are probably afflicting the lira at the moment.

The principal argument against monetary union among countries is that each country is deprived of the economic policy instrument represented by varying the exchange rate, which is greater in importance the more external shocks affect areas of an economic system with low labour mobility, as happens in Europe because of ethnic, linguistic and cultural causes.[5] It is for this reason that numerous American economists claim that, compared with the United States, Europe is not an optimal currency area. Nevertheless, in Europe the exchange rate instrument has lesser shock-compensation effects on economic areas internal to it for two reasons: the greater (compared with the United States) effective index-linking of wages, and the lesser productive specialization of the European countries compared with those in the North American Confederation.[6] Moreover, there is much less labour mobility in Europe than in the United States, even internally to individual states, and migration has a social cost which renders use of the public budget instrument preferable (the prime example being, in Italy, the *Cassa Integrazione Guadagni*).

I have already pointed out, however, that the balance between the pros and cons of monetary union depends closely on the institutional conditions applying to the single currency area in question. The conditions I refer to are monetary and budgetary. The instrument of transferring costs to the EC budget should substitute and compensate for variations in the exchange rate, as a means not only to develop areas with per-capita output lower than the average but also in order to act on incomes, rather than relative prices, in favour of areas or countries affected by demand shocks due to changing tastes and/or technologies.

The monetary institution (the ECB) raises two legitimate worries. The first concerns its statute. The Maastricht Treaty envisages that the ECB should be modelled on the pattern of the Bundesbank. The separation between the Central Bank and the Treasury has worked in countries like Germany in which there is close integration between bank and industry (so that industry is comparatively less constrained by high interest rates in its investment decisions), and in which there has been a political climate conducive to a stringent incomes policy (the deep-lying reason for the Bundesbank's 'credibility'). Conversely, in a European-scale economy, in the absence of these prerequisites, German-style 'separation' between the ECB and the federal public budget, and the single priority imposed on the ECB of an anti-inflationary policy, are bound to impose an over-tight institutional straitjacket on the European economy. The second worry is that, at the moment, the Maastricht Treaty does not equip the ECB with the traditional instruments of monetary policy: the power to change bank reserves coefficients, open market operations (i.e. the purchase and sale on the primary and secondary markets of state securities), portfolio rediscounts, and so forth. However, if the Treaty is signed, the EMI will be committed to drawing up a programme which envisages a set of monetary policy instruments at the European level for the ECB.

In short, European monetary unification can be judged favourably in economic terms the more faith one has that its institutions will adjust to a reality, that of the economy of the European countries, which is internally heterogeneous and overall different from the German economy, and the less faith one has in the automatic adjustments mechanisms represented by variations in the exchange rates among the currencies of countries preserving their monetary autonomy. It is therefore a favourable but conditional judgement.

Under the Maastricht Treaty, however, not only must unification come about under the aegis of institutions unsuited to the purpose, but, as has been said, intermediate convergence objectives have been set which, instead of mapping out the high road to monetary unification (as has been maintained by what we may call the 'Euro-orthodox' school of thought which flourishes not only in the Bundesbank but also in the German finance ministry and among the ranks of the 'institutional monetarists'), are an impediment to fulfilment of the project itself.

8. THE ERRORS OF THE EURO-ORTHODOX

The Europe of the 'Euro-orthodox' does not exist in reality. It is a Europe which must be uniform in real economic terms (production, employment, infrastructures, etc.) so that it can be equally uniform in terms of inflation, public deficits and the other Maastricht intermediate goals.

The 'Euro-orthodox' apparently want Germany to be the inspirational model for the other countries. Yet Germany today is very far from constituting such a model: many areas of the country are underdeveloped, there is substantial unemployment, high interest rates, a growing state deficit and increasing inflation. One certainly cannot say that the country is moving in the direction of the intermediate objectives set by Maastricht. Might not one argue that this was a valid reason for not unifying the two Germanies (and at, moreover, the preposterous 1-to-1 exchange rate)? Certainly not, because in this case political will prevail over financial orthodoxy. And this can and must happen also at the European level.

Europe is a dual economy, both among countries and within them, everywhere except, perhaps, France. These dualisms together with other institutional and structural facts (industrial relations, efficiency of the public administration and of the teriary sector), and hence not only central banks more or less autonomous from governments, are the principal reasons for the various hard cores of inflation, and to a significant extent (albeit certainly not exclusively) for the various public deficits among countries (Italy has deviated from normal values because of its fiscal laxity). Hence, one is faced with the decision whether to adjust the various real dynamics at the basis of most monetary-financial divergences and then proceed towards unification, or conversely whether to reach monetary union in rapid stages relaxing intermediate constraints and then adjusting the various real dynamics by means of EC budgetary instruments. The choice of the slow road means re-establishing the EMS and its system of fixed exchange rates. This, for economies like Italy's with a positive inflation differential *vis-à-vis* countries like France and Germany, would once again entail major costs in terms of high real interest rates and then, in time, the repetition of speculative situations like that of last September.

My preference is for the second option, whereas the reasons adduced by the orthodox Europeans for adopting the first are three in number: (a) the infection that the 'vicious' countries would bring to a united Europe; (b) the implicit 'virtues' represented by the external constraints on the action of governments; (c) the 'virtues' of the Bundesbank.

9. THE 'INFECTION' ENGENDERED BY THE VICIOUS COUNTRIES

In order to contest the infection thesis I shall, for reasons of space, take only the case of the relationship, apart from its objective value, between Italy's public debt and its GDP. The fact is that even now Italian state securities are bought on international markets. They are bought at high interest rates because they incorporate a twofold risk - of devaluation of the lira and default on the repayment of the credit on the maturity date. In a single-currency market, Italian state securities would continue to be bought at higher interest rates than those of gilt-edged securities in order to offset the risk of the debtor's bankruptcy. This mark-up, however, would not include the exchange risk, which is what keeps the Italian rate high today despite the fact that the lira is certainly undervalued. Reducing the interest rates on Italian state securities (which would continue to reduce the margin of insolvency risk) would be positive for Italy without being negative for the other countries. It would be up to the markets to establish the interest differentials and to adjust relative prices according to the risk of the various kinds of security, as happens in the American market. Another matter, however, would be the financial solidarity of the Europeans and their willingness to pay taxes to finance transfers to poorer regions or to weaker social groups: this solidarity may or may not exist, but it cannot be changed by imposing today financial targets on European monetary unity.

10. THE PRESUMED 'VIRTUE' OF THE CONSTRAINT

The argument that governments must be constrained by an external institution which enjoys absolute autonomy is to be treated with a great deal of scepticism, for various reasons: (a) because it is enough to live outside the non-existent world of the University of Chicago and in a real world with a certain conflict between disinflation and full employment targets, in other words with a not absolutely rigid Phillips curve, to fail to understand why choices influencing citizens' incomes and jobs must be taken by an unelected body which is not subject to the judgement of any elected one; (b) because this reasoning reverses the means/ends relationship whereby an unelected body must directly or indirectly equip the collectivity through economic costs (sometimes very high) with sanctions on the government - an inversion of levels which removes the obligation of operating on the correct plane of political sanctions on political misgovernment (it may be true that an enlightened dictator can be better than a paralysed democracy, but this is a second-best solution and as far as enlightenment is concerned, this can only be judged as such a *posteriori*); (c) capitalism reached its zenith in a period (1950-1970) of maximum cooperation, and not 'divorce', between the Central Bank and the Treasury; (d) it is true that independence from the government is necessary when the head of the Central Bank is appointed, and also when the objectives he is to pursue are formulated, but his performance must be scrutinized by the maximum elective body of the country. I believe that these ideas are not too distant from those of the Italian central bank, which has not fallen victim to Teutonic dogmatism.

11.   THE PRESUMED 'VIRTUE' OF THE BUNDESBANK

The model for the future ECB is the Bundesbank, which, in the view of the Euro-orthodox, guarantees market faith in currency, the premise for any consequent economic virtue, because of its autonomy from the government in the pursuit of anti-inflationary objectives.

The fact is, however, that this reasoning reverses the causality relationship and falsifies the conclusions to be drawn from it: it is the dynamism of German capitalism, the financial robustness of its companies, and the support they provide for the banking system with which they closely intermesh, the climate of company/trade union cooperation and, sometimes, the co-participation of workers in company administration itself which gives strength and competitiveness to the German economy, and hence strengthens the mark and gives authoritiveness to its central bank - which is' thereby enabled to pursue objectives of monetary discipline which can be sustained by a capitalism that produces technologically competitive goods. This model, however, cannot be transferred *sic et simpliciter* to an economy like that of Europe as a whole: or at least, since this is a long-drawn-out process involving a large number of areas, one cannot seek to speed it up by starting from the final outcome and imposing the Bundesbank on a Europe-wide scale.

Nevertheless, one frequently gains the impression that the Bundesbank believes that unification will either come about according to its own model or not at all. In this sense, its orthodoxy is an obstacle to the process of European unification. The Bundesbank grudgingly accepted the unification of the two Germanies because the political impetus was stronger than all its autonomies. As regards European unification, however, it has been able to raise stiffer resistance to political pressures and to delay an outcome that it does not want: monetary unification with deviant countries and the disappearance of the mark.

One must give political credit to the European will of the German political leadership (unfortunately, I cannot tell if the same applies to the German people), by convincing it to abandon the German propensity to dominance manifest in the Bundesbank's actions and in the 'cultural' hegemony of the Euro-orthodox, which sits ill with the former sentiment.

12.   CONVERGENCE, COHESION AND NEW INSTITUTIONS TO FLANK THE EMS IN THE PROCESS TOWARDS EMU

The convergence among the European economies respecting the intermediate targets set by the Maastricht Treaty which each European country must independently achieve, cannot be viewed as prerequisites for EMU; otherwise this objective will not be reached this century. The order of priorities should be reversed: the EC institutions must be designed so that they accelerate the process of convergence and cohesion among the European countries. For this purpose, it should be borne in mind that cohesion and convergence stand in a close and direct correlation with the growth of European income and employment: in periods of sustained growth the European countries tend to converge; in periods of slow growth they tend to diverge.[7]

EMU must be arrived at by giving greater flexibility to the Maastricht Treaty, by abolishing the rigidity of its intermediate objectives, and by devising instruments which prevent the weaker and more divergent economies from being forced out of a two- or more speed process. These instruments should concern EC budgetary policy and its financing. I outline below which instruments and which policies should accompany the process of monetary union and operate in a single-currency European market.

(a) First of all, during the second phase of the monetary union process, the EMI should be given a great deal of independence: it is already envisaged that the president of the EMI will not be a governor of any of central banks of the member states; however, apart from this, should the old EMS not be restructured because its radical reform would require too much time with respect to the objective of accomplishing monetary union by the end of the century, there should be some sort of ratified subordination of the 'internal' objectives of the monetary policies of the individual central banks to the 'external' objective of keeping the EMS, in order to eliminate its contradictions as set out in section 3 above.

(b) Alongside the EMI, a European Fiscal Institute (EFI) should be set up which is responsible for the fiscal monitoring of the European countries, in order to ensure that an exaggeratedly restrictive budgetary policy does not, in a highly integrated economy like Europe's, have depressive effects on the economies of other countries.

(c) The EFI should establish a European Fund for investment which finances private individuals, regions or member states in the realization of infrastructures, educational institutions and public services. In a transitional phase, these should be geared towards those areas of lower per-capita income in the countries that show greatest commitment to the fulfilment of the intermediate objectives set by the Maastricht Treaty.

(d) The EFI should also coordinate fiscal policies during transition to monetary union. It should, for example, monitor, in a restrictive fiscal sense, the countries with public deficits and public debts furthest from the Maastricht intermediate objectives; simultaneously, however, they should monitor, in the expansionary sense, the public investments undertaken by the countries that come closest to them.

(e) Just as the EMI should disappear with the institution of the ECB, so the EFI should disappear with the transformation of the present EC budgetary institutes into a real and proper European Treasury, which should also be allowed to operate at a deficit. Its regulatory statutes could make explicit reference to the Keynesian principle of a full employment budget and impose a balanced budget over a multi-year time span on the European

Treasury, allowing it to incur temporary anti-cyclical deficits.
(f) The temporary anti-cyclical deficits of the European Treasury should be financed by the ECB on agreement with the Treasury in order to determine, together with public debt policy, a system of interest rates compatible with the desired ratio between federal debt and European GDP, and compatible with the desired exchange rate between ECU and dollar.

One can envisage two scenarios of transition towards monetary union. The first preserves an EMS operating under its previous rules and to which belong only to those few countries that can comply with the conditions of the Maastricht Treaty, while the other countries maintain fluctuating exchange rates and only join the EMU when the conditions set by its intermediate objectives have been fulfilled. This is the two-speed trajectory. The second scenario envisages a cooperative system where the intermediate objectives of each country are assumed, given the close integration among the European economies, by all the economies involved in the process through institutions specially created for the purpose.

NOTES

1 A description of the EMS rules can be found in *Economia Europea*, no. 12, July 1982.
2 On German dominance in the EMS see Fratianni and von Hagen, 1990; Giavazzi and Giovannini, 1987.
3 See Giavazzi and Giovannini, 1989.
4 See Giavazzi and Pagani, 1988.
5 On the importance of labour mobility as an instrument of adjustment in a fixed exchange rate system see Mundell, 1961.
6 See Bini Smaghi and Vori, 1993.
7 This evidence was given by Pascal Petit to the annual meeting of the American Economic Association, Annaheim, 1992.

BIBLIOGRAPHY

Bini Smaghi, L. and Vori, S. (1993), 'Rating the EC as an Optimal Currency Area', *Temi di Discussione, Banca d'Italia*, no. 187.
Fratianni, M., von Hagen, J. (1990), 'German Dominance in the EMS: the Empirical Evidence', *Open Economies Review*, no. 1.
Giavazzi, F., Giovannini, A. (1987), 'Models of EMS: Is Europe a Greater Deutschmark Area?', in Bryant R.C., Portes R. (eds), *Global Macroeconomics*, St. Martin's.
Giavazzi, F., Giovannini, A. (1989), *Limiting the Exchange Rate Flexibility: the European Monetary System*, MIT Press, Cambridge, Mass.

Giavazzi, F., Pagano, M. (1988), 'The Advantage of Tying One's Hands: EMS Discipline and Central Bank Credibility', *European Economic Review*, no. 32.

Giavazzi, F., Giovannini, A. (1988), 'The Roles of Exchange Rates Regimes in Disinflation: Empirical Evidence on the EMS', in Giavazzi, F., Micossi, S., Miller, M. (eds), *The European Monetary System*, Cambridge University Press.

Mundell, R.A. (1961), 'A Theory of Optimum Currency Areas', *American Economic Review*, vol. 51.

ITALY AND THE CRISIS OF THE EMS

Luigi Bosco

1. THE CRISIS OF THE EUROPEAN MONETARY SYSTEM

In September 1992 the European monetary system was hit by serious crisis. Two leading members of the Community, Italy and Great Britain, were forced to withdraw from the system. A number of weak currencies, like the Spanish peseta or the Irish pound, were repeatedly devalued. The crisis now affecting the system comes after a relatively long period of stability, and when progress towards monetary union seemed definitively under way. The periods of turbulence that preceded and followed the crisis did not involve only the weak currencies, as witness the repeated speculative attacks on the French franc, one of the strongest of the European currencies as regards the fundamentals. The crisis of the EMS, therefore, appears to be a crisis of the system as a whole, albeit aggravated by the marked weakness of certain currencies. Analysis of the factors which provoked the crisis in a system which only shortly beforehand seemed relatively stable is therefore of particular interest, and especially in view of current debate on the third stage of the monetary unification.

There are two questions, I believe, which need answering:

(a) Was the crisis provoked by specifically contingent conditions or, conversely, did it arise because the EMS in that particular form no longer met the requirements of the European economy?

(b) If no change is made to the workings of the monetary system, is it convenient for a country like Italy to re-join the system, or should it stay out and press to have the system changed?

These questions are closely interrelated. If a model of the EMS has broken down, then a review of each country's conditions of membership, including Italy's, should be placed at the top of the agenda. On the other hand, a voluntary agreement among sovereign states, like the EMS, can only survive if it is *incentive-compatible* for each of them: if, therefore, an individual state decides that the costs of membership are higher than the benefits, this is a signal of an intrinsic weakness in the overall system.

The analysis conducted in these brief notes begins with the second of the above questions, the aim being to verify whether it is economically convenient for Italy to rejoin unconditionally the EMS. Given the close connection between the two problems, treatment of this topic will also require a review of the chief features of the European monetary system in order to assess its recent functioning.

Answering the above two questions requires analysis of the costs and benefits accruing to Italy should it rejoin the EMS. First, however, one must establish the principal characteristics of the EMS in its present form. Since its creation, in fact, the system has undergone substantial changes. Initially it was a system of fixed, but cooperatively adjustable, exchange rates, explicitly designed to be symmetric and flexible, and intended to combine the advantages of a cooperative response to possible external shocks with the advantages deriving from a certain amount of monetary independence. This early period was characterized by frequent realignments, while large inflation differentials also imposed frequent readjustments. In the next period, from 1986 onwards, the system abandoned all pretence to symmetry and was distinguished by its stability; realignments became increasingly rare until they ceased altogether between 1987 and the onset of the crisis in 1992 (if one excludes the technical, so to speak, devaluation of the lira following the narrowing of its fluctuation band in 1990).

With a certain amount of approximation, we may say that whereas in the first phase the system was not significantly different from a 'crawling peg' system, in the second phase it came more closely to resembling one with fixed exchange rates. The major difference between the two phases was the amount of credibility of the central parities. At the beginning, the credibility of exchange rate fixings was rather low, and speculative crises were therefore frequent; in the second phase the credibility of the exchange rate commitment was much more pronounced, in concomitance with a lower inflation differential between countries with high rates and those with low ones. The direction of the causal link between these two phenomena, should it exist, is one of the keys to understanding of how the EMS operates.

These notes will therefore concentrate on the economic convenience of belonging to the EMS as it is presently constituted: namely, a system with full capital mobility, with increasing financial integration, highly asymmetric 'almost completely fixed' exchange rates, in which Germany decides monetary policy for the whole system and the other countries commit themselves to maintaining the parity of their currencies against the mark.

2. ADVANTAGES OF THE EMS

Four principal arguments have been advanced in justification of the EMS:

(i)   it is an instrument which reduces uncertainty over exchange rates and therefore encourages intra-community trade;
(ii) it is a surrogate for a more complete and explicit coordination of monetary policies;
(iii) it is an instrument with which to achieve greater inflationary discipline;
(iv) it is the obligatory path towards monetary union.

To these can be added a fifth argument, one more specifically political in character and which the system's founders certainly had in mind: the EMS favours the greater integration and unity of the European countries. Political considerations also seem to have been the basis for the decision by the weaker countries, like Italy, to join: exclusion from the currency agreement was frequently perceived as exclusion from the process of European integration and, implicitly, as exclusion from the future share-out of the advantages from this integration combined with progressive economic and political marginalization. Pointing this out is important for the following two reasons. Firstly, this attitude seems to be resurfacing now that the step towards further monetary integration seems near at hand. Secondly, Britain's experience shows that its belated membership of the EMS did not prevent it from fully reaping the advantages of Community integration.

The four arguments set out above are not mutually exclusive, except for (ii) and (iii). More in general, they represent the chief interpretations of the EMS; interpretations which are often in conflict with one other because they are two different and opposing ways of resolving the problem known as the 'paradigm of n degrees of freedom'.[1] In a particular currency area, there can be one and one only monetary authority. Therefore, either political and economic independence is granted to only one country (Great Britain during the period of the Gold Standard, the United States during the Bretton Woods period) thus giving rise to a hegemonic system, or the responsibility for monetary policy is divided equally among the countries in the union, giving rise to a cooperative system.

This is not the place for examination of the above arguments one by one, or for extensive analysis of the debate between the advocates of the disciplinary and cooperative interpretations of the EMS. The reader is referred to a number of recent publications for detailed treatment of the topic.[2] I shall instead seek to assess how far these arguments exert a positive influence on the decision to rejoin the EMS.

2.1. EXCHANGE RATE UNCERTAINTY AND INTRA-COMMUNITY TRADE

Numerous empirical studies have confirmed that the EMS has brought significant reductions in uncertainty over exchange rates among member countries[3]. Still controversial, however, is the question of whether this important outcome has been achieved at the cost of increased uncertainty over other variables, for instance short-term interest rates.[4]

More relevant to my present purposes is Fratianni and von Hagen's[5] finding that there is a trade-off between uncertainty about exchange rates within the EMS and uncertainty about exchange rates among currencies internal and external to it. Obviously, the importance of this phenomenon depends on the share of intra-community trade of each individual economy. According to Fratianni and van Hagen, reduced uncertainty over intra-EMS exchange rates has been accompanied by increased uncertainty over the dollar, yen and sterling exchange rates. This result squares with the observation that variance in the effective exchange rate has not changed for the SME countries.[6]

The extent to which reduced uncertainty over exchange rates among the EMS member countries has stimulated intra-community trade is, to say the least, ambiguous. Inspection of the figures in Table 1 seems to suggest a perverse and negative effect. The fall in export shares within the EMS, however, can be partially explained by the lower rate of growth achieved by the European countries compared with the other industrialized countries.

Table 1 - Relative shares of EMS exports in percentages

	Belgium	Denmark	France	Germany	Italy	Holland	EMS
1976	79.3	34.3	66.3	57.5	64.3	76.0	64.1
1978	77,3	40.3	65.2	55.6	62.6	76.6	63.1
1980	74.8	42.8	64.8	55.8	62.8	77.0	63.3
1982	72.5	41.6	61.4	54.5	59.3	74.8	60.9
1984	70.3	37.0	58.0	50.3	54.6	72.9	57.3
1986	72.5	39.3	58.1	48.2	55.6	71.5	56.4
1988	74.9	49.8	61.6 ·	54.3	57.5	75.3	59.9
1990	75.9	52.1	62.8	54.5	58.6	77.3	61.4
1991	76.0	54.1	63.6	55.0	59.4	76.9	

Note: relative shares are given by the ratio between exports to EMS countries and total exports.

Source: Fratianni and van Hagen 1990b updated with EUROSTAT figures.

As regards Italy, its membership of the EMS seems to have reduced the penetration of the European market by Italian exports to a relatively greater extent. The main reason for this is the continuous real revaluation of the Italian lira within the EMS, which has eroded the competitiveness of Italian-produced goods.

2.2. THE EMS AND THE CREDIBILITY OF MONETARY POLICY

The interpretation of the EMS as an instrument with which to apply inflationary discipline on errant member countries acquired increasing plausibility during the 1980s.[7]

The basic idea stems from Barro and Gordon's[8] model: a positive level of equilibrium inflation comes about when the central bank is unable to make credible commitment to a policy of zero inflation. Because the rate of inflation depends directly on the preferences of the policy maker, Rogoff[9] proposes the appointment of a 'conservative' central banker; i.e. a governor with strong anti-inflationary preferences as an effective anti-inflationary measure. Countries with low credibility may, by undertaking to fix their parities to the mark, delegate their monetary policy to the Bundesbank, which under this arrangement assumes the role of conservative governor.

For an explanation of this kind to be coherent, the following hypotheses must be confirmed:

(a) the credibility lacking on the side of monetary policy must be present on that of exchange policy;
(b) the fixed exchange rate agreement must be advantageous to the member countries;
(c) inflation must be entirely the result of the monetary authority's inability to commit itself to optimal policies;
(d) the system must operate asymmetrically: Germany decides monetary policy for the entire area, and each country fixes its parity with the mark.

2.2.1. THE CREDIBILITY OF THE EXCHANGE RATE ARRANGEMENT

Even if Barro and Gordon's model is accepted, one must still explain why fixing the exchange rate is a policy able to achieve the credibility that a policy of fixing monetary policy instead lacks. The reason cannot be the fact that the exchange rate is a variable which is more easily observed and monitored, because Barro and Gordon's model presupposes that also the quantity of money, or other possible indicators of monetary policy, are perfectly known to private agents. The explanation must lie externally to the model and must postulate that devaluation incurs costs of a political nature which balance out the incentive of the monetary authority to devalue unexpectedly. These costs may be justified by the fact that (a) devaluation is usually perceived as a failure of government policy, and (b) the entire community regards devaluation as a blow to the country's international prestige.

2.2.2. THE ADVANTAGES OF THE EXCHANGE RATE ARRANGEMENT

Even if the exchange rate policy is taken for granted, the economic convenience for both the high inflation country, say Italy, and the low inflation country, say Germany, of adhering to a rigid exchange rate agreement does not follow automatically. Under the hypothesis that Germany does not change its policy after the agreement, the advantages for Italy are assured: it obtains an inflation rate lower than what it could achieve with flexible rates, and without costs in terms of lower output.[10] This hypothesis, however, is untenable in Barro and Gordon's model: the exchange rate agreement alters the trade-off between inflation and output perceived by the German policy-maker by diminishing the costs in terms of inflation of an unannounced increase in the money supply. The Bank of Italy follows the Bundesbank's monetary policy and therefore 'imports' part of the inflation generated by German monetary expansion. Which means that the rate of inflation of the whole system is higher than Germany's would be in a regime of flexible exchange rates. This outcome raises two problems: the advantage to Italy is no longer guaranteed, but now depends on the parameters of the model;[11] the disadvantage to Germany is, instead, unequivocal. One has to explain, therefore, why Germany should decide to adhere to an exchange agreement of this kind with Italy. Once again the explanation, if it exists, lies externally to the model.[12]

From what has been said, it appears that the theoretical justification for the EMS as an instrument with which to achieve otherwise impossible monetary discipline is incomplete and unsatisfactory. Of course, this does not mean that the EMS has not played a part in reducing and converging the inflation rates of the member countries. In order to evaluate the effectiveness of this role of the EMS, analysis of the empirical results is required.

Figure 1 compares the average trend of inflation in the countries that belong to the EMS with those of the principal countries that do not. Whereas in the first phase of the EMS, the performance of the EMS countries was clearly inferior to that of the non-EMS ones, from 1987 onwards the average inflation rate of the EMS countries was lower than that of the non-EMS ones. At first sight, therefore, these figures seem to confirm the view that the EMS operates as a disciplinary instrument. In the second phase of the EMS, in fact, when the fixing of parities gained credibility, this mechanism came into operation. Some remarks, however, are in order.

Appreciable disinflation and the downwards convergence of inflation rates are not features exclusive to the countries belonging to the EMS.[13] Although, therefore, a reduction in inflation more or less comparable to that achieved by the EMS countries was also obtained by non-EMS countries in Europe - Great Britain and Spain for example - the disciplinary approach can still be defended by arguing that the costs of disinflation have been lower in the EMS countries.

The studies so far carried out in this regard, however, fail to support this thesis. Giavazzi and Spaventa[14] and Dornbusch[15] have calculated 'sacrifice ratios' inside and outside the EMS without finding significant differences between the two blocks of countries.[16] De Grauwe[17] has used a 'misery index' - unemployment plus inflation - as a measure of the cost of disinflation. This index has always been higher in the EMS countries than in certain OECD countries, both before and after 1979, and, more interestingly, it increased after 1980 in the EMS countries.[18]

Figure 1 - Disinflation inside and outside the EMS

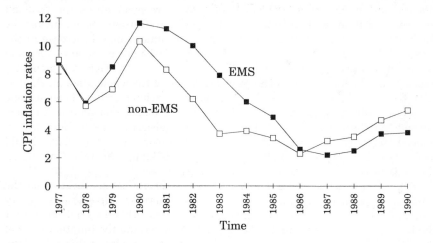

2.2.3. The 'Excess of Credibility' Hypothesis

Should inflation prove to have causes which differ at least partially from the monetary authorities' lack of credibility, a fixed exchange rate policy would have higher costs in real terms and lower advantages in terms of inflation. In this case, in fact, the inflationary differential would tend to persist, thereby creating a tendency towards the revaluation of the real exchange rate; and the inflation differential would, moreover, weaken the credibility of the commitment to exchange stability.

Figure 2 shows the differential between the inflation rates of Italy and Germany. The tendency for the differential to diminish is obvious; it slows noticeably after 1987 and reverses direction in 1990. This pattern contradicts the theory, given that it was precisely in this latter period that the nominal exchange rate between the lira and the mark remained stable. This testifies to the credibility acquired by the fluctuation band and indicates that the EMS as an instrument of monetary discipline should function better. The persistence of an inflationary differential seems to show that Italian inflation is caused by factors other than the ability of the Italian authorities to pursue credible anti-inflationary policies. Should this be confirmed, on the one hand the costs in terms of output of a disinflation policy based on fixed exchange rates would increase, because of the continuous revaluation of the exchange rate; on the other, the system would be balanced on a knife-edge. In fact, as soon as the market realized that the inflation differential was destined to persist, incurring excessive costs in terms of competitiveness and payments imbalances for the economy with the higher inflation, expectations of devaluation would intensify and the central parity would no longer be defensible.

Figure 2 - Inflation rate of Italy and Germany

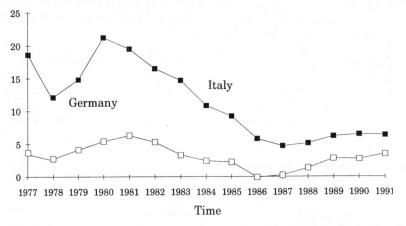

The following explanation of the persistence of an inflation differential has been proposed. When central parities gain credibility, and expectations of the devaluation of the currencies of the countries with high inflation are therefore reduced to the minimum, nominal interest rates rapidly converge, while real rates tend to be lower in the higher-inflation countries: an effect in itself perverse and which, by stimulating demand in the high-inflation countries, would slow down the reduction of the inflationary differential. In the recent past, Alan Walters[19] has cited this perverse effect to advise against English participation in the EMS. A similar argument has been subsequently advanced by several writers[20] and labelled the 'paradox of excessive credibility'. The crucial point in this argument is that the impact of credible commitment on exchange rate stability is greater on the financial markets than on the commodities and labour markets, where expectations are revised more slowly. However, should anyone seek empirical confirmation for these hypotheses, they will find it difficult to come by: although it is undeniable that demand in real terms has grown more in Italy than in Germany, a result which confirms the hypothesis, real interest rates have tended to increase in both absolute terms and relative to Germany's during the years of Italy's membership of the EMS, and this contradicts the hypothesis.[21] The further observation concerning the presistence of a high differential in nominal long-term rates is difficult to reconcile with the hypothesis of excessive credibility.

2.2.4. THE GERMAN DOMINANCE HYPOTHESIS

For the interpretative hypothesis of the EMS as an instrument of monetary discipline to be coherent, the European monetary system must function in a perfectly asymmetric manner: Germany fixes monetary policy for the entire area and the other countries fix their currencies according to the mark. This has been called the German Dominance Hypothesis (GDH).

The empirical evidence so far available,[22] however, refutes this hypothesis. The position of the Bundesbank in the EMS seems better described as one of long-term independence, not one of dominance.[23]

This result should be interpreted with caution, since at first sight it may appear contradictory. The paradigm of the n degrees of freedom entails that the independence of the German monetary authority must inevitably be accompanied by the dependence of the other central banks. This contradiction, however, is only apparent if one remembers the two release valves that the system frequently used until the 1990s: the realignment of exchange rates, and the restriction of capital movements by means of administrative controls. These two mechanisms ensured that German independence did not automatically turn into dominance. This, however, obliges us to conclude that in a situation in which these two release valves were definitively closed, German hegemony would effectively come about.

However, the stability of a system of fixed exchange rates under German dominance, in which monetary policy was determined exclusively by the Bundesbank, and in which inflation differentials tended to persist, would be rather low, unless one assumes that one of the aims of the Bundesbank was to guarantee the stability of the system by refraining from policies which would undermine its stability. In this case, however, the interpretative model would no longer be the one based on German dominance and it would instead become a system based on cooperation among monetary policies.

2.2.5. THE PERSISTENCE OF AN INFLATIONARY DIFFERENTIAL: AN ALTERNATIVE EXPLANATION

The persistence of an inflationary differential comes as much less of a surprise if one abandons the rather simplistic hypothesis of the existence of one sole good - a hypothesis that has been overworked in the most recent models of international finance. If, instead, one also considers goods that are not internationally tradable, the rate of inflation of one country may remain higher than that of another - even in the presence of fixed nominal exchange rates - if the relative price of non-tradable goods persistently rises.

The price level is equal to a weighed average of the price of tradable goods (p^T), which the fixed exchange rate equalizes, and of non-tradable goods (p^{NT}):

$$p_t = \omega p_t^T + (1-\omega)p_t^{NT}$$

Dividing both members by the price of tradable goods, we obtain:

$$\frac{p_t}{p_t^T} = \omega + (1-\omega)\frac{p_t^{NT}}{p_t^T}$$

It becomes obvious that in order for the rate of inflation in a country to be higher than that in another country (so that p_t / p_t^T increases over time), the relative price of non-tradable goods, p_t^{NT} / p_t^T, must increase in a persistent manner. Figure 3 shows that this increase in the relative price of non-tradable goods has, in fact, been the main force working against the convergence of Italian inflation towards the German and French ones. This figure shows the ratio between the value added prices in the service sector and in the industrial sector: whereas this increases in Italy, it tends to decrease in both Germany and France.

Figure 3 - Growth differentials between value added prices of services and of goods: (1985 prices = 1)

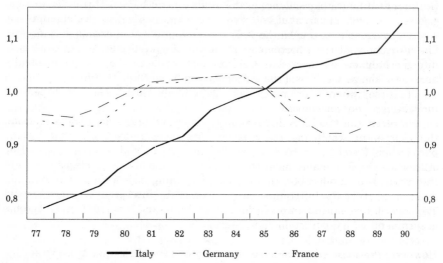

Source: Visco (1992), fig. 7.

It is therefore evident that, far from being entirely due to the monetary authorities' lack of credibility, Italian inflation also stems from structural factors sustaining the endogenous component of inflation. Exhaustive treatment of these mechanisms would be beyond the scope of this article.[24] It is clear, however, that the low rate of productivity growth in services, combined with an adjustment of the levels of wages growth to those obtaining in industrial sectors, where productivity growth has been higher, is a major cause of the increase in the relative price of services.

The most important consequence of the persistence of inflationary differentials concerns the stability of the system and the credibility of the central parities. Given the entirely free movement of capital, the credibility of the central parities appears to be crucial for the stability of the system.

However, in the presence of permanent inflationary differentials, this credibility rapidly disappears due to costs in terms of lost competitiveness for the country with the highest inflation, and due to the trade disequilibria that derive from it.

2.2.6. THE EMS AS AN INSTRUMENT OF INFLATIONARY DISCIPLINE

Theoretical analysis and empirical evidence seem to agree in stressing that the EMS, at least until the mid-1980s, was unable to perform the role of an instrument of inflationary discipline that the theory advocated. The countries belonging to the EMS did not show a disinflationary process significantly different from that of countries outside the agreement; they did not sustain significantly lower costs (indeed some studies maintain the contrary); the German dominance hypothesis, necessary for the coherence of the theory, was rejected by econometric studies; the underlying theoretical model appeared weak and unable to explain the phenomenon. When subsequent financial liberalization and the rejection of the realignment instrument rendered this interpretative model theoretically viable, the EMS displayed high instability because of the persistence of the inflationary differential.

Of course, this does not mean that the exchange rate system played no role in the disinflation process. Certainly, on the one hand the political superstructure of the EMS and its functioning mechanism with, on the other, the short-term stabilizing role that the fluctuation bands can fulfil when parities are credible, enabled Italy to pursue a policy of a strong lira which otherwise would probably have been impossible. Membership of the EMS and the refusal to undertake compensatory devaluations of the inflationary differential broke the inflation/deflation spiral that typified the decade 1975-85. The external constraint imposed by the EMS, moreover, provided the Italian government with justifiction for its unpopular policies and rendered it less susceptible to demands for compensatory policies by the social partners. However, the most important reasons for the disinflation process in Italy lie elsewhere. Giavazzi and Spaventa[25] have stressed that certain politico-social events, such as the 1984 referendum on the wage-indexing system (scala mobile), had a much more marked effect on expectations of inflation caused by membership of the EMS.[26]

The consequences of the argument so far can be summarized as follows. If one entirely accepts the credibility hypothesis, then a 'hard' EMS, i.e. one with practically immutable parities, becomes essential to maximize the benefits of belonging to the EMS. If, instead, one assumes a somewhat less critical attitude towards the credibility hypothesis, then also a 'soft' EMS, one which does not dispense with the realignment instrument, may provide valid assistance in the struggle against inflation. While the former option raises serious problems of stability and rigidity, the latter appears relatively more stable and certainly more flexible.

2.3. THE EMS AS THE OBLIGATORY PATH TO MONETARY UNION

The European monetary system has often been described as a necessary component in the transition phase towards more complete monetary union. The costs of belonging to an exchange arrangement, therefore, must be assessed not only in terms of the advantages of the EMS in itself, but also and principally in terms of the future advantages of monetary union. Of course, this assertion only makes sense if one considers the present system to be a credible path towards complete monetary union.[27]

The Treaty of Maastricht, which in part endorses and in part modifies the celebrated Delors Report of 1989, describes the three phases required to achieve monetary union. The first phase, by now concluded, involves complete financial liberalization among the countries of the Community. The third phase involves the birth of monetary union; that is, it stipulates that exchange rates should become irrevocably fixed, although what the actual features of this union should be, whether national currencies are to remain or whether they are to be superseded by a single European currency, is not made clear. The second phase comprises the crucial period of transition towards monetary union, and it warrants closer examination.

There are two possible paths to monetary union. The more rapid path, based on shock therapy, envisages the rapid realization of monetary union;[28] most of the monetary unions in history have followed this path.[29] The monetary unification which recently took place in Germany came about suddenly and, technically, with success.[30]

The path chosen by the EEC countries with the Maastricht Treaty, though, is that of a slow and gradual approach; a path which raises two rather important problems.

In the absence of close coordination of economic policies, and with the persistence of full political and economic autonomy, each national government will be induced to pursue policies apparently incompatible with the objective of the monetary stability of the future union. In other words, there will be an incentive for each country to present itself on unification day with an inflation rate, a public deficit and a stock of public debt standing higher than the average of the other countries, so that it can offload part of the adjustment costs on its European partners. To overcome this obstacle, the treaty envisages that passage to union will not be automatic, but that it will instead be conditional on the satisfaction of certain convergence criteria.[31] The currency constraint imposed by the EMS with its narrow fluctuation bands may, first, make it easier to achieve these objectives, both directly in the case of the inflation rate convergence, and indirectly by the restrictions it would impose on fiscal authorities. Second, it represents, within the logic of the treaty, the ideal environment for a gradual approach to monetary union.

The following proposition seems to underlie this position: the European countries do not exhibit real and profound divergences and disequilibria, neither internally nor among themselves, and the only source of turbulence and instability is their national governments.[32] The best policy in this case is to limit to the maximum the discretionary powers of the economic policy-makers, by constraining their action to that of an external institution which enjoys full autonomy: while the exchange agreement constrains the monetary authorities, the non-entry clauses constrain the fiscal policy-makers. Only from this point of view can the reversal of the means-end nexus underlying the Maastricht Treaty be understood: it is not monetary union that enables disequilibria and disparities to be overcome and induces convergence of macroeconomic indicators; rather, it is the convergence of these indicators that makes monetary union possible.

The other problem concerns the instability intrinsic to the Treaty itself.[33] One of the convergence criteria required of countries qualifying for EMU is that they maintain exchange rate stability (defined as keeping their currencies within their EMS fluctuation bands without severe tensions for a minimum of two years prior to the onset of monetary union). A speculative attack forcing a devaluation that prevents a country from satisfying this requirement might, by eliminating the allure of EMU membership, induce its government to abandon the current policy regime. Since the country, once driven out of the EMS, might no longer qualify for EMU, it would have no incentive to continue pursuing the policies of austerity necessary to gain entry. A speculative attack, then, may prove self-fulfilling. The theoretical underpinning of this explanation is the literature on balance of payment crisis that uses the notion of self-fulfilling speculative attacks and multiple equilibria.[34]

These considerations lead to the conclusion that a 'hard' EMS - that is, one with narrow bands, without frequent realignments, and hegemonic in character (i.e. one in which monetary policy is decided by the Bundesbank for the purpose of internal equilibrium) - does not seem a viable route towards monetary union. The sacrifice of an economy which decides to sustain the high costs of EMS membership by counting on the future benefits of a monetary union appears, in the light of the above, a sacrifice most likely to be in vain.[35]

The question arises at this point as to why the authorities of the EEC countries should have chosen an uncertain and risky route to monetary union. The answer can only be political in nature, and as such lies beyond the scope of these brief notes. Nevertheless, mention must be made of the fact that a gradual approach allows postponement of the crucial political decision, just as political responsibility for the failure of the process can be shifted onto non-fulfilment of the non-entry clauses.

2.4. THE EMS AS A COOPERATIVE INSTRUMENT

There is no doubt that at the moment of its creation, the EMS was conceived as a surrogate for more explicit cooperation over monetary policy. This is evident not only when one reads the documents and declarations that led to the birth of the EMS, but also when one analyses the initial features of the system. These were designed to ensure the more efficient absorption of shocks exogenous to the economy of the European countries: a cooperative policy eliminates recourse to 'beggar-thy-neighbour' exchange policies, whether devaluationary (to improve the trade balance) or revaluationary (to blunt inflation by exporting it).

The fixing of the exchange rate is, from this point of view, a specific form of coordination among monetary policies with the advantages that it is easy to monitor, discourages the forms of cheating possible in cooperative regimes, and does not entail the costs of frequent renegotiations of common policy. By contrast, it has the disadvantage of being sub-optimal with respect to a complete form of coordination. How distant this surrogate is from the original depends, of course, on the nature of the external shocks that affect the system and the amount of interdependence among the national economies. Major asymmetric shocks affecting economies with a low amount of interdependence require that adjustment of the exchange rate must be an important ingredient of optimal policy, whereas symmetric shocks affecting closely integrated countries may be effectively dealt with without altering the parity.

The advantage of the cooperative interpretation of the EMS is that it explains Germany's participation in the exchange arrangement: the desire to build a system that can provide a common European response to an American monetary policy often viewed as highly unstable.

It should be remembered that this interpretation of the EMS does not entail that the system must function symmetrically. Even a system operating in an asymmetric manner can be more beneficial, both to the countries which peg their parities to the mark and to Germany, than one in which there are decentralized monetary policies and flexible exchange rates. The German central bank, however, cannot operate with complete independence, given that the shocks affecting the other member countries will affect, directly or indirectly, Germany as well. This explanation therefore seems more compatible with the empirical results that indicate a less than perfect asymmetry.

Within this framework, a crisis of the system arises when asymmetric shocks (German unification, for example) make alteration to the parity rate essential for correct readjustment, particularly as regards those countries, like Italy, which are not yet closely integrated with the German economy.

3. THE COSTS OF THE EMS

The costs of membership of a fixed exchange rate arrangement essentially take the form of a loss of monetary independence and of the inability to use the exchange rate instrument. Therefore, in order to assess the costs of membership of the EMS we must specify the degree of exchange rate rigidity and the degree of monetary independence. I have already mentioned on several occasions that the EMS has passed through two stages: in the first, the possibility of frequent realignments and the existence of controls on capital movements meant that membership of the system had not completely compromised monetary independence; in the second, instead, commitment to non-realignment and the free circulation of capital almost entirely eliminated monetary autonomy.[36] The costs of EMS membership should therefore be judged according to the model of the EMS considered.

3.1. THE EXCHANGE RATE

When two countries are hit by asymmetric shocks - for example, a shift in international demand - the optimal solution may be to change the exchange rate. This use of the exchange rate instrument is justified in cases where there is a rigidity of prices and wages and low mobility of the production factors. If, in fact, prices and wages adjust immediately, a movement in relative prices will come about such as to balance out the demand effect and prevent it from affecting income and employment. Otherwise there may be a shift in manpower away from the country with falling demand towards the one with rising demand. Conversely, in the case where prices and wages are not flexible and the workforce has low mobility, a variation in the exchange rate may resolve the problem created by the initial shock.

There are, however, other policies which can be used instead of the exchange rate: notably, the fiscal instrument. Fiscal administration can be used to transfer resources from the country which has benefited from the shift in consumer demand to the country which has paid the price for it. This, though, presupposes the existence of a federal fiscal system or of a coordination of fiscal policies between the two countries. In fact, it is the existence of a federal fiscal system which distinguishes the case of two countries joined in currency union from that of two different regions of the same national state.[37] Sachs and Sala-i-Martin, for example, maintain that the American federal tax system responds appreciably to regional shocks by offsetting them to around 35% by means of lower tax revenues and greater transfer.[38]

There is no such mechanism at the moment in Europe, and the plan to accompany monetary unification with an expansion of the Community budget has been shelved. A currency union which cannot count on the shock-absorber function of a relatively wide-ranging fiscal apparatus, therefore, does not seem an efficient solution.

We have so far taken it for granted that varying the nominal exchange rate is an effective measure. Indeed it is so, but only as a first approximation and only in the short term. As regards the long term, it is necessary to establish whether a variation in the *nominal* exchange rate is able permanently to alter the *real* exchange rate. In the above case in which a country experiences a drop in demand for its products, in the short term nominal devaluation of the exchange rate corrects the negative shock, but in the long term it causes an increase in domestic inflation which counterbalances the first positive effect.

The rapidity and importance of this counter-effect depend on the degree of wage index-linking and the extent of the economy's openness. The more open the economy and the greater the wage index-linking of the country which has devalued, the more rapidly will the positive effect of the devaluation fade.

The cost of belonging to a currency union in terms of the loss of the exchange rate instrument depends on the openness of the economy concerned: the less open the economy, the more it has to lose by joining a monetary union.

Table 2 shows that there are wide differences among the degrees of openness of the EEC countries. In particular, Italy's openness compared with the other European nations is rather low, and it will therefore have to pay a very high cost should it decide to join a system of fixed exchange rates with the other European countries.

If one also remembers that Italy recently abolished its system of automatic wage index-linking, one may conclude that Italy would incur a very high cost from losing exchange rate flexibility.

Table 2 - Intra-community exports by EEC countries (as a percentage of GDP)

Ireland	50.1
Belgium	49.8
Holland	40.0
Portugal	19.6
Germany	16.1
Denmark	13.9
France	12.5
Greece	11.6
Great Britain	9.5
Italy	9.4
Spain	7.1

Source: EC Commision (1990).

3.2. THE INFLATION RATE

A system of rigid exchange rates presupposes that the inflation differential is very close to zero. We have already examined the possible consequences of a situation of slowly-converging inflation rates for the systemic stability and the economic competitiveness of a higher-inflation country. This section will briefly deal with the economic convenience for two structurally different countries to have the same rate of inflation.

When it was believed that there was a long-term trade-off between inflation and unemployment, the inflation rate was made to depend on the slope of the Phillips curve and on the preferences of economic policy-makers. In this case it was perfectly possible for two countries to have different desired inflation rates, and there was no rational reason for forcing the differential down to zero.[39] Now that faith in a long-term stable Phillips curve has faded, and the thesis of its long-term verticality is widely accepted, no reasonable defence of the thesis of monetary independence can be advanced, and the objective of a convergence of inflation rates towards the long-term minimum is accordingly difficult to criticise. However, this does not mean that, in the short period, an individual country is prevented from choosing its own convergence path towards the minimum of inflation. Short-term trade-offs may differ for the two countries, and this may justify their adoption of different short-term policies and different inflation-reducing strategies. Membership of a fixed exchange rate system, therefore, presupposes acceptance not only of a long-term trade-off between inflation and unemployment, but also acceptance of the convergence path towards monetary stability. The economic convenience of this choice, which cannot be established *a priori*, should be assessed by setting the advantages in terms of greater credibility against the possible costs arising from the choice of a convergence path other than that desired. For example, when the inflation differential is particularly high - which means that expectations of inflation are high and sluggish - the advantages, in terms of credibility, of belonging to a fixed exchange rates system for the country with higher inflation are considerable; indeed, probably higher than those of a loss of monetary autonomy in the short period.

The modern theory of optimal public finance suggests another reason why inflation rates may diverge.[40] A government will draw on different sources of fiscal revenue in order to equalize their marginal cost. If the marginal cost of fiscal revenue is greater than zero, as is likely, then seigniorage too can be used as an instrument of fiscal revenue. Two countries with different structures of fiscal administration may have different levels of seigniorage and therefore different levels of inflation.

A country like Italy, which has a backward tax system with widespread evasion, pays the price of a lower-than-optimal level of seigniorage in order to join a fixed exchange rate arrangement.

4. Costs and Benefits Compared

The European monetary system, in the form that it has taken in recent years, is a system with 'almost completely' fixed exchange rates operating asymmetrically, in which Germany establishes monetary policy for the entire area and the other countries peg their currencies to the mark. Dominance-based international monetary systems work as long as the dominant country provides the public good that justifies its role. During the 1980s, Germany performed this task by supplying the credibility of its anti-inflationary monetary policy as the public good. In the 1990s, however, the general macroeconomic picture has changed, the high inflation rates of many European countries have disappeared, and the public good provided by the Bundesbank has diminished in value.

The above sections have analysed the costs and benefits of a system with 'almost' completely fixed exchange rates. The benefits are mainly the possibility of anchoring monetary policy to German monetary policy; the costs derive from the loss of exchange rate flexibility and of autonomous monetary policy. There is an obvious contradiction here. For the benefits to emerge there must be credible commitment to exchange rate stability, which means that there is a credible renunciation of exchange rate variation. The rigidity of the exchange rate necessary to create this credibility, however, raises the costs of belonging to the system. Both costs and benefits tend to increase with an increase in the degree of rigidity of the exchange rate.

This does not apply to all countries in the same way, however. In some countries, the loss of monetary autonomy is not a high cost, both because they have economic policy objectives very similar to Germany's and because they have economies very open to Germany's, so that a variation in the nominal exchange rate has entirely temporary effects.

It is possible to draw interesting comparisons between two Italys. The first Italy, that of the early 1980s, is characterized by robust inflation - inflation kept high, amongst other things, by strong inflationary expectations - by a high level of real wage indexation, and by a somewhat low stock of public debt. The first of these features indicates that the advantages to be gained from anchoring Italian monetary policy to German policy are high in terms of the stabilization of inflationary expectations. The second feature indicates that the possible advantages deriving from varying the exchange rate, in terms of altering the relative prices of domestically produced goods, are extremely short-lived - given that the wage increases induced by index-linking push up domestic production costs. Finally, the third feature enables flexible use to be made of the interest rate to stabilize the exchange rate, particularly during periods of tension on the foreign currency markets.

The other Italy, that of the 1990s, is characterized by a slight inflationary differential which has persisted despite a credible exchange rate arrangement - a differential apparently caused by, so to speak, structural factors - by a very low degree of real wage indexation, by increasingly weak and less combative trade unions, and by an enormous stock of public debt, consisting mostly of short-term securities. In this case, whereas the advantages of an exchange rate arrangement appear to be modest, and may even turn into costs when the persistent differential undermines the competitivenes of Italian exports, the exchange rate instrument appears to be highly effective, given the rigidity of nominal wages. The high stock of public debt, moreover, renders the use of the interest rate to stabilize the exchange rate in moments of crisis rather inflexible and/or very costly.

Whereas for the first Italy the advantages of the exchange rate system are presumably greater than the costs, for the second Italy the order of preferences is reversed: the loss of monetary independence, especially in the presence of a highly restrictive policy by the leader country, seems to be anything but off-set by the modest advantage of greater credibility.

5. THE FUTURE OF THE EMS

The new EMS was unable to withstand the second major crisis in the summer
of 1993: the width of the bands' of fluctuation dramatically increased from
±2.25% to ±15%. It is self-evident that the new bands width is such that what
remains of the EMS can hardly be called a fixed exchange rates system. There
are various economic explanations for the crisis of the system, each of which
contains part of truth; yet the most important reason seems to be the power of
speculation in the international foreign exchange market.

The technical reason for the strength of speculative attacks is the lack of
any form of capital controls. This makes the size of the official reserves
ridiculous with respect to the huge amount of capital available for speculative
movements. Within this framework, the instrument interest rate appears much
more effective against speculative attacks. Raising the interest rate, however, is
not a cost-free policy, given its effect on the production level, on public finance
and on the stability of the financial structure. Not coincidentally, the first two
countries forced to leave the system were the ones which because of the high
level of its outstanding public debt, Italy, and because of its role in the
international capital markets, Great Britain, were particularly reluctant to use
the interest rate instrument.

The reasons that prompt speculative attacks are various and they played
different roles in the different countries involved in the crisis. The first is that a
realignment was overdue and had been delayed because of the misguided belief
that a *hard EMS* had achieved enough credibility to sustain existing parities
until full convergence occurred. Therefore in some countries, mainly Italy, an
inflation-differential had accumulated and their currencies had become
overvalued. Secondly, most of the countries were hit by the asymmetric shock
represented by German economic and monetary union. Response to this
disturbance should have required an appreciation of the Deutschmark (a fall in
prices and costs in other EMS countries relative to those prevailing in
Germany). Some EMS countries, and mainly France, denied Germany the
option of revaluing its currency and therefore rendered necessary either a burst
of inflation in Germany and stable prices elsewhere, or a stable price in
Germany and a burst of deflation elsewhere. A third and simpler option was to
devaluate the other European currencies. According to this interpretation, the
crisis was a way to force reluctant governments to accept the exchange rate
correction. The third explanation for the crisis points to public opposition to the
Maastricht Treaty, which was fuelled by the worsening of the general economic
conditions. Under this view, the markets simply anticipated the abandonment
of the too tight policies required by the Treaty. Lastly, the Maastricht Treaty in
itself may have had a destabilizing role, as I have already discussed.

In conclusion, brief examination of the implications of the analysis for the
future of the EMS may be of some interest. There are two ways forward, if one
excludes the possibility of the rapid achievement of monetary union.

In the first scenario, the system tries to survive with the existing broad band of fluctuations, waiting for better times to come.[41] Wider fluctuation bands discourage, at least partially, speculative attacks, as the experience of the EMS has amply shown.[42] In addition, they ensure a certain degree of monetary policy autonomy, at least in the short period.[43] The main criticism raised against this option regards the difficulty of ensuring the European single market when the nominal exchange rate can vary around 30% without any intervention by the Central Banks. Moreover, they exacerbate credibility problems. In a period of international recession, a strong incentive to pursue a 'beggar-thy-neighbour' policy may emerge via competitive devaluations.

The view that the excessive variability of exchange rates may jeopardise economic union and the single market prompts some authors to suggest the rapid return to narrower bands. The turbulence in the foreign exchange market, however, and the strength of speculation in the absence of capital controls makes this option hardly sustainable. To overcome this obstacle and to provide the monetary authority with a minimum of autonomy in conducting monetary policy, some authors[44] have revived Tobin's idea of 'putting sand' in the foreign exchange markets. What they suggest is not a revival in administrative control, no longer possible under the provisions of the Maastricht Treaty and the Single European Act, but rather an explicit or implicit tax - via non-interest-bearing deposits requirements - on foreign exchange transactions. Both measures work by raising the cost of cross-border capital flows and they penalise short-term capital movements more heavily than longer-term investments. They could support weak currencies in the short-term, and this would provide time to organise orderly realignments in the case of persistent disequilibria, without jeopardising the overall stability of the system.

In my opinion, however, both proposals miss the main point, which needs to be clarified in order to breathe new life into the project of European monetary union: the problem of conducting monetary policy within the area. This ambiguity remains unresolved because both options leave some autonomy to the national monetary authorities. This point was implicitly solved during the years of the new EMS by means of the asymmetric nature of the system, where the Bundesbank set the monetary policy for the entire area and other countries defended the parities of their exchange rates. The interpretations of the EMS as a disciplinary device provided the theoretical anchor for this political choice.

The analysis proposed in previous sections shows that the asymmetric management of economic policy is justified neither on theoretical grounds nor on empirical ones. Moreover the asymmetric management of the monetary policy seems to be one of the main reasons for the outbreak of the crisis.

This leads to the conclusion that the EMS structural crisis can be solved only by means of an institutional innovation process which leads to the creation of a European Central Bank which assumes control of monetary policy in the whole area. The cooperative management of monetary policy for the whole of the European Community, entrusted to a European Central Bank, would increase the advantages of participating in the agreement, in terms of increased efficiency in the absorption of exogenous shocks to the European economy, and could ensure greater stability for the system. The same outcome, however, could also be obtained, while maintaining the present structure, if the leader country, Germany, took it upon itself to conduct a monetary policy able to minimize tensions within the currency area. This would probably incur a cost for Germany compared with the present situation. The threat of a return to decentralized policies that would induce the breakdown of the exchange rate agreement might provide the necessary incentive for Germany to cooperate.

NOTES

1 If n countries join a currency union, in which exchange rates are fixed, only n-1 parities can be predetermined and there is a degree of freedom in fixing the common monetary policy.

2 See, for example, De Grauwe, 1992; Fratianni and von Hagen, 1992; Gross and Thygesen, 1992.

3 See Fratianni and von Hagen, 1990a; Rogoff 1985a; Artis and Taylor, 1988; Weber 1990.

4 Artis and Taylor, 1988; Rogoff, 1985a.

5 Fratianni and von Hagen, 1990b.

6 Ungerer et al. 1986.

7 Giavazzi and Pagano 1988; Giavazzi and Giovannini 1987, 1988, 1989.

8 Barro and Gordon, 1983.

9 Rogoff, 1985b.

10 This does not explain the advantageousness to Germany of this arrangement. See below, however.

11 It has been shown that the greater the integration between the two countries, the less Italy benefits from participating in a fixed exchange regime.

12 It has been suggested, for example, that Germany draws advantage, in terms of trade, from the tendency of other currencies to be overvalued in real terms with respect to the mark: Melitz, 1988; Giavazzi and Pagano, 1988. Although not without a certain validity, this explanation has two consequences which should be stressed. First, it presupposes that the Italian inflation rate is slow in converging with the German rate, and this contradicts the base hypotheses of Barro and Gordon's model, and in any case only holds for the adjustment period. Second, it confers chronic instability on the system by hypothesising persistent trade imbalances.

13 Two important factors account for this widespread process. First, all countries, belonging to the EMS or otherwise, were affected during the 1980s by the same inflation-reducing shocks. Second, these years were marked by a general change in both the politico-social equilibria that restricted the growth of labour costs and in the attitudes of the economic policy authorities, which became increasingly less willing to sustain the

economy by expanding internal demand.

14 Giavazzi and Spaventa, 1989.

15 Dornbusch, 1988.

16 The 'sacrifice ratio' is the ratio between the amount of unemployment accumulated since a base year and the total reduction in inflation.

17 De Grauwe, 1990.

18 According to De Grauwe, this result can be explained by the slower process of disinflation in the EMS countries. Countries outside the EMS mostly resorted to shock therapy which provoked a sharp but short-lived recession. In the EMS countries, however, disinflation was more gradual and extended the economic costs over a longer time-span. Only by assuming a high degree of policy shortsightedness among the EMS countries, i.e. a high intertemporal discount rate, can one maintain that the costs of disinflation have been lower in the EMS countries.

19 Walters, 1986.

20 Giavazzi and Spaventa, 1990; Bini Smaghi and Micossi, 1990.

21 The recent empirical study by Artis, 1992, confirms this scepticism.

22 See, for example, Fratianni and von Hagen, 1990a; Cohen and Wyplosz, 1989; Weber, 1990.

23 Fratianni and von Hagen, 1992.

24 See Barca and Visco, 1992; Visco, 1992.

25 Giavazzi and Spaventa, 1989.

26 Note that this statement raises doubts over the theory that holds inflation results from a lack of credibility: limiting the wage index-linking in the models used by theoreticians of this school should have the opposite result, given that it positively adjusts the trade-off perceived by the policy-maker between inflation and employment.

27 I shall not go into the debate on the advantages and disadvantages of monetary union, taking it as granted (with a goodly dose of optimism) that a monetary union with a single currency brings net advantages.

28 From a strictly theoretical point of view, the recipe is simple. On a specified day the citizens of the European countries convert their national currencies into, say, ECUs at a specific rate of exchange. Thereafter the ECU is the sole currency of the Community. The European Central Bank becomes the issuing institution and the authority of monetary policy.

29 Information on monetary unification in Germany and Italy is given in Holtfrerich, 1989, and Sannucci, 1989.

30 On German monetary union see Kalmbach, 1992, and Wills, 1991.

31 A country can join the EMU only if: (i) its rate of inflation is not more than 1.5% higher than the average of the lowest three rates of inflation among the EMS countries; (ii) its long-term interest rate is not more than 2% higher than the average rate of the three countries with lowest inflation; (iii) it has devalued in the three years leading up to the union; (iv) its public deficit does not exceed 3% of its GDP; (v) its public debt

does not exceed 60% of its GDP.

32 Of course, this hypothesis fits well with the above-mentioned Barro and Gordon model, where the main cause of inflation is not economic but political: namely, the lack of institutional instruments with which to tie the hands of future governments.

33 Eichengreen and Wyplosz, 1993.

34 Obstfeld, 1986.

35 The conclusion may be different if, instead of a hard and hegemonic EMS, one considers an EMS with broader and cooperatively managed bands of fluctuation.

36 Note that their loss of monetary independence should not be considered a cost for all the countries concerned. If inflation is engendered by the monetary authorities' lack of credibility, the loss of independence to a more credible external institution is a positive development.

37 Sachs and Sala-i-Martin, 1991; Eichengreen, 1990.

38 Von Hagen, 1992, has reported different results.

39 The possibility of autonomously fixing the inflation rate was one of the principal reasons why during the Bretton Woods period many monetarists were in favour of a flexible exchange rate regime which guaranteed maximum monetary independence.

40 Fischer, 1982; Grilli, 1989.

41 The legal interpretation of the Maastricht Treaty becomes important at this stage. Do the new fluctuation bands satisfy the cited exchange rate criterion of the Maastricht Treaty? In other words could they be interpreted as *normal* fluctuation bands?

42 One need only point to what happened in the first years of the EMS: the French franc, which fluctuated in a narrow band, came under much more vigorous attack by speculators than the Italian lira, which enjoyed a broader band. Were the central parity to be changed and the band made wide enough, the change could take place without discrete jumps in the value of the exchange rate which represents the best source of profit for speculators.

43 A recent paper by Svensson, 1992, provides theoretical support for this argument.

44 Eichengreen and Wyplosz, 1992.

BIBLIOGRAPHY

Artis, M.J. (1992), 'Counter-Inflationary Policy in the Framework of the EMS', *CEPR Discussion Papers*, no. 649.

Artis, M.J., Taylor, M.P. (1988), 'Exchange Rates, Interest Rates, Capital Controls and European Monetary System: Assessing the Track Record', in Giavazzi, F., Micossi, S., Miller, M. (eds), 1988.

Barca, F., Visco, I. (1993), 'L'economia italiana nella prospettiva europea:

terziario protetto e dinamica dei redditi nominali', in Micossi, S., Visco, I. (eds), 1993.

Barro, R., Gordon, D. (1983), 'Rules, Discretion, and Reputation in a Model of Monetary Policy', *Journal of Monetary Economics*, 12, pp. 101-21.

Bini Smaghi, L., Micossi, S. (1990), 'Monetary and Exchange Rate Policy in the EMS with Free Capital Mobility', in De Grauwe, P., Papademos, L. (eds), 1990.

Bryant, R.C. et al. (eds) (1989), *Macroeconomic Policies in an Interdependent World,* Brookings Institute.

Bryant, R.C. Portes R. (eds) (1987), *Global Macroeconomics,* St. Martin's Press.

Cohen, D., Wyplosz, C. (1989), 'The European Monetary Union: An Agnostic Evaluation', in Brayant, R.C. *et al.* (eds), Macroeconomic Policies in an Interdependent World, Brookings Institute.

Committee on the Study of Economic and Monetary Union (Delors Committee) (1989), *'Report on Economic and Monetary Union in the European Community'*, Office for Official Publications of the European Community.

De Cecco, M., Giovannini, A. (eds) (1992), *A European Central Bank? Prospectives on Monetary Unification after ten Years of the EMS,* Cambridge University Press.

De Grauwe, P. (1990), 'The cost of Disinflation and the European Monetary System', *Open Economies Review* 1, pp. 147-73.

De Grauwe, P. (1992), *The Economics of Monetary Integration,* Oxford University Press.

De Grauwe, P., Papademos, L. (eds) (1991), *The European Monetary System in the 1990s,* Longman.

Dornbusch, R. (1988), 'The European Monetary System, the Dollar and the Yen', in Giavazzi, F., Micossi, S., Miller, M. (eds), (1988).

Eichengreen, B. (1991), 'One Money for Europe? Lessons from US Currency Union', *Economic Policy*, 10, pp. 119-86.

Eichengreen, B., Wyplosz, C. (1993), 'The Unstable EMS', *CEPR Discussion Papers*, no. 817.

Fair, D., de Boisseux, P. (eds) (1991), *Fiscal Policy, Taxes, and Financial System in an increasingly Integrated Europe,* Kluwer Academic Press.

Fischer, S. (1982), 'Seigniorage and the Case for a National Money' *Journal of Political Economy*, 90, pp. 295-307.

Fratianni, M., von Hagen, J. (1990a), 'German Dominance in the EMS: The Empirical Evidence', *Open Economies Review*, 1, pp. 67-87.

Fratianni, M., von Hagen, J. (1990b), 'The European Monetary System Ten Years After', *Carnegie-Rochester Conference Series on Public Policy*, 32, pp. 173-241.

Fratianni, M., von Hagen, J. (1992), *The European Monetary System and European Monetary Union,* Westview Press.

Giavazzi, F., Giovannini, A. (1987), 'Models of EMS: Is Europe a Greater Deutschmark Area?', in Bryant, R.C., Portes, R. (eds), 1987.

Giavazzi, F., Giovannini, A. (1988), 'The Role of Exchange Rate Regimes in

Disinflation: Empirical Evidence on the EMS', in Giavazzi, F., Micossi, S.,
   Miller, M. (eds), 1988.
Giavazzi, F., Giovannini, A. (1989), *Limiting the Exchange Rate Flexibility: The
   European Monetary System*, MIT Press.
Giavazzi, F., Micossi, S., Miller, M. (eds) (1988), *The European Monetary
   System*, Cambridge University Press.
Giavazzi, F., Pagano, M. (1988), 'The Advantage of Tying One's Hands: EMS
   Discipline and Central Bank Credibility', *European Economic Review*, 32,
   pp. 1055-82.
Giavazzi, F., Spaventa, L. (1989), 'Italy: The Real Effects of Inflation and
   Disinflation', *Economic Policy*, 5, pp. 133-71.
Giavazzi, F., Spaventa, L. (1990), 'The "New" EMS', in De Grauwe, P.,
   Papademos, L. (eds), 1990.
Grilli, V. (1989), 'Seigniorage in Europe', in De Cecco, M., Giovannini, A. (eds),
   1989.
Gros, D., Thygesen, N. (1992), *European Monetary Integration*, Longman.
Holtfrerich, L.C. (1989), 'The Monetary Unification Process in Nineteenth-
   Century Germany: Relevance and Lessons for Europe Today', in De Cecco,
   M, Giovannini, A. (eds), 1989.
Kalmbach, P. (1992), 'Two years After the German Monetary Union: The
   Transition to a Market Economy with the Help of a Rich Uncle' *Annali
   Scientifici del Dipartimento di Economia*, 1992, University of Trento.
Melitz, J. (1988), 'Monetary Discipline, Germany and European Monetary
   System: A Synthesis', in Giavazzi, F., Micossi, S., Miller, M. (eds), 1988.
Micossi, S., Visco, I (eds) (1993), *L'economia italiana nella prospettiva europea*,
   Il Mulino.
Obstfeld, M. (1986), 'Rational and Self-Fulfilling Balance of Payment Crisis',
   American Economic Review, Lxxvi, pp. 72-81.
Rogoff, K. (1985a), 'The Optimal Degree of Commitment to an Intermediate
   Monetary Target', *Quarterly Journal of Economics*, 100, pp. 1169-89.
Rogoff, K. (1985b), 'Can Exchange Rate Predictability be Achieved without
   Monetary Convergence? Evidence from the EMS', *European Economic
   Review*.
Sachs, J., Sala-i-Martin, X. (1991), 'Fiscal Federalism and Optimum Currency
   Areas: Evidence for Europe from the United States', *NEBR Working Paper*,
   no. 3855.
Sannucci, C. (1989), 'The Establishment of a Central Bank: Italy in the
   Nineteenth-Century', in De Cecco, M., Giovannini, A. (eds), 1989.
Svensson, L. (1992), 'Why Exchange Rate Bands? Monetary Independence in
   Spite of Fixed Exchange Rates', *CEPR Discussion Paper*, no. 742.
Ungerer, H., Evans, O., Mayer, T., Young, P. (1986), 'The European Monetary
   System: Recent Developments', *IMF Occasional Papers*, no. 48.
Visco, I. (1992), 'Caratteri strutturali dell'inflazione italiana (1986-91)', paper
   presented at the XXXIII Meeting of the *Società degli Economisti*, mimeo.
Von Hagen, J. (1991), 'Fiscal Arrangements in a Monetary Union: Evidence

from the US', in Fair, D., de Boissieux (eds), 1991.

Walters, A. (1986), *Britain's Economic Renaissance*, Oxford University Press.

Weber, A. (1990), 'European Economic and Monetary Union and Asymmetries and Adjustment Problems in the EMS: some Empirical Evidence', CEPR Discussion Papers.

Welfens, P. (ed.) (1991), *European Monetary Integration,* Springer-Verlag.

Wills, M. (1991) 'German Monetary Unification and European Monetary Union: Theoretical Issues and Strategic Policy Problems', in Welfens, P. (ed.), 1991.

INDEX